Palgrave Studies in Indigenous Psychology

Palgrave Studies in Indigenous Psychology aims to introduce psychologists and social scientists to the indigenous psychology movement and to major theoretical and practical issues discussed in this tradition. It publishes books that make significant contributions to psychology in the era of globalization by asking important questions about the discipline, profession, and practice of psychology. The series critically appraises cultural assumptions and theoretical frameworks; sheds light on the dialectics of the universal and the particular in human subjectivity; goes beyond Western psychology in researching the ontological, epistemological, ethical, spiritual, and aesthetic dimensions of the mental life; addresses issues of structural oppression in the globalizing era; and explores possibilities for a more equitable global psychology. Given the interdisciplinary nature of indigenous psychology, this book series welcomes contributions from all disciplines in the social sciences and the humanities. In particular, it welcomes scholarship that embodies a critical thinking that is informed by the local knowledge, and inspired by the spiritual strivings of a culture. If you would like to discuss a book idea prior to submitting a proposal please contact Editor-in-Chief Louise Sundararajan via Commissioning Editor Beth Farrow (beth.farrow@palgrave.com)

Zed Zhipeng Gao • Maria I. Medved
Editors

Global Perspectives on Cultural Politics in Indigenous Psychology

palgrave
macmillan

Editors
Zed Zhipeng Gao
Department of Psychology, Health and Gender
The American University of Paris
Paris, France

Maria I. Medved
Department of Psychology, Health and Gender
The American University of Paris
Paris, France

ISSN 2946-4692 ISSN 2946-4706 (electronic)
Palgrave Studies in Indigenous Psychology
ISBN 978-3-031-96812-9 ISBN 978-3-031-96813-6 (eBook)
https://doi.org/10.1007/978-3-031-96813-6

This Palgrave Macmillan imprint is published by the registered company Springer Nature Switzerland AG.
The registered company address is: Gewerbestrasse 11, 6330 Cham, Switzerland

Contents

Notes on Contributors

Stephen Baffour Adjei is Associate Professor of Psychology in the Department of Psychology, University of Oslo, Norway. Before joining the University of Oslo, he was Associate Professor of Psychology and the Acting Dean of Student Affairs at Akenten Appiah-Menka University of Skills Training and Entrepreneurial Development (AAMUSTED) in Ghana, where he taught and conducted research for eight years. He applies cultural psychological theories, African communitarian philosophy and theory of personhood, and decolonial perspectives to understand the interaction among culture, context, and psychological processes. His research interests include critical/indigenous African psychology, decolonizing knowledge and being, cultural psychology of child development and learning, and cultural grounding of intimate partner violence. He has taught, conducted research, and directed programs at universities and research institutions in Ghana and abroad, including Malawi, Zambia, Denmark, Germany, Norway, the Netherlands, and the United States. He is Associate Editor at *Psychological Science*, a Review Editor at *Frontiers in Psychology*, Academic Editor at *Perspectives in Psychiatric Care*, Editorial Advisory Board member at the *Journal of HARM*, and a member of the Editorial Board of *Personality and Social Psychology Review* (*PSPR*). He was the World Academy of Sciences (TWAS) and the German Research Foundation's (DFG) Visiting Scholar at Ruhr University Bochum, Germany, in 2021, and the 2023 Inaugural Editorial Fellow and Associate Editor for *PSPR*. He is currently coediting a Special Issue for *PSPR*, which aims at highlighting indigenous personality and social psychological theory from Majority World contexts.

Mark Standing Eagle Baez the President of the Society of Indian Psychologists and an associate professor at Bemidji State University, is in the clinical and counseling program. Baez is a licensed psychologist with a small private practice. With over 18 years of experience in mental health and wellness and impactful research among Indigenous people across the lifespan, he has inspired significant change in the field of Indigenous mental health. Baez has advocated for culturally strengths-based approaches to serving Indigenous people and hopes to change community-based approaches among AI/AN peoples by weaving together culture, traditional methods, and Western approaches to improve Indigenous well-being. He believes the Western approach is only one perspective on mental health services among Indigenous populations, and incorporating traditional Indigenous methods is crucial to effectively addressing the mental health needs of marginalized Indigenous communities. Thus, weaving traditional methodologies is vital in working with marginalized populations across Indian Country. He has developed a culturally responsive approach called the "Sweetgrass Method," which focuses on weaving the best evidence-based practices and the best Indigenous strength-based approaches for the clients served. Baez can assess and diagnose behavior and learning in adolescents and children, incorporating culturally responsive methods into his services.

C. Allison Baez is a Training and Technical Coordinator with Tribal Tech, LLC. She is a member of the Tap Pilam Coahuiltecan Nation. Baez has shared her expertise with K-12 and higher education environments for over 25 years. Her research focuses on Native populations that implement the best practices with their cultural lens. Her services strengthen and empower American Indian/Alaska Native individuals, families, and communities. She continues serving Indigenous populations, sharing, collaborating, and educating on culturally responsive approaches and methodologies. She received her doctorate from the University of the Incarnate Word in San Antonio, TX.

Fortidas Bakuza is an associate professor at the Aga Khan University's Institute for Education Development East Africa in Dar-es-Salaam, Tanzania. He is also the Associate Dean of research and partnership at Aga Khan University. He specializes in teaching and learning in early childhood education, teacher education, and curriculum and teaching. His research focuses on early childhood education leadership and policies with emphasis on evidence-based policies and programs on early childhood education leadership. He calls for investment in capacity building of early childhood service providers from government and civil society organizations, especially in developing countries.

Umesh Bharte is an assistant professor in the Department of Applied Psychology, Mumbai University, Mumbai (India). He holds an MPhil and a PhD from Jawaharlal Nehru University (JNU), New Delhi, with an interdisciplinary flavor of psychology and economics. His interest areas include international student migration, behavior economics, and social psychology. He has many national and international journal articles and many book chapters to his credit. His recent publications include "Working Through the Politics of Indigeneity: Decolonising Psychology by Way of a Dialectical Approach" (with A. K. Mishra), "Psychology and Developing Society," Sage; and a book chapter, "Putting Psychology Back into Migration Research: A Case of Indian Student Mobility," in an edited volume by Springer Nature, Switzerland.

Katherine Bischoping is an Associate Professor of Sociology at York University, Toronto, and holds a PhD from the University of Michigan. Her research collaborations examine the awkward moments of methodologists, apply diverse narrative and discourse analysis strategies to interview data on cultural-political topics, and help expand the theatrical canon to include more works by women around the globe. With Amber Gazso (York University), she coauthored *Analyzing Talk in the Social Sciences: Narrative, Conversation, and Discourse Strategies* (Sage UK), and with Yumi Isshi (University of Tokyo), she coedited a special issue of *Oral History Forum d'histoire orale* entitled "Generations and Memory: Continuity and Change."

Arthur W. Blume is an Indigenous American and Professor of Clinical Psychology at Washington State University. He has been honored with the Joseph E. Trimble Award for Distinguished Contributions to Native and Indigenous Psychology, Rockefeller Foundation and Brocher Foundation Fellowships in Europe, and as a fellow of the American Psychological Association. A consultant for the World Health Organization on The State of the World's Indigenous Peoples (SOWIP) Report, and widely published in the areas of Indigenous psychology, he is currently completing a contracted book discussing the intersection of Indigenous psychologies with health equity.

Cheryl Cadogan-McClean is an Industrial/Organizational Psychologist who views employee wellness as the secret to a productive workplace. She is a seasoned educator, facilitator, and researcher with over 20 years of experience teaching at the tertiary level. She is a lecturer at the University of the West Indies, Cave Hill Campus in Barbados, and a certified Health and Wellness Coach. Her research focuses on workplace wellness, employee well-being, work stress, and ethical decision making in the Caribbean. An experienced scholar/practitioner, she has engaged in consultancies and conducted training in stress management and other Human Resources-related areas for corporate entities.

Fei Bi Chan is Research Assistant/Doctoral Student in Counseling Psychology, University of Louisville, Louisville, KY.

Chan is a third-year doctoral student in counseling psychology at the University of Louisville. Chan is Chinese and originally from Malaysia. Her research experiences and expertise focus on Asian Americans, Asians, social justice beliefs, activism, liberation, and Indigenous psychology.

Nuria Ciofalo is Professor and Co-founder of the Community, Liberation, Indigenous, and Eco-Psychologies Specialization at Pacifica Graduate Institute. Born in Mexico, she holds an MA in Psychology from the University of Munich, Germany, MA in Planning, and a PhD in Community Psychology from the University of Hawaii. She has worked with Indigenous communities in Hawaii and Mexico for several decades. She has published on participatory action research, evaluation, decoloniality, community psychology, and Indigenous psychologies. Her book, *Indigenous Psychologies in an Era of Decolonization* (2019), was written with Maya Lacandon youths and community leaders of the Lacandon Rainforest in Chiapas.

Zed Zhipeng Gao is Assistant Professor in the Department of Psychology, Health and Gender at the American University of Paris in France. He holds a PhD in historical, theoretical, and critical studies of psychology and has conducted postdoctoral research in sociology and anthropology.

Gao studies Chinese immigrants' cultural identity and belonging. He applies interdisciplinary methods to situate cultural identity in racial relations, which are in turn embedded in (trans)nationalism and (de)globalization. Additionally, Gao has published on China's communist movement.

Gao has published over 20 journal articles and book chapters, and guest edited two special issues of journal *Integrative Psychological and Behavioral*

Science (Springer) and journal *Theory & Psychology* (Sage) on the topics of Indigenous psychology and globalization. He has received awards in international psychology, the history of psychology, theoretical psychology, and qualitative inquiry from the American Psychological Association and other academic societies.

Logan Hamley (Ngāti Rangi, Whanganui) is a senior researcher at Whakauae Researcher Services, a Ngāti Hauiti-led research center that focuses on Māori health. His research explores the intersections of Indigenous youth identity, masculinity, and well-being. He is passionate about systems transformation, and the possibilities for Indigenous ways of being and knowing to create a more just and equitable world.

Tumelo Kgolo is a psychology lecturer at the University of Botswana with a strong interest in cross-cultural neuropsychology. A member of the International Neuropsychology Society (INS) Cultural Special Interest group, she actively contributes to fostering cultural awareness within the realm of neuropsychology, ensuring that assessments are conducted with a deep understanding of cultural nuances. Her research focus has primarily been on the development of neuropsychology test norms for a Botswana population, as well as the neuropsychological impact of epilepsy on mental health. Beyond academic and research endeavors, she actively works toward expanding the landscape of neuropsychology in Botswana. Her efforts contribute to the development of culturally informed practices, ensuring that the field evolves to be inclusive and responsive to the needs of diverse populations.

Andrian Liem Originally from Indonesia, Andrian Liem holds a doctoral degree from the School of Psychology, the University of Queensland, Australia. For his PhD thesis, Liem investigated Indonesian clinical psychologists' knowledge, attitude, and experience related to integrative medicine. After graduating, he worked as a postdoctoral fellow at the University of Macau, Macao (SAR), to assist a project on digital mental health intervention for overseas Filipino workers. He then continued his work at the Monash University Malaysia to explore the experiences of Indonesian migrant domestic workers in caring for older adults in Asian countries.

Rashelle Litchmore is a Jamaican-Canadian immigrant and an Assistant Professor of Human Development at Connecticut College. Her research spans the areas of cultural psychology, education policy, Black and racialized adolescent identities, and systems transformation. Her research is conducted through critical, theoretical, and analytical frameworks including post-structuralism, critical discursive social psychology, Black Feminist Theory, and Critical Race Theory. Litchmore was previously a Senior Policy Advisor with the Anti-Racism Directorate of Ontario, Canada, where she supported government decision making in addressing disparities faced by racialized and Indigenous people in Ontario.

Laurie D. McCubbin PhD, LP, is the Chair/Professor at the University of Kentucky and is an Indigenous/multiracial scholar (Native Hawaiian/Japanese/European American). Her research expertise includes resilience and well-being among Indigenous peoples and people of color, cultural identity development, and stress and coping processes among multiracial families.

Maria I. Medved is Professor of Psychology and Chair of the Department of Psychology, Health and Gender at The American University of Paris in France. She is also a licensed psychologist. Before starting her existing position, she worked at the University of Manitoba, Canada, where she partnered with indigenous peoples, a collaboration that continues to the present. Her work is informed by the practical realities and need of the communities she works with, and her interdisciplinary approach, which integrates qualitative, theoretical, and quantitative methods, emerges from psychology but extends beyond it.

Her research explores narrative as a functional and performance mode of thought that is manifest in how we understand ourselves and our being in the world. More specifically, she studies, across diverse cultural contexts, narratives of risk, resilience, and resistance told by individuals, families, and communities. She has published on topics including family narratives of illness, gendered narratives of health and healing, mental health treatment seeking, and suicidality in First Nations communities in Canada.

Arvind Kumar Mishra teaches social psychology at the Jawaharlal Nehru University, New Delhi, India. He has coedited *Interrogating Development: Insights from the Margins* (OUP, 2010); *School Education, Pluralism and Marginality: Comparative Perspective* (OBS,2012); *Dynamics of Inclusive Classroom: Social Diversity, Inequality and School Education in India* (OBS, 2017); *The Marginalized Self: Tales of Resistance of a Community* (Primus, 2020); and *The Social Context of Learning in*

India: Achievement Gaps and Factors of Poor Learning (Routledge, 2023). His research interests include resistance to modernity, decolonization of psychology, philosophy of social research, self and identity processes among marginalized communities, and academic experiences of disadvantaged students.

Seth Oppong was, until his untimely demise on February 17, 2024, a professor in the Department of Psychology, University of Botswana, Gaborone, Botswana. He was a visiting professor in the Department of Psychology, University of the Witwatersrand, South Africa. He was also a co-convenor of the Knowledge Generation Working Group of African Union CESA ECED Cluster. He was an international visiting scholar to North Carolina State University, Raleigh, and a fellow of Africa Early Childhood Network, Nairobi. He is viewed by many as a thinker and a theoretician in psychology in Africa. His research interests include cultural, historical, philosophical, and theoretical (CHPT) domains of psychology and African psychology, as well as decolonizing early childhood science and practice. In collaboration with some ECD practitioners and researchers, he has coauthored a practical resource on how to enhance cultural relevance of early childhood development interventions in Africa. He was a cochairperson for the Ernst Strüngmann Forum titled "Early Childhood Development: Toward a Truly Global Science."

Christine Park is an assistant professor at Adler Graduate School, Honolulu, HI.

Park is a second-generation Korean, third-generation Chinese, and fourth-generation Portuguese in Hawai'i. She is a certificated teacher in general and special education, a licensed mental health counselor, and a nationally certified counselor. Park has worked as an educator and counselor for disadvantaged and marginalized youth and adults, Native Hawaiians, in the public education system.

Carl Ratner is a cultural psychologist who emphasizes the political basis of human psychological processes. Two of his books have been translated into Chinese. His recent work examines political implications of psychological phenomena that are prominent in social-political movements, such as anti-racism.

E. San Juan Jr. is Emeritus Professor of English, Ethnic Studies and Comparative Literature, University of Connecticut, Storrs, USA, AM and PhD (English), Harvard University

E. San Juan Jr. was previously a fellow of the W.E.B. Institute, Harvard University, and Fulbright professor of American Studies at Leuven University, Belgium. He was visiting professor of Cultural Studies at Polytechnic University of the Philippines and the University of the Philippines. His latest books are *Maelstrom over the Killing Fields* (Pantax Press) and *Peirce's Pragmaticism: A Radical Perspective* (Lexington Press). He is completing a book on the Hegel-Spinoza debate within a pragmaticist/cognitive science perspective, and also a monograph on the world-historic significance of the thought of Apolinario Mabini, one of the key intellectuals responsible for the establishment of the first Philippine Republic in 1899 and the resistance to US colonization of the Philippines.

Chetan Sinha teaches at the OP Jindal Global University. He holds a PhD in Social Psychology from Jawaharlal Nehru University. His academic interests include social psychology of education, political psychology, and questions regarding interdisciplinarity. His approach is derived from social identity theory, social representation theory, and critical pedagogy. He has authored a book *Power Dynamics in Education: Shaping the Structure of School Education in India* from Routledge (2023).

Edmund Siu is an independent scholar and holds a Specialized Honors BA from York University. His research aims to shed light on the factors driving mobilization of and electoral support for the radical right in North America. His undergraduate honors thesis identifies the concerns and discourses mobilized by those opposed to pandemic-related masking and lockdowns, anti-vaxxers, the far right, and anarchists on MeWe, an alternative social media platform. He has also coauthored an article in *University Affairs* about virtual versus in-person learning experiences during the COVID-19 pandemic.

Rachel Sing-Kiat Ting Originally from Malaysia, Rachel Ting holds a PhD in Clinical psychology from an APA accredited institution (Fuller Graduate School of Psychology) and worked in the United States, China, and Malaysia in capacities as an academician and practitioner since 2006. She is an adjunct associate professor in the Psychology Department at Monash University (Malaysia campus). Spearheading indigenous psychology research network in Southeast Asia (SEAIP), developing culturally responsive mental health services, and mentoring next generation elites in indigenous psychology have been her current passions of life.

List of Figures

CHAPTER 1

Introduction: Cultural Politics in Indigenous Psychology

Zed Zhipeng Gao and Maria I. Medved

Progress and Challenges

Since its emergence in the 1960s, Indigenous Psychology has been part and parcel of the Indigenous rights movement, drawing momentum and inspiration from it while also contributing to it through scholarly inquiry. As such, it is impossible to evaluate the progress of Indigenous Psychology in isolation from the broader Indigenous rights movement. Over the decades, there has been significant progress in this movement across continents. In 2007, the United Nations adopted the *Declaration on the Rights of Indigenous Peoples*, a landmark global instrument that outlines the rights of Indigenous peoples, addressing issues such as land and resource use, cultural preservation, and participation in decision-making processes (Allen & Xanthaki, 2011). The Indigenous rights movement finds further manifestation in increased representation of Indigenous interest in parliaments, the establishment of research centers, as well as

Z. Z. Gao (✉) • M. I. Medved
Department of Psychology, Health and Gender, The American University of Paris, Paris, France
e-mail: zgao@aup.edu; mmedved@aup.edu

Z. Z. Gao, M. I. Medved (eds.), *Global Perspectives on Cultural Politics in Indigenous Psychology*, Palgrave Studies in Indigenous Psychology, https://doi.org/10.1007/978-3-031-96813-6_1

greater media attention to the welfare of Indigenous peoples. The popularized land acknowledgment statement serves as a powerful occasion for recognition, respect, and encouragement for action.

Now, let us return to Indigenous psychology. Since its peak in the 1980s, Indigenous Psychology has promoted intellectual sensibilities that have significantly influenced the broader field of psychology. These include a critique of universalistic, overgeneralizing theories; an emphasis on local cultural ecology; a commitment to social justice; and a favourable view of qualitative modes of inquiry. Over time, these ideas have made inroads into mainstream psychology. The "WEIRD" acronym, which underscores the disproportionate focus of psychology research on Western, Educated, Industrialized, Rich, and Democratic populations, is now widely recognized in academic circles (Henrich et al., 2010). It is hard to imagine the popularity of the WEIRD concept without the contribution of Indigenous psychology. In 2010, the Task Force on Indigenous Psychology came into being under the sponsorship of the Society for Humanistic Psychology (Division 32 of the American Psychological Association). This taskforce has since brought renewed energies to scholarly discussion. In 2023, the works of Indigenous psychologists culminated in a major breakthrough when the American Psychological Association (APA) made its first official apology to the First Peoples in the United States (The Indigenous Apology Work Group, The American Psychological Association, 2023). In this apology, the APA acknowledged that the field of psychology has caused significant harms to First Peoples through its complicity in colonialism. This declaration marks a historic juncture, signaling the APA's willingness to engage in self-reflection and its commitment to reconciliation.

However, one must remain vigilant against the danger of complacency. Since the 2008 financial crisis, the world entered a new cycle of instability and disintegration (Gao & Teo, 2023). The process of globalization experienced significant setbacks, as evidenced by events such as Brexit and trade wars. The COVID-19 pandemic has exacted a tremendous toll on public health and the global economy. Wars in Ukraine and the Middle East were among the greatest challenges to global peace since World War Two. The various social, economic, and political challenges have contributed to a broader conservative shift. Various populations' prior enthusiasm for ethnic and cultural diversity is increasingly giving way to protectionist agendas, heightened security concerns, and renewed emphasis on national identity. Western countries have strengthened borders to curb immigration. In North America, diversity, equity, and inclusivity (DEI) initiatives are losing ground, not only in institutional frameworks but also in public opinion. Amid this sweeping tide of change, how confident can we be that Indigenous Psychology will remain unaffected?

Culture and Politics in Indigenous Psychology

At this critical juncture, we would like to reflect on the mission of Indigenous Psychology through the lens of "cultural politics". The field of Indigenous Psychology is founded on two conceptual pillars: culture and politics. On the one hand, culture shapes the mentality of local communities, differentiating Indigenous psychology from universal psychology. On the other hand, Indigenous Psychology originated as a political project amid the decolonization movement, which opposed the deliberate or unwitting spread of Western norms under the guise of universality. However, the precise relations between culture and politics have not yet been sufficiently theorized.

One might argue, for example, that culture is an intrinsically normative system that we draw on to fashion our sense of self, negotiate social relations, enliven economic activities (consider Max Weber's writing on the Protestant ethic and capitalism), and decide which political party to vote for. As a culture evolves through history, its various components may become canonized, hybridized, appropriated, or tabooed—all of which may signal power dynamics. It is thus not surprising that China's communist movement culminated in a "Cultural Revolution" targeting culture as an obstacle to political goals, or that a far-right xenophobic group in France recently proclaimed: "Ni kebab ni burger, vive le jambon-beurre" ("Neither kebab nor burger, long live the ham and butter sandwich"). This relation is not always negative, but can also be positive. To give one example, many Indigenous communities' spiritual attachment to nature offers promising solutions to the climate crisis humanity is experiencing.

The Incorporation of Culture in Studies of Politics

To understand the convergence between culture and politics, we need to trace two separate genealogies, as both concepts have undergone major transformation and debates over the recent decades. Let us begin with "politics". Originating in the Anglophone world, the meaning of "politics" has expanded significantly. "Politics" used to designate formal governmental processes at the level of nation-state; its expanded meaning now encompasses both formal and informal relations of power (Nash, 2001). One illuminating example is the coinage of the slogan "the personal is political" during the second-wave feminism. The 1960s and 1970s witnessed several surging movements including the Civil Rights movement and the Anti-Vietnam War movement. Participants of these movements saw themselves as engaging with political matters according to the traditional definition of "politics". Consequently, they dismissed the Women's Liberation Movement, claiming that feminists' demands—such as those concerning sex, appearance, and abortion—were personal matters outside of the scope of politics. The slogan "the personal is political" came into being as a critical response to this narrow definition of politics (Hanisch, 1969). The significance of this slogan extends beyond the feminist movement, as it ruptured the pre-existing private/public dichotomy and expanded the traditional notion of "politics" to encompass personal, subjective issues.

Second-wave feminism uniquely presents a clearly defined moment when the definition of politics was expanded. Other processes through which political discourses incorporated "culture" have been much messier. In short, all these processes have culminated in the modern concept of cultural politics. According to Nash (2001), the key assumption is that culture is constitutive of social relations and identities. But which social relations and identities? One thing is national identity. According to the identity-border-order (IBO) model, if a nation-state is defined by a shared identity, encircling borders, and a stable social order (Albert et al., 2001), culture largely sustains the identity component by defining who a nation is. The question of national cultural identity gained particular political significance during the decolonialization movement, as the recognition and preservation of Indigenous culture became a major condition for self-determination in the face of colonialism's detrimental impact. At the same time, several schools influenced by Marxism also integrated culture into their approach to political economy. According to Marx, culture is part of the "superstructure" that reflects and reinforces the economic "base". Building on Marxism, Gramsci (1971) developed the concept of "cultural hegemony" to explain how ruling classes maintain dominance through ideas, beliefs, and values. The Frankfurt School analyzed how the cultural industry and mass media reproduce dominant ideologies (Horkheimer et al., 2002; Marcuse, 2013). Bourdieu's (2006) conceptualization of cultural capital explains how one's cultural taste contributes to class stratification. These academic theorizations coincided with a series of real-world developments. The process of globalization—most notably international migration and digital media—brought cultural differences to the forefront of political life (Hermans & Kempen, 1998). Additionally, political polarizations often revolve around "culture wars" over a range of cultural norms that regulate, for example, gender, religion, and individual rights (Thomson, 2010). All of these developments have contributed to the "cultural turn" in studies of politics (Nash, 2001). Given the feminist idea "the personal is political", it is not far-fetched to say "the cultural is political".

The Critical Turn in Cultural Studies

So far we have discussed how studies of politics have increasingly incorporated cultural analysis. But this is only one side of the story. The other genealogy involves how scholars in culture-related fields have increasingly politicized their topics. "Culture" is notoriously difficult to define (Baldwin et al., 2006). As early as in the 1950s, Kroeber and Kluckhohn (1952) collected 164 definitions of the term. The structuralist approach to culture aims to identify various elements of culture—such as human behaviors, ideas, and cultural products specific to one population—and subsequently establish the underlying structures that organize these elements. This approach is largely descriptive, focusing on depicting culture. In contrast, the functionalist approach contains a normative agenda. This harks back to the Latin origin of the term "culture": *culturare*, meaning "to cultivate". This semantic root evolved into the eighteenth-century German definition of *kultur*, referring to the cultivation of individuals through the "general process of intellectual, spiritual, and aesthetic development" (Williams, 2014, p. 90). The English counterpart was formulated in great earnest: that culture is "a pursuit of our total perfection by means of getting to know, on all the matters which most concern us, the best which has been thought and said in the world" (Arnold, 1869, p. viii). What makes culture and the process of individual enculturation so important? The answer is that culture is functional: "every culture is designed to perpetuate the group and its solidarity, to meet the demands for an orderly way of life and for satisfaction of biological needs" (Kluckhohn, 1949, pp. 24–25).

Both structuralism and functionalism would eventually encounter powerful pushback (San Juan Jr.'s chapter being part of the critique). Since the 1970s, studies of culture have taken a critical turn (Baldwin et al., 2006). Similar to developments in political studies, scholars in cultural studies incorporated Marxist analysis to examine how culture reproduces dominant ideologies and maintains social status quo. Their Marxist analysis of social conflict challenged the functionalists' harmonious portrayal of culture: perhaps culture indeed functions in certain ways, but to whose benefit and at whose expense? Meanwhile, the rise of poststructuralism challenged the tenets of structuralism. Rather than merely identifying structures of culture in an empiricist fashion, poststructuralist scholars began asking: how do we use conceptual structures to demarcate the world and justify domination? Nowadays, the impact of poststructuralist thinking on the public is clearly discerned in the popularized skepticism surrounding gender and racial categories.

The Perspective of Cultural Politics

In light of the convergence of culture and politics over the past half-century or so, in this edited volume, we explicate the multiple ways in which culture and politics are entangled in Indigenous psychology. This task is particularly pressing given that the critical potential of Indigenous Psychology has been tempered by its recent positioning of culture as the core of its identity (Gao, 2022). We approach this project through the lens of "cultural politics", a critical interdisciplinary perspective that has attracted the attention of leading theorists such as Spivak (2012) and Ahmed (2013). Unlike traditional political studies, which focus on central institutions of power such as the State, law, partisanship, and capitalism, cultural politics is concerned with what Schiller (1997) describes as "the processes through which relations of power are asserted, accepted, contested, or subverted by means of ideas, values, symbols, and daily practices" (p. 3).

When it comes to psychology, the cultural politics perspective extends to the question of subjectivity. We might ask: how is power embodied and transmitted through culture and becomes something that we quasi-intuitively feel and identify with, as opposite to the power of social institutions and law, which is reinforced through coercive means (Foucault, 1979)? The cultural politics perspective invites a return of critical inquiry to the everyday—those things that we hold too dear to our hearts to give up or that we overlook too easily for their banality. Nevertheless, the focus on the grassroots level should not prevent us from asking significant questions, such as those related to globalization, racial relations, and power dynamics. By using the broad category of "politics", we aim to cover a broad range of critical social issues. Anti-colonialism is the indisputable core of Indigenous Psychology (as discussed by Blume). At the same time, contributors of this volume address issues including environmentalism (McCubbin, Park and Chan), culture and religion (San Juan Jr.; Sinha, Bharte, and Mishra), capitalism (Ratner; Ciofalo), poverty (Ting and Liem), diaspora (Litchmore & Cadogan-McClean; Bischoping, Gao & Siu), youth identity (Hamley), the philosophy/sociology of science (Adjei, Bakuza, Kgolo, and Oppong), and mental health (Baez and Baez).

Global Perspectives

This edited volume comprises twelve chapters. The contributors—some of whom are leading experts in the field and some with emerging, innovative research programs—hail from five continents and represent a wide range of Indigenous populations. We use the term "global perspectives" to highlight the geographical scope covered by the contributions.

That said, there is a more important theoretical question at stake. The term "global perspectives" evokes "global psychology", a long-standing proposal within Indigenous Psychology (Sundararajan et al., 2020). To begin with, Indigenous Psychology prioritizes localized investigation (Kim & Berry, 1993). In Sundararajan's (2019b) nimble phrasing, it is a psychology "of the local, by the local, and for the local" (p. 82). But, Indigenous Psychology does not stop at the local. Since the 1990s, Yang (1997) famously made the proposal that various local Indigenous Psychologies should eventually be integrated into a global psychology. We applaud the motivation to replace the domination of Western psychology with a more equitable global psychology. But we have reservations about whether global psychology is truly achievable. One key issue is the politics of representation.

The Politics of Representation

Yang's proposal of global psychology is meant to address the lack of representation of colonized and developing societies in the discipline of psychology. Yet, who is actually represented in the Indigenous Psychology literature? The reality is that Indigenous Psychology is only possible in places with sufficient economic and institutional support. Some countries that host Indigenous Psychology are on their way to becoming major regional or global powers. In contrast, many countries remain absent from the literature of Indigenous Psychology. Here, the disparity among nations, which is unlikely to disappear in the near future, poses the first challenge to the vision of global representation. Speaking of "nation" as a unit of representation, this concept itself raises the second challenge: will we reach global psychology in an imagined future when every nation is represented? Not necessarily (Ting & Sundararajan, 2017). As discussed in two chapters (Ting and Liem; Sinha, Bharte & Mishra), hegemonic national discourses tend to overshadow ethnic and religious minorities within the nation. And what about diasporas located outside of the nation (Litchmore & Cadogan-McClean; Bischoping, Gao & Siu)? The concept of "nation" is troubled by analytic units both above and below it. A third question is how representation should be achieved. Significant diversity exists within Indigenous Psychology with regard to what topics, types of data, methods, analytic strategies, etc. are preferable. Indeed, one might argue that due to its unique position within the scientific, cultural, and political worlds, Indigenous Psychology is well-suited to engage with a wide range of ontological and epistemological questions that have troubled philosophers and social scientists for centuries and are unlikely to be solved any time soon. The vitality of Indigenous Psychology, in our view, lies in its epistemology of the marginalized. The promise of "global psychology" risks glossing over, rather than fostering and sustaining, such critical engagement. Fourth and finally, what is the purpose of representation? While Indigenous psychologists have promoted the representation of Indigenous cultures as a pathway to their recognition and appreciation, they have remained aware of the potential danger of excessive demands for representation leading to nationalism or racial division (Long, 2019). Another potential pitfall is that acts of representation may essentialize Indigenous identity, depriving it of the possibility of evolution (Sundararajan, 2019b). If, as Geertz (1973) suggests, culture is open-ended, how can we creatively envision the future of Indigenous Psychology without idealizing a pristine past where Indigenous culture is frozen in time? This point is addressed by Hamley in this volume.

In short, we do not envision global psychology as a finishable project for Indigenous psychologists. As long as history continues to unfold, new social actors, conditions, and challenges will emerge and demand renewed representations. Indigenous Psychology will remain in constant flux. There is no end to Indigenous Psychology, just as there is no end to history. In this volume, we instead use the "global" term to express an interest in inclusivity. We recognize that every Indigenous group, regardless of how it is defined, deserves a voice and has something valuable to share. Essentially, what we find valuable in the concept of "global" is that it allows for pluralism.

Pluralism

Pluralism is a poststructural condition that contrasts with previous homogeneous worldviews. Various components of globalization in the second half of the twentieth century—such as immigration, new technologies of transportation and communication, international trade, and diplomacy—have powerfully challenged homogenous cultures in individual societies, replacing them with frequent intercultural exchange and hybridization. In response, many scholars have embraced pluralism, celebrating its associated cosmopolitan, multicultural worldview as a replacement for the previous universalizing concepts of "progress" or "civilization", which tend to subjugate cultures deemed "backwards" or "inferior" (Ferguson, 1997).

Thus, with a poststructuralist spirit, we disagree with Jahoda's (2016) criticism of Indigenous Psychology. Jahoda (2016) is dissatisfied with the fact that Indigenous Psychology lacks a singular, consensual definition and that Indigenous psychologists' multiple perspectives, typologies, and goals do not always cohere with one another. We would like to point out that the very discipline of psychology itself has been suffering chronic fragmentation and has never reached a single, unified definition (Leary, 1979; Yanchar & Slife, 1997). Yet, these problems never prevented psychology from becoming one of the most popular disciplines. Wittgenstein's (2009) discussion of family resemblance or Deleuze and Guattari's (1987) notion of rhizome easily solve the problem of definition. The real question is not conceptual clarity. It is instead one of worldview: a homogenous, universalizing worldview versus a pluralistic one. Jahoda's (2016) criticism stems from a lack of understanding that it is precisely the modernist attempt to develop an universal grand narrative that helped construct colonialism in the first place. In this volume, we highlight plural "perspectives" to combat this universalizing tendency. The recognition of plural perspectives helps us conceptualize a "global" psychology that is not "universal" (Danziger, 2009; Long, 2019). Some relevant discussion can be found in the chapter by Adjei, Bakuza, Kgolo, and Oppong.

Relativism: The Need of Political Analysis

While celebrating pluralism, we do recognize that it brings about an alternative set of questions (Eck, 2015). In the following, we would like to discuss two: relativism and identity politics. To begin with, relativism is part of what that enables pluralism. The co-existence of multiple cultures does not necessarily lead to a harmonious multiculturalism. As mentioned before, we have often witnessed Enlightenment-style dismissal of non-Western cultures as something backward or inferior. It is only relativism—a suspicion of the Eurocentric hierarchy—that permits the possibility to view the non-European/American cultures on equal ground. This is a key point made by poststructuralist scholars (see elaboration by Ciofalo). According to poststructuralism, we conceptualize the world through binary oppositions such as good/evil, man/woman, and modern/traditional. Further, each of the dichotomies contains one category that dominates the other (such as good dominating evil, man dominating woman, and modern dominating traditional). One major contribution made by poststructuralism is that it replaced the hierarchical organization of dichotomies with a relativist organization. This relativist view helped Indigenous peoples free themselves from subjugated positions.

However, critiques of relativism never ceased (Parker, 1999). One major concern is that it undermines epistemological and ethical foundations. If "anything goes", how can we distinguish truth from falsehood? How we can distinguish good from evil? Indigenous Psychology faces the same challenge. As Ratner questions in his chapter: is indigenous psychology/culture *a priori* superior? Is it free from abuse? This is where we argue that the category of "culture" is insufficient on its own. While cultural norms and ideals prescribe what is right or wrong, such criteria originate from inside of the culture itself. We still need external criteria to evaluate individual elements of a culture: for example, what social functions they perform and whose interests they serve. In so doing, we introduce "politics" into the picture. Political analysis is necessary for us to identify and evaluate the function of power through culture. As Sinha, Bharte, and Mishra argue, critical engagement with culture must be directed toward social justice and human liberation.

Identity Politics: An Intersectional Remedy

Another question is identity politics. Identity politics refers to "a wide range of political activity and theorizing founded in the shared experiences of injustice of members of certain social groups" (Heyes, 2002, p. 1). Well-known components of identity politics include feminism, the racial minority rights movement, and the LGBTQ rights movement. Typically championing progressive causes, identity politics has frequently come under malicious attack from the right wing. What is notable, however, is that some concerns originate from the left wing as well. Fraser (2008), for example, famously cautioned against the risk of identity-based demands for *recognition* overshadowing systematic injustices in *redistribution*. Arfken (2012) made a similar argument with regard to the internationalization of psychology. Such critiques touch on the question of pluralism: what if the left wing of society, instead of uniting around common progressive causes to confront a growing right wing, evolves into a Tower of Babel that collapses and fractures into many pieces?

In his chapter, Ratner urges us to return to Marx's analysis of political economy, which underlies various forms of exploitation, including that of Indigenous People. This proposal resonates with Fraser's (2024) latest work where she argues that gender, race, and class are three interconnected faces of capitalist labor. Here, Fraser makes it clear that "intersectionality" holds the promise of rebuilding common ground for progressive pursuits. Intersectionality is a theoretical framework that examines how various forms of social identity—such as race, gender, and religion—intersect to create overlapping systems of oppression. Several chapters in this volume apply the intersectional approach: Ting and Liem address questions of poverty and employment among Indigenous groups in South Asia, while Ciofalo analyzes how Indigenous rights movement has incorporated feminist pursuits. One advantage of the intersectional approach is its ability to overcome the limitations of essentialist thinking, an alternative response to pluralism. When faced with pluralism, conservatives often resort to essentialist perspectives: such as returning to a bounded, uncontaminated notion of national or cultural identity to the exclusion of ethnic minorities. The intersectional approach, in contrast, promises to nurture a political common that is as inclusive as possible. Rather than being defined by an essentialist core, this political common functions like a meeting place that accommodates diverse participants and agendas. Here, we heed Sundararajan's (2019a) caution that Indigenous psychologists often become self-absorbed within their own cultural worlds. We further propose that the solutions should not only involve collaboration among different Indigenous Psychologies but also adopt an intersectional approach that explicitly re-embeds culture within social and political realms.

An intersectional approach to Indigenous Psychology requires us to revisit the question of identification. Typically, Indigenous people relate to their own community through cultural identification in that they draw on the same system of culture or social identification though shared ancestry and community ties. However, challenges arise both within and above the "people" unit. Who are considered part of the people? What about urban Māori youths who do not speak the Māori language (Hamley)? How about dislocated individuals without clearly defined Indigenous ancestry (Ratner)? How to develop solidarity among different indigenous communities (Blume)? Also, how do we understand diasporic identification with their country or culture of origin (Litchmore & Cadogan-McClean; Bischoping, Gao & Siu)? Another critical question is how Indigenous people can extend the project of anti-colonialism and form alliance with marginalized groups along other axes of oppression. While existing social psychology literature offers extensive discussions on in-group/out-group dynamic, it is less clear on how individuals identify themselves or others along intersecting dimensions such as race, gender, and class. Moreover, examining identification practices may require moving beyond psychology literature, as these practices often occur within broader legal, political, and popular discourses.

The Art of Translation

One last question remains: how should we actually implement the intersectional approach? As Blume reminds us, if different Indigenous communities can fall into the trap of "colonial splitting" and end up conflicting with one another, the challenges become even greater when it comes to broader alliances between the Indigenous rights movement and other social movements. Given that various groups occupy different social locations and face distinct forms of oppression, how can we foster shared understanding and empathy toward solidarity building? In response, we would like to highlight the question of translation.

Translation has long been a challenge in the history of colonialism. When early anthropologists (and sometimes psychologists) rendered foreign cultures comprehensible to Western audiences, they often simultaneously problematized or exoticized these cultures. What we are referring to here is not limited to the conventional definition of translation as the creation of commensurability between languages. Rather, the question of translation often involves the exertion of power relations; the process of meaning-making can sometimes produce epistemological violence (Teo, 2011). The Indigenous rights movement revisited a set of questions about translation: who performs the translation (the insider/outsider tension)? To which audience (with regard to writing, publishing, and application)? And for what purpose (the problematization vs. recognition of Indigenous culture)?

In order to address these questions, we must move from a conventional view of translation as a logocentric, linguistic activity to a broader understanding of translation as a praxis informed by the ethics of care. While translation might appear to have a definitive object—the text being translated—it can actually participate in a wide range of sociopolitical dynamics such as globalization and human rights. The translator must remain sensitive to the political repercussions involved in rendering a culture intelligible to a target audience.

Translation occurs not only between cultures but also between different kinds of phenomena. For example, how does power-saturated social relations translate into lived experiences such as dignity, hope, and grief? And how does culture mediate such process by informing how we are supposed to feel (Hochschild, 1979)? In addressing these questions the translator needs to navigate the dilemma between commonality and difference. On the one hand, what common human experience allows different groups to understand and empathize with one another (Gair, 2012)? On the other hand, the translator must respect each group's alterity, ensuring that sociocultural differences are not erased in an eager pursuit of universality. In this regard, we celebrate the recent rise of qualitative inquiry, which holds a strong presence in our edited volume. From a translational point of view, the strength of qualitative inquiry lies in its sensitivity to cultural difference, its attentiveness to social context, its holistic thinking style that promises to bring together fragmented findings of individual studies, and its agility in formulating critical questions.

Synopsis

The volume is divided into four parts. The first part is titled "The Many Faces of Colonialism". It contains two chapters that explore various mechanisms in which colonialism continues to exert power over Indigenous populations. Chapter 2 is on the psychology and politics of colonial splitting. In this chapter, Blume is primarily concerned with how social relations are structured to the disadvantage of Indigenous people. To begin with, Blume argues, colonialism is enabled by a culture of meritocracy, White settlers' belief that they are entitled to take over land and resources from Indigenous territory. In the meantime, Indigenous peoples often find themselves in a weak position for self-defense because of colonial splitting, the chapter's focus. According to Blume, colonial splitting refers to "a form of manipulation that generates divisiveness among different disempowered groups victimized by colonialism". Colonial splitting could take different forms: sometimes through cultural and religious assimilation, and other times through competition over economic resources. Most notably, the blood quantum approach to enrollment in Indigenous citizenship has been a flashpoint within Indigenous communities. Many were unable or unwilling to enroll due to various reasons: specific blood quantum, intermarriage outside of the nation, or lost lineage following displacement. The economic consequences of enrollment have led to much friction between and within the Indigenous nations. In spite of their shared history of oppression, Indigenous populations face challenges in forming an alliance. How to overcome colonial splitting? Blume offers several answers. One is to recognize how materialistic, individualistic culture brought by capitalism undermines Indigenous solidarity. Another is to identify the harm of populist, nationalist thinking, which underpins an exclusionary White identity (even though low SES White citizens have much in common with oppressed minoritized groups). With vigilance with these problematic cultures, Blume argues, we can begin to build a culture of responsibility, egalitarianism, and reconciliation.

In Chap. 3, Ting and Liem performs a two-layered analysis to complicate our understanding of colonialization. To begin with, similar to many other Indigenous scholars, they are critical of blind borrowing of Western theories to conceptualize mental health in Asia. Next and importantly, Ting and Liem move on to identify the phenomenon of self-colonization in the field of psychology, sometimes even in Indigenous psychology. That is, many studies conducted in Asia collect samples from the mainstream population (namely Westernized, urbanized, educated, rich, and liberal) while excluding marginalized minorities. For example, while Chinese psychologists and Filipino Psychologists champion their versions of Indigenous Psychology (against Western psychology), they at the same time exclude ethnic minorities in their own countries. The construction of national Indigenous psychology, while resistant to Westernization, often contains an assimilative agenda that erases the cultures of ethnic minorities within the nation. Applying this two-layered framework, Ting and Liem analyze two groups that suffer oppression not only from the West but also from dominant ethnicities inside of Asia. The first marginalized group is Temiar, an Indigenous tribe of Malaysia, who suffer from loss of ancestral land as well as natural resources and cultural identity associated with it. Additionally, the Temiar have been pressured by the Malaysian government to make religious conversion. The second group comprises migrant domestic workers from Indonesia and Philippines. They move to high-income countries in Asia, such as Hong Kong, Taiwan, and Singapore, for a better life, but in reality often face poor working conditions and mental health struggles.

The second part of the book presents, as suggested by its title, "Theoretical Reflections". The three chapters offer reflections from various angles, some calling for continued efforts in decolonizing the discipline of psychology, and others pointing out weak points of current scholarship of Indigenous Psychology toward future improvement. In Chap. 4, Adjei, Bakuza, Kgolo, and Oppong revisit the tension between two camps of child development researchers: the universalists who claim that child development is largely regulated by general, biologically based laws; and the contextualists who emphasize the role of culture and ecology in co-determining developmental outcomes. The two camps disagree over a range of developmental questions including developmental trajectories, nutrition, attachment, and intelligence. Adjei et al. point out that the universalists tend to promote a Western ideal that children should be fully agentive, consistently autonomous, and vocal, and such an ideal is often accompanied by the perception that childhood in developing societies is backward, prone to risk, and lacking a future. Further, using a social epistemology perspective, Adjei et al. argue that the universalists tend to dominate the contextualists along three popularly received hierarchies of knowledge: The first hierarchy privileges knowledge produced in the affluent, powerful West. The second hierarchy privileges biomedical fields over culturally related research. And the third hierarchy privileges quantitative knowledge over qualitative knowledge. In conclusion, Adjei et al. propose that the strategy of "glocalization" holds promise to reconcile the tension between the universalists and the contextualists.

In the next chapter, Marxist scholar Ratner argues that Indigenous Psychology should have been more progressive. From a Marxist historical-materialist perspective, all cultures, including indigenous cultures, are part of superstructure that is shaped by the political-economic base. One implication is that, to combat colonialism, it is insufficient to merely focus on culture as a self-contained system; instead, scholars must analyze how culture performs economic and political functions. Transforming political-economy is crucial for achieving a democratic, collectivist culture. A second implication is that culture might be part of the distorting ideology that serves the interest of the ruling classes by concealing exploitation. This Marxist view of culture-ideology potentially subjects all cultures under scrutiny, including Indigenous cultures. According to Ratner, even though Indigenous culture/psychology deserves support in front of Western colonial oppression, it might still be subject to abuse, as indicated in existing scholarly writings. What is the political-ethical foundation to evaluate various components of a culture? The answer, according to Ratner, lies in Marxist historical-materialism. Ratner argues that historical-materialism offers conceptual clarity as well as concrete strategies to identify modes of oppression—including the colonial ones—and to invent pathways to emancipation. For example, internationalism is one promising approach to understand globalized labor and production, a key component of colonialism.

In Chap. 6, Sinha, Bharte, and Mishra seek to problematize Indigenous psychology's current status and offer an alternative perspective for its theorization and applications in the Indian context. Their review of the history of psychology in India indicates that although Indigenous Psychology flourished in the 1980s and the 1990s, as of today it has not yet fulfilled its promise. Instead, Indigenous Psychology has become taken over by cross-cultural psychology. Sinha et al. argue that there are several reasons behind the setback: many psychologists approach Indigenous Psychology with nationalist motivation; much writings remain speculative and abstract, without formulating concrete research questions; and a narrow, selective focus on Hinduism. Additionally, Indian psychology continues to be dominated by universalistic, natural-scientific approach to psychology that emanates from the West. In light of such reviews, Sinha and colleagues offer critical reflection that as useful as the concept "indigeneity" could be, it is a flexible, messy construct subject to potential problems: oversimplifying conceptualization of Indigenous Psychology as the polar opposite of Western psychology; homogenous definition of "indigeneity" that favors the dominant regions and castes within the Indian nation; as well as the abuse of Indigenous Psychology toward the maintenance of unjust status quo. In order to critically evaluate specific understandings and uses of "indigeneity", Sinha et al. envision a critical Indigenous psychology. At the intellectual level, critical Indigenous Psychology would examine its philosophical assumptions as well as the political implications of its knowledge. At the level of action, it should not be satisfied with merely critiquing mainstream psychology but endeavor to initiate societal changes toward justice and liberation. Relationally, critical Indigenous psychologists should collaborate with activist members of the Indian society on the ground level.

In Chap. 7, San Juan Jr. discusses Filipino psychology (Sikolohiyang Filipino). San Juan Jr. contextualizes Filipino psychology within the 400 years of colonialism first under Spain and then under the United States, sometimes through violent conquer and other times through modes of persuasion, including language and religion. Against this backdrop, San Juan Jr. shifts to the complicity of the social sciences, including psychology, in colonialism. In particular, San Juan Jr. is critical of structuralism and functionalism for their roles in maintaining the social status quo and in promoting capitalism. Next, drawing on the works of Virgilio Enriquez, the progenitor of Filipino psychology, San Juan Jr. points out how Western psychologists have misunderstood the minds of the Filipinos by imposing Western dualistic, rational thinking while ignoring the local cultural context. The program developed by Enriquez, in contrast, affirms communal values based on lived experience under the guidance of the conceptual metaphor *kapwa* (mutuality or shared humanity). According to San Juan Jr., by understanding the "embodied mind" (*diwa*) of the emergent Filipino identity, Indigenous Filipino psychology displays the potential to resist Western hegemony and contributes to the struggle for democracy and national sovereignty. That said, San Juan Jr. cautions that Enriquez has not provided a substantive analysis of the colonizing ideological mechanisms. Also, in-depth treatment of sexuality, gender, marital relations, and so forth in the indigenizing agenda is yet missing. A rigorous critique of historical and socioeconomic determinants is needed for the indigenizing project to avail in front of repressive social conformity and neoliberal market economy.

The following part of the book focuses on "Indigenous Identities and Social Positions" and is interested in the manifestation of Indigenous identities in particular social positions. Conventional literature of Indigenous Psychology tends to equate the scope of one Indigenous Psychology with that of a nation or a society. For example, the idea that Filipino psychology is located in the Philippines. Contributions in this part move beyond the culture/nation equation and examine Indigenous Psychology in unexpected social positions, such as the urban space and in the diaspora.

In Chap. 8, Hamley explores how urban Māori youth navigate Māori identity. Due to the impact of colonialism, many Māori individuals display less identity markers that would qualify them as part of the Māori community: such as their knowledge of the Māori language (te reo Māori), and their engagement with the Māori ancestral complex (marae). This phenomenon is particularly pronounced among Māori youths who are immersed in the dominant culture in an urban environment. As shown in Hamley's interview research, many urban Māori youths reject the derogatory label of "plastic Māori" and make efforts to perform more authentic Māori identity. Yet, in so doing, their very discourses and actions reinforce the "plastic" concept, as well as the underlying distinction between an "upper class" and a "lower class" Māori. Additionally, their various attempts to "reconnect" with the Māori community often prove to be futile and even counterproductive. According to Hamley, the root cause of these problems is the static understanding of "authentic" Māori identity: that one must fully embody the pre-colonial Māori culture in order to be deemed an authentic member of the community. Hamley calls such search for historic, outmoded Indigenous identity "strategic essentialism". It is essentialist in that it is premised on a fixed view of culture. Such essentialism is problematic in that it could potentially further the colonial agenda of gradual elimination of the Māori people. In response, Hamley calls for a more fluid view of Māori identity and diversified means of engagement with the Māori culture.

In Chap. 9, Litchmore and Cadogan-McClean theorize a Black diasporic Indigenous psychology. Their analysis begins with the notion of "black", an initially discriminatory label that was later reclaimed by Black people to signify racial pride and solidarity. What Litchmore and Cadogan-McClean found limiting about the "Black" concept is that it is often interpreted to mean "African American". Correspondingly, the field of Black psychology is largely concerned with the American context. How to account for Black psychology's circulation and manifestation in the broader diaspora? To answer this question, Litchmore and Cadogan-McClean identify two interlinked groups: Black-Caribbean and Black-Caribbean-Canadian populations, both of which deviate from the American context yet inextricably tethered to it due to geographical, social, and cultural proximity. By locating Indigenous Psychology within the Black diaspora, Litchmore and Cadogan-McClean explore cultural fluidity, hybridization, and dispersion amid transnational movement and global media access. They suggest that a Black diasporic Indigenous Psychology should explicitly consider epistemological and ontological questions in framing and carrying out their research; recognize the socio-politico-historical contexts that shape the shared meanings and beliefs of the Black diaspora; incorporate decolonial and intersectional approaches; address social problems toward greater social justice; and collaborate with other Indigenous psychologists.

In Chap. 10, Bischoping, Gao, and Siu analyze how Chinese immigrants use Indigenous cultural resources to negotiate their diasporic belonging. The focus of their inquiry is a family of roots-related metaphors that center around the expression "*luoyeguigen*" [fallen leaves return to the roots], which is popularly used in Chinese culture to express an individual's affective attachment and moral obligations to one's geographical, cultural, or national origin. Bischoping et al. approach *luoyeguigen* using two methods. First, they review existing literature to establish a transnational genealogy of *luoyeguigen*, with the conclusion that the cultural ideal it depicts has become increasingly politicized by the Chinese state to promote ethno-nationalist belonging. Second, they conduct interviews with Chinese living in Canada, and their findings suggest that the roots-related metaphors permit flexible usages in accordance with Chinese immigrants' diverse, sometimes conflicting, modes of belonging. For example, while some adopt the hegemonic, essentializing discourse of *luoyeguigen* sponsored by the Chinese state, other opt for the counter discourse of *luoyeshenggen* (meaning "[leaves/seeds] fall to/land on the ground and take root") to assert alternative senses of belonging. Bringing these research findings together, Bischoping et al. argue that the roots-related metaphors constitute one example of cultural politics. Culture, as a historically evolved repertoire of meanings and ideals, often serves political functions. The roots-related metaphors, for example, offer certain pre-structured definitions about one's entitlement and obligation with regard to his/her country of origin. Yet, cultural politics is not deterministic; it is possible for social actors to exercise agency and tap into existing cultural resources toward flexible ends.

The fourth and last part of the book addresses "Indigenous Resistance". Contributions analyze how indigenous resistance takes place and the important lessons we can learn from that. In Chap. 11, McCubbin, Park, and Chan discuss native Hawaiians' acts of Indigenous resurgence concerning environmental issues. Their analysis begins with the central place of land ('āina) for the overall wellness of the Native Hawaiians (Kānaka 'Ōiwi). Native Hawaiians lost land stewardship through two historical processes. First, the overthrow of the Hawaiian Kingdom deprived the people of their autonomy and subjected them to colonial rules. Second, the introduction of capitalism into Hawai'i led to the commodification of the Hawai'i land, resources, and human labor at the expense of the original ecological system. One telling example is that the colonial settlers dismissed the traditional Hawaiian farming practices as inferior, ignoring that these practices were rooted in conservation and responsibility to the land and future generations. The settlers instead preferred environmentally destructive farming methods that yield immediate economic gains. Indigenous resurgence thus centralizes land and environmental protections. McCubbin et al. then go on to examine three cases of activism. The first case was concerned with the reclamation of Kaho'olawe, a sacred Hawaiian Island occupied by the US Navy for decades. The second case was with regard to the ongoing conflict over Mauna Kea. Being one of the tallest mountains in the world, Mauna Kea attracted the proposal of a telescope construction project which could cause economic and cultural damages. The third case is about the Red Hill fuel storage facility which was recently responsible for the pollution of drinking water. According to McCubbin et al., Indigenous insurgence is a form of healing, and the healing of the land is simultaneously the healing of the Hawaiian community and its cultural traditions after colonial damage.

In Chap. 12, Ciofalo analyzes the various forms of "power" in light of a Mexican Indigenous movement. To begin with, Ciofalo argues that colonialism exercises its power partly through dichotomous categories: such as "primitive-civilized", "nature-culture", and "irrational-rational". Divided along the racial line, these dichotomies contain normative impulses and justify the colonization of the supposed inferior races. Another mechanism is capitalism which facilitated the extraction of human labor and natural resources in Mexico. How to combat the colonial powers? According to Ciofalo, one answer lies in "popular power", a force exercised by collective organizations to foster shared goals for social change and political participation in defense of the people's legitimate interests. When effectively mobilized, popular power constitutes a form of "contra-power" in that it resists external agents such as state institutions and corporate capital. Ciofalo illustrates these power dynamics by revisiting the Zapatista movement in Mexico. The Zapatista movement instantiates a new form of community empowerment as a cultural-political philosophy and pedagogy of *lekil kuxlejal, buen vivir* (good living). Deeply rooted in Indigenous knowledge, axiology, and praxes, the Zapatistas have created autonomous educational and health systems and a good government. In addition to bolstering Indigenous self-determination, the Zapatista movement also strengthened women's rights. Toward the end of the chapter, Ciofalo discusses how the Zapatista movement can help us think about Participatory Action Research, a critical methodology that interweaves knowledge generation, community involvement, and social change at the same time.

In Chap. 13, Baez and Baez present a culturally sensitive therapeutic approach, Sweetgrass Method, in response to the mental health needs of American Indians and Alaska Natives. With a history of colonial victimhood and continued oppression in the present, American Indians and Alaska Natives display disproportionally high rates of mental health issues. Psychologists attempted to tackle these problems by introducing Western evidence-based strategies, but the outcomes have been limited. It is clear that the Western models fail to recognize the Indigenous values embedded within the sociopolitical and historical context of American Indians and Alaska Natives. In response, Baez and Baez developed a culturally responsive approach called the Sweetgrass Method. American Indians/First Nations people have held sweetgrass (Óhonte Wenserákon) sacred for a long time. Sweetgrass is used to purify oneself—mentally, emotionally, physically, and spiritually. Specifically, the Sweetgrass Method comprises three threads. The first thread refers to "introspection", a life-long commitment to self-reflection, cultural humility, and attitude. The second thread is on "communication", a commitment to building relationships and partnerships with people and groups to address mental health concerns. The third and last thread is about "continuation", ongoing support, and strategies for clients and their communities that foster long-term success. Deviating from the popular biomedical model, the Sweetgrass Method represents a culturally responsive framework and a community-based participatory practice approach.

References

Ahmed, S. (2013). *The cultural politics of emotion*. Routledge.
Albert, M., Jacobson, D., & Lapid, Y. (2001). *Identities, borders, orders: Rethinking international relations theory*. University of Minnesota Press.
Allen, S., & Xanthaki, A. (2011). *Reflections on the UN declaration on the rights of indigenous peoples*. Bloomsbury Publishing.
Arfken, M. (2012). Scratching the surface: Internationalization, cultural diversity and the politics of recognition. *Social and Personality Psychology Compass, 6*(6), 428–437.
Arnold, M. (1869). *Culture and anarchy: An essay in political and social criticism*. Smith, Elder & Co. https://doi.org/10.1515/9780691213118-013
Baldwin, J. R., Faulkner, S. L., & Hecht, M. L. (2006). A moving target: The illusive definition of culture. In *Redefining culture* (pp. 27–50). Routledge.
Bourdieu, P. (2006). Distinction: a social critique of the judgement of taste. In D. Grusky (Ed.), *Inequality: Classic readings in race, class, and gender* (pp. 287–318). Routledge.
Danziger, K. (2009). The holy grail of universality. In T. Teo, P. Stenner, A. Rutherford, & E. Park (Eds.), *Varieties of theoretical psychology* (pp. 2–11). Captus Press.
Deleuze, G., & Guattari, F. (1987). *A thousand plateaus: Capitalism and schizophrenia* (B. Massumi, Trans.). University of Minnesota Press.
Eck, D. L. (2015). Pluralism: Problems and promise. *Journal of Interreligious Studies, 17*, 54–62.
Ferguson, J. (1997). Anthropology and its evil twin. In F. Cooper & R. Packard (Eds.), *International development and the social sciences: Essays on the history and politics of knowledge* (pp. 150–175). University of California Press.
Foucault, M. (1979). *Discipline and punish: The birth of the prison* (A. Sheridan, Trans.). Random House.
Fraser, N. (2008). Social justice in the age of identity politics: Redistribution, recognition, and participation. In *Geographic thought* (pp. 72–89). Routledge. https://www.taylorfrancis.com/chapters/edit/10.4324/9780203893074-8/social-justice-age-identity-politics-nancy-fraser
Fraser, N. (2024, November 4). *Three faces of capitalist labour*. Critical theory 101: Future directions and new challenges. The American University of Paris.
Gair, S. (2012). Feeling their stories: Contemplating empathy, insider/outsider positionings, and enriching qualitative research. *Qualitative Health Research, 22*(1), 134–143. https://doi.org/10.1177/1049732311420580
Gao, Z. (2022). Indigenous psychology: Difficult engagements with culture and power. *Theory & Psychology, 32*(6), 974–976.
Gao, Z., & Teo, T. (2023). Introduction: Theorizing the psychology of deglobalization. *Theory & Psychology, 33*(2), 163–174.

Geertz, C. (1973). *The interpretation of cultures: Selected essays*. Basic Books.

Gramsci, A. (1971). *Selections from the prison notebooks of Antonio Gramsci: Ed. and Transl. by Quintin Hoare and Geoffrey Nowell Smith* (G. Nowell-Smith & Q. Hoare, Trans.). International Publishers.

Hanisch, C. (1969). *The personal is political*. http://www.carolhanisch.org/CHwritings/PIP.html

Henrich, J., Heine, S. J., & Norenzayan, A. (2010). The weirdest people in the world. *Behavioral and Brain Sciences, 33*(2–3), 61–83.

Hermans, H., & Kempen, H. J. G. (1998). Moving cultures: The perilous problems of cultural dichotomies in a globalizing society. *American Psychologist, 53*(10), 1111–1120. https://doi.org/10.1037/0003-066X.53.10.1111

Heyes, C. (2002). *Identity politics*. https://plato.stanford.edu/Entries/identity-politics/

Hochschild, A. R. (1979). Emotion work, feeling rules, and social structure. *American Journal of Sociology, 85*(3), 551–575.

Horkheimer, M., Adorno, T. W., & Noeri, G. (2002). *Dialectic of enlightenment*. Stanford University Press.

Jahoda, G. (2016). On the rise and decline of 'indigenous psychology. *Culture & Psychology, 22*(2), 169–181. https://doi.org/10.1177/1354067X16634052

Kim, U. E., & Berry, J. W. (1993). *Indigenous psychologies: Research and experience in cultural context*. Sage Publications. https://psycnet.apa.org/record/1993-98753-000

Kluckhohn, C. (1949). *Mirror for man: The relation of anthropology to modern life*. Routledge.

Kroeber, A. L., & Kluckhohn, C. (1952). *Culture: A critical review of concepts and definitions*. Peabody Museum.

Leary, D. E. (1979). Wundt and after: Psychology's shifting relations with the natural sciences, social sciences, and philosophy. *Journal of the History of the Behavioral Sciences, 15*(3), 231–241.

Long, W. (2019). Indigenous psychology: Going nowhere slowly? *Journal of Theoretical and Philosophical Psychology, 39*(2), 115–119.

Marcuse, H. (2013). *One-dimensional man: Studies in the ideology of advanced industrial society*. Routledge.

Nash, K. (2001). The 'cultural turn'in social theory: Towards a theory of cultural politics. *Sociology, 35*(1), 77–92.

Parker, I. (1999). Against relativism in psychology, on balance. *History of the Human Sciences, 12*(4), 61–78. https://doi.org/10.1177/09526959922120496

Schiller, N. G. (1997). Cultural politics and the politics of culture. *Identities: Global studies in culture and power, 4*(1), 1–7. https://doi.org/10.1080/1070289X.1997.9962580

Spivak, G. C. (2012). *In other worlds: Essays in cultural politics*. Routledge.

Sundararajan, L. (2019a). Introduction to the special issue on "indigenous psychology: What's the next step?". *Journal of Theoretical and Philosophical Psychology, 39*(2), 65.

Sundararajan, L. (2019b). Whither indigenous psychology? *Journal of Theoretical and Philosophical Psychology, 39*(2), 81.

Sundararajan, L., Hwang, K.-K., & Yeh, K.-H. (2020). *Global psychology from indigenous perspectives: Visions inspired by K. S. Yang*. Palgrave Macmillan.

Teo, T. (2011). Empirical race psychology and the hermeneutics of epistemological violence. *Human Studies, 34*(3), 237–255.

The Indigenous Apology Work Group, The American Psychological Association. (2023). *Report on an offer of apology, on behalf of the American Psychological Association, to first peoples in the United States*. The American Psychological Association.

Thomson, I. T. (2010). *Culture wars and enduring American dilemmas*. University of Michigan Press. https://library.oapen.org/handle/20.500.12657/30571

Ting, R. S.-K., & Sundararajan, L. (2017). *Culture, cognition, and emotion in China's religious ethnic minorities: Voices of suffering among the Yi*. Springer.

Williams, R. (2014). *Keywords: A vocabulary of culture and society*. Oxford University Press.

Wittgenstein, L. (2009). *Philosophical investigations* (G. E. M. Anscombe, P. M. S. Hacker, & J. Schulte, Trans.). Blackwell Publishing.

Yanchar, S. C., & Slife, B. D. (1997). Pursuing unity in a fragmented psychology: Problems and prospects. *Review of General Psychology, 1*(3), 235.

Yang, K. (1997). Indigenizing westernized Chinese psychology. In M. H. Bond (Ed.), *Working at the interface of cultures: Eighteen lives in social science* (pp. 62–76). Routledge.

PART I

The Many Faces of Colonialism

CHAPTER 2

The Psychology and Politics of Colonial Splitting: Moving from Division to Transformation

Arthur W. Blume

Introduction

Colonialism has viewed the world as inherently hierarchical, and therefore justified the conquest and colonization of people and entities deemed as culturally inferior (Blume, 2020). Modern colonialism has been driven by the desire to enhance political power and material wealth of the European ruling class. Christian church leaders sanctioned colonial conquest beginning with the Crusades, and the targeting of non-Christian peoples for conquest, enslavement, and exploitation of resources that were codified by the papal edicts of Dum Diversas (1452) and the Doctrine of Discovery (1493) as a divine duty to the church (Dunbar-Ortiz, 2014; Echo-Hawk, 2013).

Colonial assumptions of natural hierarchies contributed to beliefs of entitlement for the privileged, exploitation of the natural world and its

A. W. Blume (✉)
Department of Psychology, Washington State University, Vancouver, WA, USA
e-mail: art.blume@wsu.edu

Z. Z. Gao, M. I. Medved (eds.), *Global Perspectives on Cultural Politics in Indigenous Psychology*, Palgrave Studies in Indigenous Psychology, https://doi.org/10.1007/978-3-031-96813-6_2

natural resources, oppression, and racism and other group-based "-isms" that suggested inferiority of other demographics when compared to the privileged (Blume, 2020). First-generation colonial nations such as Spain, Portugal, England, France, Germany, Russia, Belgium, Norway, and Denmark felt justified and compelled to colonize the rest of world (Murrey, 2020). Eventually, a second generation of colonial nations (such as the US, Canada, Australia, New Zealand, South Africa, and Rhodesia) emerged from areas colonized by the first-generation nations, populated by colonial settlers that ultimately gained their independence from first-generation colonial nations, but continued colonizing policies against Indigenous people.

Modern colonization has broad global impact. The power and coercive influence of first- and second-generation colonial nations have culturally, environmentally, and politically impacted at least 84 percent of the land area of the world during the last six centuries (Hoffman, 2015). Colonial values have been spread globally through assimilation efforts, such that hierarchical beliefs and practices have been incorporated to various degrees into the cultures and politics of nations negatively impacted by European colonization. Some nations that were initially colonial victims have since become colonizers in their own ways, such the People's Republic of China and Israel. Other colonial victims have resorted to populist and nationalistic policies that look very much like those reflected in the colonial powers of history (e.g., India and Türkiye; Blume, 2022a).

The hierarchical assumptions of colonialism consequentially resulted in a self-oriented and reductionistic cultural perspective famously presented by Cartesian philosophy (Descartes, 1637). The self-interests of colonists often clashed with the collective interests of those they conquered. A reductionistic viewpoint inevitably prioritizes self and therefore self-interests over others, which naturally promotes divisiveness between self and others (Blume, 2020). The conquest and subjugation of others for the benefit of a privileged few has unsurprisingly resulted in societies of perpetual conflict and divisiveness (Blume, 2022a).

Exercising superiority and privilege in colonial nations has created generations of dispossessed, underprivileged, impoverished, and politically disempowered peoples. As an example, the First Peoples of the Americas have suffered greatly from colonization, essentially losing most of their liberties, much of their cultures, and almost all their material resources. Intergenerational poverty and health inequities have been common consequences (Blume, 2019; Presidential Task Force on Psychology and Health

Equity, 2023). Exploitation of the few natural resources that Indigenous people continue to hold has been widespread, often generating health-threatening pollution and degradation of land, water, and air (Blume, 2020; Lewis et al., 2017). Indigenous people have not been the only groups that experienced intergeneration colonial consequences in the US. Many immigrants experienced colonial oppression as slaves, indentured servants, or otherwise exploited workers. The US Constitution was written in such a way to ensure liberties, including voting rights, property ownership, and religious freedom, were extended only to a certain privileged group that excluded all minoritized groups, women, and children or those in early adulthood until very recent times (e.g., Blume et al., 2020; Echo-Hawk, 2013). Even today, the extension of rights to all citizens remains fluid and subject to the whims and manipulations of the privileged (Noggle, 2021).

Minoritized peoples are the most obvious victims of hierarchy, but people of European descent have also been exploited by hierarchy. Not all European immigrant families and their progeny have shared in the political power and wealth of the most privileged in colonial societies. The privileged of the US have propagated a myth referred to as the "American Dream" to advance the belief of national exceptionalism and entice its citizens to believe in meritocracy—that class migration is not only possible but common, despite evidence to the contrary (Chetty et al., 2018; Smeeding, 2016). Many White Americans largely continue to buy into the myth of the American dream, despite having more in common with other minoritized groups than with the crème de le crème of the American social order. Consequentially, White Americans from the lower socioeconomic class often side politically with privileged White Americans in ways that work against their own best interests for social advancement (Blume, 2020; Metzl, 2019). What can explain this phenomenon of misalliances?

Colonialism: Attack, Control, and Manipulate and Distract

Colonial proponents have relied extensively on three tactics to achieve their goals of seizure and subjugation. The first tactic has been to attack, which has resulted in brutal consequences such as physical violence, death, and sometimes attempts at extermination and genocide. Colonists, often significantly outnumbered in their colonial exploitations, would often use divide et impera strategies to prevail in wars. However, attacks have also taken the form of economic and cultural assaults and political powerplays that have harmed and threatened minoritized peoples *after* they have been conquered or subdued. The second tactic has been to control by use of assimilation, indoctrination, restriction of rights, and economic and political neglect. The use of attack and control of the Indigenous First Peoples of the US (i.e., Indigenous Americans) has been widely discussed by scholars.

The third tactic, manipulation, has been subtler in its expression and widely used by colonists when wanting to deceive. Colonial manipulators often use distraction to cover their intentions, including when engaging in *colonial splitting* (Blume, 2020, 2022a, 2022b), a form of manipulation that generates divisiveness among different disempowered groups victimized by colonialism. *Splitting*, a term that may have different meanings in Western psychology, is used here to describe interpersonal (relational) behavior when a person manipulates two or more people against one another to get their needs met, often encouraging disagreement or conflict between the individuals being split. *Colonial splitting* often involves intentional acts by those who would politically benefit from the manipulation of the splitting, but sometimes the consequences of colonial splitting may take on a life of their own. Colonial splitting is not a strategic tactic of wartime to turn enemies against one another like divide et impera, but rather strategic use of manipulation in non-warring circumstances to control and disempower those deemed inferior by the privileged of society, which has the effect of maintaining the hierarchical status quo.

The function of colonial splitting is to disempower minoritized people politically and economically to maintain hierarchies and to protect and benefit the privileged of colonial societies. The privileged intentionally manipulate disempowered groups through direct or indirect messaging that portrays another group as a threat or potential political or economic rival. Colonial splitting tactics also weaponize economic disempowerment to elevate divisions within and between groups.

Colonial America used colonial splitting in highly effective ways to disempower Indigenous Americans. A wide variety of colonial splitting tactics encouraged divisions and enlisted collaborators during the colonial era. "Whiskey" treaties were one tactic used by the US federal government during the period of conquest. During these negotiations, the liberal flow of alcohol made it easier to manipulate and split nations such that collaborators were perceived as betraying their people during treaty negotiations (e.g., the Treaty of Greenville, which included US historic icons Meriwether Lewis and William Clark as participant-witnesses; Dunbar-Ortiz, 2014; Owens, 2002). Sometimes within-nations conflict resulted from acts of colonial splitting (e.g., Conser, 1978). Colonial splitting tactics were used to promote animosity between citizens who were considered "full blooded" and those who were of "mixed blood" (i.e., White and Indigenous; Anderson & Woolworth, 1988), a distinction that has been used historically to divide Indigenous American nations. Sometimes colonial splitting tactics under the guise of cultural assimilation were meant to divide communities generationally, such as the use of residential schools to split children from families, communities, and their cultures through coercive and abusive educational assimilation (Bureau of Indian Affairs, 2022). President Vladimir Putin used a modern version of this colonial splitting tactic by imposing Russian citizenship on children taken from Ukraine during wartime (BBC, January 6, 2024).

Another tactic of colonial splitting was to grant special (false) privileges within Indigenous nations to collaborators who would promote and enforce colonial policies on reservations. Collaborators would eventually be coerced to help round up children for boarding schools (Bureau of Indian Affairs, 2022), a colonial splitting activity that has scarred communities for generations. Additionally, the US government might grant collaborator privileges and feigned acceptance to mixed bloods over full bloods (or vice versa) to encourage further splitting of the nation, sometimes resulting in nations being split during conflicts with the US army (e.g., Anderson & Woolworth, 1988). However, when collaborators are of no further use to the privileged of colonial societies, they are routinely abandoned, suggesting that the privilege and acceptance assigned to collaborators is a fleeting and illusory proposition.

Colonialism has always been closely aligned with material goals (ownership, wealth seeking, etc.). One of the primary tenets of colonialism, supported by the church doctrines of Dum Diversas (1452) and the Doctrine of Discovery (1493), was the persistent belief that colonists had a divinely sanctioned right to seize resources from Indigenous people and claim them for their own. Colonists have often exploited and manipulated Indigenous citizens to advance their own material wealth. One notorious example of this type of deceit and manipulation included White Americans marrying and manipulating relationships with Osage citizens to gain tribal rights to petroleum extraction from tribal lands, including some who resorted to murder to gain those financial interests (Grann, 2017).

The privileged of colonial materialistic societies have often used economic incentives as tools for colonial splitting. The economic incentives are used to encourage an Indigenous nation to engage in an economic venture with those off the reservation. Inevitably, due to clashes between the hierarchical and self-interested assumptions of colonial culture and the holistic assumptions of Indigenous culture, individuals may reap the short-term benefits of these incentives, but the collective whole may not receive sustained benefits, enhancing community divisiveness. Conflict often ensues when economic collaboration is interpreted as betrayal of the collective whole. Unfortunately, pie in the sky incentives offered by colonial manipulators may only last if the colonial corporations find the partnership profitable.

Economic acts of colonial splitting against Indigenous communities continue. Sometimes colonial splitting pits different communities with similar circumstances against one another with the promises of material gains for some communities at the expense of others. The Biden administration committed such an act, unwittingly or not, by approving the Willows oil project that benefited some Alaska Native communities financially but threatened environmental degradation to others (Thiessen & Brown, March 16, 2023). Blaming the collaborators becomes a typical response by those who feel victimized and betrayed, which is exactly the distraction and conflict desired by those who have manipulated the circumstances to their benefit. In reality, both the betrayed and the collaborators are victims, having been manipulated by the colonial privileged who have leveraged the divisions to advance their own wealth-building agenda.

Blood Quantum, Enrollment, Colorism, and Colonial Splitting

The US Congress enacted the Dawes Act in 1887 to start the process to fully assimilate the survivors of the colonial conquest such that the extinction of Indigenous American cultures would result (Dunbar-Ortiz, 2014; US National Archives, February 8, 2022). The Dawes Act and subsequent legislation gave the illusion of providing and protecting land and resources for Indigenous nations and their citizens, but instead contributed to tremendous losses of land, resources, and culture. The Dawes Act also began a federal process of identifying and splitting Indigenous people by blood quantum as another method to weaken the Indigenous people. Later, the

Indian Reorganization Act of 1935, enacted during the height of the eugenics movement, codified the use of blood quantum to define who were federally recognized as Indigenous Americans in the US, leaving decisions for how to define blood quantum requirements for citizenship to individual nations (Spruhan, 2006). The Indian Reorganization Act was used to expand the concept of enrolled citizenship to all federally recognized nations. Defining and registering Indigenous people by statute was not limited to the US, but also occurred in other colonial nations (e.g., Canada; Parrott, 2022; South Africa; Breckenridge, 2014).

The enrollment process facilitated the ability of the federal government to monitor and control those listed on the enrollment lists. Shifting enrollment processes to individual nations on the surface appeared to be a step toward self-determination, but the federal government shrewdly pitted citizens against one another by promoting hierarchical blood quantum considerations for citizenship that became a flashpoint within the communities. Enrollment as a method for colonial splitting has survived to the present day, enhancing conflict within nations, communities, and even within families and clans concerning citizenship and racial identity, and generating ethical concerns about methods that may inevitably result in population attrition (e.g., Lussenden, 2023).

Native Americans remain the only racial demographic in the US to be defined by blood quantum and enrollment, a notably racialized classification system that originated during the era of eugenics and in the context of White supremacy movements. The assimilation policies of the US federal government became a template for another colonial society oriented toward White supremacy, Germany. The Nazi Party studied and coopted American policies toward the assimilation of Native Americans, ultimately developing their own enrollment lists to control and attack Jewish citizens (Miller, 2020).

Enrollment policies have also divided Indigenous people over economic resource concerns. The long history of nations sharing the meager resources provided by the US government has generated tremendous competition and understandably contributed to defensive postures by nations to protect those resources. The colonial government, by weaponizing those limited resources, exacerbated concerns about any perceived threat to those resources. As a result, there have been periods of serious tensions between those who are enrolled with those who are not enrolled and claiming Indigenous roots that are perceived as a threat. Clearly, some who claim Indigenous roots are lying or misinformed, but not all.

However, there are many legitimate historical circumstances that would contribute to Indigenous Americans claiming ancestry while not being enrolled. Children referred to as *lost birds* by Indigenous communities were adopted away from their nations without any sense of their family history. Many Indigenous Americans were coerced or strongly encouraged to move away from their traditional lands and peoples and those connections may have been lost. Some may have moved away from their nations prior to the process of enrollment. Some may have intermarried outside the nation, perhaps to a person of another race, and their children will no longer meet the tribal quantum requirements for enrollment. Some who married other tribal citizens could have children who are majority Indigenous but do not qualify for quantum requirements in either the father's or mother's nation. Some may have made personal choices not to seek enrollment because of the historical circumstances. Others may have been unenrolled during an internal political squabble, and some of those squabbles may have been the result of racialized motives for disenrollment (e.g., "Black Indians;" Inniss, 2015). Some nations were disenrolled by the federal government by its termination policies meant to assimilate and dissolve sovereignty and confiscate their treaty lands (Galanda, September 12, 2018). Other nations are recognized by states but not the federal government and therefore not officially recognized as Indigenous. Many of these unenrolled people strongly identify as Indigenous and as allies of enrolled Indigenous people, yet sometimes viewed with scorn by enrolled citizens for being unenrolled. Enrolled citizens could have easily been unenrolled themselves if the chaotic circumstances of colonialism had gone just a bit differently

Many people are not enrolled due to chance rather than choice. There are many historical reasons why those who claim heritage might not be enrolled, and arguably most if not all those circumstances have been due to the consequences of colonial oppression. The feuding between those who are enrolled and those who are not has been strongly manipulated by those with colonial privilege to create yet another barrier to thwart Indigenous unity. Enrolled citizens lose the human capital of those who were lost over time to their nations, who might be allies amid a treacherous society. The opportunity for widespread acts of colonial splitting inherent in the enrollment policies has victimized both the enrolled and those not enrolled. The squabbles between the enrolled and the not enrolled are victories for the colonial oppressors.

Colonial splitting policies have promoted competition and feuding between and within the nations over who accesses the extremely limited resources provided by the federal government to enrolled citizens. Colonial entities have routinely manipulated and controlled Indigenous nations by weaponizing those limited resources into the modern era. The dependence of Indigenous nations on the US federal budget due to conquest and assimilation is so profound that government shutdowns typically harm Indigenous nations in ways that other demographic groups are not impacted (e.g., Denetclaw, September 28, 2023). The federal government has never provided the resources they promised in treaties or needed to end poverty and promote health equity. Indian Health Services has been historically underfunded and underprioritized in federal budgets (Gone & Trimble, 2012). Inequity in healthcare, inadequate resources, economic inequities, and acts of racism have ensured intergenerational health disparities (Blume, 2019; Presidential Task Force on Psychology and Health Equity, 2023). Assimilation legislation such as the Dawes Act and the Indian Reorganization Act of 1935 created policies that have weaponized economic promises to control, manipulate, and prevent the social advancement of Indigenous peoples. These policies are colonial relics that have enabled over a century of colonial splitting of Indigenous Americans, hindering the ability to rise above the inherent divisions of competition to act with unity.

Colonial nations have also been adept at wielding colorism, or the relative comparison of skin tone, as a tool of colonial splitting. The history of colorism in the US has its roots in eugenics and hypodescent policies where "one drop" of blood of color disqualified a person from being considered "White." The use of colorism as a tool for colonial splitting has created a history within minoritized communities to also look to skin color as a subjective assessment of identity credibility or level of cultural belongingness. The challenges of colorism are profound for bi- or multiracial individuals, where the consequences of colonial splitting have made it difficult to identify with any racial-ethnic community (Hud-Aleem & Countryman, 2008). The psychological circumstances of colorism have been linked with unhealthy efforts to fit into a group, such as using skin lightning agents to appear White (Daftary et al., 2023).

Encouraging Colonial Splitting Between Different Groups

The US colonial government was also particularly good at using colonial splitting to divide different demographic groups who would be natural allies if circumstances were different. An economic manifestation of colonial splitting has been to manipulate the threat of competition between different disempowered groups for scarce resources, when both were suffering from a lack of resources due to exploitation by the privileged in society. Colonial influencers have adeptly spread disinformation to deflect responsibility for the economic inequities of society, projecting perceptions of threat and blame on others.

Stereotyping of groups has been used to fuel the fire of divisiveness between minoritized groups. Xenophobia has been fostered to manipulate one group against another, through racialized dog whistle statements or in depicting immigrants as a threat to colonial societies (Blume, 2022a). The privileged of society developed legal and economic systems to consolidate wealth and protect privilege that has contributed to extreme social inequities (Echo-Hawk, 2013; Presidential Task Force on Psychology and Health Equity, 2023). Colonial proponents have manipulated those inequities, deflecting blame to disempowered groups who are portrayed as economic and political rivals to distract from the reality that it is the colonial system's social order that victimizes.

Colonial splitting has not been limited to race or ethnicity and has been used to divide any demographic group deemed inferior by the privileged elite of colonial societies (by ableism, ageism, heterosexism, sexism, etc.). For example, colonial splitting between religious groups has been used to divide and disempower people of certain minoritized religious perspectives viewed as a threat to the colonial majority. Indigenous peoples in the US did not receive religious freedom protections until 1978 because traditional religions were considered empowering and threatening, but assimilation through Christianity was encouraged (Blume et al., 2020). The US has not been alone in using these tactics. Modern examples exist, such as colonial splitting of Hindus from other religious groups in India and Chinese efforts to control and manipulate Tibetan Buddhism. Due to the global extent of colonialism, colonial splitting has been widely used as a method to control Indigenous peoples.

Exercising Liberties to Advance Colonial Splitting

Privilege in colonial societies is a natural consequence of the hierarchical assumptions of superiority and exceptionalism. Colonial privilege advances the notions that the elite have special entitlements to how they act and live that are not extended to the whole of those societies, and that the rules of society applied to common citizens are not necessarily applicable to the privileged. Colonial elites have historically assumed that liberties are divinely sanction rights and entitlements. The US Constitution has many examples of divinely sanctioned liberties and entitlements extended to a select few but not the whole, such as voting rights and freedom of religion. The privilege of elite citizens in colonial nations affords many advantages, including the ability to exercise their liberties without the fear of retribution (Blume, 2020). Due to beliefs of superiority and exceptionalism, the privileged often exercise their liberties with little concern for how it impacts others, especially those viewed as irrelevant or inferior. During the COVID-19 pandemic, people of privilege exercised their liberties in ways that increased health risks to others, especially minoritized groups (Blume, 2022a).

Freedom of speech has been used liberally by the privileged (such as politicians or social influencers) as an essential weapon to advance colonial splitting, often spreading misinformation or advancing disinformation to increase tensions between diverse groups of people (Blume, 2022a). Social media has been a reliable and rapid conduit for colonial splitting, and the privileged rights of freedom of speech have been used as justification even when colonial splitting resulted in conflict, harm, and violence. An excellent example is how privileged influencers-manipulators have successfully leveraged racialized threats to convey threat to lower SES Whites related to both economics and political power, even though low SES White citizens have much more in common with oppressed minoritized groups than the privileged elite (Blume, 2020; Metzl, 2019).

Elon Musk illustrates an excellent example of privilege weaponizing liberties by defending the power of free speech to the potential detriment of others on "*X*." Mr. Musk made the decision to reinstate the account of "social influencer" Alex Jones who has notoriously spread hate under the guise of freedom of speech, even though reinstating the Jones account might hurt his company financially (Duffy, December 10, 2023). His actions have suggested that freedom of speech as an entitlement of privilege was more important to him than the consequences of that freedom of speech. Exercising liberties despite their harmful consequences to others naturally occurs in a hierarchical society that sanctions privileged entitlement.

Populism and Nationalism as Political Methods for Colonial Splitting

Colonial populism and nationalism have been used effectively as tools for colonial splitting of minoritized groups including Indigenous peoples. Populism appeals broadly to protecting the interests of common citizens and may appear superficially to be a benign grassroots movement. However, populists typically manipulate a false narrative that a group (often the societally empowered ingroup) is being victimized by others and then portray their movement as designed to protect those perceived victims. Populists often falsely promote an anti-establishment movement (Ashutosh, 2021), even though leaders are typically representative of the privileged elite or prone toward an evolution of elitism themselves. However, the colonial roots of populism are apparent in its hierarchically divisive assumption that the people it represents (common or otherwise) are the rightful heirs to power and privilege that allegedly is being threatened by others. A populist movement may feign advancing equality but eventually results in division and conflict due to its implicit hierarchical tenets concerning justice.

Populism is often associated with nationalism (Blume, 2022a; Heiskanen, 2020; Singh, 2021), both which foundationally reflect tenets endorsing group superiority. Indigenous people are commonly victimized by populist-nationalism since they are typically excluded from the populist-nationalist identity. They are not alone in that exclusion. Nationalistic identity is often derived from within the conqueror-colonizer perspective (Blume, 2022a; Filc, 2015). Populist-nationalism may appeal to Indigenous peoples for their political support, promising economic or political advances for the people, but rarely have those promises materialized historically, as suggested by the continued inequities in Indigenous communities (Blume et al., 2020). Even when a populist-nationalistic movement proposes to advance an equitable Indigenous political order, those movements tend to drift toward exclusivity and may inequitably resort to protecting the implied needs of the populist-nationalistic group at the expense of others (de la Torre, 2016; McKay & Colque, 2021).

Psychological Consequences of Colonial Splitting

The divisiveness and disunity promoted by colonial splitting has resulted in significant and intergenerational psychological consequences, particularly trauma and dehumanization, for Indigenous American communities. For example, colonial splitting acts of religious assimilation have created tensions between those practicing colonial Christian beliefs and those practicing traditional spiritual practices. Another source of community tensions has been from economic colonial splitting, where certain members have benefitted from capitalistic ventures and others have not. Individual ownership and wealth building were not traditional cultural values in many communities, but some Indigenous Americans have assimilated to colonial values regarding ownership. Today, Indigenous American communities live in completely different realities often due to the duress of colonial splitting methods.

Assimilation processes coerced Indigenous Americans to adapt to colonial cultural assumptions to survive. Egalitarian collective peoples were coerced to adapt to a culture that emphasized hierarchies and self-interests—coerced to internalize colonial values. Internalized colonization coerced people for whom ownership and materialism was foreign to adapt to a materialistic culture, in a process I refer to as material assimilation. Because of colonial splitting, collectivistic people were coerced into a process of individualization through acts of individual assimilation, manipulated and cajoled into adapting to a colonial culture of self-interests. Material and individual assimilation through colonial splitting have magnified envy and jealousy, a self-interested outcome linked to community disharmony. Colonial splitting encouraged the development of factions within nations that remain today and can be the source of internal conflict. Leaders may be tempted to follow colonial hierarchical models rather than traditional egalitarian expressions of leadership due to internalized colonization (Blume & Trimble, 2024).

Colonial proponents have succeeded in some ways at sowing discord within and between Indigenous communities due to the splitting tools of manipulation, deceit, and the blaming of others. The externalizing tactics of blaming have been assimilated into our communities, tactics that run contrary to Indigenous internalizing processes for advancing health, wellness, and personal learning and growth (Blume, 2020). Externalization often involves blaming or scapegoating others for circumstances of life leaving one vulnerable to the tactics that assign blame or scapegoat others, whereas internalization takes personal responsibility for attitudes and behaviors, thus minimizing the risk of manipulation. Internalized interpretations and returning to our collective, communal, and egalitarian roots will be important to reversing the damage of colonial splitting within Indigenous American communities.

Decolonizing the Consequences of Colonial Splitting

Decolonizing the traumatic and dehumanizing consequences of colonial splitting requires systematic reconciliation and restoration. The first step is to expose colonial splitting when it occurs, remembering its colonial intent to divide victims against one another. When conflict and division emerge, minoritized groups must identify who might stand to gain from the consequences of division, conflict, and mistrust—who initiated and benefitted from the division and how those benefactors are manipulating the situation now. If the manipulation is not transparently evident, communities must look to how the privileged might benefit from the divisiveness for interpretation.

Second, decolonizing the consequences of colonial splitting requires reconciliation. Reconciliation is the daily process of reclaiming sacredness in one's relationships with others, and the process includes a return to internalized interpretations of what is my social responsibility to others in this interaction rather than externalized interpretations of what others are doing to me. Reconciliation is an important process that promotes psychological wellness. Indigenous American Psychology specifies seven steps for reconciliation to promote harmony and balance in relationships, two that may be particularly helpful processes to decolonizing the impact of colonial splitting: reconciling social systems to all people and reconciling diverse groups of people (Blume, 2020, p. 154). Reconciliation as a daily goal promotes harmony and balance in relationships with others, rather than conflict and division. Daily acts of reconciling social systems to equitably serve all victimized peoples and of reconciling restorative justice and peace with one another will make it increasingly less likely that colonial splitting will be successful.

Third, decolonizing the consequences of colonial splitting requires exposing colonial hierarchical culture as an enemy of the people. Colonialism harms everyone through its attacks, controls, and manipulations and distractions, and cultural beliefs in natural hierarchies and meritocracy promote broad-based inequities and injustices that adversely impact the physical and psychological wellness of the planetary system (Blume, 2020). Colonial splitting is a risk for any society that assumes hierarchical assumptions that result in supremacist or exceptionalist values that inevitably lead to the subordination of others. Decolonization of hierarchical beliefs and values helps to ensure that privilege and entitlement expectations arise in where entitlement justifies the exploitation of others or in which others might be viewed as a potential threat to privilege that needs to be controlled. An egalitarian model of social organization is an essential element for transforming the risk of colonial splitting and ensuring the psychological wellness of the collective (Blume, 2020). Reclaiming sacredness in relationships contributes to restoration of the Indigenous values of egalitarianism that expose hierarchies as a house of cards waiting to fall under its own weight of manipulation and deceit. Those who have been targeted by colonialism can reclaim the lenses of egalitarianism that will aid in the decolonization process, including those who identify with the majority but have not flourished under its colonial social contract.

Fourth, colonial splitting is decolonized by a restoration of social responsibility as a guiding principle of daily living is a crucial step to learning life transforming lessons. Personal challenges must be observed and interpreted internally rather than assigned to external factors such as blaming others, meaning that challenges are meant to promote rather than impede personal growth. Externalization is a key factor for why colonial splitting tactics are effective—externalizing promotes discord and disharmony. Internalized interpretations of life examine the opportunities in the moment rather than the barriers and promote optimism rather than frustration and despair (Blume, 2020).

Fifth, the restoration of healthy relationships with others will promote healthy allyship between groups. Colonial splitting may breed disunity and conflict, but decolonization promotes unity and alliances. Restoration and reconciliation processes open the eyes of those being targeted for colonial splitting as to where the real threat lies. The enemy is the colonial mindset that has been indoctrinated into colonial social orders. The splitting influencers are the proponents of colonialism, invested in protection of the privilege of the few. Disempowered peoples rising together as allies to oppose the acts of colonial splitting is the next step of decolonization beyond restoration and reconciliation. Understanding that the acts are purposefully intended to attack, control, and manipulate and distract those who are targeted, makes it easier to ally against those acts.

Indigenous people have a shared kinship when it comes to colonial attack, control, manipulation, and distraction. Indigenous peoples have shared many commonalities in their histories, such as the consequences of colonialism including colonial splitting, manipulation, and deceit. Indigenous individuals have historically used their community's traditional healing practices and ceremonies to facilitate reconciliation and restorations with others. One historic example of reconciliation by some communities was to covertly merge traditional spiritual ceremonies and practices into Christian rituals, or to engage in ceremonies and practices in community churches when Western clerics were not present. At the community or national level, coalitions of Indigenous groups have emerged to work on decolonization efforts. Indigenous psychologists, for example, have been working collaboratively to address issues such as colonial splitting and its consequences through the Global Psychology Alliance and other similar organizations, or advancing collaborative relationships independent of formal organizational structures.

Some Indigenous Americans have expressed concerns that efforts to seek unity of purpose smack of pan-Indigenous cultural diffusion, threatening sovereignty and disrespecting cultural differences. Seeking allies across the nations would be strengthened by coming together as a coalition of sovereigns that understand and appreciate their shared sacred and communal interests in advancing decolonization. Furthermore, global Indigenous allies who have shared in the experiences of colonization would also be immensely helpful to advancing global decolonization from a position of collective strength.

From Survivance to *Thrivance*

Indigenous peoples have shared experiences of victimization and survivance (Vizenor, 1993) that bind and strengthen us without threatening sovereignty. Those shared experiences will motivate the creation of powerful alliances in support of the decolonization process. Survivance represents the strengths of overcoming the consequences of colonial attacks, controls, and manipulations and distractions (Vizenor, 1993). Survivance has been a collective response to a collective threat. Colonial splitting has coerced many people into acts of survivance, but decolonization requires movement beyond survivance to positions of strengths-based *thrivance*

(Walters et al., 2020). A holistic Indigenous perspective suggests that seeking thrivance must be a collective effort. The decolonization healing processes of exposing colonizing methods including colonial splitting, reconciliation of relationships with others and social systems, exposing colonial hierarchical culture as the shared enemy of the people, restoration of social responsibility as a guiding principle of daily living, and the restoration of healthy relationships with others will put us on the collective pathway to healing, resulting in a movement from individual survivance to collective thrivance. Seeking thrivance is the next step on our collective journey to psychological healing of the individual and collective traumas that have occurred as a result of the divisiveness of colonial splitting.

Conflict of Interest: the author declares that there is no conflict of interest.

References

Anderson, G. C., & Woolworth, A. R. (Eds.). (1988). *Through Dakota eyes: Narrative accounts of the Minnesota Indian War of 1862.* Minnesota Historical Society Press.

Ashutosh, V. (2021). Populism and nationalism: An overview of similarities and differences. *Studies in Comparative International Development, 56*(2), 131–147. https://doi.org/10.1007/s12116-021-09332-x

BBC. (2024, January 6). *Ukraine-Russia war: Putin citizenship decree violates children's rights, Ukraine* says. https://www.bbc.com/news/world-europe-67901567

Blume, A. W. (2019). Seeking health and well-being for Indigenous North American men. In D. E. Griffith, M. A. Bruce, & R. L. Thorpe (Eds.), *Men's health equity: A handbook* (pp. 472–485). Routledge Press.

Blume, A. W. (2020). *A new psychology based on community, equality, and care of the earth: An Indigenous American perspective.* Bloomsbury.

Blume, A. W. (2022a). *Colonialism and the COVID-19 pandemic: Perspectives from Indigenous Psychology.* Springer Nature.

Blume, A. W. (2022b). Promoting new psychological understandings by use of an Indigenous American Psychological Paradigm. *Journal of Humanistic Psychology, 62*(4), 540–562.

Blume, A. W., Morse, G. S., & Love, C. (2020). Human rights and psychology from Indigenous perspectives. In N. Rubin & R. Flores (Eds.), *The Cambridge handbook on psychology and human rights* (pp. 258–272). Cambridge University Press.

Blume, A. W., & Trimble, J. E. (2024). "What really matters is that you have a beautiful spirit": Selected Native American Indian traditional leadership styles.

In J. L. Chin, J. E. Trimble, & J. Tan (Eds.), *Building bridges to inclusive leadership through the lens of cultural narratives.* Cognella Academic Publishing.
Breckenridge, K. (2014). The book of life: The South African population register and the invention of racial descent, 1950–1980. *Kronos, 40*, 225–240. http://www.jstor.org/stable/24341941
Bureau of Indian Affairs. (2022). *Federal Indian boarding school initiative investigative report.* US Department of Interior. https://www.bia.gov/sites/default/files/dup/inline-files/bsi_investigative_report_may_2022_508.pdf
Chetty, R., Hendren, N., Jones, M. R., & Porter, S. R. (2018). *Race and economic opportunity in the United States: An intergenerational perspective.* Harvard University. http://www.equality-of-opportunity.org/assets/documents/race_paper.pdf
Conser, W. H. (1978). John Ross and the Cherokee resistance campaign, 1833–1838. *The Journal of Southern History, 44*(2), 191–212. https://doi.org/10.2307/2208301
Daftary, K., Poondru, S., Patel, N., Shramuk, M., Muhammad, L., & Kundu, R. V. (2023). Colorism attitudes and use of skin lightening agents in the United States. *International Journal of Women's Dermatology, 9*, e092. https://doi.org/10.1097/JW9.0000000000000092
de la Torre, C. (2016). Populism and the politics of the extraordinary in Latin America. *Journal of Political Ideologies, 21*(2), 121–139. https://doi.org/10.1080/13569317.2016.1150137
Denetclaw, P. (2023, September 28). Government shutdowns deeply impact tribal nations. *Indian Country Today.* https://ictnews.org/news/government-shutdowns-deeply-impact-tribal-nations
Descartes, R. (1637). *Discourse on the method.* Translated in 1983 by V. R. Miller and R. P. Miller (Springer-Verlag).
Duffy, C. (2023, December 10). *'The people have spoken': Elon Musk restores the X account of conspiracy theorist Alex Jones after poll.* https://www.cnn.com/2023/12/09/business/alex-jones-restored-x-elon-musk-poll/index.html
Dunbar-Ortiz, R. (2014). *An Indigenous peoples' history of the United States.* Beacon Press.
Echo-Hawk, W. R. (2013). *In the light of justice: The rise of human rights in Native America.* Fulcrum.
Filc, D. (2015). Latin American inclusive and European exclusionary populism: Colonialism as an explanation. *Journal of Political Ideologies, 20*(3), 263–283. https://doi.org/10.1080/13569317.2015.1075264
Galanda, G. S. (2018, September 12). Disenrollment IS a federal action. *Indian Country Today.* https://ictnews.org/archive/disenrollment-is-a-federal-action

Gone, J. P., & Trimble, J. E. (2012). American Indian and Alaska Native mental health: Diverse perspectives on enduring disparities. *Annual Review of Clinical Psychology, 8*, 31–60. https://doi.org/10.1146/annurev-clinpsy-032511-143127

Grann, D. (2017). *Killers of the flower moon*. Vintage Books.

Heiskanen, J. (2020). The nationalism-populism matrix. *Journal of Political Ideologies, 26*(3), 335–355. https://doi.org/10.1080/13569317.2020.1825280

Hoffman, P. (2015). *Why did Europe conquer the world? Princeton economic history of the Western World*, J. Mokyr Series Editor, Princeton University Press. https://doi.org/10.2307/j.ctvc778hd

Hud-Aleem, R., & Countryman, J. (2008). Biracial identity development and recommendations in therapy. *Psychiatry, 5*(11), 37–44.

Inniss, L. B. (2015). Cherokee Freedmen and the color of belonging. *SMU Scholar, 5*(2), 100–118. https://scholar.smu.edu/cgi/viewcontent.cgi?article=1433&context=law_faculty

Lewis, J., Hoover, J., & MacKenzie, D. (2017). Mining and environmental health disparities in Native American communities. *Current Environmental Health Report, 4*(2), 130–141. https://doi.org/10.1007/s40572-017-0140-5

Lussenden, A. (2023). Blood quantum and the ever-tightening chokehold on tribal citizenship: The reproductive justice implications of blood quantum requirements. *California Law Review, 111*, 287–324. https://doi.org/10.15779/Z386Q1SJ11

McKay, B. M., & Colque, G. (2021). Populism and its authoritarian tendencies: The politics of division in Bolivia. *Latin American Perspectives*. https://doi.org/10.1177/0094582X211052980

Metzl, J. (2019). *Dying of whiteness*. Basic Books.

Miller, R. J. (2020). Nazi Germany's race laws, the United States, and American Indians. *St. John's Law Review, 94*(3), 751–817. https://scholarship.law.stjohns.edu/lawreview

Murrey, A. (2020). Colonialism. In A. Kobayashi (Ed.), *International encyclopedia of human geography* (2nd Ed., pp. 315–326). https://doi.org/10.1016/B978-0-08-102295-5.10804-2

Noggle, R. (2021). Manipulation in politics. In W. R. Thompson (Ed.), *Oxford research encyclopedia of politics*. Oxford University Press. https://doi.org/10.1093/acrefore/9780190228637.013.2012

Owens, R. M. (2002). Jeffersonian benevolence on the ground: The Indian land cession treaties of William Henry Harrison. *Journal of the Early Republic, 22*(3), 405–435. https://doi.org/10.2307/3124810

Parrott, Z. (2022). Indian Act. *The Canadian Encyclopedia*. https://www.thecanadianencyclopedia.ca/en/article/indian-act

Presidential Task Force on Psychology and Health Equity. (2023). Report of the American Psychological Association Presidential Task Force on Psychology and Health Equity. *American Psychologist, 78*(2), 259–267. https://doi.org/10.1037/amp0001125

Singh, P. (2021). Populism, nationalism, and nationalist populism. *Studies in Comparative International Development, 56*(2), 250–269. https://doi.org/10.1007/s12116-021-09337-6

Smeeding, T. M. (2016). Multiple barriers to economic opportunity for the "truly" disadvantaged and vulnerable. *RSF, 2*(2), 98–122. https://doi.org/10.7758/RSF.2016.2.2.04

Spruhan, P. (2006). Legal history of blood quantum in federal Indian law to 1935. *South Dakota Law Review, 51*(1), 1–50.

Thiessen, M., & Brown, M. (2023, March 16). *Willow oil project approval intensifies Alaska Natives' rift*. Associated Press. https://apnews.com/article/oil-drilling-willow-alaska-natives-biden-41a725010e9500628318cd9c56e0d700

US National Archives. (2022, February 8). *Dawes Acts (1887)*. https://www.archives.gov/milestone-documents/dawes-act

Vizenor, G. (1993). The ruins of representation: Shadow survivance and the literature of dominance. *American Indian Quarterly, 17*(1), 7–30. https://doi.org/10.2307/1184777

Walters, K. L., Johnson-Jennings, M., Stroud, S., Rasmus, S., Charles, B., John, S., Allen, J., Kaholokula, J. K., Look, M. A., de Silva, M., Lowe, J., Baldwin, J. A., Lawrence, G., Brooks, J., Noonan, C. W., Belcourt, A., Quintana, E., Semmens, E. O., & Boulafentis, J. (2020). Growing from our roots: Strategies for developing culturally grounded health promotion interventions in American Indian, Alaska Native, and Native Hawaiian Communities. *Prevention Science, 21*(Suppl 1), 54–64. https://doi.org/10.1007/s11121-018-0952-z

CHAPTER 3

Constructing an Indigenous Psychology for the Political Minorities: Challenges and Resilience of the Indigenous Tribe and Migrant Domestic Workers in Asian Regions

Rachel Sing-Kiat Ting and Andrian Liem

Introduction

Globalization has brought both opportunities for many Asian countries for exchange with the Western countries. However, some Southeast Asian countries that fall on the low- and middle-income (LMIC) range would need to climb the ladder to find its resources and protection from the politically stronger countries in the West due to power disparity. While economic inequality drives the migration movement from rural to city, from city to foreign countries, traditional values and social ecology face

R. S.-K. Ting (✉)
Department of Psychology, Jeffrey Cheah School of Medicine and Health Sciences, Monash University Malaysia, Subang Jaya, Malaysia
e-mail: ting.singkiat@monash.edu

Z. Z. Gao, M. I. Medved (eds.), *Global Perspectives on Cultural Politics in Indigenous Psychology*, Palgrave Studies in Indigenous Psychology, https://doi.org/10.1007/978-3-031-96813-6_3

tremendous challenges and risk of disruption. Many sufferings of the ethnic minorities group are the consequences of their poor fit with the domestic political agenda and globalized neoliberalism (Ting & Sundararajan, 2018; Thong et al., 2021). Especially the Indigenous people in Southeast Asia are left to compete with the resources of the political majority domestically, including financial income, healthcare system, education opportunity, and housing (land). For example, Temiar (an Indigenous tribe of Malaysia) is facing poverty due to unsecure land rights for their forest conservation which is the source of their livelihood supply and cultural identity. Yet, their suffering is inseparable from the colonial history from the West that used to exploit their natural resources and dehumanize them. Another minority group that is often neglected in the Indigenous psychology (IP) literature among LMIC Southeast Asian countries is the migrant domestic workers, who are mainly from Philippines and Indonesia and hired by high-income Asian countries, such as Hong Kong, Taiwan, and Singapore. Some call them "maids", but they are often the unprotected female labor force that forged the economy of higher-income Asian countries through short-term or long-term employment. Both internal politics in their home countries (e.g. corruption, classism) and international politics (e.g. ex-colonization and Westernization) are forcing them to migrate to a more advanced country for survival.

The rationale behind focusing on these two groups together lies in their shared experiences of marginalization, exploitation, and colonialism within the broader context of politization. For the Indigenous people (Orang Asli, OA) in Malaysia, this includes the loss of ancestral lands and continued marginalization despite being recognized as "*Bumiputra*" (sons of the soil) in Malaysia. For migrant domestic workers (MDWs), the colonial histories of economic exploitation in Indonesia and the Philippines have led to structural inequalities that drive them to seek employment abroad under often exploitative conditions. Economic pressures are also a significant factor for both groups. The OA struggle with poverty and lack of access to basic resources due to systemic neglect and land dispossession. Similarly, MDWs migrate to escape economic hardship but often end up in precarious working conditions with low wages, long hours, and limited legal protections. Furthermore, the OA experience cultural erosion and

---

A. Liem
Jeffrey Cheah School of Medicine and Health Sciences, Monash University Malaysia, Subang Jaya, Malaysia
e-mail: andrian.liem@monash.edu

social displacement due to modernization and forced assimilation into mainstream society. Similarly, MDWs face social isolation and cultural dislocation as they live and work in foreign countries, often under restrictive and abusive conditions. Both groups face systemic discrimination rooted in historical and colonial legacies.

Our chapter is structured in two parts. First, addressing the self-colonizing agenda (see below) in psychology through critical reflexivity on the challenges of mental health among the Indigenous people (OA; Orang Asli in Malaysia) and migrant domestic workers (MDWs) from Indonesia and the Philippines. Second, proposing a decolonizing blueprint for IP research and services that promote resilience of the minority communities. We posit that major challenges faced by these minorities, such as health jeopardy, mental health crisis, relocations, and poverty, are the prices they paid to keep the political status quo of keeping both the domestic and international dominant groups' welfare.

Self-colonization of Psychology in Addressing Political Minorities

While we try to reclaim the global marginalized knowledge and decentralize psychology or social sciences, we first critically review the existing Indigenous psychologies (plural) literature, research, and practices that could contribute significantly to this agenda. Movement of Indigenous psychology (IP) emerged in the 1960s and peaked in the 1980s, with multiple non-Western scholars claiming Indigenous wisdoms and epistemology in their respective continents and countries in contrast to the "Western psychology" (Allwood & Berry, 2006). This terminology (IP) was later contextualized in Northern America, Australia, and New Zealand (settlers countries) with explicit focus on the Indigenous people, hence fostering the development of Indigenous (people) Psychology, led by native scholars or proponents of native culture (e.g. Dudgeon & Walker R., 2015; Gone, 2004).

However, IP studies are inevitably repeating self-colonization, when the researchers are "mimicking" the settler's mentalities by excluding the minorities from their psychological realm. Their study samples often consist of cultural majorities who are Westernized (English-speaking), urbanized, educated, rich, and liberal, even in the Asian setting, leaving out those who are marginalized and from lower social classes due to poor literacy to survey questionnaires (Ting & Thong, 2020). For example, Chinese Psychology and Filipino Psychology has been criticized for not being inclusive of the marginalized populations from remote areas and the ethnic minorities. The imposition of "national IP" constructed by the majority group often contains a political agenda to hegemonize the marginalized into "national discourse", inevitably forcing them to give up their original identity and adopt one that is appealing to the mainstream. This self-colonization in academia unconsciously leads to "colonization of others" when the political minorities are being treated as a little "colony" to the mainstream structure, discarding their cultural particularities. To resolve this plight, moving to a greater diversity in our psychological study should begin with adequate attention to the classism in the society (Moghaddam, 2022), which is why we focus on the "political others" from the post-colonial region of Southeast Asia (in contrast to the West) in this chapter.

Besides academic self-colonization within the field of psychology, the service model of self-colonization is also quite prevalent and evident. For example, blindly importing mental health theory developed in the West (e.g. CBT, ACT, REBT, psychoanalysis) to conceptualize illness and wellness in Southeast Asian countries is being seen as the trend. Not many local psychologists are trained to criticize the Western mental health interventions exported to the global society which are mainly individual focused with little cultural relevance. Terminologies of "self-esteem", "self-efficacy", "self-love" have been used by popular psychology in the region to promote well-being during the COVID-19 pandemic, whereas little has been done to address systemic injustice that created the barrier of accessibility and acceptability of mental health services for the political minorities during the health crisis (e.g. ethnic minorities, refugees, migrant workers). This "psychologization" of society has been accelerated by mental health professionals through social media and promotion of the "Western" model of mental health literacy. Therefore, we shall move to critical reflexivity, by asking ourselves how we are treating "political others" in the Asian context, as a test to the commitment of the decolonial psychology movement.

Decolonizing Psychology in Southeast Asia Through Political Minorities

Reflexivity on the Suffering of the Indigenous People (Orang Asli) in Malaysia

Who are the truly Indigenous people in Malaysia? The Indigenous populations of Peninsular Malaysia are referred to as "Orang Asal" (OA, Indigenous people) and are considered the earliest dwellers of Peninsular Malaysia (Masron et al., 2013). Historically their indigenous land was taken after hundreds of years of colonization by Spain, Portugal, Britain, and Japan to build tea plantation, dam, and mining land. OA was later differentiated from the Malays group[1] by British colonizers, when power to reign was passed to the Malays who have claimed to be the majority as "bumiputra" (*sons of the lands/soils*) in the newly independent country of Malaysia (formed in 1963). Though OA are politically grouped together as "bumiputra" with the majority Malays, to this day, they are living in settlements without full ownership over their ancestral lands in West Malaysia.

With an estimated population of 146,412, the OA were streamed into three primary tribal groups during British colonization: the Semang (Negrito), Senoi, and Proto Malay (Aboriginal Malay) and include 18 ethnic groups that engage in varied ways of life (Masron et al., 2013). According to available statistics, approximately 76.9% of OA remain below the poverty line despite government poverty-reduction attempts, with 35.2% categorized as "hard-core poor" (Department of Statistics Malaysia, 2010). Resettlement schemes and development have also led to lifestyle changes for the OA, affecting their livelihood, diet, and culture (Abdullah et al., 2014). Thus the OA of Peninsular Malaysia, similar to Indigenous peoples worldwide, endure adversity associated with colonialism from the settlers (e.g. Dutch, British, Japanese) and continued marginalization (from the current ruling class), including dispossession of land and

[1] *Malay* is a loose term used in the late nineteenth century and early twentieth century to describe the Austronesian peoples that shared the Malay language and resided in Indonesia and Malaysia. According to the British colonial officer, Stamford Raffles, Malay is used to refer to the people of a large yet unspecified part of the South East Asian archipelago. Though one of the Indigenous group in Malaysia is termed as "proto-Malay", they are being categorized as OA (who shared similar feature as Malay), rather than true "Malay" (Aliran, 2014; Reid, 2001).

environmental destruction from resource extraction and disruptive infrastructure development in their traditional territories by state and private businesses (Salamanca, 2019). The inability to obtain acknowledgment and possession of land titles has left most of OA land vulnerable to outside interests with deforestation, depletion of natural resources, environmental degradation, and increasing tensions and conflicts over resources and land ownership (Aiken & Leigh, 2011).

In this sociopolitical context, as a second-generation Chinese born in Malaysia, I aim to reach out to this "poorest of the poor" and underrepresented citizens of our country. In partnership with a nonprofit organization (who call themselves "Friends of OA"), we decided to enter the Temiar community in Ulu Perak as a starting point. The Temiar are a Senoic group and one of the largest OA tribes. Over five years of fieldwork using ethnography, participant observation, in-depth interviews, and focus groups with religious and community representatives, we found that major adversities for the Temiar community included a lack of basic needs, lack of land rights and unjust treatment from authorities, destruction of the forest environment and livelihood, and lack of accessibility and resources, which were attributed to the authority's negligence of responsibilities, increasing human-animal conflict, environmental threats, and imposed lifestyle changes. Faced with this adversity, the Temiars endeavored to survive by working crops and gathering forest resources. They utilized resources from family, fellow villagers, external agencies, and spiritual-religious traditions (Ting & Thong, 2023; Thong et al., 2023a, 2023b).

Political Factors Threatening the Resilience of OA

From a grounded theory analysis of 23 Semai tribe OA (Indigenous) community members, Chua et al. (2021) established the Semai's model of family resilience. Findings revealed that the Semai's concept of family encompasses an extensive network of individuals with their shared relationship with *nyenang* (spirit ancestors) and cultural heritage, which in turn leads them to have a deep sense of shared family identity and connectedness. This worldview guided the Semai's family processes and functioning, captured by the following five dimensions: sharing obligations and responsibilities, making collective decisions, prioritizing community's welfare, sharing of knowledge and resources, and willingness to work with everyone. These factors facilitate a conducive and supportive environment aimed at maintaining existing family relationships. This is similar to our study of OA among the Temiar tribe, where "spirituality" is the center of their "semangat" (resilience).

According to anthropological observation, many OA have engaged in healing practices involving familial spirits, encountered either in dreams or channeled through performers in song and dance ceremonies (*sewang*) (Roseman, 1993). For example, Temiars believe that spirits inhabit natural elements and this influences the way they perceive and interact with their forests and surroundings with particular respect and reverence (Benjamin, 2014). This ecology underlies their spirituality as well as their collective identity. All plants and animals have spirits (*jiwa*) in them, and it is a taboo to offend them in the jungles, as it might cause illness or injury. The Temiar also believe in other spiritual forces such as a deity called the thunder god (known as *Karei*) who controls humans and their behavior, punishing those who transgress cultural norms and social rules (Masron et al., 2013).

When asked about their healthcare and healing methods, many Temiar mentioned "traditional ways of healing", including using *ubat hutan* (herbal plants in the forests) and consulting "*bomoh*" (spirit mediums) for *jampi* (spell casting) (Ting et al., 2023b). Besides seeking *bomoh* for personalized healing rituals, Temiars regularly engaged in communal *sewang* (dance ceremony) for healing, thanksgiving, and blessings. We participated in several *sewang* occasions at the villages and found great variation in this ceremony based on the villagers' assimilation of other religious traditions (such as Bahai or Islam). It is a dynamic rather than a fixed or scripted ceremony. Some *sewang* were done on a small scale with only family members, some were done in the *sewang* house (ceremonial hut) and lasted two hours with elaborate rituals in the dark (modern technology was not allowed in the worship house). The *sewang* involves the Indigenous healers (*bomoh*) praying in Temiar, using bouquets made of wildflowers and certain weeds, to cleanse themselves. The healers stand in circles, dancing and stamping their feet while chanting and singing their prayer out loud following a certain rhythm, while the women sit at the side stamping the bamboo and repeating the chant as chorus. Toward the end, the women join the men in going through a "cleansing ritual" by squeezing a special cane hanging on the ceiling until the juice wets their hair.

While traditional healings are still held in Temiar communities, there have been several challenges to sustaining their cultural heritage due to modernization and pressure to assimilate (Ting & Thong, 2023). First, there is an increase in conversions to proselytizing religions such as Islam and Christianity (Toshihiro, 2009). The Malaysian government historically has pursued a policy of assimilation through Muslim conversion (Endicott, 2016). Consequently, about 20% have converted to Islam and 10% to Christianity (JAKOA, 2018). These conversions have given rise to a myriad of cultural changes that mirror the larger globalization movement. For example, some Temiar-Muslims participate in the celebratory *sewang*, without joining the feast because the foods were non-halal. Some Temiar-Christians do not participate in the *sewang* at all due to conflicting beliefs about the "spiritual realm". What used to bind the Temiar community has become fragmented due to changes in religious identification.

The Temiars continue to grapple with tensions between colonial healthcare methods and their traditional ways of healing. Many still prefer the traditional modes of healing, which are more natural and less intrusive than modern medicine. One middle-aged male interviewee expressed an intense fear of having his body pierced by needles or subjected to surgical procedures if he was hospitalized. Many mourned for the loss of knowledge and availability of their *ubat hutan* (forest medicine) and flowers bouquet for sewang ceremony due to deforestation (e.g. illegal logging activities) and passing of the older generations. The younger generations were no longer interested in finding herbal treatment from the forest due to the modern education (going to boarding school) and healthcare system (thinking Western medicine as a sign of improvement). The connection with the spiritual realm and awe for nature is slowly diminishing in the younger Temiar generation. For urban OA, traditional healing is not easily accessible because it is deeply intertwined with the forest ecology nonexistent in the city. The urban OA also starts adopting psychological explanations of their illnesses due to exposure to the modern mental health system (Ting et al., in press). While many OA continue to seek resources from both old and new ways of healing, Malaysian psychology is yet to acknowledge and integrate the traditional wisdom in our practice that could enhance holistic health of this political minority. In contrast to the internal displacement faced by Indigenous people, many Southeast Asians are compelled to leave their home countries as migrant workers due to economic pressures that will be discussed in the following section.

The Impact of Post-colonialism and Neoliberalism on Indonesia and Philippines Workforce

The International Labour Organization (ILO) estimated that 164 million people were migrant workers, which covers 64% of migrants worldwide in 2017. Despite their significant socioeconomic contributions to the countries of origin and destination, there is still inadequate social protection for migrant workers including access to health services (Liem, et al., 2020). Moreover, migrant workers have to cope with the acculturative stress that is worsened by discrimination in destination countries (Liem et al., 2021). Abundant studies on migrant workers' health have been published (e.g. Hargreaves et al., 2019; Hasan et al., 2021; Kaur-Gill, 2020' Lee et al., 2022; Loganathan et al., 2020; Oliva-Arocas et al., 2022), which highlighted the health injustice experienced by the migrant workers because of the unfair policy in destination countries (i.e. barriers in accessing mental health services).

However, most of the psychological studies only addressed the gap of mental health services from the majority group perspectives, without looking into the political dynamics interplaying with the mental health issues of these workers. Borrowing critical lenses from sociology and anthropology, we would like to apply a decolonized approach in studying migrant workers' mental health issues through critical reflexivity of the potential structural bias and power imbalances (Jaggar, 2020; Haskins & Lowrie, 2014). This section will focus on "migrant domestic workers" (MDWs) as they are the most precarious group of all types of migrant workers (ILO, 2021), and based on the second author's lived experiences interacting with them since 2019, particularly in Macau (SAR), Malaysia, and Republic of China (Taiwan).

In the simplest definition, MDWs are understood as individuals who cross their country border (international migration) to work in a household setting with typical jobs including but not limited to undertake "3C" (cleaning, cooking, and care for children, elderly, and disabled people) as well as gardening, driving, and guarding private households, with these tasks varying across countries and time periods (ILO, 2021). Indonesia and the Philippines are the two main countries who send their MDWs across the globe. The historical legacies of colonization in these two countries contribute significantly to the phenomenon of MDWs in both countries (Balmores-Paulino et al., 2023).

The exploitation of domestic workers is a phenomenon deeply rooted in historical dynamics that go beyond the context of colonization in Indonesia and the Philippines. Hence politicization of MDW issues is necessary, which means making the struggles and rights of domestic workers a matter of public and political concern, thereby challenging their exclusion from key labor legislation and advocating for their rights and protections. This process is essential for transforming their status from being invisible and vulnerable to being recognized and protected under the law. This process of politicization is also evident in the history of liberating domestic workers in the United States. Historically marginalized and predominantly female domestic workers in the United States have a complex legacy shaped by factors such as slavery, post-Civil War economic transformations, and immigration patterns (Harzig, 2017; Sarti, 2014). African American women were systematically employed as domestic workers (or more popular as maids at that time), contributing significantly to the US economy while facing severe exploitation and limited legal protections. The experience of Indonesian and Filipina MDWs are similar to those African American women in the US history, when the exclusion of domestic workers from key labor legislations (i.e. the Fair Labour Standards Act of 1938) further perpetuated their vulnerable status. This "modern slavery" is happening to Indonesian and Filipina MDWs at a large scale in Asia (Platt, 2014; Rother, 2017), which desperately needs to be liberated.

The colonial histories of economic exploitation, social hierarchies, and cultural impositions in Indonesia and the Philippines has left a deep imprint on the socioeconomic structures of these nations. Structural inequalities established during the colonial period contribute to the complex relationship between the economic aspirations that drive MDWs to seek opportunities abroad and the political dimensions of labor policies and international relations. The Philippines, under Spanish and later American rule, experienced socioeconomic inequalities that continue to drive Filipinos to work abroad, including in domestic roles. Similarly, in Indonesia, the Dutch colonial legacy has influenced migration patterns, with economic inequalities driving individuals, particularly women, to also seek domestic work opportunities abroad. However, despite this similarity of colonization histories, currently, only the Philippines as a country in the Asian region has ratified the convention concerning decent work for domestic workers known as C-189. Adopted by the International Labour Organization (ILO) in 2011, C-189 represents a landmark effort to establish comprehensive standards for the fair treatment of domestic workers worldwide (ILO, 2023).

The continuing impact of post-colonization from the West on MDWs from Indonesia and the Philippines is evident at the intersection of historical dynamics, labor migration, and political discourse. The experiences of MDWs are intricately woven into a larger political narrative that places migration issues at the center of diplomatic negotiations and policymaking. As they cross geographical and cultural boundaries, their narratives become intertwined with the dynamics of global labor migration (Hellgren & Hobson, 2021; Spitzer, et al., 2023). The politicization of MDWs in both countries would need the formulation and negotiation of migration agreements, labor laws, and bilateral relations with destination countries.

Invisible Labor, Visible Struggles: Reflexivity on the Suffering of Migrant Domestic Workers from Indonesia and the Philippines

MDWs face multiple life struggles, including mental health challenges, which could be even started from the recruitment process, arising from deep-rooted structural inequalities, discriminatory practices, and gaps in legal protection. Situated in live-in condition with the employers make MDWs domesticated and invisible from the society. However, these blurred lines of private and professional space in homes put MDWs in a precarious situation of modern slavery (Azmi, 2022). We identified several key political challenges and plights faced by the MDWs that are expounded below in bold.

First, some MDWs are victims of ***unsafe migration practices*** that include human trafficking, fraudulent recruitment practices, and unsafe migration routes. These MDWs may be physically and emotionally abused during the recruitment process and in their destination countries, as demonstrated by MDWs from East Nusa Tenggara, Indonesia (Zero Human Trafficking Network Research Task Force, 2021). This abuse could lead MDWs to exploitative working conditions, including long hours, low wages, lack of overtime pay, and inadequate rest periods. Their work often extends beyond normal working hours as they may live in the households where they are employed, blurring the boundaries between work and private life. This situation was captured in studies during the COVID-19 pandemic and among MDWs who also cared for the elderly who they worked for about 14 hours per day on average (Liem, 2023).

Furthermore, legal frameworks in both sending and receiving countries may not adequately protect the rights of MDWs, which leave them with ***limited legal protection***. Many MDWs work in informal or unregulated sectors, which means they lack the legal protections afforded to other workers and leaves them vulnerable to abuse and exploitation. For example, MDWs in Hong Kong were suddenly fired by their employers who escaped from the city lockdown during the COVID-19 pandemic, which made these MDWs stranded and homeless (Carvalho, 2020a). Furthermore, this inadequate legal protection could be from a systematic issue like discrimination toward domestic workers in The Malaysian Employment Act 1955 (Amnesty International Malaysia, 2020). The condition is worsened because when faced with abuse or exploitation, MDWs may face challenges in accessing legal recourse. These ***lack of mechanisms for legal redress*** include language barriers, fear of retaliation, and unfamiliarity with the legal systems of host countries that can hinder their ability to seek justice. Example of this situation came from Macau where migrant workers were handed a letter written in Chinese which they did not understand but asked to sign during the COVID-19 pandemic (Beitler, 2020). The employers stated that the letter was about temporary housing but it turned out to be a resignation letter.

Psychologically, MDWs often experience ***social isolation and lack of social support*** as they live in private homes away from their own families and communities. This isolation can contribute to feelings of loneliness, depression, and lack of emotional support. The pandemic was worsening this situation, for example, as MDWs in Hong Kong were not allowed by their employers to leave the house for taking their day off, which they usually used to meet fellow MDWs at the park (Carvalho, 2020b). Furthermore, some MDWs may experience ***restricted mobility and being "controlled"*** as their passports are confiscated by employers or agents despite this being an illegal practice (BNP2TKI, 2019; Kavurmaci, 2022). As a result, their ability to leave abusive situations is restricted, exposing them to the risk of becoming undocumented migrant workers. Unfortunately, MDWs may also have ***inadequate healthcare and living conditions***, including limited access to health services and substandard housing. Poor living conditions can have a negative impact on their physical and mental health. For example, the social security protection for MDWs in Malaysia was only applied in June 2021, and they had no basic health protection let alone maternity protection before that (Ganesan, 2022; SOCSO Malaysia, 2021).

Future Blueprint in Constructing an Equitable Indigenous Psychology for the Political Minorities

To promote decolonial practice in mental health research and practice, recognition and reflexivity from the psychologists and redistribution or sharing of power and resources from the stakeholders are essential (Fraser & Honneth, 2003). To meet these needs, changes in Western psychology also have an important role to play. Following are the four principal actions we learn from our lived experiences and work with the OA and MDW communities, which could serve as a future blueprint in decolonizing psychology movement with the political minorities:

Action 1. Decolonizing research agenda: From our experiences, employing storytelling and narrative approaches to elicit the lived experiences of participants is better than a top-down questionnaire or structured interview questions. This method allows individuals to share their stories in their own words, providing a more authentic representation of their experiences and challenges. The use of these approaches in psychology is grounded in the recognition that individuals hold unique, culturally embedded narratives that shape their identities, experiences, and perspectives. Particularly in working with OA and MDWs, storytelling and narrative approaches are culturally relevant and resonate with many Asian traditions. In various cultures, storytelling has been a fundamental way of transmitting knowledge, preserving histories, and fostering a sense of community. By incorporating these approaches, psychologists acknowledge and respect the cultural significance of participants' lives and their resilience.

Additionally, researchers should partner with cultural insiders in designing research agendas and actions. For example, in our OA field trips, permission and approval was gained from the village head, one by one, through the introduction of our NGO partners. Field trips usually involved an extended stay in the village homestay or being "adopted" by the families who welcomed us, without assumptions of payment. Eating and feasting with them, accepting whatever they offered us, following their lead of home visit, joining in their ceremony, bathing with them in the river etc. all are our attempts to experience the "cultural insider" perspectives. When we are being given local names (e.g. local floral or animal labels) by the OA, that is a sign of being accepted. After in-depth cultural immersion, we could have a more authentic assessment of their needs in directing the goal of our research projects. This will help avoid the possibility of researchers' "imposition and colonization".

Action 2. Decolonizing psychological intervention: Empowering MDWs and OA through ensuring their access to education and skills development is vital. Psychologists could implement empowerment and advocacy programs within the community, fostering leadership and self-advocacy skills among participants. This not only supports individual well-being but contributes to broader social change and challenges systemic inequalities, because empowerment programs could also equip individuals with the tools and knowledge needed to articulate their needs, navigate systems, and advocate for their rights. By fostering self-advocacy within the community, political minorities could gain a sense of agency and autonomy in addressing the challenges they face. They are encouraged to identify and challenge systemic barriers, advocating for changes at the institutional and policy levels that perpetuate inequalities. The core objective of empowerment and advocacy programs is to address systemic inequalities by creating a platform for collective action that would be more sustainable and self-determinant. This will in turn reduce internalized stigma of the political minorities, and externalize their discrimination experiences to societal injustice.

Action 3. Decolonizing researchers language and mental space: Decolonization extends to cultural spheres and requires recognition and respect for the diverse backgrounds of MDWs and OA. Cultural sensitivity training for employers and public awareness campaigns can foster an inclusive environment that values their contributions and challenges negative stereotypes. In research and psychological practices, using local language and framing to avoid "colonial" terms that reinforce power imbalances is crucial. For example, "maid" and "servant" are words with historical baggage of slavery that should not be used for describing MDWs. Instead, the term "domestic worker" is more appropriate in the context, which emphasizes that domestic work is an "occupation" that deserves civil rights and responsibilities. For OA, some prefer to refer to themselves as "Orang Asal" (Original people) over "Orang Asli" (Indigenous people) nowadays as the former recognizes their land autonomy. Some would prefer to identify themselves with specific tribal groups (such as Bateq, Penan, Temiar, Semai, etc.) rather than lumping them all under the political umbrella of OA. The introduced term "Negrito" (during British colonial) in referring to one of the OA subgroups (which has features like African descents) might also have a racist connotation that needs further examination by anthropologists. Learning the local self-reference would help researchers move away from false assumptions and unconscious political pride.

Action 4. Decolonizing legal space: Lastly, we can't deny that decolonizing the plight of political minorities requires robust legal reforms that provide comprehensive protections. For MDWs, this includes the establishment of comprehensive labor laws, anti-discrimination policies, and anti-trafficking measures in the host countries. Successful models, such as the ratification of C-189 by the Philippines Government and the Domestic Workers' Bill of Rights in the United States, can serve as blueprints. For OA, this requires gazetting their lands under national law as customary land and reforming the *Aboriginal Peoples Act (APA) 1976* (Malaysia) with the objective of safeguarding the welfare and progress of the OA. Inviting Indigenous people into the legal sphere in determining their own needs has been implemented by Australia and New Zealand. Southeast Asian psychologists could lend our voices to the political minorities by being active advocates on social media and other scholarly platforms.

Conclusions

In the past, Indigenous psychology (IP) movement aimed to critique Western psychology theory by examining psychological concepts or disciplines in the non-Western context (Kim et al., 2006) and to study the impact of culture and other social processes on people's intrapsychic processes and behavior. In recent years, IP has advocated for "giving voices to the voiceless" by empowering local psychologists to conduct culturally relevant studies and services, to improve the lives of local communities, especially among the Global South, who still live in poverty (Bhatia & Priya, 2019). The intersectionality of East and West in Southeast Asia (due to the imprint of colonization) provides a myriad of opportunities to witness the whole spectrum of cultural transformation and transactions. Its unique multiracial and multireligious landscape provides the context in which to develop a global understanding of the complex dynamics between different cultural groups. However, in the past, most of the international and Indigenous psychological publications in Asian regions have been dominated by high-income and homogenous countries, such as Hong Kong, Mainland China, Taiwan, Korea, and Japan (Ting et al., 2023). This chapter showcases the sociopolitical factors embedded in the sufferings and resilience among two types of political minorities (OA and MDWs), particularly in Southeast Asian regions, through a reflexive and systemic analysis from IP scholars. Both groups face systemic discrimination rooted in historical and colonial legacies as minorities and reflect the potential harm of colonialism in the region. Actions were called for cultural psychologists and mental health practitioners to contextualize our practices and research agenda to construct a more just and equitable Indigenous psychology.

Acknowledgement We would like to acknowledge our NGO partners Rimbunan Hijau (led by Hubert Thong) who connected us with the Orang Asli communities in Hulu Perak, and the Temiar community who entrusted us with their stories and narratives. We are grateful to all migrant workers who have been sharing their life experiences, particularly Indonesian migrant domestic workers at IMWU Macau and Hong Kong, PERTIMIG Malaysia, and GANAS Community Taiwan.

Conflicts of Interest We have no conflict of interest to be declared.

References

Abdullah, R., Acciaioli, G., Ramle, N. H., & Mat Rasat, M. S. (2014). Forest significant and conservation among the Semoq Beri tribe of orang Asli in Terengganu State, Malaysia. *Australian Journal of Basic and Applied Sciences, 8*, 386–395.

Aiken, R. S., & Leigh, C. H. (2011). In the way of development: Indigenous land-rights issues in Malaysia. *Geographical Review, 101*(4), 471–496. https://doi.org/10.1111/j.1931-0846.2011.00113.x

Aliran. (2014, January 19). *Pseudo-theory on origins of the 'Malay race'*. Retrieved November 30, 2020, from https://aliran.com/web-specials/pseudo-theory-malay-race.

Allwood, C., & Berry, J. (2006). Origins and development of indigenous psychologies: An international perspective. *International Journal of Psychology, 41*(4), 243–268.

Amnesty International Malaysia. (2020). End culture of violence, discrimination against domestic workers. *Malaysia Kini*. https://www.malaysiakini.com/letters/543986

Azmi, A. B. (2022). Rethinking foreign domestic worker in Malaysia: A modern form of slavery? Retrieved December 03, 2022, from https://www.ideas.org.my/rethinking-foreign-domestic-worker-in-malaysia-a-modern-form-of-slavery/

Balmores-Paulino, R. S., Suryani, A. O., Hta, M. K. Z., Pamoso, A. H. G., Liem, A., & Ting, R. S. K. (2023). The relationship of stigma and social support to quality of life in Indonesia and the Philippines during the COVID-19 pandemic. *International Perspectives in Psychology: Research, Practice, Consultation, 12*(3), 175–188. https://doi.org/10.1027/2157-3891/a000078

Beitler, D. (2020). Workers face termination in underhanded letter. *Macau Daily Times*. https://macaudailytimes.com.mo/workers-face-termination-in-underhanded-letter.html

Benjamin, G. (2014). *Temiar religion, 1964–2012: Enchantment, disenchantment and re-enchantment in Malaysia's uplands*. National University of Singapore Press.

Bhatia, S., & Priya, K. R. (2019). From representing culture to fostering 'voice': Toward a critical indigenous psychology. In K. H. Yeh (Ed.), *Asian indigenous psychologies in the global context* (Palgrave Studies in Indigenous Psychology). Palgrave Macmillan. https://doi.org/10.1007/978-3-319-96232-0_2

BNP2TKI. (2019). *Data Penempatan dan Perlindungan TKI Periode 1 Januari - 31 Maret 2019*. Pusat Penelitian Pengembangan dan Informasi BNP2TKI. http://portal.bnp2tki.go.id/read/14229/Data-Penempatan-dan-Perlindungan-TKI-Periode-1-JANUARI-S.D-31-MARET-2019.html

Carvalho, R. (2020a). 'It's chaos': Hong Kong's domestic workers call for help amid coronavirus outbreak. *South China Morning Post*. https://www.scmp.com/print/week-asia/health-environment/article/3048893/its-chaos-hong-kongs-domestic-workers-call-help-amid

Carvalho, R. (2020b). Stressed, isolated: Migrants face increased mental health risks amid coronavirus crisis. *South China Morning Post*. https://www.scmp.com/week-asia/people/article/3052929/stressed-isolated-migrants-face-increased-mental-health-risks-amid

Chua, R. Y., Kadirvelu, A., Yasin, S., & Park, M. S.-A. (2021). An exploratory model of family resilience processes and functioning: A cultural perspective of the Semai indigenous communities in Perak, Malaysia. *Journal of Cross-Cultural Psychology, 52*(6), 567–582. https://doi.org/10.1177/00220221211028297

Department of Statistics Malaysia. (2010). *Population and housing census of Malaysia 2010: Preliminary count report*. Department of Statistics Malaysia.

Dudgeon, P., & Walker, R. (2015). Decolonising Australian psychology: Discourses, strategies, and practice, special thematic section on "Decolonizing Psychological Science". *Journal of Social and Political Psychology, 3*(1), 276–297. https://doi.org/10.5964/jspp.v3i1.126. jspp.psychopen.eu | 2195–3325.

Endicott, K. (2016). *Malaysia's original people: Past, present and future of the Orang Asli*. NUS Press. http://www.jstor.org/stable/j.ctv1qv35n

Fraser, N., & Honneth, A. (2003). *Redistribution or recognition? A political-philosohical exchange*. Verso.

Ganesan, R. R. (2022, June 26). Remove 'discriminatory' clauses against domestic workers, HR ministry told. *Free Malaysia Today*. https://www.freemalaysiatoday.com/category/nation/2022/06/26/remove-clauses-against-domestic-workers-in-law-hr-ministry-told/

Gone, J. P. (2004). Mental health services for Native Americans in the 21st century United States. *Professional Psychology, Research and Practice, 35*(1), 10–18.

Hargreaves, S., Rustage, K., Nellums, L. B., McAlpine, A., Pocock, N., Devakumar, D., Aldridge, R. W., Abubakar, I., Kristensen, K. L., Himmels, J. W., Friedland, J. S., & Zimmerman, C. (2019). Occupational health outcomes among international migrant workers: A systematic review and meta-analysis. *The Lancet Global Health, 7*, e872–e882. https://doi.org/10.1016/S2214-109X(19)30204-9

Harzig, C. (2017). Domestics of the world (unite?): Labor migration systems and personal trajectories of household workers in historical and global perspective. In E. R. Barkan (Ed.), *Immigration, incorporation and transnationalism* (pp. 39–62). Routledge.

Hasan, S. I., Yee, A., Rinaldi, A., Azham, A. A., Farizah Mohd, H., & Nordin, A. S. A. (2021). Prevalence of common mental health issues among migrant workers: A systematic review and meta-analysis. *PloS One, 16*(12), 1–21. https://doi.org/10.1371/journal.pone.0260221

Haskins, V. K., & Lowrie, C. (2014). Decolonizing domestic service: Introducing a new agenda. In V. K. Haskins & C. Lowrie (Eds.), *Colonization and domestic service: Historical and contemporary perspectives* (pp. 1–18). Taylor & Francis Group.

Hellgren, Z., & Hobson, B. (2021). Welfare markets and home-based domestic/care services: Market Dynamics and mechanisms in two different institutional contexts—Spain and Sweden. In C. Ledoux, K. Shire, & F. van Hooren (Eds.), *The dynamics of welfare markets: Private pensions and domestic/care services in Europe* (pp. 105–131). Springer International Publishing. https://doi.org/10.1007/978-3-030-56623-4_4

ILO. (2021). *Making decent work a reality for domestic workers: Progress and prospects ten years after the adoption of the Domestic Workers Convention, 2011 (No. 189)*. The International Labour Organization. https://www.ilo.org/global/topics/domestic-workers/publications/WCMS_802551/lang%2D%2Den/index.htm

ILO. (2023). *Ratifications of C189 - Domestic workers convention, 2011 (No. 189)*. https://www.ilo.org/dyn/normlex/en/f?p=NORMLEXPUB:11300:0::NO::P11300_INSTRUMENT_ID:2551460

Jabatan Kemajuan Orang Asli (JAKOA). (2018). *Statistik penduduk masyarakat orang asli mengikut daerah*. http://www.data.gov.my/data/ms_MY/dataset/statistik-penduduk-masyarakat-orang-asli-mengikut-sub-etnik

Jaggar, I. A. M. (2020). Decolonizing Anglo-American Political Philosophy: The Case of Migration Justice. *Aristotelian Society, 94*, 87–113. https://doi.org/10.1093/arisup/akaa008

Kaur-Gill, S. (2020). The COVID-19 pandemic and outbreak inequality: Mainstream reporting of Singapore's migrant workers in the margins [Original Research]. *Frontiers. Communication, 5*(65). https://doi.org/10.3389/fcomm.2020.00065

Kavurmaci, A. (2022). Filipino migrant women in domestic work: A comparative evaluation among Turkiye, East Asian, and Middle Eastern countries. *Journal of Social Policy Conferences, 82*, 357–382. https://doi.org/10.26650/jspc.2022.82.1105587

Kim, U., Yang, K.-S., & Hwang, K.-K. (2006). Contributions to indigenous and cultural psychology: Understanding people in context. In U. Kim, K.-S. Yang, & K.-K. Hwang (Eds.), *Indigenous and cultural psychology: Understanding people in context* (pp. 3–25). Springer.

Lee, W.-C., Chanaka, N. S., Tsaur, C.-C., & Ho, J.-J. (2022). Acculturation, work-related stressors, and respective coping strategies among male Indonesian migrant workers in the manufacturing industry in Taiwan: A post-covid investigation. *International Journal of Environmental Research and Public Health, 19*(19), 1–11.

Liem, A. (2023, September 19). *EXploring the experiences of Indonesian migrant domestic workers in caring for older adults in Asia.* Seminar from The National Ageing Research Institute - Visiting Scholar, Melbourne, Australia. https://www.nari.net.au/event/seminar-19th-september

Liem, A., Renzaho, A. M. N., Hannam, K., Lam, A. I. F., & Hall, B. J. (2021). Acculturative stress and coping among migrant workers: A global mixed-methods systematic review. *Applied Psychology: Health and Well-Being, 13*, 491–517. https://doi.org/10.1111/aphw.12271

Liem, A., Wang, C., Wariyanti, Y., Latkin, C. A., & Hall, B. J. (2020). The neglected health of international migrant workers in the COVID-19 epidemic. *The Lancet Psychiatry, 7*, pe20. https://doi.org/10.1016/S2215-0366(20)30076-6

Loganathan, T., Rui, D., & Pocock, N. S. (2020). Healthcare for migrant workers in destination countries: A comparative qualitative study of China and Malaysia. *BMJ Open, 10*(12), 1–13. https://doi.org/10.1136/bmjopen-2020-039800

Masron, T., Masami, F., & Ismail, N. (2013). Orang Asli in Peninsular Malaysia: Population, spatial distribution and socioeconomic condition. *Journal of Ritsumeikan Social Sciences and Humanities, 6*, 75–115.

Moghaddam, F. (2022). How psychologists failed. In *How psychologists failed: We neglected the poor and minorities, Favored the rich and privileged, and got science wrong* (Progressive Psychology, p. I). Cambridge: Cambridge University Press.

Oliva-Arocas, A., Benavente, P., Ronda, E., & Diaz, E. (2022). Health of international migrant workers during the COVID-19 pandemic: A scoping review. *Front Public Health, 10*, 1–9. https://doi.org/10.3389/fpubh.2022.816597
Platt, M. (2014). Foreign domestic workers in Singapore: Historical and contemporary reflections on the colonial politics of intimacy. In V. K. Haskins & C. Lowrie (Eds.), *Colonization and domestic service: historical and contemporary perspectives* (pp. 131–145). Taylor & Francis Group.
Reid, A. (2001). Understanding Melayu (Malay) as a source of diverse modern identities. *Journal of Southeast Asian Studies, 32*(3), 295–313. https://doi.org/10.1017/S0022463401000157
Roseman, M. (1993). *Healing sounds from the Malaysian rainforest: Temiar music and medicine*. University of California Press.
Rother, S. (2017). Indonesian migrant domestic workers in transnational political spaces: Agency, gender roles and social class formation. *Journal of Ethnic and Migration Studies, 43*(6), 956–973. https://doi.org/10.1080/1369183X.2016.1274567
Salamanca, A. (2019, October 28). *Indigenous peoples of Southeast Asia reaffirm their rights*. https://www.sei.org/perspectives/indigenous-peoples-of-southeast-asia-reaffirm-their-rights/
Sarti, R. (2014). Historians, social scientists, servants, and domestic workers: Fifty years of research on domestic and care work. *International Review of Social History, 59*(2), 279–314. https://doi.org/10.1017/S0020859014000169
SOCSO Malaysia. (2021). *Frequently asked questions (FAQ): Extension of social security coverage to domestic workers*. https://www.perkeso.gov.my/images/pekerja_domestik/280721_-_FAQ_Domestic_Workers.pdf
Spitzer, D. L., Thambiah, S., Wong, Y. L., & Kaundan, M. K. (2023). Globalization and the health and well-being of migrant domestic workers in Malaysia. *Global Health, 19*(1), 29–44. https://doi.org/10.1186/s12992-023-00925-w
Thong, J. J. A., Ting, R. S. K., Teo, S. L. (2021). Causal-attribution and emotion-expression of suffering among Southeast Asian indigenous peoples: A systematic review study. *Online Publication on Journal of Humanistic Psychology*. https://doi.org/10.1177/00221678211036333
Thong, J. J. A., Ting, R. S. K., Takeuchi, T., Jobson, L., Phipps, M. E. (2023a). A qualitative study exploring the epistemology of suffering within a Malaysian indigenous tribe. *Transcultural Psychiatry, 62*, 305–321.
Thong, J. J. A., Ting, R. S. K., Jobson, L., & Sundararajan, L. (2023b). In the wake of religious conversions: Differences in cognition and emotion across three religious communities of an indigenous tribe in Malaysia. *Psychology of Religion and Spirituality*, 16(2), 182–192. https://doi.org/10.1037/rel0000493

Ting, R. S. K., Azlan, D., Liem, A., Thong, J., Krishnan, L., Ortega, A., Phipps, M., & Su, T. T. (In press). A qualitative study on the perceptions towards illness and modern healthcare among Indigenous people in Peninsular Malaysia. *AlterNative.*

Ting, R. S. K., & Sundararajan, L. (2018). *Culture, cognition, and emotion in China's religious ethnic minorities: Voices of suffering among the Yi.* Palgrave Macmillan. https://doi.org/10.1007/978-3-319-66059-2

Ting, R. S. K., & Thong, J. J. A. (2020). Global psychology: Symphony or elephant. In L. Sundararajan, K. H. Yeh, & K. K. Huang (Eds.), *Global psychology from indigenous perspectives: Visions inspired by K. S. Yang* (pp. 225–244). Palgrave Macmillan Publication. https://doi.org/10.1007/978-3-030-35125-0_13

Ting, R. S. K., & Thong, J. J. A. (2023). Do not pluck that flower: The forest and cultural identity for the hunter-gatherer tribe (Temiars) of Malaysia. Sundararajan, L., & Dueck, A. (Eds). *When the gods have fled: Being human in the age of machine and the market* (pp. 225–244). Palgrave Macmillan Publication.

Ting, R. S. K., Yeh, K. H., & Jones, E. (2023). Special issue: Building an equitable global psychology: Giving voice to the indigenous psychology in Southeast Asia. *International Perspectives in Psychology: Research, Practice, Consultation, 12* (2), 61–133. ISSN: 2157-3883 eISSN: 2157-389

Toshihiro, N. (2009). *Living on the periphery: Development and Islamization among the Orang Asli in Malaysia.* Publisher: Center for Orang Asli Concerns.

Zero Human Trafficking Network Research Task Force. (2021). *The impact of the Moratorium of Indonesian Migrant workers placement on society attitudes Towards human trafficking in East Nusa Tenggara* (Retno Agustin, Meifita Handayani, Yovi Arista, & Zulyani Evi, Eds.). Migrant CARE.

PART II

Theoretical Reflections

CHAPTER 4

Indigenizing Child Development Science: Cultural Politics between Contextualists and Universalists

Stephen Baffour Adjei, Fortidas Bakuza, Tumelo Kgolo, and Seth Oppong

---

We dedicate this chapter to our late friend and colleague, Professor Seth Oppong. To us, you were more than a co-author. We will eternally remember your dedication to African Indigenous knowledge about child development practices, and the guidance and leadership you provided in writing this chapter. Rest well, Seth!

S. B. Adjei (✉)
Department of Psychology, University of Oslo, Oslo, Norway

Akenten-Appiah-Menka University of Skills Training and Entrepreneurial Development, Kumasi, Ghana

F. Bakuza
Aga Khan University, Dar es Salaam, Tanzania

T. Kgolo
University of Botswana, Gaborone, Botswana

S. Oppong
University of Botswana, Gaborone, Botswana

University of the Witwatersrand, Johannesburg, South Africa

Z. Z. Gao, M. I. Medved (eds.), *Global Perspectives on Cultural Politics in Indigenous Psychology*, Palgrave Studies in Indigenous Psychology, https://doi.org/10.1007/978-3-031-96813-6_4

Introduction

There have been a longstanding tension and controversy about universal claims of developmental pathways for childhood development and contextual or culture-specific claims of child development. For example, based on samples from Minority World contexts, and the scientific lens of Minority World researchers, mainstream White-centric developmental science, particularly developmental psychology and neuroscience, continues to make universal claims about natural developmental mechanisms and trajectories that are believed to characterize childhood development everywhere (e.g., McCoy et al., 2022a, 2022b). The Euro-American global view of childhood is seen as legitimate knowledge that transcends culture and contexts. While we use the term Majority World to refer to non-Western societies in Africa, Asia, Latin America, and the Caribbean where most humans live (Alam, 2008; Kagitcibasi, 2002), the term Minority World is used here to mean Western societies which make up the minority of the world's population (Khan et al., 2022). The dominant perspective on child development is often promoted by institutions such as the World Health Organization (WHO), United Nations Children's Fund (UNICEF), the World Bank Group (WBG), and LEGO Foundation (Oppong, 2023; Scheidecker et al., 2023) and the scholars who authored the authoritative *The Lancet's series Advancing Early Childhood Development*. We shall refer to this group as the universalists for their theoretical orientation and programming approach that tends to assume, more or less, a one-size-fits-all approach.

On the other side of the divide are cultural or contextual developmental scientists and cultural anthropologists who believe that behaviors and developmental outcomes of children are culture specific (De Gioia, 2009; Fleer, 2006; Funk et al., 2023; Keller, 2017; Keller & Kärtner, 2013; Nsamenang, 1992, 2006; Oppong, 2015, 2022; Oppong et al., 2022; Oppong & Strader, 2022; Scheidecker et al., 2022, 2023; Serpell & Nsamenang, 2014; Weisner, 2002, 2014). These cultural developmental psychologists and anthropologists argue for the foregrounding of childhood studies and analyses in Indigenous knowledge and practices because, to them, local environmental circumstances, household structures, and societal values define the everyday experiences of the child. In essence, the contextualists regard human development in general and child development in particular as a *bio-eco-cultural process* (see Keller, 2017; Oppong & Strader, 2022; Weisner, 2002). This implies that the development of a human being is codetermined by the person's biology, ecological conditions of living, as well as the culture into which she or he is born. We shall refer to this group as the contextualists for their theoretical orientation and programming approach that tends to emphasize a sensitivity to the culture and ecology based on a strong anthropological and cultural psychological evidence of cultural differences across the world. The contextualists do not have the same level of institutional representation as do the universalists.

For the universalists, child development is primarily a biological process and children everywhere show fairly the same normative characteristics in their developmental pathways (Britto et al., 2017; Mesman et al., 2017). The universalist view of childhood, though based on the cultural and historical background of Europe and America, has contributed to and influenced the framing of international conventions and legislation on children, such as the United Nations Convention on the Right of the Child (UNCRC). The universalized Euro-American perspective of the child is considered as the most influential and valid representations of the state of affairs in childhood studies and child development science, and has thus become the prevailing standard used to develop international benchmarks for assessment of all children globally. The Euro-American biomedical view and evidence of childhood is projected as naturalized in child development science and appropriated by Western development agencies as international policy imperatives for all (see Oppong, 2023; Scheidecker et al., 2023). Essentially, based on the culture-specific view of the West, and through the axes of coloniality of power, children become codified as policy subjects and material substances for future healthy societies (Quijano, 2007). The consequence of the globalization of the universalized models of childhood is further reinforced by cultural politics and intellectual narratives that overtly and covertly prioritize the "more human" agentic and civilized childhood practices from native/indigenous and backward ones (Araneda-Urrutia, 2022; Quijano, 2007). We use the term cultural politics to mean the "processes through which relations of power are asserted, accepted, contested, or subverted by means of ideas, values, symbols, and daily practices" (Schiller, 1997, p. 2). We shall return to the concept of cultural politics in the next section.

Apparently, to a very large extent, the global geopolitical narratives influence the cultural politics of knowledge production on childhood (de Castro, 2020; Oppong, 2013, 2023). The epistemic power imbalances between the Minority and Majority Worlds and the subaltern position of the Majority World in knowledge production affect narratives around childhood in the child development science literature (de Castro, 2020). The growing body of research on childhood and their families tend to come from Minority World contexts as "there is a paucity of such information available within and about Africa" or from the rest of the Majority World (Pence et al., 2008, p. 4). As a result, the historically systematic social, cultural, political, and geographical exclusion of the voices of the Majority World from the hierarchy of knowledge and power essentially determines what topics are studied and whose view on childhood matters in developmental sciences (Oppong, 2013; Scheidecker et al., 2024). Eventually, the cultural narratives of the influential Minority World frame discussions around childhood and become the domineering voice in the child development science and practice, ignoring evidence from the Majority World and preventing the scientific community, educators, and practitioners from seeing past the universal frames and ideals set by the Minority World. In the view of Nsamenang (2008, p. 135) there is a need "to extend the dialogue and substantiate the importance of cultural conceptualizations of childhood by introducing child development theories and practice that follow from Africa (Majority World) ways of acting in and understanding the world."

There have been previous studies that have challenged psychological and anthropological claims of human universals (e.g., Danziger, 2009; Norenzayan & Heine, 2005). These studies have raised questions about the default assumption that empirical findings obtained from specific geographical locations offer an acceptable and valid basis for theoretical generalizations across time and space (Danziger, 2009). The goal of this chapter is to build on previous studies by critically evaluating the perspectives and controversies that characterize the ongoing conversations in the child development science. We particularly highlight the power and cultural politics between the universalists and contextualists on the issue of the universality or context specificity of child development. We engage with and attend to the nature and use of cultural politics and dominant narratives in the extant child development literature in order to illustrate how power relations are constructed, asserted, accepted, and contested in the discussions about the science and practice of child development. We further integrate the perspectives into a unified narrative of "glocalization" that orients toward and emphasizes a globally representative and inclusive child development science and practice for effective and meaningful childhood intervention efforts. In the sections that follow, we first provide a synoptic discussion of cultural politics as a relevant framework for understanding knowledge claims and power relations in child development science. We then discuss the perspectives and debates between the contextualists and the universalists in child development science, and further integrate their perspectives into a unified narrative of "glocalization" that underscores the need for a more representative and inclusive child development science and practice. We finally provide concluding thoughts.

Cultural Politics as a Framework for Understanding Knowledge Claims and Power Relations in Child Development Science

As indicated earlier, cultural politics generally involves mechanisms by which relations of power are asserted, accepted, contested, or subverted by means of ideas, values, symbols, and everyday practices (Schiller, 1997). Cultural politics is an analytical framing of politics in society that recognizes "the cultural" as an important site for struggles over meaning, a site for different people and groups to negotiate questions about identity, belonging, inclusion, and exclusion (Korf, 2020). It is a "struggle for control of the means of cultural production and conflict over meaning" (Rudolph, 1992, p. 1489). Cultural politics is the politics of meaning (Rudolph, 1992), which involves symbolic as well as material practices (Korf, 2020). Thus, cultural politics, in the context of this chapter, involves the use of symbolic language and cultural narratives as a framework for constructing and making knowledge claims of legitimacy about children and normative childrearing practices. The claims of knowledge legitimacy and the politics of meaning between contextualists and universalists do not exist independent of the material and social world, they are situated and culturally contextualized activities (Adjei, 2013, 2019). As Rudolph (1992) argues, cultural politics is "constituted and contested through the means and processes of public culture," which deals with what is read, heard, and seen in the print, film, and electronic media, as well as what is published in the press, books, and journals (p. 1489).

It is important to note that mainstream Western-centric psychology and Indigenous psychology both involve and appropriate cultural politics to legitimize their knowledge claims. The cultural politics and the construction of power in child development science manifest in ways in which the experiences of Majority World's children are interpreted via the "theoretical canons, vernaculars and institutions of northern academia" (Abebe et al., 2022, p. 255) and the privileging of quantitative research evidence as the gold standard for studying child development. A further manifestation of the cultural politics in child development studies is the ways in which contextualists contest the universalists' claims of legitimacy of evidence and the Euro-American universalized interpretations of the experiences of children based on quantitative and global comparable data to standardized measurement. For example, the universalists' view of child development almost always ignores differentiating factors such as cultural, contextual, temporal, and individual aspects of child development, and proceed on Euro-centric dominant narratives that universalize child development goals as ultimately a pursuit of personal, social, and political autonomy, independence and self-sufficiency (Lansdown, 2005). Consequently, the Western developmental science literature and multinational childhood development policy directives increasingly intellectualize and position globally desirable children as those who are fully agentive, consistently autonomous, and vocal (Hanson et al., 2018). On the other hand, context-conscious child development psychologists and cultural anthropologists have contested and rejected the universal scientific claims that are mostly based on quantitative evidence from the West (Keller, 2021; Nsamenang, 2005; Oppong, 2015; Scheidecker et al., 2021, 2022, 2023; Weisner, 2002). The contextualists assert that the concepts and experiences of childhood are not static, they are changing in many parts of the world, partly due to developments in education and urbanization (Ansell, 2005). There is a concern that the "global model" of childhood that is widely presented as ideal affects children's experiences. As Ansell (2005, p. 74) argues, "childhood remains culturally and historically specific and is never simply an exported Western Institution." This implies that child development cannot be separated from the culture and context in which children are brought up.

Thus, the understanding of cultural politics and narratives in child development science allows one to appreciate the political or constitutive effects of social actions (Graham, 2011), and further provides a relevant analytical frame to appreciate how the universalists and contextualists engage in cultural politics and construction of power in child development science. It enables an understanding of the epistemic claims of universalists about children and normative childrearing practices, and how these narratives and epistemic claims are accepted, contested, and counteracted by the contextualists with alternative Indigenous perspectives on child development practices. When cultural politics is utilized as an analytical framework, it helps to appreciate and articulate the ways in which both contextualists' and universalists' narratives and representations in child development science constitute mundane practices that are utilized to construct and condition the exercise of epistemic power and control over knowledge production on children and their development, and over meaning of good science. The use of cultural politics as an analytical framework in this chapter does not necessarily reveal a definitive truth in the narratives and counter-narratives of the universalists and the contextualists, but rather it explores the underlying cultural and political dynamics that shape these perspectives, and as a means of legitimation of knowledge claims.

Perspectives and Debates in Child Development Science

There are a number of perspectives and obvious controversies that characterize child development science. The universalists and the contextualists differ in perspectives on such important issues in child development science as child nutrition (Funk et al., 2023; Scheidecker et al. 2021), developmental trajectories or pathways (Oppong, 2015; Oppong et al., 2022; Scheidecker et al., 2021, 2022; Weisner, 2002, 2005), attachment (Keller, 2021; Keller et al., 2018; Mesman et al., 2017), and intelligence (Nsamenang, 2006; Oppong, 2020; Serpell, 1993, 2000, 2011; Serpell & Haynes, 2004). In the midst of this cultural politics, both the universalists and the contextualists draw on such terms as best available evidence, scientific evidence, randomized controlled trials, evidence-based, data-driven, global consensus, global, international, international standards, international frameworks, culture-specific, ecological validity, indigenous evidence, ethnographic accounts, among others, as important instruments for the struggle for the means of control over knowledge production, and the negotiation and contestation of power. For instance, the universalists tend to construct and/or appropriate the power contained in such words or phrases as best available evidence, scientific evidence, global consensus, randomized controlled trials, and the like. They do so in order to command respect or ascribe believability to their opinions, data, analysis, recommendations, and conclusion. Perhaps, it is important to note that the words and phrases used by the universalists have societal currency (inherent scientific authority and credibility) already and are well-established powerful terminologies that can sway the opinions of laypeople and policy makers. The societal currency it assumes may imply broad agreement and validation from respected institutions and experts, fostering trust and legitimacy. On the other hand, terminologies associated with and used by the contextualists to describe opinions, data, analysis, recommendations, and conclusions have lower currency of power in the scientific community and among policy makers. This means that, despite their valuable insights, contextualists' methods are perceived to be less rigorous, with context-specific findings regarded as less broadly applicable and thus receiving less visibility and dissemination in high-impact journals and media. Such terms as qualitative evidence, ethnographic evidence, indigenous evidence, to mention a few, are regarded as very subjective, less rigorous and scientific, and of lower applicability (though the trend is changing slowly).

Again, the hierarchies of evidence seem to suggest that qualitative evidence is at the bottom of level of quality of evidence—at the same level as expert opinions, case reports, case studies, and bench research (Burns et al., 2011; Wallace et al., 2022). It needs to be said that these hierarchies of evidence were created by scholars in the biomedical field as guides in formulating clinical protocols in their practice. Thus, the universalists construct power by employing such cultural frameworks knowingly or unknowingly. Interestingly, the various hierarchies were also constructed based on informed opinion (Burns et al., 2011), calling into question the very bases for these hierarchies. It is also as if expert opinion produces a hierarchy that ascribes to the expert opinion a lower status—disrespecting itself in the process. Thus, the cultural politics of child development tends to appropriate the existing frameworks that seem to suggest that any evidence up in the hierarchies of evidence constructed on expert opinion is more useful, powerful, and requires little defending than those lower in these hierarchies. In particular, the universalists tend to present evidence that aligns with a certain level in the hierarchy to increase the credibility of their epistemic claims. This appears to be so because child development research and practice tends to be dominated by scholars from pediatrics and related disciplines allowing them to transport medical ontologies and epistemologies (such as the hierarchies of evidence) into a field characterized by a bio-eco-cultural process. Given that language can be mobilized as an important instrument of social practice to elevate a certain type of evidence and claims (Adjei, 2013), Oppong (2023) used the term "qualitative scientific evidence" to contest and assimilate the powerful influence of the term "scientific evidence" to elevate the level of scientific authority and credibility of qualitative evidence as different but not deficient type of scientific evidence.

The universalists child development model is characterized by a conception of a normative sequence of child development. Central to the dominant narrative and cultural framing of the universalists are broad claims about universal normative child development practices and global childhood interventions that are believed to be capable of helping children, especially those in Majority World contexts, reach their optimum "developmental potential" (Grantham-McGregor et al., 2007, p. 62) and improve the development of their "brain structure and function" (Britto et al., 2017, p. 97) in order to forestall "intergenerational transmission of poverty" (Engle et al., 2007, p. 229). For the universalists, according to the "best available scientific evidence," children in all cultures develop along a common trajectory into adulthood and that all cultures have the same goals and aspirations for child development. For example, the bond between an infant and a specific caregiver, particularly the mother (Bowlby, 1969), and a caregiver's sensitive responsiveness (a caregiver's ability to notice infant signals, to interpret and respond to them correctly and promptly; Ainsworth et al., 1974) is widely believed by many universalists as a universal aspect of parenting in infancy that is related to positive child development outcomes (Bowlby, 1969; Mesman et al., 2016, 2017). Based on Western ontological perspectives, such universal claims, such as secure infant–mother attachment, is unreflectively projected in the child development science and practice as the most standard parenting strategy capable of promoting positive and healthy infant development.

Furthermore, from the universalists' standpoint, difference in child development is a deficiency. For this reason, many international and national child intervention efforts proceed with the goal to promote universal child development practices by pathologizing many disadvantaged communities and their Indigenous cultures or attempt to "rescue" such children from perceived "harmful" practices (See Lansdown, 2005). The universalists' claim about responsive caregiving has influenced international early childhood development (ECD) intervention frameworks such as the Nurturing Care Framework (NCF) proposed and implemented globally by WHO, UNICEF, and WB. These so-called international ECD frameworks serve to construct comparable polarities (such as that between the colonized and the colonizer) between the global and the local, and further work to obscure the complex processes of child development practices. As previous studies have claimed, Indigenous childhood practices and children from the Majority World are represented in some Western child development science literature as backward, uncivilized, risky, and lacking a future (Balagopalan, 2019; De Castro, 2020; Oppong et al., 2022; Scheidecker et al., 2022). Thus, to be accepted as a healthy and normal child, societies across cultures and contexts must subscribe to the biopolitical control and the cultural politics of the global child development science that universalizes a desirable uniform childhood framework as a natural precondition for all (Burman, 2008).

The global template for able-bodied child (humanness) is presented as "international" and "evidence-based" intervention framework to which societies, especially those in low- and middle-income countries (LMICs) must aspire (Araneda-Urrutia, 2022; Hanson et al., 2018; Scheidecker et al., 2023). However, certain beliefs from the Minority World about children and their care, which tend to be presented as "universal," are often lacking the global evidence to prove and support those claims (Pence & Benner, 2015). It is instructive to note that, implicit in such terms as "international," "global," or "scientific evidence" lies a complex variety of cultural assumptions and politics about human nature and the type of care that children everywhere must receive to be truly "human." Such terms as international intervention, global consensus, and best practices do not only help us understand how particular dominant narratives are appropriated to systematically construct a version of the social world (Hodges et al., 2008) but they also highlight how such narratives and the knowledge they produce are culturally embedded (Adjei, 2019; Raby, 2002). Apparently, the universalists' biopolitical model that systematizes childhood taxonomies and differentiates "good" childhood science and practices from "unhealthy" or "poor" childhood practices (re)produce patterns of coloniality of power and domination that helped Western imperial powers to distinguish and rank their humans (the colonizer) from the "less than human" natives (the colonized) that inhabited their possessions (Maldonado-Torres, 2007; Quijano, 2007).

On the other hand, the contextualists contest the epistemic frames and ontological approaches that are central to, and broadly define and influence, knowledge production in global childhood studies. For example, the contextualists object to the claims about widespread cognitive and socio-emotional deficiencies among children in Majority World settings because, according to them, such claims are deeply drawn from dominant Western child development literature and "excludes research from anthropology, cultural psychology, and related fields that could provide crucial insights about childrearing and children's development in the targeted communities" (Scheidecker et al., 2023, p. 3; also see Scheidecker et al., 2024). Indigenous cultural psychology and anthropology provide valuable consideration of the holistic interaction between physical, emotional, cognitive, and spiritual growth, often emphasizing communal responsibility and cultural practice in child development (e.g., Nsamenang, 1992, 2006; Oppong, 2022). The contextualists believe that the universalists' universalized and biomedical view of children which inform international public policy on children across geopolitical contexts is part of the cultural politics of child development science which perpetuates coloniality of power (Quijano, 2007). For example, universal child nutritional policy interventions that are mostly promoted by Euro-American research and practice and believed to increase the bodily abilities of children in all contexts have been seen by some Majority World and Indigenous decolonial child development scientists as a biopolitical, social justice imperative facilitated through coloniality of power (Araneda-Urrutia, 2022). These contestations and counter-narratives of the contextualists, though not the dominant view in the field, are also part of the cultural politics and framing that assert minority view in child development science and practice. The contextual scientists believe that the dynamics of child development, such as the timing of developmental milestones and developmental pathways, as well as developmental precursors and consequences, differ from culture to culture, and even within a given community (Keller & Kärtner, 2013; Nsamenang, 2006; Weisner, 2002).

Accordingly, many of these contextual social scientists have long argued for the conceptualization of child development practices and research as a cultural process and a product of specific ecocultural, socio-economic, and historical processes (Keller, 2017; Woodhead, 1999; Super & Harkness, 1982, 1986). For example, the contextualists contest and reject the universalists' claim of sensitive responsiveness, warmth, and other attachment qualities as a universal characteristic of caregivers. Rather, the contextual scientists argue that warmth and sensitive responsivity of parents only reflect a "culture-specific ideal of good parenting in relation to a view of healthy infants as emotionally expressive, entitled, independent agents" (Keller et al., 2018, p. 1), a parenting model that is found mostly among Western caregivers (Arnett, 2008; Henrich et al., 2010). Also, Super and Harkness (1986) have articulated the need for *developmental niche* as a foundational framework for child development science and practice. This framework identifies three socio-ecological elements that influence the development of children: (1) the physical and social settings children inhabit, such as the family, social patterns, and organization of their daily lives; (2) the culturally regulated customs and childrearing practices such as normative arrangements for care and education, attitudes toward play, discipline, and training; and (3) the beliefs or ethno-theories of the parents in terms of the goals and priorities they have for children's development and their views on how these can be achieved.

For cultural psychologists, anthropologists, and other contextual scientists, child development science and practice "must be embedded within a nexus of cultural logic" and "based on ecologically valid childrearing values and beliefs" (Keller et al., 2018, p. 1). For example, to understand child development and intelligence, particularly among West African children, Nsamenang (2006) has proposed social ontogenesis as the most effective framework. Founded on the contextualists' tradition of ecological and cultural theorizing, social ontogenetic framework notes that different developmental pathways and intelligences are located within the ecological and social systems in which children are nurtured. The social ontogenetic paradigm contrasts the Western universalized independent or autonomous frame for understanding child intelligence and cognitive functioning as abstractions. Rather, it focuses on the foundational principle of interdependent relational script and social maturity or competence of children. The view of these Indigenous African developmental psychologists and theorists is that children discover knowledge by participating in social interaction, cultural life, economic activities, and daily routines (Nsamenang, 2006; Oppong, 2020; Serpell, 2000, 2011). They posit that cognitive development of children unfolds during the participation in which children develop the abilities to "generate the knowledge and skills with which to responsibly and increasingly engage with the world" (Nsamenang, 2006, p. 296). Thus, to understand the social cognition and intelligent behavior of Africans, one has to pay attention to and capture the "shared routines and participatory learning, rather than in completing school-based instruments" (Nsamenang, 2006, p. 296). It is thus important to emphasize that culture is central and "embodied in the ways that children are raised and the environment where they grow and develop" (Ball, 2010, p. 1). Children's identities are shaped early in life in the context of family, and communities where they grow and get socialized.

Perhaps, assessment of child developmental outcomes deserves a special emphasis. Assessment of child developmental outcomes relates to measurement and evaluation of growth, change or improvement in cognitive, physical, and socio-emotional domains. Of particular interest is cognitive outcome assessment in child development science and practice. The universalists' perspective is that we can utilize universal assessment tools to measure the developmental outcomes across cultures and still have meaningful data for comparison. Cultural psychology, cross-cultural psychology, and cross-cultural neuropsychology challenge the universalists' perspective by highlighting the significant influence of culture on cognitive processes and brain functioning (Ardila, 2005; Oppong, 2020, 2023; Oppong et al., 2022). Mathew (as cited in Ardila, 1995, p. 144) emphasized that the universalists' narrative is

> a very limited kind of neuropsychology, appropriate to only a fraction of the world's population, is presented to the rest of the world as if there could be no other kind of neuropsychology, and as if the educational and cultural assumptions on which neuropsychology is based were obviously universals that applied everywhere in the world.

Despite belonging to the universalists' camp, McCoy (2022) asserts that child development cohort studies in Minority World settings employ measurements focusing on a narrow set of skills assumed to be culturally consistent, thereby restricting their scope and results. Despite attempts to validate these tools, there is minimal evidence supporting their complete cross-cultural equivalence. It is important to note that although the basic cognitive processes are, to some degree, shared among human beings, their development and expression vary across cultures (Manly, 2008). The influence of culture extends beyond cognition to actual brain functioning, as evidenced by differences in brain activation patterns between individuals from different cultures during various cognitive tasks (Chiao et al., 2008; Kitayama & Park, 2010). Given that the universalists' and contextualists' perspectives are not apolitical, and that they both make valid knowledge claims that are important to ignore, the next section integrates their views into a perspective called "glocalization" which combines the strengths of the two opposing sides.

Toward Glocalization in Child Development Science

Scientific debates, if not properly carried out, can either paralyze the field or foster scientific progress and breakthrough (Mesman et al., 2017). The universalists' view of childhood research and interventions and the contextualists' Indigenous perspectives are both too important to ignore. Child development processes are dynamic and complex and require multidisciplinary approaches and multicultural perspectives to its study. There are many strengths and weaknesses in both the universalists' universal view and the contextualists' culture-specific perspectives in child development science to the extent that a rigid cultural political bifurcation of the two views will not be beneficial to the field. The dichotomy between the universalists' universal view and the contextualists' culture-specific perspectives underscores the need for a nuanced and integrative approach. Instead of a simplistic linear conception of child development science and practices as involving either a universal/global or contextual/culture-specific processes, we believe that what the field needs is a shift toward "glocalization." Glocalization is a meaningfully genuine, progressive, and valuable marriage between the universalists' (global) conceptions and the contextualists' (local) notions about childhood and childrearing practices. The proposal for "glocalization" in child development science represents a shift away from a rigid adherence to global perspectives, recognizing the limitations of a one-size-fits-all approach. Emphasizing a more inclusive and nuanced understanding, glocalization advocates for a balanced integration of universalist and contextualist views.

Originally, the term glocalization was introduced into the social science discourse by Sociologist Roland Robertson (1994) as a linguistic blend of *globalization* and *localization*. For Robertson (1994, 2013), globalizing (universalists) ideas do not exist "out there" and that their articulation cannot and should not be decoupled from that of the local or culture-specific views. In the same vein, the local is never quite "pure," outside or separable from the global (Robertson, 1994, 2013), they are importantly interlinked. In modern social, political, and economic discourses, glocalization has come to represent the simultaneous occurrence of both universalizing and culture-specific or particularizing tendencies of a given phenomenon or practice (Blatter, 2022). We utilize glocalization in this chapter to reject the essentialists' cultural politics and the controversy of polarities between the universalists' and contextualists' narrow understanding of child development science and practice. We further believe that glocalization leverages the indispensable interconnectedness among disciplines and knowledges, and the valued exchange of expertise between the universalists and the contextualists for a fruitful future of the field. To this end, glocalization ensures that child development science and practices are more inclusive and broadly conceptualized to reflect the diversity of contexts, values, topics, methods, epistemologies, researchers, and populations that mostly define the realities of the field and its subject matter.

The primary focus of glocalization should be to learn useful lessons from and leverage the applied resources of the universalists and the contextualists to achieve more positive and sustainable child development outcomes. Attempts should be made to systematically analyze the benefits from both ends and, where possible, learning should reciprocate to allow knowledge and skills in childrearing practices and parenting to come from both ends and to be built on in an open and trusting relationships. Glocalization rejects a simplistic binary division between global and local, advocating for a progressive and valuable linkage that considers the diversity of contexts, values, and epistemologies that shape the realities of child development. There are many obvious shortcomings of Indigenous knowledge as well as many pragmatic usefulness of external knowledge, and that utilizing local knowledge "as inspiration for child development process does not necessarily imply an uncritical and a wholesale acceptance of all contextual knowledge as worthy and a blanket rejection of all external knowledge (universalists) as inferior" (van Vlaenderen & Neves, 2013, p. 453). We strongly believe that the strength and progress of child development science and practice rests not on universal knowledge claims traversing continents and contexts, but rather on plurality of perspectives and the complementarity of indigenization and culture-specific notions. Ultimately, the goal is to generate knowledge that is not only more balanced and enduring but also reflective of the diversity inherent in the field. Glocalization articulates and yields a unified narrative that fosters epistemic harmony between the universalists and the contextualists. This harmony further ensures that childhood and development are circumscribed around the biology of children as well as their culture, context, and the social constructions and the family they inhabit. It harmonizes disciplinary boundaries, concepts, and approaches by drawing robust scientific evidence from such disciplines as pediatrics, developmental psychology, child studies, developmental neurosciences, behavioral economics, sociology of childhood, philosophy of childhood, cultural anthropology, cultural psychology, and other relevant fields to define what constitutes "healthy child development" and "optimal childcare."

There are a number of practical and concrete ways by which child development scientists can work toward the realization of epistemic harmony and to achieve glocalization. For example, epistemic harmony and glocalization may be achieved through targeted forums, conferences, and workshops that bring people of the opposite sides of the debate to discuss areas of agreement and disagreement in order to fashion out ways to resolve such disagreement. Another pragmatic way to realize glocalization could be instituting editorial policies that require authors and potential authors to compulsorily include citation statements that indicate that manuscripts submitted for publication cite evidence from both sides of the controversy. Also, there could be book projects that bring both the contextualists' and the universalists' framings together, or research collaborations and projects undertaken between and among members from both sides of the divide, with diverse cultural backgrounds and disciplinary perspectives. By fostering partnerships across different regions and academic disciplines, researchers can facilitate the exchange of knowledge and expertise, leading to a more comprehensive understanding of child development that incorporates global and local insights. Additionally, we can work to achieve epistemic harmony and glocalization through deliberate funding policies that equally favor context-conscious research projects that apply qualitative and ethnographic methodological approaches to the study of children. Further, creating platforms for community engagement and participatory research can empower local communities to contribute their perspectives and priorities to the narratives on child development. This grassroots approach not only enhances the relevance and applicability of research findings but also promotes a more inclusive and equitable research process. These practical steps, if adhered to, will give equal voice to both sides of the divide to improve child development outcomes, and researchers can move closer to realizing the vision of glocalization, where global and local perspectives converge to create a more holistic understanding of child development that reflects the richness and diversity of human experiences.

To this end, the goal of glocalization will be to help generate a more balanced, useful, enduring, and trustworthy knowledge that will be of interest to a broad audience in the child development field. As it has been observed, child development is a bio-eco-cultural project in the sense that the biological processes of development interact with cultural processes to ultimately influence and produce the type of person the child will grow into as an adult (Morelli et al., 2018; Nsamenang, 2006; Oppong, 2015; Serpell & Nsamenang, 2014). There is an urgent necessity of hearing the voices of diverse researchers from diverse socio-historical backgrounds and disciplinary perspectives on child development matters, especially considering that both local and international/global perspectives are crucial to a balanced and integrative knowledge of child development science and practice. However, we caution against the current privileging of the universalists' framing of child development and the potential and continued privileging of that framing as we attempt to integrate both claims to produce a truly global child development science and practice.

Conclusion

In this chapter, we have argued for and foregrounded the relevance of culture and context in understanding child development science and practice. We have cautioned against the prevailing cultural politics in child development science and practice, and the tendency for generalizing knowledge about childrearing practices, values, and expectations based on a one-sided Euro-centric biomedical understanding, which often leaves out the contextual and culture-specific notions of child development. It is significant to recognize that child development theories developed in one part of the globe may not be suitable in studying cultural and social practices of children in other parts of the world. The most forward-looking approach to the study and practice of child development is glocalization, which ensures the production of balanced, integrative, and sustainable knowledge on child development practices, and, ultimately, reflects the inherent diversity in child development science. It is more beneficial for child development researchers and practitioners, as well as multinational child development agencies, to work to prioritize multiple voices from diverse researchers in different socio-cultural contexts and disciplinary perspectives on child development matters because both local and global perspectives are crucial for a healthy child development science and practice. It is important to understand and recognize that the social and cultural context in which children grow and develop is as important as the biological processes of their development, and should thus be taken into account when planning appropriate and sustainable childhood intervention strategies and programs for all societies.

Conflict of Interest The authors declare that there is no conflict of interest.

References

Abebe, T., Dar, A., & Lysa, I. M. (2022). Southern theories and decolonial childhood studies. *Childhood, 29*(3), 255–275.

Adjei,S.B.(2013).Discourseanalysis:Examininglanguageuseincontext. *TheQualitative Report, 18*(50), 1–10. https://doi.org/10.46743/2160-3715/2013.1502

Adjei, S. B. (2019). Conceptualizing discursive analysis as a culturally contextualized activity. *The Qualitative Report, 24*(9), 2233–2243. https://doi.org/10.46743/2160-3715/2019.4020

Ainsworth, M. D. S., Bell, S. M., & Stayton, D. J. (1974). Infant–mother attachment and social development. In M. P. Richards (Ed.), *The introduction of the child into a social world* (pp. 99–135). Cambridge University Press.

Alam, S. (2008). Majority world: Challenging the West's rhetoric of democracy. *AmerasiaJournal, 34*(1), 88–98. https://doi.org/10.17953/amer.34.1.l3176027k4q614v5

Ansell, N. (2005). *Children, youth and development.* Routledge.

Araneda-Urrutia, C. (2022). The invention of the "weird" southern child: Mapping coloniality in the political problematization of disadvantaged children's lives in the global South. *Childhood, 29*(3), 292–306.

Ardila, A. (1995). Directions of research in cross-cultural neuropsychology. *Journal of Clinical and Experimental Neuropsychology, 17*(1), 143–150.

Ardila, A. (2005). Cultural values underlying psychometric cognitive testing. *Neuropsychology Review, 15*(4), 185–195.

Arnett, J. J. (2008). The neglected 95%: Why American psychology needs to become less American. *American Psychologist, 63*(7), 602–614.

Balagopalan, S. (2019). Why historicize rights-subjectivities? Children's rights, compulsory schooling, and the deregulation of child labor in India. *Childhood, 26*(3), 304–320.

Ball, J. (2010). Culture and early childhood education. In R. E. Tremblay, M. Boivin, & R. DeV. Peters (Eds.), *Encyclopedia on early childhood development* [online] (pp. 1–8). Centre of Excellence for Early Childhood Development and Strategic Knowledge Cluster on Early Child Development.

Benner, A., & Pence, A. (2015). *Complexities, capacities, communities: Changing development narratives in early childhood education, care and development.* University of Victoria.

Blatter, J. (2022). *Glocalization.* Encyclopedia Britannica. https://www.britannica.com/money/topic/glocalization

Bowlby, J. (1969). *Attachment and loss* (Vol. 1). Basic Books.

Britto, P. R., Lye, S. J., Proulx, K., Yousafzai, A. K., Matthews, S. G., Vaivada, T., Perez-Escamilla, R., et al. (2017). Nurturing care: Promoting early childhood development. *The Lancet, 389*(10064), 91–102.

Burman, E. (2008). *Developments: Child, image, nation.* Routledge/Taylor & Francis Group.

Burns, P. B., Rohrich, R. J., & Chung, K. C. (2011). The levels of evidence and their role in evidence-based medicine. *Plastic and Reconstructive Surgery, 128*(1), 305–310. https://doi.org/10.1097/PRS.0b013e318219c171

Chiao, J. Y., Iidaka, T., Gordon, H. L., et al. (2008). Cultural specificity in amygdala response to fear faces. *Journal of Cognitive Neuroscience, 20*, 2167–2174.

Danziger, K. (2009). The holy grail of universality. In T. Teo, P. Stenner, A. Rutherford, et al. (Eds.), *Varieties of theoretical psychology* (pp. 1–11). Captus University Publications.

de Castro, L. R. (2020). Why global? Children and childhood from a decolonial perspective. *Childhood, 27*(1), 48–62.

De Gioia, K. (2009). Parent and staff expectations for continuity of home practices in the child care setting for families with diverse cultural backgrounds. *Australasian Journal of Early Childhood, 34*(3), 9–17.

Engle, P. L., Black, M. M., Behrman, J. R., Cabral de Mello, M., Gertler, P. J., Kapiriri, L., Martorell, R., Young, M. E., & International Child Development Steering Group (2007). Strategies to avoid the loss of developmental potential in more than 200 million children in the developing world. *Lancet* (London, England), *369*(9557), 229–242. https://doi.org/10.1016/S0140-6736(07)60112-3

Fleer, M. (2006). The cultural construction of child development: Creating institutional and cultural intersubjectivity. *International Journal of Early Years Education, 14*(2), 127–140. https://doi.org/10.1080/09669760600661294

Funk, L., Scheidecker, G., Chapin, B. L., Schmidt, W. J., Ouardani, C. E., & Chaudhary, N. (2023). *Feeding, bonding, and the formation of social relationships: Ethnographic challenges to attachment theory and early childhood interventions.* Cambridge University Press. https://doi.org/10.1017/9781009306300

Graham, L. J. (2011). The product of text and 'other' statements: Discourse analysis and the critical use of Foucault. *Educational Philosophy and Theory, 43*(6), 663–674.

Grantham-McGregor, S., Cheung, Y. B., Cueto, S., Glewwe, P., Richter, L., & Strupp, B. (2007). Developmental potential in the first 5 years for children in developing countries. *The Lancet, 369*(9555), 60–70. https://doi.org/10.1016/S0140-6736(07)60032-4

Hanson, K., Abebe, T., Aitken, S. C., Balagopalan, S., & Punch, S. (2018). 'Global/local' research on children and childhood in a 'global society'. *Childhood, 25*(3), 272–296. https://doi.org/10.1177/0907568218779480

Henrich, J., Heine, S. J., & Norenzayan, A. (2010). The weirdest people in the world? *Behavioral and Brain Sciences, 33*(2–3), 61–83. https://doi.org/10.1017/S0140525X0999152X

Hodges, B. D., Kuper, A., & Reeves, S. (2008). Discourse analysis. *British Medical Journal, 337*, a879. https://doi.org/10.1136/bmj.a879

Kagitcibasi, C. (2002). A model of family change in cultural context. *Online Readings in Psychology and Culture, 6*(3). https://doi.org/10.9707/2307-0919.1059

Keller, H. (2017). Culture and development: A systematic relationship. *Perspectives on Psychological Science, 12*(5), 833–840. https://doi.org/10.1177/1745691617704097

Keller, H. (2021). *The myth of attachment theory*. Routledge.

Keller, H., Bard, K., Morelli, G., Chaudhary, N., Vicedo, M., Rosabal-Coto, M., Scheidecker, G., Murray, M., & Gottlieb, A. (2018). The myth of universal sensitive responsiveness: Comment on Mesman et al. (2017). *Child Development*. https://doi.org/10.1111/cdev.13031

Keller, H., & Kärtner, J. (2013). Development: The cultural solution of universal developmental tasks. In M. J. Gelfand, C.-y. Chiu, & Y.-y. Hong (Eds.), *Advances in culture and psychology* (pp. 63–116). Oxford University Press. https://doi.org/10.1093/acprof:oso/9780199930449.003.0002

Khan, T., Abimbola, S., Kyobutungi, C., & Pai, M. (2022). How we classify countries and people-and why it matters. *BMJ Global Health, 7*(6), e009704. https://gh.bmj.com/content/7/6/e009704

Kitayama, S. & Park, J. (2010). Cultural neuroscience of the self: Understanding the social grounding of the brain. *Social Cognitive and Affective Neuroscience, 5*(2–3), 111–129. https://doi.org/10.1093/scan/nsq052

Korf, B. (2020). Cultural politics. In A. Kobayashi (Ed.), *International encyclopedia of human geography* (2nd ed., pp. 111–116). https://doi.org/10.1016/B978-0-08-102295-5.10808-X

Lansdown, G. (2005). The evolving capacities of the child. *Innocenti Insights*, no. 11,

Maldonado-Torres, N. (2007). On the Coloniality of Being: Contributions to the Development of a Concept. *Cultural Studies, 21*(2–3), 240–270.

Manly, J. J. (2008). Critical issues in cultural neuropsychology: Profit from diversity. *Neuropsychology Review, 18*(3), 179–183.

McCoy, D. (2022). Building a model of cultural universality with specificity for global early childhood development. *Child Development Perspectives, 16*(1), 27–33. https://doi.org/10.1111/cdep.12438

McCoy, D. C., Seiden, J., Cuartas, J., Pisani, L., & Waldman, M. (2022a). Estimates of a multidimensional index of nurturing care in the next 1000 days of life for children in low-income and middle-income countries: A modelling study. *The Lancet. Child & Adolescent Health, 6*(5), 324–334. https://doi.org/10.1016/S2352-4642(22)00076-1

McCoy, D. C., Wolf, S., & Tsinigo, E. (2022b). Improving early childhood development on a global scale: Best practices for intervention. *JAMA Pediatrics, 176*(4), 337–338. https://doi.org/10.1001/jamapediatrics.2021.5351

Mesman, J., Minter, T., Angnged, A., Cissé, I. A. H., Salali, G. D., & Migliano, A. B. (2017). Universality without uniformity: A culturally inclusive approach to sensitive responsiveness in infant caregiving. *Child Development, 89*(3), 837–850. https://doi.org/10.1111/cdev.12795

Mesman, J., Van IJzendoorn, M. H., & Sagi-Schwartz, A. (2016). Cross-cultural patterns of attachment: Universal and contextual dimensions. In J. Cassidy & P. R. Shaver (Eds.), Handbook of attachment: Theory, research, and clinical applications (3rd ed., pp. 852–877). Guilford.

Morelli, G., Quinn, N., Chaudhary, N., Vicedo, M., Rosabal-Coto, M., Keller, H., Murray, M., Gottlieb, A., Scheidecker, G., & Takada, A. (2018). Ethical challenges of parenting interventions in low- to middle-income countries. *Journal of Cross-Cultural Psychology, 49*(1), 5–24. https://doi.org/10.1177/0022022117746241

Norenzayan, A., & Heine, S. J. (2005). Psychological universals: what are they and how can we know?. *Psychological Bulletin, 131*(5), 763–784. https://doi.org/10.1037/0033-2909.131.5.763

Nsamenang, A. B. (1992). *Human development in cultural context: A third world perspective*. Sage.

Nsamenang, A. B. (2005). Educational development and knowledge flow: Local and global forces in human development in Africa. *Higher Education Policy, 18*(3), 275–288.

Nsamenang, A. B. (2006). Human ontogenesis: An indigenous African view on development and intelligence. *International Journal of Psychology, 41*(4), 293–297.

Nsamenang, A. B. (2008). (Mis) understanding ECD in Africa: The force of local and global motives. In M. Garcia, A. Pence, & J. Evans (Eds.), *Africa's future, Africa's challenge early childhood care and development in sub-Saharan Africa*. World Bank.

Oppong, S. (2013). Indigenizing knowledge for development: Epistemological and pedagogical approaches. *Africanus, 4*(2), 34–50. https://doi.org/10.25159/0304-615X/2300

Oppong, S. (2015). A critique of early childhood development research and practice in Africa. *Africanus, 45*(1), 23–41. https://doi.org/10.25159/0304-615X/252

Oppong, S. (2020). Towards a model of valued human cognitive abilities: An African perspective based on a systematic review. *Frontiers in Psychology, 11*, 538072. https://doi.org/10.3389/fpsyg.2020.538072

Oppong, S. (2022). Raising a new generation in a postcolonial era through decolonised early childhood development and care services. *Contemporary Issues in Early Childhood, 23*(2), 182–197. https://doi.org/10.1177/1463949120970238

Oppong, S. (2023). Promoting global ECD top-down and bottom-up. *Ethos: Journal of the Society for Psychological Anthropology, 51*(3), 321–325. https://doi.org/10.1111/etho.12393

Oppong, S., Scheidecker, G., Chaudhary, N., Röttger-Rössler, B., & Keller, H. (2022). Different is not deficient: Respecting diversity in early childhood development—A response to Seiden et al. and Black and Richter. *Refubium-Repositorium der Freien Universität Berlin.* https://refubium.fu-berlin.de/handle/fub188/37259

Oppong, S., & Strader, S. (2022). *Interventions that matter start with local cultures: Issues and strategies in early childhood care and education interventions in Africa.* An ECCE Project Supported by Spencer Foundation/Boston College. https://afecn.org/blog/2022/5/23/interventions-that-matter-start-with-local-cultures-issues-and-strategies-in-early-childhood-care-and-education-interventions-in-africa

Pence, A., Evans, J. L., & Garcia, M. (2008). In M. H. Garcia, A. Pence, & J. Evans (Eds.), *Africa's future, Africa's challenge: Early childhood care and development in sub-Saharan Africa.* World Bank.

Quijano, A. (2007). Coloniality and modernity/rationality. *Cultural Studies, 21*(2–3), 168–178.

Raby, R. C. (2002). A tangle of discourses: Girls negotiating adolescence. *Journal of Youth Studies, 5*(4), 425–448. https://doi.org/10.1080/1367626022000030976

Robertson, R. (1994). Globalisation or glocalization? *The Journal of International Communication, 1*(1), 33–52.

Robertson, R. (2013). Situating glocalization: A relatively autobiographical intervention. In G. S. Drori, M. A. Ho¨llerer, & P. Walgenbach (Eds.), *Global themes and local variations in organization and management: Perspectives on glocalization* (pp. 25–36). Routledge.

Rudolph, L. I. (1992). The media and cultural politics. *Economic and Political Weekly, 27*(28), 1489–1496. http://www.jstor.org/stable/4398634

Scheidecker, G., Chaudhary, N., Keller, H., Mezzenzana, F., & Lancy, D. F. (2023). Poor brain development in the global South? Challenging the science of early childhood interventions. *Ethos, 51*, 3–26.

Scheidecker, G., Chaudhary, N., Oppong, S., Röttger-Rössler, B., & Keller, H. (2022). Different is not deficient: Respecting diversity in early childhood development. *The Lancet. Child & Adolescent Health, 6*(12), e24–e25. https://doi.org/10.1016/S2352-4642(22)00277-2

Scheidecker, G., Oppong, S., Chaudhary, N., & Keller, H. (2021). How overstated scientific claims undermine ethical principles in parenting interventions. *BMJ Global Health, 6*(9). https://doi.org/10.1136/bmjgh-2021-007323

Scheidecker, G., Tekola, B., Rasheed, M., Oppong, S., Mezzenzana, F., Keller, H., & Chaudhary, N. (2024). Ending epistemic exclusion: Toward a truly global science and practice of early childhood development. *The Lancet. Child & adolescent health, 8*(1), 3–5. https://doi.org/10.1016/S2352-4642(23)00292-4

Schiller, N. G. (1997). Cultural politics and the politics of culture. *Identities: Global Studies in Culture and Power, 4*(1), 1–7.

Serpell, R. (1993). *The significance of schooling: Life-journeys in an African society*. Cambridge University Press.

Serpell, R. (2000). Intelligence and culture. In R. J. Sternberg (Ed.), *Handbook of intelligence* (pp. 549–577). Cambridge University Press. https://doi.org/10.1017/CBO9780511807947.026

Serpell, R. (2011). Social responsibility as a dimension of intelligence, and as an educational goal: Insights from programmatic research in an African society. *Child Development Perspectives, 5*(2), 126–133. https://doi.org/10.1111/j.1750-8606.2011.00167.x

Serpell, R., & Haynes, B. P. (2004). The cultural practice of intelligence testing: Problems of international export. In R. J. Sternberg & E. L. Grigorenko (Eds.), *Culture and competence: Contexts of life success* (pp. 163–185). American Psychological Association. https://doi.org/10.1037/10681-007

Serpell, R., & Nsamenang. A. B. (2014). *Locally relevant and quality ECCE programmes: Implications of research on indigenous African child development and socialization*. Early childhood Care and education working papers series, 3. United Nations Educational, Scientific and Cultural Organization (UNESCO).

Super, C., & Harkness, S. (1982). Cultural perspectives on child development. In D. Wagner & H. Stevenson (Eds.), *Cultural perspectives on child development* (pp. 170–198). W.H Freeman.

Super, C. M., & Harkness, S. (1986). The developmental niche: A conceptualization at the interface of child and culture. *International Journal of Behavioral Development, 9*, 545–569.

van Vlaenderen, H., & Neves, D. (2013). Participatory action research and local knowledge in community contexts. In D. Hook, N. Mkhize, P. Kiguwa, & A. Collins (Eds.), *Critical psychology* (pp. 445–464). Juta and Company Ltd.

Wallace, S. S., Barak, G., Truong, G., & Parker, M. W. (2022). Hierarchy of evidence within the medical literature. *Hospital Pediatrics, 12*(8), 745–750. https://doi.org/10.1542/hpeds.2022-006690

Weisner, T. S. (2002). Ecocultural understanding of children's developmental pathways. *Human Development, 45*(4), 275–281. https://www.jstor.org/stable/2676368

Weisner, T. S. (2014). Culture, context, and child well-being. In A. Ben-Arieh, F. Casas, I. Frønes, & J. Korbin (Eds.), *Handbook of child well-being* (pp. 87–103). Springer. https://doi.org/10.1007/978-90-481-9063-8_3

Weisner, T. S. (Ed.). (2005). *Discovering successful pathways in children's development: Mixed methods in the study of childhood and family life*. University of Chicago Press.

Woodhead, M. (1999). Reconstructing developmental psychology: Some first steps. *Children and Society*, *13*, 3–19.

CHAPTER 5

The Conservative Politics of Indigenous Psychology and Decolonial Psychology

Carl Ratner

Indigenous Psychology (IP) and Decolonial Psychology (DP) present themselves as progressive intellectual and political praxes for understanding and opposing the colonial psychology of oppression. I shall demonstrate that IP and DP fail to comprehend the fundamentally political-economic basis of colonialism and the psychology of oppression, and they fail to elucidate the need to transform this basis into a humane political-economy. My critique is a Marxist critique of IP and DP.

The standard format of a critique is to first present an issue and then explain its flaws and necessary solutions. My editors have suggested that it would be easier for my readers to follow my critique of IP and DP if they could see it in advance and then utilize it to understand the details of IP and DP. I have adopted this approach of presenting the Marxist solution before explaining the IP/DP conundrums.

My critique is organized around Marxist cultural psychology which I have developed from Marxist political philosophy called historical-materialism. I name my approach "Macro Cultural Psychology" (Ratner,

C. Ratner (✉)
Institute for Cultural Research & Education, Trinidad, CA, USA
e-mail: cr2@humboldt1.com

Z. Z. Gao, M. I. Medved (eds.), *Global Perspectives on Cultural Politics in Indigenous Psychology*, Palgrave Studies in Indigenous Psychology, https://doi.org/10.1007/978-3-031-96813-6_5

2008, 2011, 2012, 2014, 2018, 2019, 2022; Marcus & Fischer, 1999; Lutz, 1988). The main principles of this political philosophy/cultural theory are that culture is a coherent system that is based in a specific political-economy. This grounding imbues cultural factors—including linguistic and psychological factors—with a political-economic ethos and telos. This is what makes cultural factors concrete. Let us see how this is all pertinent to understanding the culture and psychology and emancipation of oppressed people.

Marx's historical-materialist conception of culture-psychology is depicted in Fig. 5.1.

Historical-materialist culture generates a logical, congruent model of emancipation. It entails solving social problems by tracing their formative cultural factors to their political-economic base, and then utilizing this collective focus from cultural-psychological factors to transform that base to erect a new cultural-psychological system. Figure 5.2 depicts this transformation.

This emancipatory process applies to all countries and all social problems. (Kristen Ghodsee (2018) has adopted this perspective to explain Why Women Have Better Sex Under Socialism.) This model of emancipation rejects direct, horizontal reforms of particular cultural elements—for

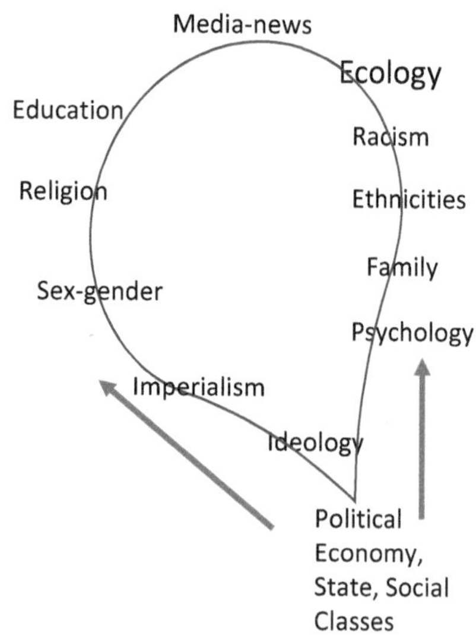

Fig. 5.1 Historical-materialist model of culture

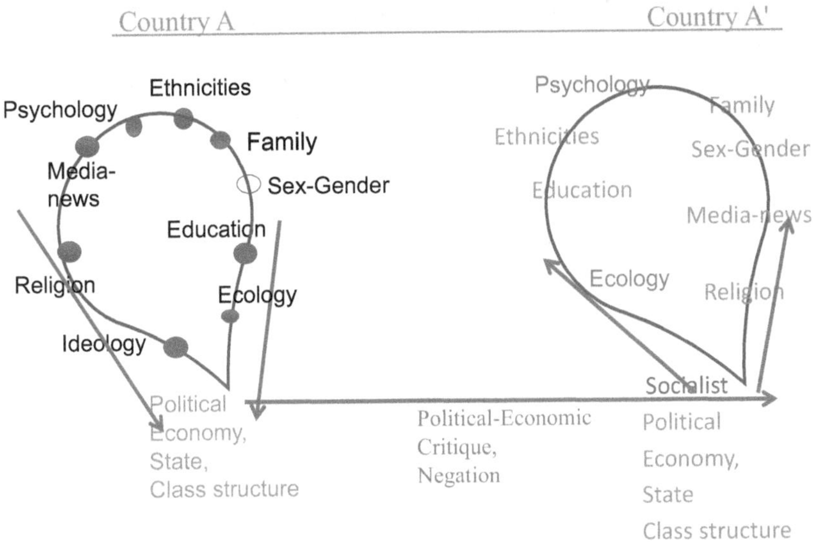

Fig. 5.2 Historical-materialist social improvement

example, changing education or ecology or ethnicities from A to A′—without changing their political-economic basis. Individual countries internalize socialism as their common telos for national liberation. This culminates in a world of A' + B' + C' + D' + E' countries, which is International Socialism.

This was the model of The International Workingmen's Association (IWA), often called the First International (1864–1876). It was an international organization which aimed at uniting the international working classes of all countries against capitalism. Its mission: "is not ... a mere improvement that is contemplated, but nothing less than a regeneration, and that not of one nation only, but of mankind." Marx was a representative of German workers to the first Congress. He wrote the "Inaugural Address of the IWA, and the Provisional Rules of the International Working Men's Association." It said, "To save the industrious masses, co-operative labor ought to be developed to national dimensions, and, consequently, to be fostered by national means." National means will be utilized to develop socialist society. IWA expanded to 860,000 members in 1869.

Marx defined some important elements of socialism:

- Abolish private property and replace with public property where workers collectively own and control their labor, rather than working for capitalists who buy and control it
- Abolish social classes
- Abolish wage labor
- Abolish commodity production and market exchange.

The IWA sought to educate the masses to understand this analysis. It hinges on recognizing that throughout the kaleidoscope of manifest social oppressions runs the coherent telos and ethos of the "mute, brute compulsion of capital" (Mau, 2023). Likewise, the kaleidoscope of particular social struggles to emancipate particular, cultural phenomena (and people) must be informed by the concrete negation of the mute, brute compulsion of capital, that is directed by the collective, democratic, ethos and telos of global socialism. The Marxist model encompasses colonialism and its psychology of oppression. "Ethnicities" in Fig. 5.2 represents colonized peoples who have been exploited by colonial, capitalist powers, and who need democratic, collective socialism in order to negate colonial capitalism and realize their humanity.

According to Marx, socialism is the historically available alternative to capitalist exploitation in all its forms. Transforming the political-economy is crucial because it (a) provides a concrete direction/strategy and content for overcoming oppression, (b) provides a material support system for realizing this direction/strategy, and (c) eliminates obstacles to transformation which reside in the existing political-economy and its cultural system.

Denying this, and identifying and changing cultural factors apart from their political-economic base—as native, racial, gendered, religious, psychological—impede intellectually comprehending them and politically improving them. These failures are fostered by a lack of (a) concrete direction, strategy, and features that negate the essence of social oppression; (b) material support for realizing this deep (radical), comprehensive, powerful direction/strategy. These errors characterize the vast majority of social theory and practice. These errors plague the work of indigenous psychologists and decolonial psychologists.

Indigenous Psychology

Indigenous psychology is a polysemous term like psychology itself. It refers to (a) ordinary peoples' psychological phenomena—their emotions, perceptions, mental illness, cognitions, self-concept, imagination, motivation, sexuality (I call this indigenous psychology with a small "p"); and (b) the disciplined study of ordinary psychology by academicians, clinicians, and religious figures (I call this indigenous Psychology with a capital "P"). Indigenous Psychology includes theories/constructs about psychology, the methodologies for studying psychology, the interventions that advance psychology which are employed by practitioners of psychology in diverse countries, and political-cultural assumptions which guide all of these.

This essay is more about Indigenous Psychology than indigenous psychology. I seek to elucidate and improve upon the manner in which IP conceptualizes, defines, circumscribes, explains, describes, and emancipates peoples' indigenous psychologies.

Definitions and Political Assumptions of Indigenous Psychology Shape Its Praxis

The term (or construct) "indigenous" denotes a birthplace; it is being native to a place, endogenous to it, and developing there. In Latin, the "gen" in indi*gen*ous, is the "gen" in *gen*erative. Indigenous implies being naturally generated by an organic, benevolent condition. For example, redwood trees are indigenous to Northern California. The tree has grown from, is adapted to, thrives in, expresses, and is functional for its native, benevolent, supportive, ecological context. Mutual symbiosis governs indigenous phenomena and their ecologies. Indigenous is synonymous with aboriginal. This conception is espoused in Kim and Berry's early book on the subject: *Indigenous Psychologies* (1993, p. 2) which conceives of indigenous psychologies "as the scientific study of human behavior (or the mind) that is native, that is not transported from other regions, and that is designed for its people."

Indigenous psychologists became interested in indigenous psychology because it had been brutalized by socio-economic-political-cultural colonialism. Indigenous Psychology arose as an element of anti-colonialism that respected, validated, and recuperated/restored indigenous peoples' original, authentic, native, autonomous, cultural-psychology, and condition. Indigenous Psychology regarded indigenous psychology as a political human rights issue of opposing colonialism. Some 5,000 living, indigenous groups have been identified, containing hundreds of millions of people in total. They are all minorities within the states in which they live.

We now utilize Marxist historical-materialism/Macro Cultural Psychology to evaluate IP/DP's viability for comprehending and liberating indigenous, colonized people, and their psychology. Our primary criticism is that while IP/DP correctly condemns colonialism's unjust, immoral treatment of indigenous people, and rightfully empathizes with them, this standpoint does not constitute a scientific psychological understanding of indigenous psychology, or a scientific, viable political venue for emancipating indigenous people from oppression. Indeed, the IP/DP psychological and political narratives manifest limited rationale or clarity.

IP/DP brush aside Marx's careful analysis of human society, class exploitation, and a logical, dialectical, socialist alternative. They replace it with a new narrative of indigenous people who live in "the global South," being colonized by white people who live in the "global North." The United Nations extols this orientation in the 2007 *United Nations Declaration on the Rights of Indigenous Peoples*; the United Nations General Assembly 1993 declaration of the International Year of the World's Indigenous People; and 1995–2004 as the Decade of the World's Indigenous People which declared: "Indigenous Peoples are inheritors and practitioners of unique cultures and ways of relating to people and the environment."

This new formulation is questionable because it ignores Marxist historical-materialism which successfully explains colonialism and an emancipatory alternative. Moreover, IP/DP's psychological and political constructs are poorly formulated with limited rationale or clarity.

The basic construct "Indigenous People" refers to people who have a historical relationship with people who inhabited a territory prior to colonialization. It does not designate a specific social organization in which one lives. It is simply a historical lineage to pre-colonial times. This is uninformative about the culture and psychology that such an individual may have today. The problem appears in The American Bureau of Indian Affairs' criterion of the genetic composition that qualifies a person as being Indian. Given the intermingling of races in contemporary times, the Bureau recognized that it could not confine Indian to 100% Indian genotype. It reduced the criterion to 25%—that is, a person's blood must contain at least one-fourth Indian blood to qualify as an Indian and receive government benefits. This allows a person to qualify as Indian even when s/he is genetically 75% non-Indian. This renders the definition of Indian problematic. Indigenous life is rarely assessed through an objective analysis of the social practices. This is necessary in determining whether they should be validated as an alternative to colonialism. In fact, these are quite often oppressive.

Walter Rodney (2018, p. 73) informs us that much of the great material and spiritual artifacts of indigenous (pre-colonial) African civilization were premised on a developed division of labor in which ruling aristocracies emerged, seizing control of the means of production, thereby becoming "a social stratum above the clans which previously existed."

Indigenous African societies also included an active, domestic, slave economy, which sold slaves to European and American plantation owners on the trans-Atlantic slave trade. A detailed historical study of a domestic African slave economy found that "the rise and expansion of the Aro merchant group and their organization as a trade diaspora [which] were pivotal to the massive expansion of the Biafra [slave] trade in the mid-eighteenth century." "As a small group, the Aro depended economically on slaves as both merchandise and laborers." "Endogenous sociocultural practices, such as slavery, means of enslavement, and conceptions of the Atlantic world helped to shape the composition of export captives." "Their value system celebrated the ownership and proliferation of people and encouraged the sale of captives into Atlantic slavery." "The unusual gender structure of the Biafra slave trade [was organized] by patterns of domestic consumption, ritual, warfare, gender division of labor in agriculture, and long-distance trade" (Nwokeji, 2010, pp. xviii, 2, my emphasis).[1] Similarly, British colonial rule in India used existing caste distinctions as instruments of colonial domination.

Chinese dynasties—such as the Ming (1368–1643)—are similarly included as indigenous societies when they were structured into social classes which exploited the common people—the Ming ruling class imposed exorbitant taxes on the Ming peasants which caused them to revolt. Chinese indigenous cultures also practiced oppressive foot-binding of certain classes of women for 1,000 years.

[1] Idealizing "indigenous culture-psychology" minimizes its negative features. It also exaggerates the violence of cultural outsiders such as colonists who are blamed for all indigenous oppression. African slavery is almost always attributed to White, Anglo-Americans invading Africa and enslaving its population, without fully appreciating Africans' indigenous slave trade.

These examples devastate the IP paradigm. For, they were endogenous, and endogenous is presumed to be a priori benevolent (valuable, unique, respected, symbiotic), which means that the indigenous examples were benevolent. IP/DP has no logical objection to this. Actually, the real logic of Indigenous Psychology is the opposite: slavery was endogenous to Africa, slavery is bad; therefore, endogenous behavior is not necessarily good, which refutes the indigenous paradigm of glorifying endogenous behavior-psychology.[2]

Conservative Psychological and Cultural Features of Indigenous Psychological Constructs

Wang and Greenwood (2016) explain how unemployed Chinese workers draw upon traditional Chinese concepts as psychological tools to detrimentally deal with their misfortune. "In China the xiagang [unemployment] problem became a national crisis. 25.5 million workers were laid off from State owned enterprises between 1997 and 2003" (p. 52). Wang & Greenwood identified four psychological themes that laid-off workers experienced: (a) feeling of loss, (b) feeling of physical pain, (c) feeling of fatalism, and (d) accepting unemployment and seeking to overcome it. These experiences are concretely (historically) organized by, and expressed (symbolized) in, indigenous Chinese concepts. Feeling of loss is dominated by loss of face (diu mianzi). Physical pain is a cultural somatization of mental pain. Fatalism is defined by Chinese ancient theocratic concept of Tian Ming.

Nearly all the interviewees said that their first response to being laid off involved losing face (diu mianzi). This cultural template, or framing, of

[2] The reason indigenous cultures include oppression is that they are relatively recent—they are defined as pre-colonial which is pre-sixteenth century. Violence was commonplace long before that date. Violence is characteristic of class society, not only colonial society. Class society emerged with agriculture, about 12,000 years ago. Before then, societies were nomadic and classless. Class society existed for about 12,000 years before colonialism. Consequently, many pre-colonial societies were typically class societies which were hierarchical and violent. Marx described them as follows: "The sporadic application of co-operation on a large scale in ancient times, in the middle ages, and in modern colonies, reposes on relations of dominion and servitude, principally on slavery" (Capital, chapter on Cooperation). IP/DP mistakenly equates pre-colonial, indigenous societies with classless, non-oppressive societies. This accounts for the idealization IP/DP makes about indigenous cultures and indigenous psychology.

their loss generated a series of negative psychological feelings toward themselves and family. They enclosed themselves in their own world of distress, without much communication with the outside world. For example: "I felt I had no face to meet my families, friends, neighbors after being laid off. I felt I was shameful and inferior to my friends. Therefore, I tried to avoid seeing them. … What made me very shameful was that my daughter felt she lost face in front of her classmates due to my layoff" (Li Ming, 48 years old, male, married, p. 56).

We can see that the indigenous cultural construct "losing face" exacerbates the tragedy of unemployment. It blames the worker for the job loss that was instigated by a bureaucratic decision. This deflects criticism of the State that was responsible for the crisis. It blocked Li Ming from resenting, criticizing, or rebelling at the system. Utilizing this cultural construct to explain Li's unemployment additionally led Li's daughter to blame her father rather than the State. Emotional shame is a conservative emotion that maintains the status quo by blaming and punishing individuals for negative behavior (Lin, 2012).

This example shows that indigenous cultural-psychological constructs may legitimate social oppression rather than symbiotic growth. Anthropologist Jie Yang makes this Foucauldian point explicitly:

> In Changping, workers' displays of anger and discontent have been directly engaged by local authorities through medicalized discourse, feminization, reemployment, shaming, comradery … and Confucianist and Daoist approaches to anger management. My analysis examines both the domestication of anger and the personalization of politics, for example, by counselors; both are state organized interventions designed to shift blame from policies that aggravate injustice towards problems of the individual. (Yang, 2016 p. 120; see also Yang, 2012, 2015, 2017)

An important Chinese social-political reform movement of 1915 critiqued indigenous Chinese culture-psychology for this reason: the "New Culture Movement" was critical of Confucian social-political values like hierarchy, paternalism, obedience, and unquestioning respect (Matthyssen, 2021, p. 282).[3]

[3] Indigenous Confucian philosophy reveals the limitations of indigenous constructs for everyday psychology and as explanatory and analytical frameworks for a science of indigenous Psychology.

Indigenous cultural institutions and psychology become altered by contemporary social forms. Yet, these are masked by using the term "indigenous" which connotes pre-colonial behavior. For instance, most Indigenous people in the Americas now do not live in peasant or rural communities but in urban areas. Some Native American tribal governments and members have even embraced extractive industries like oil and coal on their reservations. Calling these "indigenous" obscures their modern forms, and renders them acceptable as behavior of "indigenous people."

Wang and Jiang (2022) insightfully explain that "While every Minzu (ethnicity) in China claims to have a 'time-honoured history' and 'splendid culture,' most ethnic minorities today are not the natural continuation of a Minzu in the past but are a result of the construction of contemporary Chinese ethnic politics" (p. 8). "Traditional culture has been systematically redeveloped as a tourism resource, especially since the emergence of cultural tourism. These reinvented public cultural products are reintroduced into the ethnic group's own cultural system and become accepted by the cultural owners as part of the local culture" (pp. 13–14).

Hui (2024) explains that Dai Buddhism is such a case. "The lives of monks and Buddhist masters have become increasingly secularized; many previously strictly observed commandments have been gradually broken. Buddhist rituals through which the Dai people expressed their beliefs have become increasingly secularized and are now more like a form of folk entertainment with fewer and fewer religious components." The spiritual, immaterial, indigenous, Dai Buddhist ethos has become commodified by charging a monetary fee to explore spiritual temples (p. 165). This commodification is then accepted as indigenous, and respected and validated

(a) It is not a systematic analysis of Confucian society. It does not explore society's political-economic structure, or ideologies.
(b) Nor does Confucianism emphasize its own origin and function as the imperial ideology of emperors that legitimizes the political state and subjects the populace to it.
(c) Nor does Confucianism recognize how Confucian society generates Confucian psychology, and
(d) how and why Confucian psychology blinds indigenous people and indigenous Psychologists to their oppressive society and to their own cultural-political suppression.

Describing and explaining Confucianism and indigenous cultural-psychological constructs must be achieved by an external, scientific macro cultural Psychology which elucidates their cultural-political origin, mechanisms, character, and functions.

as an emancipatory alternative to modern capitalism. Indigenization coopts people into embracing capitalism in indigenous form. It is a wolf in sheep's clothing.

Anthropologists and historians need to establish criteria for indigenous customs and psychology that are similar to criteria for indigenous personhood. They must ask whether Dai Buddhism can qualify as an indigenous cultural ethos even if it has renounced 30% or 50% or 75% of its ancient ethos.

Marx's Correction of Indigenous Ideology

Marx provides a corrective to the faulty indigenous paradigm. He was interested in the dynamics of human civilization that provided a material and cultural-psychological ground for world socialism. Marx saw socialism as the culmination of a historical dynamic that commenced with a primordial socialism which he called "primitive communism." Primordial communism was a social system of collectivism, egalitarianism, and cooperation; it preceded class society (as footnote #2 describes) and legitimated the possibility of a future classless socialism. Modern socialism was to be a dialectical advance (aufhebung) over primitive communism; it emerges from advanced capitalism's extensive coordination of production which lends itself to democratic collectivization by the working class (see The People's Republic of Walmart: How The World's Largest Corporations Are Laying The Foundation for Socialism, 2019, for an example). Marx did not pin socialism on conditions and acts that were "primitive," "aboriginal," "indigenous," "native," "synergistic," "unique," "autonomous," and "pre-colonial," because (1) they no longer existed; (2) they are laden with social class hierarchy and oppression; (3) they are devoid of the capacity to analyze and negate capitalism which is central to genuine emancipation.

Indigenous Psychology and Decolonial Psychology

Indigenous Psychology seeks to counterpose local, self-made, cultural forms of psychology to Western forms. This has made the former an element of political resistance to Western colonialism. This political form of Indigenous Psychology is called decolonial Psychology.

Unfortunately, the errors of IP have permeated decolonial Psychology and weakened its political and scientific power. DP shares IP's ambiguous definition, and opposition to foreign psychologies.

IP/DP reduces concrete social factors of oppression and emancipation to abstract acts which are not political or economic. For example, Ngwane et al. (2017) describe populist movements in the global south. While their descriptions recognize certain exploitive features of capitalism, their decolonial approach reframes these as empty abstractions. In Mexico, September 2013, "the Zapatistas denounced neoliberalism as a system intended to annihilate human dignity." This culminated in a "March of Dignity" that demanded the right to work, education, justice, and peace (pp. 82–83).

The contrast with the historical-materialist paradigm is obvious. Capitalist politics and economics consists of an imperialist, capitalist class exploiting a global working class to generate surplus value; this political-economic system is negated by the global working class which produces the world's means of subsistence and has the power to transform the productive system into socialism. IP/DP emphasizes colonialists destroying the dignity of indigenous people in the global south, which is restored by marginalized indigenous people in the global south, decolonializing themselves by de-linking from colonialism. All the elements in the IP/DP model are abstractions lacking specific definition, power, and direction.

Even the term "Decolonialism" is an abstraction. It implies non-colonialism rather than a concrete, historical-materialist alternative, such as socialism. Reddy, et al. only mention capitalism once, as "tethered to coloniality" rather than to profit, commodification of wage-labor, private property, and class struggle. They never mention socialism as a solution. Decolonialism also lacks a process for how to de-link from global capitalism which provides people with most of the products they use (including food), and avidly works to defeat defectors from the system by power and cooptation. ["Walter Rodney was among midcentury thinkers deeply influenced by Marxism who argued that formal independence from colonial powers did not entail actual emancipation. Instead, it led to a 'neocolonial' order" (Raza & Ali, 2024).]

Decolonial emancipation is simply "de-linking from" colonial culture-psychology by engaging in local, traditional customs + newly created activities by the people. Decolonialism carves out a protective niche of respect, support, and autonomy for certain ethnic peoples within capitalism. However, assertions about emancipatory decolonialism and decolonial psychology are not supported by empirical or theoretical reason.

For example, Harvard Divinity School, on March 23, 2016, issued a bulletin entitled "Decolonizing Voice." It reported the work of Grace Nono, HDS Visiting Lecturer in Women and Shamanism, who links shamanism to decolonialism, indigenous Psychology, and liberation. "Asserting the power of voice as site of decolonization, Grace punctuated her talk with performances of oral chants with sacred themes that were taught to her by several babaylan and other oralist singers." The report never explains how shamanism is decolonial, and what its emancipatory effects are. Mere difference (de-linking) from colonial behavior qualifies as decolonial and emancipatory, regardless of what the new form or content is.

These conundrums within decolonial Psychology are manifested in an article by Reddy, et al. (2021).

I. "Decolonial perspectives take Southern and majority-world settings as a privileged standpoint from which to better understand general processes that remain obscure when viewed from gated-community enclaves of global modernity in the Global North. The goal of decolonial perspectives is a general psychology—to advance theoretical insights from a Southern standpoint about reality at large, including psychological life in Eurocentric global modernity."

The authors fail to identify a "Southern standpoint" on psychology/Psychology. Nor do they document how it is superior to psychological approaches from the Global North for understanding and emancipating general psychology. On the contrary, examples of oppressive indigenous, Southern standpoints are plentiful, as they are in indigenous cultures. One case is the indigenous Gambian treatment of women, which consists of removing the clitoris and labia minora of girls between the ages of 10 and 15. This is perpetrated as an indigenous religious obligation. It is also perpetrated by indigenous female relatives of girls, who invoke indigenous psychological concepts of cultural autonomy to defend it. Reddy, et al., would claim that this "indigenous, Southern cultural-psychological standpoint" better understands and supports global Southern and Northern women than Northern epistemology does.

Decolonial, indigenous ideology is similarly utilized to attack homosexuality in various African countries. "Uganda's Constitutional Court on April 3, 2024, upheld a sweeping anti-gay law that calls for life imprisonment for anyone who engages in gay sex. The law is popular in Uganda. Religious and political leaders say that homosexuality is a Western import.

A few weeks after it was introduced in Parliament, the law was quickly passed with only two lawmakers opposing it" (New York Times, April, 3, 2024). Indigenous African culture/religion is marshaled to resist Western homosexuality which is said to be a colonial, oppressive "other."

II. Political emancipation that ensues from DP is indefinite and subjectivistic: "The Decolonial attitude invites psychologists to get up from their desk and join the protest, not as leaders but in solidarity with community organizations." This political activism is silent about who formulates political activity, who carries it out, and what their programs are.

- Decoloniality additionally seeks to objectify these conflicting standpoints in global geography. Colonialism is construed as wealthy white people from Northern and Western countries conquering poor people of color who reside mostly in the "Global South" (North-White-colonialist-wealthy; South-Colored-colonized-poor). This geographical, racial, economic framing of colonialism is incoherent.
- "The global north" and "the global south" are geographic areas without any definite political or economic characteristics. Countries in each geographical zone consist of completely different conditions—some autocratic, some democratic, some wealthy, some poor, some theocracies, some secular, some black, some white. Burundi is an African country whose population is half the population of the city of Shanghai. One Chinese capitalist is wealthier than Burundi's entire GDP of $2.7 billion. Burundi is the poorest country in the world! Yet Burundi and China are categorized together as associates of the Global South, with common interests, "standpoint," and psychology.
- The "Global South" incongruously includes Northern hemisphere countries of India and China. Conversely, Australia is excised from the Global South.
- Most African countries are north of the equator, yet Africa is considered to be the Global South. Algeria, which was brutally colonized by France, is north of the equator.
- Global North countries include desperately poor States, such as Afghanistan, which sits on the same geographic latitude as Florida but has two-thirds of its population impoverished.

- Many Global South countries (identified by decolonial theory) are classified by the World Bank as upper-middle income, not poor: China, Argentina, Brazil, South Africa, Guatemala. Uruguay has high income, high wealth equality, and stability.
- American colonialists decimated American Indians who lived in the Global North, not the South which is supposed to bear the brunt of Northern colonialism.
- Japan invaded China in the 1930s despite the fact that both countries are people of color in the geographic North.
- Japan bombed the United States despite the fact that both were Northern. Aggressor Japan was non-White while the victim United States was white.
- White capitalists exploit white labor in the Northern hemisphere, in addition to colored labor in the Southern hemisphere.

The Scientific and Political Value of Indigenous Psychology/Decolonial Psychology

IP and DP espouse superficial, incoherent causes of, categories of, and solutions to, colonialism. Notions of the Global North and Global South make it impossible to know how to treat countries which the theory associates with them. For IC/DC, the causes of colonialism are race, geography, and colonialists oppressing indigenous people. Its solutions are: de-linking colonialism and recuperating native, indigenous customs plus newly created activities (Naicker, 2023). These constructs are not the essential causes and solutions to colonialism. Those include the political-economic profit motive, private ownership of property and resources, commodifying labor and the natural environment, exploiting labor and nature, financialization, private equity, declining rate of profit, and the capitalist class structure—all of which must be negated in concert by socialism, as depicted in Fig. 5.2.

Colonialism does not exist as an independent phenomenon with its own mechanisms and players. Its particular features are forms of capitalism. IP/DP obfuscates the causes, forms, perpetrators, victims, and solutions to colonialism by misconstruing them as independent phenomena, mechanisms, and players whose characteristics are not explained. Examples include indigenous people, colonists, native customs, Global South, "racial capitalism," white racism, de-linking, and community.

Historical-materialism (i.e., Macro Cultural Psychology) corrects this error by replacing abstract, autonomous, restricted terms such as colonist with the broader political-economic term "capitalist" who exploits everyone, everywhere. Marx explained slavery in terms of capital. Foster et al. (2020) note: Marx explained that slave labor was embedded within "a situation of capitalist production. The same person is capitalist and landowner."

Marxists translate "de-linking" into concrete political-economic negations of capitalism, such as "de-commodifying," "de-classing," "de-privatizing," and "de-militarizing." "Colonizer," "indigenous people," "colonized people," "people of color," and "community of people" are forms of social class. This socialist critique is followed by positive, socialist terms that Marx proposed (see Das, 2023 for a socialist program). Gumede (2023, p. 445) explains the historical-materialist solution to colonialism that Fig. 5.2 depicts. He says: "delinking is associated with a transition—outside capitalism and over a long time—towards socialism. This political-economic-cultural movement must be specific and cogent enough to oppose neoliberal, capitalist pressures in post-colonial countries" (Bond, 2013, 2023, pp. 315, Bond & Garcia, 2015).

Neiman (2024, p. 20) similarly explains that "Fanon's view of the Algerian revolution was not just an anti-colonial struggle but a social revolution. ... Fanon allied with the most open-minded group in the Algerian National Liberation Front, Marxists who believed that national revolution was only worthwhile as a prelude to social revolution," that is, socialism. (Walter Rodney expressed the same conclusion in Raza & Ali, 2024.) This is depicted in Fig. 5.2, where "ethnicities" contribute to illuminating the existing political-economy and to transforming it into global socialism. "National autonomy" is not emancipatory because it is indefinite and can include reactionary populism, dictatorship, and national inequality.

Social class is the quintessential dialectical phenomenon. Social class is the concrete mechanism of oppression/exploitation, and also the concrete mechanism of emancipation. The capitalist class's exploitation of working class labor is the generative mechanism of capital's wealth and power, and its general destructiveness (that includes indigenous people, people of color, and community). The transformation of social class to classlessness by the working class is the mechanism of general emancipation for all oppressed people; it is also the expression/measure of emancipation.

Forms of emancipation in diverse cultural-psychological domains and populations must ultimately be forms of socialist classlessness. Indigenous people cannot wave good-bye to their systemic oppression, and re-link to native customs in the belly of the beast. This fallacy is objectified in phrases such as "Recognition As Resilience: How An Unrecognized Indigenous Nation Is Using Visibility As A Pathway Towards Restorative Justice" (Renoir & Covert, 2024). This is an orientation to liberation that utilizes an apolitical, abstract strategy of "visibility" to "restore justice" as a means of "historical redress and reconciliation" as well as "a pathway for reasserting identity, rights, and a collective future" (see Tauri, 2022 for critique). These abstract signifiers replace viable, material solutions to political-economic problems for native people. They ignore rapacious, neoliberalism that imposes austerity, precariousness, decimation of social services, commodification, and alienation on native (as well as all) laboring people. Actually, the empty terms of Indigenous Psychology have been filled by neoliberalism: Recently, 23 First Nation and Metis communities used their autonomy and community to acquire an 11.57% interest in seven Enbridge-operated gas-oil pipelines in the Canadian province of Alberta. (As I am writing this in December 2024, an Enbridge pipeline is spilling 70,000 gallons of oil in Wisconsin.) In the Pacific coastal province of British Columbia, another consortium of First Nations, known as the Western Indigenous Pipeline Group, is seeking to purchase the Trans Mountain Pipeline. More than 90% of First Nations along B.C.'s proposed northern pipeline routes have signed agreements.

Indigenous people must heed the words of Franz Fanon: "The struggle does not give back to the national culture its former values and shapes; this struggle aims at a fundamentally different [new] set of relations between men; it cannot leave intact either the form or content of the people's culture." Martin Luther King (1961) explained the true political-economic telos of IP/DP: *"We must see now that the evils of racism, economic exploitation and militarism are all tied together ... you can't really get rid of one without getting rid of the others ... the whole structure of American life must be changed."*

Conflict of Interest The author declares that there is no conflict of interest.

References

Bond, P. (2013). Sub-imperialism as lubricant of neoliberalism: South African 'deputy sheriff' duty within BRICS. *Third World Quarterly, 34*(2), 251–270.

Bond, P. (2023). 'Nothing has changed, South Africa's sub-imperialist role has been reinforced': Samir Amin's durable critique of apartheid/post-apartheid political economy. *Politikon: South African Journal of Political Studies, 50, 4*, 314–333.

Bond, P., & Garcia, A. (2015). BRICS: An anti-capitalist critique. South Africa Jacana Media. https://www.researchgate.net/profile/Ana-Garcia-287/publication/349928435

Das, R. (2023). Marxism and revisionism in the world today. *Capital & Class, 47*, 383–406.

Foster, J., Holleman, H., & Clark, B. (2020, July–August). Marx and slavery. *Monthly Review, 72*, 3. https://monthlyreview.org/2020/07/01/marx-and-slavery/

Ghodsee, K. (2018). *Why women have better sex under socialism.* Vintage Books.

Gumede, V. (2023). Post-colonial development in Africa – Samir Amin's lens. Politikon,: South African Journal of. *Political Studies, 50*(4), 438–451. https://doi.org/10.1080/02589346.2023.2300893

Hui, C. (2024). *Between tradition and modernity: Study on the symbiosis between monastic education and school education of the Dai in Xishuangbanna.* Routledge.

Lin, D. (2012). Working to be worthy: Shame and the Confucian technology of governing. In A. Kipnis (Ed.), *Chinese modernity and the individual psyche* (pp. 169–186). Palgrave.

Lutz, C. (1988). *Unnatural Emotions.* University of Chicago Press.

Marcus, G. E., & Fischer, M. M. (1999). *Anthropology as cultural critique: An experimental moment in the human sciences.* University of Chicago Press.

Matthyssen, M. (2021). *Ignorance is bliss: The Chinese art of not-knowing.* Palgrave.

Mau, S. (2023). *Mute compulsion: A Marxist theory of the economic theory of capital.* Verso.

Naicker, N. (2023). The problem of epistemological critique in contemporary Decolonial theory. *Social Dynamics, 49*, 220–241.

Neiman, S. (2024, June 6). Fanon the universalist. *New York Review of Books, 71*(10), 19–21.

Ngwane, T., Sinwell, L., & Ness, I. (2017). *Urban revolt: State power and the rise of people's movements in the global south.* Haymarket.

Nwokeji, G. (2010). *The slave trade and culture in the Bight of Biafra.* Cambridge University Press.

Ratner, C. (2008). *Cultural psychology, cross-cultural psychology, and indigenous psychology.* Nova Publishers.

Ratner, C. (2011). Macro cultural psychology, the psychology of oppression, and cultural-psychological enrichment. In P. Portes & S. Salas (Eds.), *Vygotsky in 21st Century society: Advances in cultural historical theory and praxis with non-dominant communities* (pp. 87–112). Peter Lang.

Ratner, C. (2012). *Macro cultural psychology: A political philosophy of mind.* Oxford University Press.

Ratner, C. (2014). The psychology of oppression. In T. Teo (Ed.), *The encyclopedia of critical psychology* (pp. 1557–1570). Springer.

Ratner, C. (2018). Macro cultural psychology: Its genesis, science, and politics. In G. Jovanović, L. Allolio-Näcke, & C. Ratner (Eds.), *The challenges of cultural psychology: Reviving historical legacies, engaging for future responsibilities*. Routledge.

Ratner, C. (2019). *Psychology's contribution To Socio-Cultural, Political, and Individual Emancipation*. Palgrave Macmillan.

Ratner, C. (2022). *Cultural psychology, racism, and social justice*. Springer.

Raza, S., & Ali, N. (2024, January 24). Walter Rodney's Radical legacy. *Boston Review* https://www.bostonreview.net/articles/walter-rodneys-radical-legacy.

Reddy, G., Suffla, S., Adams, G., Ratele, K., & Stevens, G. (2021). General psychology otherwise: A decolonial articulation. *Review of General Psychology, 25*(4), 339–353.

Renoir, M., & Covert, S. (2024). Recognition as resilience: How an unrecognized indigenous nation is using visibility as a pathway towards restorative justice. *The American Historical Review, 129*(4), 1567–1598.

Rodney, W. (2018). *How Europe underdeveloped Africa*. Verso (Originally published, 1972).

Tauri, J. M. (2022). What exactly are you restoring us to? A critical examination of indigenous experiences of state-centred restorative justice. *Howard Journal of Crime and Justice, 61*, 53–67.

Wang, B., & Greenwood, K. (2016). 'Face' and psychological processes of laid-off workers in transitional China. *Family Medicine and Community Health, 4*(3), 51–63.

Wang, W., & Jiang, L. (2022). *Ethnic identity of the Kam People in contemporary China: Government versus local perspectives*. Routledge.

Yang, J. (2012). Song wennuan, 'sending warmth': Unemployment, new urban poverty, and the affective state in China. *Ethnography, 14*, 104–125.

Yang, J. (2015). *Unknotting the heart: Unemployment and therapeutic governance in China*. Cornell University Press.

Yang, J. (2016). The politics and regulation of anger in urban China. *Culture, Medicine, Psychiatry, 40*, 100–123. https://doi.org/10.1007/s11013-015-9476-1

Yang, J. (2017). Virtuous power: Ethics, Confucianism, and psychological self help in China. *Critique of Anthropology, 37*(2), 179–200.

CHAPTER 6

Critical Indigenous Psychologies in India: Striving for Human Liberation

Chetan Sinha, Umesh Bharte, and Arvind Kumar Mishra

Introduction

The contemporary global knowledge system, including scientific psychological knowledge, has started showing inadequacy in addressing human and social problems. The superiority of the enlightenment worldview in improving the well-being of people and society has been questioned in the face of incidents such as the two World Wars, the Cold War, global terrorism, religious and ideological fundamentalism, the breakdown of community ties, and an increase in economic inequalities. Similarly, there is now an increasing awareness of the limitations of mainstream psychology as reflecting the experiences of people only from Western, Educated,

C. Sinha (✉)
Jindal Global Law School, OP Jindal Global University, Sonipat, India
e-mail: csinha@jgu.edu.in

U. Bharte
Department of Psychology, University of Mumbai, Mumbai, India

A. K. Mishra
Zakir Husain Centre for Educational Studies, Jawaharlal Nehru University, New Delhi, India

Z. Z. Gao, M. I. Medved (eds.), *Global Perspectives on Cultural Politics in Indigenous Psychology*, Palgrave Studies in Indigenous Psychology, https://doi.org/10.1007/978-3-031-96813-6_6

Industrialized, Rich, and Democratic (WEIRD) societies and their role as observers within the discipline (Henrich et al., 2010). Moreover, the applications of psychological theories in addressing the problems related to mental health, education, child-rearing practices, and social-political conflicts have invited scepticism among the stakeholders (Fox et al., 2009; Kincheloe et al., 1999; Mohanty, 2015; Sinha, 2015). Some scholars argue that this failure of academic psychological knowledge can be viewed as the refusal of existentially variegated human experiences to be articulated in a post-Enlightenment worldview. Ironically, instead of accepting that the philosophical lop-sidedness and ethical blindness of its knowledge base are responsible for this sorry state and showing a willingness to rectify its dominant practices, the votaries of the discipline have adopted a strategy of accommodating various Indigenous psychologies. Now, it is being realized that all psychologies are essentially Indigenous psychology, and mainstream psychology can be articulated as the Indigenous psychology of the privileged section of people from Western societies. However, it is projected as universal knowledge about the nature and functioning of human mental processes and behaviour, and the adjective 'Indigenous' is used only for the psychologies of non-Western societies.

It is no secret that various Indigenous psychologies do not have the same status and prestige as mainstream psychology among career-oriented students and professionals, government officials, and corporate managers. Only those versions/constructions of Indigenous psychologies get recognition in academia that co-exist with mainstream psychology without exposing the latter radically. This asymmetrical power relations between mainstream psychology and Indigenous psychologies reflect the hierarchical power relations existing in current global politics. The role of Indigenous psychologists is to adopt activism for social change, empower the oppressed, and become a facilitator of their rights by making them feel like leaders of their movement. However, the question, 'Can the subaltern speak?', raised by Gayatri Chakravorty Spivak (1988), indicates the complexity and difficulty in achieving this goal. How much is the opportunity of space available to the oppressed to express? Who are we to provide space? Is not the space of expression located in the collective memories and collective movement? These led us to the question what is redundant and lifeless in the development of Indigenous psychology. Our metatheory is constructed on the lines of decolonization of dominant imperialism along with a pathway as laid down in the vision of the Constitution of India, which was drafted under the chairpersonship of B.R. Ambedkar, a leader who championed the cause of the subaltern/oppressed section of Indian society.

This chapter seeks to problematize Indigenous psychology's current understanding and practices and offers an alternative perspective for its theorization and applications in the Indian context. To achieve this goal, this chapter is organized into three sections. The first section situates the history and practices of Indigenous psychology in India and critically examines its present status. Following this discussion, the second section critically examines the cultural politics of Indigeneity among the public and academic scholars. It argues that Indigenous psychology is a political project and should aim to ensure social justice, liberation, and re-humanization of the people. The third section offers an outline of critical Indigenous psychology, wherein an argument is provided that an essentialist and pure notion of Indigeneity or any progressive political enterprise will prove problematic and, therefore, such construction needs to be revisited and deconstructed.

Growth and Limitations of Indigenous Psychology in India

At least two major forces appear to have exerted considerable influence on the emergence of Indigenous psychologies, especially in Third World countries. First, the post-colonial critique that resulted in a serious rethinking of Western or Eurocentric systems of knowledge and paved the way for "other ways" of appreciating human psyche. Second, the exploration of cultural pluralism in human conduct in anthropology during the 1960s and 1970s (Raina, 2016). This trend in anthropology regarded human agency as embedded in each socio-cultural context rather than treating culture and behaviour in the independent-dependent dichotomy of variables. Thus, this move in anthropology "was away from a view of culture as objectively knowable and describable to a more interactive and creative relationship between individuals and their sociocultural surroundings (Berry, 1997, p. xi)". Such anthropological exploration seems to have played an instrumental role in stimulating indigenizing psychologies in different parts of the world. The very promise of Indigenous psychologies in Third World countries in general, and in India in particular, was to develop a culturally sensitive and socially relevant psychological perspective. Since most Western psychologists of the nineteenth and twentieth centuries showed little interest in non-Western traditions of psychological thought, it was hoped to understand psychological phenomena in their ecological, historical, philosophical, religious, political, and cultural contexts. This was in sharp contrast with the knowledge generated by certain geopolitical sites such as North America and Western Europe. Not only those knowledge claims were considered authentic and valid but also unquestionably universally applicable. As Danziger (2009) observes, especially during the second half of the twentieth century, there was a unidirectional and asymmetrical flow of psychological knowledge from a geographical centre, the United States, to its periphery—other parts of the world and not back. This resulted in what Mignolo (2000) called the "geopolitics of knowledge" and desperate efforts to achieve "the holy grail of universality" (Danziger, 2009).

Against this backdrop, Indigenous psychology promised to adopt a cultural psychological perspective, viewing culture as a practical system of knowledge, concepts, and symbols that are inherent in human action and that allow people to give meaning to their world, their self, and their existence (Chakkarath, 2021). Although cultural psychology and Indigenous psychology share many perspectives, the latter "is resulted from the dissatisfaction with the historically and politically rooted dominance of certain other psychological disciplines (including cultural psychology)" (Chakkarath, p. 72). The call for re-orienting psychological science has occupied a central place in post-colonial and Indigenous reflections and is clearly aligned with a critical intent.

As we know, colonial powers exerted tremendous influence in India, substantially transforming the country's economic, social, and cultural milieu. Colonization did not remain confined to trade only, but in due course of time, it also resulted in intellectual colonization. It was soon realized that it was not just the conquest of the land, but it represented an invasion of epistemological space (Nandy, 1988; Cohn, 1996), or what Teo (2010) calls "epistemological violence (p. 295)". The discourse of Orientalists presents itself as a form of knowledge that is both different from and superior to the knowledge the Orientals have of themselves (Said, 1978). And it "invariably places the Europeans in a relationship of intellectual dominance over the Easterners" (Inden, 1990, p. 39). Following the philosophical tradition of Locke, Hume, Berkeley, and Husserl, they claimed their knowledge to be rational, logical, scientific, realistic, and objective, and more importantly, applicable across cultures.

In the Indian context, Durganand Sinha (1981, 1986, 1997, 1998) was one of the most noteworthy figures in the post-independent era who alarmingly pointed out the apparent limitations of mainstream American-Eurocentric psychology to understand and deal with local realities. It would not be an exaggeration to argue that any discussion of Indigenous psychology in India starts with his incredible efforts to redirect psychological studies towards the rich tradition of Indian thought and wisdom. He also played an instrumental role, albeit in collaboration with his contemporary scholars from India and other parts of the world, in making Indigenous psychology a *movement*. Sinha (1981) identified four threads underlying the set of definitions he considered. He concluded that psychological knowledge should (a) arise from within the culture, (b) reflect local behaviour, (c) be interpreted within a local frame of reference, and (d) yield results that are locally relevant. Although Sinha (1997) was much more critical of Western or imported knowledge, he was not against Western scholarship and its insights into understanding human behaviour. Instead, he believed, "Indigenization by its very definition does not imply cultural duality of knowledge, and essentially endeavours to bring about an interface of the two to their mutual advantage" (p. 159). Many psychologists in the country seriously took up the call of Sinha during the post-colonial period. The call was against the backdrop of our colonial encounter on both the ontological and epistemological fronts.

Following Sinha's call during the post-independent era in India, many psychologists tried to refrain from merely testing Western theories on Indian samples and being imitative. Instead, they strived for Indigenous psychology aimed at focusing on local concepts, problems, and hypotheses, giving due attention to the socio-cultural realities and language of the people. Accordingly, it called for serious and creative ways to respond to socially and culturally important themes in India (Sinha, 2003; Dalal, 2011). Especially during the 1980s and the 1990s, many important works having an Indigenous flavour appeared, such as leadership styles (Habibullah & Sinha, 1980); context sensitivity in organizational behaviour (Sinha & Kanungo, 1997); ethics in management (Chakraborty, 1995); self and identity in modern India (Paranjpe, 1998); conception of stress (Palsane et al., 1986); human development (Saraswathi, 1999), self and well-being (Misra, 2009), personal harmony and peace (Bhawuk, 1999); and non-attachment styles (Pandey & Naidu, 1992). The work of Kakar on religion and mysticism (1991), traditional healing practices (2003), and culture and the Indian psyche (2008) can also be cited as good examples of Indigenous psychology. Similarly, Rao (1988) discusses early Buddhist psychology with special reference to transcendence.

Although this is not an exhaustive list of works that have been produced and highlighted the richness of Indian intellectual traditions to appreciate human behaviour, it provides a glimpse of psychological explorations local in nature, mostly during the period from the 1980s to the 1990s. Accordingly, it can be argued that these appeared to be 'flourishing decades' for Indigenous psychology in India. After Sinha's call and following other related developments in psychology, many psychologists in India (and Asia) were very much convinced about the inevitable place of culture in understanding human behaviour. This was also the period when cross-cultural psychology was becoming popular in Asia (Sinha, 1997), and it provided an opportunity for many Indian psychologists to explore the role of culture in appreciating the human psyche. In a critical review, while discussing the influence of culture, Sinha (1997) takes stock of the famous trend of cross-cultural study of knowledge in psychology, focusing on various socially important themes in the Indian context, ranging from mental health, socialization, family structure, deprivation, values among youths, issues related to farmers to poverty. However, the cross-cultural explorations in the Indian context, as noted by Sinha (1997), only led to the testing of Western theories on Indian samples, making Asia largely a target for cross-cultural data. Similarly, in their comment on the place of culture in psychological science, Misra and Gergen (1993) observe that, to a large extent, cross-cultural psychology remained a methodological enterprise and culture remained a peripheral concern. So, after the period of the 'flourishing decades', the promise of Indigenous Indian psychology seemed to be unfulfilled and taken over by cross-cultural psychology. This unfortunately resulted in taking a disembedded form of culture and human agency.

The same tendency seems to be continued in the later generations of psychologists in the country. For example, let's pay attention to the survey of research in psychology commissioned by the Indian Council of Social Science Research (ICSSR). The first two surveys of research in psychology by Mitra (1972) and Pareek (1980, 1981) revealed that a review of numerous studies conducted by Indian psychologists across various domains tended to be imitative of the Western models, both theoretically and methodologically, lacking severe cultural suitability. The recent third survey by Pandey (1989) also reports a somewhat similar picture with respect to the development of Indigenous psychology in India. Compared to the first two, the third survey was more comprehensive, published in three volumes, and comprised sixteen thematic review papers on recent developments in psychological research and theory in the country. The goal of the third survey was "To assess the extent to which the researchers in the field have been able to respond to the Indian context and to further the goal of scientifically and systematically Indianizing psychology" (Mohanty, 1990, p. 133). The third survey reported that although there is some significant groundwork and encouraging emerging trends, contributions by Indian psychologists generally lack (a) conceptual clarification and theory building, (b) methodological sensitivity to the socio-cultural context, and (c) application value. By and large, the third survey did not find psychology in India fully Indigenized, and Western influence still seems to dominate.

Even today, as aptly observed by Paranjpe (2024), "It is also common in India (and perhaps elsewhere too) where psychologists become alien to their own culture and accept a Western import in the name of a universal 'science' of psychology". Although a small group of dedicated scholars have been engaged in doing Indigenous psychology grounded in intellectual and spiritual traditions in India, blind imitation of Euro-American models continues (Paranjpe, 2024). So, although with a promising start during the decades of the 1980s and the 1990s, what went wrong? Why has the promise of Indigenous psychology in India not been fulfilled? And, more importantly, where are we heading?

We could identify and locate multiple reasons for the unfulfilled promise of Indigenous psychology in India. With a few noteworthy exceptions, as mentioned earlier, many psychologists' attitudes towards Indigenous psychology remained attached to nationalist sentiments rather than being rationally based (Jahoda, 2016). Most of them did not develop logically theoretical accounts or models to represent the unique character of the Indian psyche. Additionally, the discourse of Indigenous psychology in the country continued to be largely speculative high-level abstractions, leading to no specific research questions or ideas (Jahoda, 2016). One important way to arrive at Indigenous psychology is by drawing on existing traditional sources within one's culture. However, many psychologists erroneously equated focusing on religious-philosophical texts with cultural revivalism—a tendency to view Indigenous psychology as being informed by Hinduism only and its revival. However, it's important to emphasize here that Indigenous psychology in India is constitutive not only of Hinduism but also of such religious-philosophical traditions as Buddhism, Jainism, the *Bhakti* movement, Sufism, etc. Another problem that could be pointed out concerning the development of an Indigenous understanding is that most of the psychologists in India have been trained predominantly in the Western tradition. Very little or no exposure to our traditional wisdom and knowledge systems rooted in philosophical-religious texts and various other forms has been given to them. Further, there has been a great discussion going on about arriving at a universal global psychology combining diverse Indigenous psychologies worldwide (Sundararajan, 2019). The absence of any definite solution to this specific issue might also have forced many psychologists to remain, in one way or another, away from efforts at the Indigenization of psychology.

Further, two additional issues have been raised by Paranjpe (2024). One of the most important obstacles to promoting Indigenous psychology in India, and in other former colonies, is the continuing presence of a colonial mindset. And second is the commitment to the idea of psychology fashioned after the natural sciences and the worldview of logical positivism. So, what we have today is an Asian (or Indian) psychology Western in character, albeit with a few noteworthy exceptions (Ho, 1988). What is more relevant for developing countries like India, "is not a psychology geared to the exercise of control… what is particularly needed is a psychology guided by emancipatory interests" (Paranjpe, 2002, p. 29). This necessitates not only rethinking the very Indigeneity but also critically examining the Indian version of Indigenous psychology.

Rethinking Indigeneity: Confronting the Enemy within and without

Despite having the emotional, political, and ethical significance of the notion of Indigeneity, achieving a consensus about its meaning has eluded scholars. This section aims at complicating the concept of culture and underlining the theoretical, political, and ethical challenges involved in defining the concept of Indigenous culture. To achieve this goal, we begin to propose that human culture exists in the complex matrix of lived social reality, and it is perpetually in the process of evolving due to peoples' responses to the changing social, political, and economic conditions of their society. While there is an inherent fluidity and ambiguity in human culture, people have an emotional need to view it as a stable and meaningful entity to derive a sense of certitude in life. When the culture of a society undergoes a radical change due to some external forces, such emotional need motivates people to recover and preserve its authenticity. People of a social group try to fulfil this need by perceiving certain elements of their culture as Indigenous (therefore authentic) arbitrarily, at times irrationally too, and differentiate them from the remaining elements, which are considered as sources of degeneration of the former. Studies in perception and social cognition indicate that values, needs, and ideology colour our perception and understanding of social reality (Billig, 1991; Bruner & Goodman, 1947). Further, it has been said that "perception is active, selective, constructive, elaborative, evaluative, motivated, and always takes place from the particular vantage point of the perceiving self" (Turner & Oakes, 1997, p. 367). Quite often, perceivers impose a set of restricted meanings on not-easily describable complex socio-cultural realities and contrast them with those of ideologically constructed 'other' social groups to cope with anxieties emanating from a perceived loss of Indigenous culture (see Mishra, 2023; Padalia, 2023). Nandy (1983) has observed that non-modern Indians used to feel comfortable living with ambiguous self-definition, and the tendency to define Indigenous culture as a binary opposite of other cultures has arisen under the influence of modern Western epistemology. He has drawn our attention to the danger of defining Indian culture as the binary opposite of Western culture in the following words:

> The pressure to be the obverse of the West distorts the traditional priorities in the Indian's total view of man and universe and destroys his culture's unique gestalt. In fact, it binds him even more irrevocably to the West. (Nandy, 1983, p. 73)

Moreover, insights from anthropological and cultural studies inform that there is a continuity across cultures, and they differ from one another in terms of the importance they attach to certain human tendencies. For example, while human traits such as individualism and collectivism exist in all cultures, modern culture accords more importance to individualism and traditional culture prioritizes collectivism over individualism. Moreover, if in a particular situation, the use of a certain human trait is viewed as more appropriate than the one that is normally preferred, there is flexibility in the culture to allow its people to use their judgement to deal with the situation effectively. Traditional Indian culture, in Nandy's view, allows her people such flexibility to respond to any situation according to their judgement of the situation. Therefore, it seems that Nandy is correct in observing that any attempt to oversimplify the understanding of Indian Indigenous culture as a binary opposite of Western culture runs the risk of distorting its uniqueness.

In the light of preceding discussion, it may be observed that the characteristics of human and social realities are indeterminate and elude any definite specification. However, Western scholarship has ignored a nuanced understanding of Indian culture and portrayed it pejoratively to help their ruling elites and subsequently justify their dominance over non-Western societies (Cohn, 1986; Nandy, 1983; Said, 1978). Various scholars have pointed out the complicity of science with colonialism (Nandy, 1993; Smith, 1999). Even after the end of political colonialism, *coloniality* continues to influence the lives of people of ex-colonized societies through the production of global knowledge. It is worth noting that coloniality differs from colonialism, and the former survives the latter. It refers to "long-standing patterns of power that emerged due to colonialism but that define culture, labour, intersubjective relations, and knowledge production well beyond the strict limits of colonial administrations" (Maldonaldo-Torres, 2007, p. 243). Coloniality is grounded in the assumption that the societies in the world are unevenly divided in terms of the degree of humanity their people are endowed with and strives to demonstrate that this assumption is a true description of reality with the help of educational, cultural, and political processes. They help coloniality to remain alive and impact the functioning of the contemporary world by demonstrating, through their research in psychology and other social sciences, that people of Western societies possess more developed humanity and cognitive faculties than those from non-Western societies. Similarly, mainstream psychology, in the garb of being a body of neutral and objective knowledge, also contributes to the persistence of coloniality in present times.

In an ideal sense, Indigenous psychology is required to rectify the distortions of the image of non-Western people and their societies by accurately representing their experiences and voices. However, the discipline of psychology is predicated on the ontological and epistemological assumptions of the modern Western worldview, and training in this discipline avoids critical examinations of its philosophical assumptions. This trend may be one of the factors responsible for perpetuating coloniality through this discipline. Scholars involved in developing Indigenous psychology should use the notion of Indigeneity cautiously. It is important to remind ourselves continually that the term "Indigeneity" is a messy concept, and social scientists have no consensus on one particular meaning of this term. Even then, human rights activists have deployed this concept to demand justice for Indigenous people (Gregg, 2019). Therefore, it is imperative for Indigenous psychologists to keep the goal of social justice in mind while articulating and defining Indigenous culture. However, due to the absence of a culture of critical evaluation of the philosophical assumptions of disciplinary practices and a lack of awareness of the political implications of the knowledge produced, even some well-intentioned Indigenous psychologists quite often get tempted to use Orientalists' stereotypical construction of Indigenous culture and knowledge (Said, 1978; Seth, 2007). For instance, in some versions of Indigenous psychology, it is argued that spiritualism characterizes Indian culture, while materialism is the core characteristic of Western culture. However, a closer critical examination of Indian and Western traditions reveals that both materialism and spiritualism constitute these traditions. As the issues related to Indigenous culture and knowledge do not remain confined to the academic domain, and often, they acquire emotional and political overtones, it poses a serious challenge to critically reflect on the nature and purpose of Indigenous psychology. Similarly, "anthropologists have evinced skepticism towards the very idea of an authentic, systemic, and autonomous 'Indigenous knowledge' as something to be opposed to a singular 'scientific knowledge'" (Suman Seth, 2009, p. 378). Articulating the nature and goal of Indigenous psychology requires different sensibilities that are not overwhelming by a compulsion to oppose some dominant view. Public intellectuals of societies, such as creative artists and writers, political and cultural activists, mavericks, and self-chosen 'social deviants', have the sensibilities to identify and articulate repressed/marginalized consciousness from the interstices of societies and bring them back to the shared consciousness of their respective societies. Through their works and narratives, they subvert the dominant definitions of academic and socio-political categories informing the current global consciousness. They may help restore the lost/repressed sensibilities of all—the dominant and the subordinate, the exploiter and the exploited, the rich and the poor within the Global North and the Global South. The history of social reforms in medieval India, such as the Bhakti movement, indicates that public intellectuals have played a pivotal role in raising the critical consciousness of the masses through socio-cultural movements. In the modern period, Indian social thinkers such as Tagore and M.K. Gandhi creatively interpreted and deployed the works of the Bhakti movement saint-poets to critique certain regressive social practices and build an alternative tradition.

Indigeneity is a social construction and is often used for political purposes (Gregg, 2019). While it can be deployed for progressive causes, it is equally possible to be exploited to resist social reforms and maintain the status quo of unjust societies. Unfortunately, academics trained and working in the modern university system of non-Western countries have lost the sensibilities of public intellectuals due to the pressure to meet the global standards of scholarly works, though not completely. Although academic intellectuals may also act as public intellectuals of their societies, owing to the influence of neoliberal capitalism on the governance and management of the modern university system, there is an acute scarcity of public intellectuals (and their sensibilities) in the academic space in current times. As a result, it is not surprising to observe a gap between the knowledge about human psychology available in mainstream psychology books and that in the works of public intellectuals. It is, therefore, imperative for academic psychologists to interact with the public intellectuals of their societies to remain in touch with the sufferings and aspirations of the common masses. Articulating a similar view, Bhatia (2019) has given a call to reframe Indigenous psychology. Drawing on the decolonization framework, he has argued that Indigenous psychology's academic researchers need to partner and collaborate with people on the ground who are mobilizing and creating movements for a more equal and just world. Further, he has emphasized the need to interrogate the 'culture of inequality' and find answers to the omnipresent and inescapable social inequality prevalent in most societies. "Indigenous Psychology (IP) needs to create "epistemological solidarities" among the different and scattered IP perspectives so it can participate in offering robust explanations of the cultural life of people who are living in many postcolonial societies" (Bhatia, 2019, p. 107). Further, to maintain the right framework, they need to engage with the following 'W' questions concerning the enterprise of Indigenous psychologies: What are the goals of Indigenous psychologies? Who is involved in doing it, and why are they doing it? How will it impact people's lives, particularly those who have been rendered as the 'wretched of the earth' by the dominant economic and historical forces?

Indigenous psychology, in our view, should essentially be a political project and should strive to ensure social justice and liberation for the underprivileged suffering masses. It also needs to ensure the rehabilitation of other social classes in India who are struggling and alienated due to self-imposed pressure to maintain their middle-class identities. It should not remain satisfied merely by offering a critique of mainstream psychology but should endeavour to restore human sensibilities in the discourse and practice of mainstream psychology. Further, like any other society in the world, Indian society too is diverse and unequal. The combination of diversity and inequality is at the root of the suffering, exploitation, and marginalization of her underprivileged groups, and this also contributes to the alienation and dehumanization of privileged groups. Quite often, the culture of a society tends to mask its dark reality and, at times, eulogizes certain regressive social practices too. Despite the importance of culture in individuals' psychological and spiritual growth, Indigenous psychologists should adopt a critical perspective toward the culture of their society. They should not be obsessed with only analysing the linkage between the sufferings of Indigenous people and larger global forces but also be open to casting their critical gaze at the enemy within the society, which may not be easily detectable. If the movement of Indigenous psychology aims at ameliorating the suffering and dehumanization of humankind, it must present an effective resistance to the dehumanizing forces lurking within the society and the juggernaut of ruthless neoliberal machinery pervading everywhere, and to do so, its foot soldiers and generals have to be ready to step out of the comfort zone of their academic citadels.

Towards a Critical Indigenous Psychology in India

The previous sections were intended on moving forward towards rethinking Indigeneity and starting activism at the ground level. The idealism prevalent in the Indigenous psychology in India homogenized all social groups. This stance was more skewed towards the psychology of people who occupied dominant caste groups. The call for critical Indigenous psychology seems more representative of underrepresented and marginalized groups, giving new meaning to indigeneity. This is possible when the meanings of social justice, heterogeneity, and liberation aptly converge with the psychology of the historically oppressed. The available approach to understanding Indigeneity in Indian Indigenous psychology is looking inward and understanding oneself. We do not promote cultural homogeneity in the name of developing Indigenous psychology in India. We look forward to restoring self-respect together with a balanced outlook towards the philosophies that help in our agenda of sustained social justice. The insight we gain through locating ourselves in the cultural genesis and striving to become thoroughly engrossed with the intricacies of culture depends on the socioeconomic, Varna-based system, and Vedic ritual aspects of social life (see also Kosambi, 1962; Staal, 2008). This section strongly believes in social change and rejects the cycle of oppression and caste-class-gender-based dominance through various means and channels.

In the construction of Indian Indigenous psychology, these aspects were predominant. It was generally taken as an Indigenous movement, showing an incomplete picture. We are not claiming completeness; however, there is a need to highlight the critical aspect of being Indigenous, theorizing and putting forward the agenda of Indigeneity, including the historically marginalized matters in this movement. It was seen as a movement to be collectively conscious of our past and revive it in the present and future. It is also important to acquaint the present generation with traditional values, socialize with them through various means, and sustain them in the future. The mainstream Indigenous psychology is also about the politics of self-recognition in conventional terms. The post-Western psychology and domination of knowledge is one of the critical agendas (e.g., Bharte & Mishra, 2023; Bhatia et al., 2024; Misra & Mohanty, 2002) along with the critical intricacies of Indigenous psychology (Teo & Wendt, 2020). It also underlies the possibilities of how the West is understood and how it is taken by diverse and historically oppressed groups (e.g., Khan et al., 2017; Sinha, 2016; Sophan & Nair, 2023). In the case of the possibilities of critical Indigenous psychology in India, it is also needed to understand the Indian way of thinking, which is the confluence of diversities, for example, region, religious practices, philosophies, caste-based customs, and everyday politics, including the mindset derived from the presence of coloniality and modernity (see Ramanujan, 1989).

Indigenous psychology is connected to Indigenous politics, Indigenous science, and the Indigenous way of seeing the social system. Being Indigenous must be connected to the facts of history and philosophy. The quality of Indigenous life indicates toughness, engagement with nature, and utilization of the resources that come from nature and are preserved by it. Even the emotions, if any, exist for Indigenous people, possibly following different pathways constructed in community life and oneness with nature. However, the politics of nature and imposition towards monoculturalism may be fatal unless the culture is seen in its multitude (e.g., Latour, 2007). The struggle and resistance towards naturalism indicate Indigenous people's critical politics towards colonialism, which always intrudes on and theorizes their experience. This is why Indigenous psychology is a critical enterprise. The term Indigenous is a Western construct and a much popularized one (see also Beteille, 1998; Peters & Mika, 2017). For Indigenous people, it is not the widespread labelling of their way of life but the everyday struggle with Western imperialists and dominant appropriations (Smith, 2021). To be labelled as Indigenous is itself a categorization that Indigenous people bear. Indigenous psychology is not a disconnected movement since people assert their rights in front of their oppressors, and they resist historical oppression. In India, the tribal people's assertion to be called Adivasi (see Sen, 2018) is an assertion of their social identity, which is both preserved and practised. We respect the idea of Indigenous psychology for social change, which is for reclaiming their rights over "*Jal-Jungle-Jameen*" (water-forest-land), which was lost to imperialism and at the same time, looking forward to inclusive space for social mobility. This chapter hopes for social space to consist of rightful owners, facilitating social mobility and, if possible, cultural intersection rather than dominance. However, this must be seen in a more complex way. This term has been developed into an approach and movement, and forums and groups are doing Indigenous politics for survival and preserving collectivity. Even Indigenous groups are apt to work with people of different migratory origins to fight for their cause of independence and social identity movement.

In India, Indigenous psychology is an academic advancement of Indian psychology. Its comparison with the Indigenous movement has to be critically revisited. As mentioned earlier, the wave of the Indigenous psychology movement in India was to counter imperialism. However, the method to challenge colonialism was taken through the route of Indian psychology, primarily manifested in the psychology of yoga and purity of self. The other routes, like Sufism, Adivasi, and Dalit, were left to the stakeholders. Deep-seated caste and socio-cultural hierarchies didn't form many intersectional avenues. So, Indigenous psychology was confined to one way of living, although we also encountered variations in different systems. If this is the only route, there is less doubt that untouchability and oppression are connected to this psychology when it comes to the real life of everyday social practices and rituals.

A possible avenue to rebuild Indigenous psychology is to revamp the psychology of people who were being voiceless and oppressed, bearing the brunt of neoliberalism and chronic capitalism. The agenda of historically powerful and their needs to be redefined in terms of deprived and disadvantaged groups against the corpus of colonialism also needs to be revisited, keeping in mind the foundation of Indigenous movements in terms of Indigenous. Since colonial times, Indian philosophical thoughts have had a powerful influence on students and scholars. The influx of modernity, the reading of Indian texts and scriptures by Western scholars, and the need to understand Indian culture through understanding Sanskrit[1] brought a new wave of pride among scholars and students from India. Earlier, it was their daily routine to live by their rituals. Understanding philosophy invoked new energy to know one's lost self through critical hermeneutics, venturing deeper into different schools of thought and practices. It was like becoming conscious of oneself about one's history and culture through the interpretation of the colonizer. It was a clear divide between the colonized and the colonizer. The collective feeling of powerlessness and oppression in their motherland followed different routes, but the idea was strongly connected to the humiliation of one's self. The very mention of the Indian thought system invokes a sense of spirituality and an urge to dig out the past and repressed desires to connect with the supreme consciousness (Paramatma).

The spirit of the Indigenous movement can be the same as communicating with one's history, space, time, and spirituality. However, the rise of neoliberalism, toxic individuality, and the expansion of dominant culture for economic benefit possibly led to the loss of self for the imposed ones. Indigenous history is plural and varied, as are the levels of the movements (e.g., Pickren & Tasci, 2022). To some extent, modernity gave a critical turn to inner colonialism in India and empowered the oppressed group. It provides a new desire to excel, fight for their rights, and form their own space without any interventions from the dominant and oppressive social structure. The Indigenous movement in psychology should be firmly aligned with the spirit of social justice and disentanglement from toxic colonialism from the outside. It is to clarify that Indian psychology is rooted in the non-reductive understanding of the native Indian ethos (Rao et al., 2008). It is understood that Indian psychology is a holistic approach towards understanding one's collective self. This demands a rethinking and change in understanding of the politics of Indigeneity in India, since the Indian ethos is also facilitated in the Indian Constitution.

In the Indian context, it is crucial to identify who is Indigenous and how Indigenous psychology caters to their socio-political and economic

[1] Sanskrit was considered to be the tool to understand Indian culture better

needs. During colonial times, Indigenous people, having a distinct culture and engaging with the forest for livelihood, were ascribed as tribals. Their powerful identities imposed their sense of identity (Guha, 1983; Sen, 2018). According to Sen (2018),

> Accordingly, they have generally been portrayed as subordinate/vulnerable rather marginal group of people, being subjected to various exploitations by more dominant groups. To elaborate, they were deemed as prehistoric; so their past was considered unworthy of recording. But when this was done, they were largely portrayed as a low group of people as done by the ancient Sanskrit texts and colonial writings. (p. 7)

In our case, we do not cater to the psychology which does not address the Indigenous and local culture in which people live their everyday lives. We also do not cater to psychology, which is not critical and does not address social justice issues. If cultural truism is the result of Indigenous psychology as portrayed by the dominant and upper castes, it doesn't fit the notion of liberation and psychology for social justice. This indicates the internal colonialism that has also deprived people of the Adivasi groups of their rights over their land. Their categorization as primitive people and the removal of their memories, cultural practices, and sustenance is the psychology of power, and it is natural that it does not correspond to Indigenous people's lives. Thus, to revive, reclaim, and rethink one's imposed self is a political enterprise, and if it is done by the people who were marginalized based on their marginalized culture, it is a critical Indigenous psychology we look forward to.

Even the decolonial, authentic natives of a given geographical space live with various experiences. The tribal man who works in a government office, affiliates with the political party, has a view about national culture, and recites the national anthem. His children study in state-run or private schools and may attend ceremonies and functions. This person plays many roles and lives his identity. When any tribal issue arise, his tribal identity may get activated, and he may raise his voice or remain silent. The bifurcation of roles and identities is complex since they operate under the giant umbrella of a strong culture. The presence of the natural environment is the prime factor in the theorization of Indigeneity; the rest of the concerns about the loss of self, due to the loss of culture seem futile. As we see the rise of neoliberal hegemony in intentions and acts, the loss of land to the capitalistic agenda and regular mobilization of the community to support state programmes have a remarkable impact on Indigenous psychology.

Indian psychologists interested in cultural practices have done interesting work on the tribals' lives (e.g. Mishra & Chaubey, 2002; Panda, 2008). This work was necessary on two fronts. First, they described the conditions of tribal life and their everyday affairs in dealing with their environment, and second, they compared their culture with the mainstream and formalized it. It connects the culture and Indigenous peoples, considering the varieties of affairs humans engage in with their communities. The agenda here is to broadly understand how it was descriptive of their way of life, engagement with the tools, shared culture, and deprivation.

The social aspect of Indigenous psychology in India was constructed through the philosophy of the East, which focused on sharedness, collectiveness, and higher-order consciousness. The attempt was homogenizing and, at the same time, differentiating based on caste and gender. The Indian way of understanding the self and the world is primarily based on Karma, the afterlife, spirituality, and, at the same time, materialism. Karma is based on what society expects from a person's affiliation with his community, ancestral occupations, and social roles. Karma is connected to one's religion or dharma. Since Indian society has prescribed roles for people belonging to various castes and genders, it is always bad karma if a person diverts from those ascriptions (Prabhu, 1954). Even Muslims, Christians, and other religious and cultural social identities, like Indigenous and tribal people living in different parts of the country, are somewhere affected by the dominant caste systems that have been banal in society through established power dynamics. In any way, caste hierarchies cannot be understood from a simple cultural lens since there are ample examples of experiences in which one caste dominates over another, hence the cultures. The Indigenous way in this context may be misconstrued as liberating and further stabilize the deep-seated social categorical assumption about people. In this context, we need critical Indigenous psychology which not only gives space to renounce the dominant self but also critically empowers and scaffolds the oppressed and marginalized groups to take forward their voice. Critical Indigenous psychology is not about replacing Indigenous thinking but advancing it further to have a critical and disruptive approach towards what was closed and demeaning to the oppressed. In the case of gender, social evils like Sati Pratha[2] were rampantly practised until the British government and the Indian reformer Raja Ram Mohan Roy strongly opposed it. The colonial period should also not be

[2] Tradition or custom where Hindu widow threw herself on the pyre of her dead husband.

homogenized as it was always brutal, as it has participated in reforming the psychology of people and, to some extent, modernizing it. However, there was stiff opposition from the revivalist camp to preserve what was dead and based on the logic of violence. It also shows the deservingness of politics and ignores rampant inequality based on stiff social categorization. This has directly or indirectly impacted the development of the politics of Hindu consciousness. The emptiness felt due to the rising voices of diversity reshaped identity politics into the politics of Indigeneity.

Indigenous movements are always in a state of continuity and flux. So, the meaning also gets a new understanding by including the critical metatheory of social justice. This is possible through social movements, which play a critical role in changing perceptions. The assertion of rights and collective meaning-making, bringing the collective memory of Indigenous people to the curriculum level and legitimizing it through academic intervention matter. The way things changed over time. People learn new skills and pass them on to future generations. The way new institutions, norms and social structures were formed shaped our collective consciousness. Indigenous is not a separatist movement but the balance of diversity and, at the same time, the preservation of uniqueness. Here, the connection between culture and Indigeneity in the context of social justice, liberation, and re-humanization helps develop Indigenous psychology in India. This provides a better platform to critically understand the meaning of Indigeneity, since culture is not homogenous but is practised with set rules, norms, and beliefs. Indigenous reflects lifestyle, history, social beliefs, and culture. Here, it is confined to a limited geographical space where resources and tools for everyday living can be generated and used. People are content with their lifestyle and everyday conflicts with nearby groups and are occupied with their rituals and beliefs. Their philosophy of life is rooted in the ground itself. For example, in some northeastern regions of India (e.g., Nagaland), the umbilical cord is buried in the ground of the house when a child is born. This always reminds them of their roots and a sense of responsibility towards their community.

In this chapter, we look forward to the development of critical Indigenous psychology. It critically examines the power relations among people from different social groups (e.g., Rycroft & Dasgupta, 2011; van Schendel, 2011; Gonzalez et al., 2022). It presumes that people's history before the colonial intervention and in the post-colonial times is nearly the same. For example, the status of tribal groups, Dalit groups, and Muslims continuously faces atrocities and state-sponsored deprivations despite the full constitutional rights they are endowed with. India, a composite of different groups and cultures, is a land of people with varying knowledge systems, histories, and methodologies to understand the social world. It is a complex conglomeration with the will to cooperate with the idea of oneness. When collective memories, resources, and labour are occupied with the act of colonialism, the agenda of Indigeneity becomes an activity for social justice. The agenda to liberate consciousness and Indigenous culture from colonial imposition signifies a critical Indigenous approach. The global model of liberation can be adopted for the emancipation of the self (Martin-Baro, 1994; Sinha, 2015) from the shackles of imperialism of the West and the power dominance of the upper caste model of morality. Indigenous psychology, having a critical outlook, need not always be a good boy or Satvik psychology but can also be bad psychology (see Grzanka & Cole, 2021), serving as a resistant force (e.g., Ghai et al., 2020; Jaiswal, 2016) to the oppressive ideologies which work against the preamble of the Indian constitution. To live in a Trishanku state of mind is not feasible to the idea of critical Indigenous psychology. The need for psychology, which investigates the terrain of the Indigenous way, is a decolonial stance which does not concretize the process of being and becoming. The idea of Indigenization and Indigenizing becomes more meaningful in the context of the collective movements of people disadvantaged in history due to colonialism and inner geographical cultural dominance.

Concluding Comments: Towards Indigenous, Indigenization and Indigenizing

The development of Indigenous psychology in India has followed limited pathways. It passed through the cultural memory of established traditions (dominantly a Hindu view of life[3]). We can say its orientation is status quo; however, with the varieties of indigeneity, cultural practices, and history of oppression within the cultural context, this dominant way of expressing indigeneity has not raised uncomfortable questions about Indian society. Sometimes, it portrays a dangerous form of decolonialism, which hides internal colonialism and sustains deep-seated power hierarchies. On the political front, it turns into cultural revivalism. The status quo psychology embedded in mainstream Indigenous psychology in India develops a

[3] See S. Radhakrishnan (1960). The Hindu view of life. Unwin Books.

knowledge system representing the voice of dominant identities. It was never reflexive and renouncing of the self which created a comfort zone for the powerful. The concerns and voices of Dalits, Women, and minorities got lost or devalued in the powerful discourses and practices of mainstream Indigenous psychology in India. This chapter makes a case for critical Indigenous psychologies that can be more balanced and fact-oriented but also overhaul the dominant and capitalizing Indigenous psychology. The movement of Indigenous psychology is also a movement against the internal colonialism of caste and religious-based SOCIAL hierarchy that has occupied academia and the relationship of power between the dominant East and West. The common thread between local, Indigenous, and international psychology concerns the rising voice of the powerless and historically deprived. We advocate for psychology representing the voiceless and oppressed, deconstructing the homogeneity, and going beyond essentialism and social dominance. The Indian way of thinking is in its diversity, constitutional values, and equal opportunities. We are also thoughtful about how this chapter will be taken by people directly working at the grassroots level or activists working to uplift oppressed people. We need to see the time when the past is recuperated and the voices of the marginalized, subalterns, and oppressed are louder. We need reconstruction of Indigenous psychology in India, which is sovereign, sensible, and representative. It can be the politics of doing social science, which is academic in expression and connects to the psychological humanities in both intention and activism.

Conflict of Interests All authors have no conflicts of interest.

Author Contribution All authors have contributed equally to this chapter.

Fundings There are no fundings.

References

Berry, J. W. (1997). Preface. In J. W. Berry, Y. H. Poortinga, & J. Pandey (Eds.), *Handbook of cross-cultural psychology* (Vol. 1). Allyn and Bacon.

Béteille, A. (1998). The idea of indigenous people. *Current Anthropology, 39*, 187–192.

Bharte, U. L., & Mishra, A. K. (2023). Working through the politics of indigeneity: Decolonising psychology by way of a dialectical approach. *Psychology and Developing Societies, 35*(1), 22–42.

Bhatia, S. (2019). Searching for justice in an unequal world: Reframing indigenous psychology as a cultural and political project. *Journal of Theoretical and Philosophical Psychology, 39*(2), 107–114.

Bhatia, S., Long, W., Pickren, W., & Rutherford, A. (2024). Engaging with decoloniality, decolonization, and histories of psychology otherwise. In L. Comas-Díaz, H. Y. Adames, & N. Y. Chavez-Dueñas (Eds.), *Decolonial psychology: Toward anticolonial theories, research, training, and practice* (pp. 61–85). American Psychological Association. https://doi.org/10.1037/0000376-004

Bhawuk, D. P. (1999). Who attains peace? An Indian model of personal harmony. *Indian Psychological Review, 52*(3/4), 40–48.

Billig, M. (1991). *Ideology and opinions.* Sage.

Bruner, J. S., & Goodman, C. C. (1947). Value and need as organizing factors in perception. *Journal of Abnormal and Social Psychology, 42*, 33–44.

Chakkarath, P. (2021). How India almost lost its soul: The detrimental effects of ethnocentrism and colonialism on the psychology of spirituality. In A. Dueck (Ed.), *Indigenous psychology of spirituality* (Palgrave Studies in Indigenous Psychology) (pp. 227–254). Palgrave Macmillan.

Chakraborty, S. K. (1995). *Ethics in management: Vedantic perspectives.* Oxford University Press.

Cohn, B. (1986). *An anthropologist among the historians and other essays.* Oxford University Press.

Cohn, B. S. (1996). *Colonialism and its forms of knowledge: The British in India.* Princeton University Press.

Dalal, A. K. (2011). A journey back to the roots: Psychology in India. In M. Cornelisson, G. Misra, & S. Verma (Eds.), *Foundations of Indian psychology, volume 1: Theories and concepts* (pp. 27–56). Publisher: Pearson.

Danziger, K. (2009). The holy grail of universality. In T. Teo et al. (Eds.), *Varieties of theoretical psychology* (pp. 2–13). Captus University Publications.

Fox, D., Prilleltensky, & Austin, S. (2009). *Critical psychology: An introduction.* Sage.

Ghai, R., Mishra, A. K., & Kumar, S. (2020). *The marginalized self: Tales of resistance of a community.* Primus Books.

González, R., Carvacho, H., & Jiménez-Moya, G. (2022). Psychology and indigenous people. *Annual Review of Psychology, 73*(1), 431–459.

Gregg, B. (2019). Indigeneity as social construct and political tool. *Human Rights Quarterly, 41*(4), 823–848.

Grzanka, P. R., & Cole, E. R. (2021). An argument for bad psychology: Disciplinary disruption, public engagement, and social transformation. *American Psychologist, 76*(8), 1334–1345.

Guha, R. (1983). *Elementary aspects of peasant insurgency in colonial India.* Oxford University Press.

Habibullah, A. H. M., & Sinha, J. B. (1980). Motivational climate and leadership styles. *Vikalpa, 5*(2), 85–94.

Henrich, J., Heine, S. J., & Norenzayan, A. (2010). Most people are not WEIRD. *Nature, 466*, 29.

Ho, D. Y. F. (1988). Asian psychology: A dialogue on indigenization and beyond. In A. C. E. Paranjpe, D. Y. Ho, & R. W. Rieber (Eds.), *Asian contributions to psychology* (pp. 53–78). Praeger Publishers.

Inden, R. (1990). *Imagining India.* Basil Blackwell.

Jahoda, G. (2016). On the rise and decline of 'indigenous psychology'. *Culture & Psychology, 22*(2), 169–181.

Jaiswal, S. (2016). *The making of Brahmanic hegemony: Studies in caste, gender and Vaisnava theology.* Tulika Books.

Kakar, S. (1991). *The analyst and the mystic: Psychoanalytic reflections on religion and mysticism.* University of Chicago Press.

Kakar, S. (2003). Psychoanalysis and eastern spiritual healing traditions. *Journal of Analytical Psychology, 48*(5), 659–678.

Kakar, S. (2008). *Culture and psyche: Selected essays.* Oxford University Press.

Khan, S. S., Svensson, T., Jogdand, Y. A., & Liu, J. H. (2017). Lessons from the past for the future: The definition and mobilisation of Hindu nationhood by the Hindu nationalist movement of India. *Journal of Social and Political Psychology, 5*(2), 477–511.

Kincheloe, J. L., Steinberg, S. R., & Villaverde, L. E. (1999). *Rethinking intelligence: Confronting psychological assumptions about teaching and learning.* Routledge.

Kosambi, D. D. (1962). *Myth and reality: Studies in the formation of Indian culture.* Sage Texts.

Latour, B. (2007). *Politics of nature: How to bring the sciences into democracy.* Oreint Longman.

Maldonaldo-Torres, N. (2007). On coloniality of being: Contributions to the development of a concept. *Cultural Studies, 21*(2–3), 240–270.

Martín-Baró, I. (1994). *Writings for a liberation psychology.* Harvard University Press.

Mignolo, W. D. (2000). The geopolitics of knowledge and the colonial difference. *South Atlantic Quarterly, 101*(1), 57–97.

Mishra, A. K. (2023). Thinking beyond domestication of the colonial knowledge. *Psychological Studies.* https://doi.org/10.1007/s12646-023-00779-7

Mishra, R. C., & Chaubey, A. C. (2002). Acculturation attitudes of Kharwar and Agaria tribal groups of Sonebhadra. *Psychology and Developing Societies, 14*(2), 201–220.

Misra, G. (2009). Self and well-being. *Psychological Studies, 54*(2), 85–86.

Misra, G., & Gergen, K. J. (1993). On the place of culture in psychological science. *International Journal of Psychology, 28*(2), 225–243. https://doi.org/10.1080/00207599308247186

Misra, G., & Mohanty, A. K. (Eds.). (2002). *Perspectives on indigenous psychology* (Vol. 3). Concept Publishing Company.

Mitra, S. K. (1972). Psychological research in India. In S. K. Mitra (Ed.), *A survey of research in psychology* (pp. xvii–xxxxiii). Popular Prakashan.

Mohanty, A. K. (1990). *Psychology of poverty and disadvantage*. Concept Publishing.

Mohanty, A. K. (2015). Psychology in India: Still at the crossroads? *Psychology and Developing Societies, 2*(1), 117–136.

Nandy, A. (1983). *The intimate enemy: Loss and recovery of self under colonialism*. Oxford University Press.

Nandy, A. (1988). *The intimate enemy: The psychology of colonialism*. Oxford.

Nandy, A. (1993). *Traditions, tyranny, and utopias: Essays in the politics of awareness*. Oxford University Press.

Padalia, D. (2023). Psychology in India must rethink its goals: Reflections on Sinha (1965). *Psychological Studies*. https://doi.org/10.1007/s12646-023-00747-1

Palsane, M. N., Bhavsar, S. N., Goswami, R. P., & Evans, G. W. (1986). The concept of stress in the Indian tradition. *The Journal of Individual Psychology, 5*(1), 1–12.

Panda, M. (2008). Saora culture, as-if discourse and mathematics learning. In G. Zheng, K. Leung, & J. G. Adair (Eds.), *Perspectives and progress in contemporary cross-cultural psychology: Proceedings from the 17th International Congress of the International Association for Cross-Cultural Psychology.*

Pandey, J. (Ed.). (1989). *Psychology in India: The state of the art (3 vols.)*. Sage Publications.

Pandey, N., & Naidu, R. (1992). Anasakti and health: A study of non-attachment. *Psychology and Developing Societies, 4*, 89–104.

Paranjpe, A. (2024). Challenges in the pursuit of an indigenous psychology: A self-reflection. *Review of General Psychology, 28*(1), 237–252.

Paranjpe, A. C. (1998). *Self and identity in modern psychology and Indian thought*. Plenum Press.

Paranjpe, A. C. (2002). Indigenous psychology in the post-colonial context: An historical perspective. *Psychology and Developing Societies, 14*(1), 27–44. https://doi.org/10.1177/097133360201400103

Pareek, U. (Ed.). (1980). *A Survey of Research in Psychology, 1971–76*. Popular Prakashan.

Pareek, U. (1981). *A survey of research in psychology, 1971–76, Part 2*. Popular Publication.

Peters, M. A., & Mika, C. T. (2017). Aborigine, Indian, indigenous or first nations? *Educational Philosophy and Theory, 49*(13), 1229–1234.

Pickren, W. E., & Taşçı, G. (2022). Indigenous psychologies: Resources for future histories. In D. McCallum (Ed.), *The Palgrave handbook of the history of human sciences.* Palgrave Macmillan. https://doi.org/10.1007/978-981-16-7255-2_80

Prabhu, P. H. (1954). *Hindu social organization: A study of the socio-psychological and ideological foundations.* Popular Prakashan.

Raina, D. (2016). Mainstreaming the indigenous knowledge: Genealogy of a meta-concept. In S. Hodges & M. Rao (Eds.), *Public health and private wealth* (pp. 252–268). Oxford University Press.

Ramanujan, A. K. (1989). Is there an Indian way of thinking? An informal essay. *Contributions to Indian Sociology, 23*(1), 41–58.

Rao, K. R. (1988). What is Indian psychology? *The Journal of Individual Psychology, 7*(1), 37–57.

Rao, K. R., Paranjpe, A. C., & Dalal, A. K. (Eds.). (2008). *Handbook of Indian psychology.* Cambridge University Press India/Foundation Books.

Rycroft, D. J., & Dasgupta, S. (Eds.). (2011). *The politics of belonging in India: Becoming Adivasi* (1st ed.). Routledge. https://doi.org/10.4324/9780203826010

Said, E. W. (1978). *Orientalism.* Routledge & Kegan Paul.

Saraswathi, T. S. (1999). *Culture, socialisation and human development: Theory, research and applications in India.* Sage.

Sen, A. K. (2018). *Indigeneity, landscape and history: Adivasi self-fashioning in India.* Routledge India.

Seth, S. (2007). *Subject lessons: The Western education of colonial India* (Kindle ed.). Duke University Press.

Seth, S. (2009). Putting knowledge in its place: Science, colonialism, and the post-colonial. *Postcolonial Studies, 12*(4), 373–388.

Sinha, C. (2016). Decolonizing social psychology in India: Exploring its role as emancipatory social science. *Psychology & Society, 8*(1), 57–74.

Sinha, D. (1981). Non-Western perspectives in psychology: Why, what and whither? *The Journal of Individual Psychology, 3*(2), 1–9.

Sinha, D. (1986). *Psychology in a third world country: The Indian experience.* Sage.

Sinha, D. (1997). Indigenizing psychology. In J. W. Berry, Y. H. Poortinga, & J. Pandey (Eds.), *Handbook of cross-cultural psychology* (Handbook of cross-cultural psychology: Theory and method) (2nd ed., pp. 129–169). Allyn & Bacon.

Sinha, D. (1998). Changing perspectives in social psychology in India: A journey towards indigenization. *Asian Journal of Social Psychology, 1*, 17–31.

Sinha, D. (2015). *Psychology for India.* Sage.

Sinha, J. B. (2003). Trends toward indigenization of psychology in India. *Contributions in Psychology, 42*, 11–28.

Sinha, J. B., & Kanungo, R. N. (1997). Context sensitivity and balancing in Indian organizational behaviour. *International Journal of Psychology, 32*(2), 93–105.
Smith, L. T. (1999). *Decolonizing methodologies: Research and Indigenous people.* Zed Books Ltd.
Smith, L. T. (2021). *Decolonizing methodologies: Research and indigenous peoples* (3rd ed.). Zed Books Ltd..
Sophan, A., & Nair, A. (2023). Decolonising caste in the Indian context: The psyche of the oppressor. *Psychology and Developing Societies, 35*(1), 110–130.
Spivak, G. C. (1988). Can the subaltern speak? In C. Nelson & L. Grossberg (Eds.), *Marxism and the interpretation of culture.* University of Illinois Press.
Staal, F. (2008). *Discovering the Vedas: Origins, mantras, rituals, insights.* Penguin.
Sundararajan, L. (2019). Introduction to the special issue on "Indigenous psychology: What's the next step?". *Journal of Theoretical and Philosophical Psychology, 39*(2), 65–66. https://doi.org/10.1037/teo0000124
Teo, T. (2010). What is epistemological violence in the empirical social sciences? *Social and Personality Psychology Compass, 4*(5), 295–303. https://doi.org/10.1111/j.1751-9004.2010.00265.x
Teo, T., & Wendt, D. C. (2020). Some clarifications on critical and indigenous psychologies. *Theory & Psychology, 30*(3), 371–376.
Turner, J. C., & Oakes, P. (1997). The socially structured mind. In C. McGarty & S. A. Haslam (Eds.), *The message of social psychology* (pp. 355–373). Blackwell Publishers.
Van Schendel, W. (2011). The dangers of belonging: Tribes, indigenous peoples and homelands in South Asia. In *The politics of belonging in India* (pp. 19–43). Routledge.

CHAPTER 7

Sikolohiyang Pilipino: Vicissitudes of Indigenization in the Philippines

E. San Juan Jr.

If truth is to be found in the synchronization of reason and experience, rectitude lies in the synchronization of theory and practice.
—Apolinario Mabini, The Philippine Revolution (1969, p. 8).

The seed of knowledge is the mind, the field of available consciousness—all that is present or can be called upon. The rude [mark] is experience. He who may not have felt quite sure of understanding why the entrance of the element of Form should be called [experience] will find enlightenment in thinking of the matter from this point of view.
—Charles Sanders Peirce, The Essential Peirce (1998, p. 374).

Introduction

Indigenization in late modernity, as viewed by Filipino proponents of *sikolohiyang Pilipino* (SP/Filipino Psychology), emerged as a cultural-political movement chiefly in peripheral zones, as opposed to the margin

E. San Juan Jr. (✉)
University of Connecticut, Storrs, CT, USA

Z. Z. Gao, M. I. Medved (eds.), *Global Perspectives on Cultural Politics in Indigenous Psychology*, Palgrave Studies in Indigenous Psychology, https://doi.org/10.1007/978-3-031-96813-6_7

of metropoles in world-systems theory (Wallerstein, 1974). Despite globalization in this millennium, stark differences among the geopolitical zones persist. Countries in the periphery have been colonized and dominated for centuries by Europe and the United States. Colonial subjugation either destroyed the native population and their habitat or enslaved the rest for resource extraction, trading, craft industry, etc., transferring accumulated profits to the metropole. To understand SP's origin and trajectory, it is necessary to establish its historical determinants, without which its singular narrative cannot be fully appreciated.

Spain dominated the Philippines for over 300 years, exploiting their Christianized subjects and extracting enormous wealth from the galleon trade and crop monopolies. After numerous sporadic revolts, the *indios* mounted a widespread rebellion in 1896, overthrew Spanish power, and established the first Philippine Republic in 1898 (Agoncillo & Guerrero, 1970, pp. 117–264). The Spanish-American War broke out when the Filipinos were on the verge of capturing the capital city, Manila. The technological-industrial might of the U.S. defeated feudal-theocratic Spain, bought the Philippines, and confronted the Filipino revolutionary army. After the Filipino American War (1899–1913), the United States overwhelmed the republic's forces and claimed the islands as its "possession." The Catholic Church and its religious orders, the main ideological machinery for reproducing subjects for Spanish colonialism, continued to function, reinforcing the family system and the patron–client syndrome. But its social-reproductive service was replaced by the public school and a bureaucracy trained for serving finance capital (Constantino, 1975, pp. 231–383, 1978, pp. 25–210). Neoliberal globalization today is a sequel to neocolonial governance in the Philippines (Jose, 1984; Abaya, 1984; Pforr, 2013).

Mapping the Contradictions

Over a hundred years of colonial domination ensued, resulting in today's neocolonial setup. The U.S. employed various ideological apparatuses—coercive institutions and other state agencies (schools, bureaucracy, hospitals, prisons, media, etc.)—to produce an acquiescent subject and its conformist *habitus* (Bourdieu's term, 1977, pp. 82–83) geared to promote the aims of U.S. corporate business. This has been attested by mainstream commentaries (Bonner, 1987; Karnow, 1989). To cite one study: faced with the communist Huk guerillas after World War II, George

E. Taylor noted that from the outset, U.S. finance capital crafted "the emergence of a 'colonial' type" national economy, heavily dependent on agricultural material exports and on manufactured goods and processed goods imported from the U.S. ...The problem at the heart of economic growth is the value system..." (309). And so, it's the "value system" based on the landlord–tenant clientelist setup that the U.S. preserved to coopt the local oligarchs as colonial/neocolonial overseers (Constantino, 1978, pp. 25–94; Veneracion, 1987, pp. 59–64).

Oddly enough, this feudal setup permeating the whole society is called "personalism," which underlies the "intense cynicism of the Philippine polity" (Grossholtz, 1964, p. 282; see "compadrazgo system" in Karnow, 1989, pp. 29–21). Jonathan Fast remarks on the profound impact of American "tutelage" since English was imposed as the official language in 1899: "The prevalence of U.S. cultural forms and the recently seen movement [circa 1960] to make the Philippines a U.S. state are manifestations of this deleterious ideological inheritance of the imperialist period" (1973, p. 71; for U.S. neocolonialism in the Philippines, see Pomeroy, 1970; Schirmer, 1987; Sison, 2016).

One can clearly discern how political domination subsumes the cultural subordination of the dominated and its reproduction. This is what Nina Glick Schiller envisaged when she said that cultural politics is concerned with "the processes through which relations of power are asserted, accepted, contested, or subverted by means of ideas, values, symbols and daily practices" (1997, p. 3). A more precise, adequate term to designate this transaction between cultures/politics is the narrative of the ideological struggle for hegemony. Initially by violence (the repression of recurrent peasant revolts) and then by persuasive, consensus-making strategies, U.S. authority established its hegemony over Filipinos, winning precarious majority consent in the three decades of direct colonial rule (1899–1935). But this was never uncontested, given the sustained progressive movement to recuperate lost sovereignty and empower the victims (Agoncillo & Guerrero, 1970; Constantino, 1975; for the U.S. support of the Marcos dictatorship, see Bonner, 1987; San Juan, 2007).

Without this historical framework of U.S.-sustained ascendancy, we cannot understand SP's genealogy as part of the nationalist movement in the 1970s–1980s. It is basically an emancipatory project, a counterhegemonic mobilization of popular forces initiated in the academy. Worldwide protests against the Indo-Chinese Wars and suppression of the nationalist movement during the Cold War laid the groundwork for indigenization as a mode of anti-imperialist resistance. This entailed recovering suppressed ethical traditions and legitimizing their epistemic potential as elements of a submerged national identity that needs reactivation. In this project, it sought to expose and analyze the ideological instruments of persistent U.S. intervention. Thus, its twin task was both to repudiate the colonial standards of value judgment and to affirm the urgent necessity of restoring a repressed "form of life," a recursive pattern of metabolic adjustment with the changing milieu and its natural environment.

Advent of Native Inquiry

Virgilio Enriquez, SP's acknowledged progenitor, has provided us a historical sketch of the U.S. hegemonic program carried out in the imposed colonizer's language, American English. One of the effective instruments deployed for colonial rule consists of the American educational methodologies and disciplines, among them psychology (Enriquez, 1992, pp. 3–23). Psychology as a pedagogical practice is one of the apparatuses for producing subjects whose labor power can yield profits for business and revenue for the State. Purporting to be the science of the mind, psychology began with Wilhelm Wundt, who established an experimental laboratory to study the modalities of perception, learning, motivation, memory, intelligence, and personality. At the turn of the century, Freudian psychoanalysis and other idealist theories arose, contradistinguished from mechanistic-reflexology which later evolved into positivist behaviorism (Voloshinov, 1976, pp. 17–28).

The challenge of dialectical approaches to behaviorism began not with Freud but with the Russian Lev Vygotsky (1962). Vygotsky criticized Pavlov's reflexology by emphasizing how humans "actively create their environment" and explore "new forms of consciousness" (Billig, 1983, p. 403). Social reproduction of beliefs and attendant codes of conduct is imperative for maintaining "law and order." This follows the historical-materialist focus on how the external world is reflected through complex mediations in consciousness (such as feelings, thoughts, impulses, volitions, etc.). The concept of the "embodied mind" proposed by cognitive science today (Varela et al., 2016) was previously given a Marxist articulation by Wilhelm Reich (1972), Phil Brown (1974), Lucien Seve (1978), and others. However, cognitive science's heuristic discoveries are still to be tested by its application to indigenizing initiatives such as SP.

Western social scientists have not neglected historical contexts or cultural situatedness. George Gurvitch, for example, surveyed class-based knowledges in *The Social Frameworks of Knowledge* (1971), while Maria Ossowska compared the bourgeois and nobility ethos in *Social Determinants of Moral Ideas* (1970). They are the precedents of the "embodied mind" of contemporary cognitive science (Lakoff & Johnson, 1980; Varela et al., 2016; Johnson, 2018). Eventually, however, positivist/behaviorist paradigms have focused on learning and motivation. They were supplemented later with social psychology, symbolic interactionism, etc., fusing Durkheim, Weber, and modern anthropology, as exemplified in the textbook *Character and Social Structure* by Hans Gerth and C. Wright Mills (1953). Overall, this converged with structuralist-functionalist sociology and its emphasis on stability, conformity, and the integration of individuals into prevailing norms. This sociology is rendered coherent and intelligible when sutured to an expanded systems theory of action (see the critique of structural-functionalism in Giddens, 1979, pp. 110–119).

This approach was appropriated by the American Jesuit Frank Lynch trained in the Cold War Human Area Files (specimens of this inquiry are the "country" studies by Taylor, Grossholtz, and Karnow cited here). Its main concern was the preservation of social equilibrium and status quo maintenance. Lynch organized an institute devoted to investigating the notions of reciprocity and social acceptance that purportedly define the Filipino culture, personality, and social dynamics. Changes in attitude and consequent patterns of behavior are thought to characterize the transition from a traditional to a modern society, following the European model. Lynch and his disciples avoided analyzing U.S. modernization schemes involving the commodification of labor power, marketized accounting of values, hierarchical governance, and disavowing problems of psychic breakdowns or anomie in urban industrialized regions. Muted or obscured in their research are the power asymmetries between peasant and landlord in feudal sectors, between worker and capitalist boss in factories, and between despotic patriarch and women/children in the extended family. The reality and experience of alienation in the workplace were expunged, given the focus on regularity and reproduction of routine affairs and business transactions.

Counter-Revolutionary Strategy

Amid peasant and labor-union unrest, this inquiry into Filipino personality and its motivations was highly serviceable. We can cite the use of local superstitious beliefs by the CIA agent Col. Edward Landsdale to frighten Huk guerrillas in the late 1940s (Shalom, 1987, pp. 115–16). Understanding the mechanisms of the Filipino psyche at that conjuncture proved useful in reinforcing prevailing lopsided power relations. Formulas for promoting stability and class reconciliation were easily deduced from the structural-functionalist analysis of group behavior patterns. The functionalist imperative of maintaining social equilibrium is premised on how abstract individuals internalize status quo norms, enabling authorities to regulate and control their behavior. The unconstrained buying and selling of commodities (labor power as the chief commodity) in the free market is presumed to guarantee democracy and personal liberty. There is no warrant for alarm. If any social change is registered, it refers to the internal differentiation of action patterns, not systemic transformation in terms of altering the existing social division of labor, distribution of wealth, allocation of property, etc.

Lynch's framework of mizing smooth interpersonal relations (SIR) served the U. S. Cold War program of modernization based on free market precepts. It conserved the neocolonial normative order and its unequal divisions of wealth and power. The time when Lynch occupied a position of authority was a time of crisis, when traditional values became precarious or were directly attacked. Lynch's value diagnosis attempted some kind of conflict management, a compromise formula, and an anodyne administered to pacify everyone. It sought to neutralize radical theories of class conflict and any critique of unequal property/power relations. It assumed the existence of genuine Filipino sovereignty and equitable representation of the majority in the government. Thus, the reality of feudal and capitalist exploitation of Filipinos was rendered invisible. In the Lynch school's reductive optic, Filipino "traits" such as *hiya, utang-na-loob,* and other accommodative responses serve as the keys to understanding how Filipinos behave, think, feel, and conduct themselves as "rational" human beings (1973).

In almost every tourist guide available today, the identity of the Filipino and their modes of interacting with others are constructed by selecting a few folkways claimed to be typical of the group. Customary rituals of middle-class citizens are deemed to represent the entire nation. The framework of generalization followed by these guidebooks derives from the doctrine of Western utilitarianism and its calculus of pleasure/pain. They take precautions to depict the neocolonial landscape as exotic and bewitching, or at least nonthreatening. Take the claim that one typical quality of Filipino "smooth" interaction is epitomized by *pakikisama*, "the ability to get along and implying camaraderie and togetherness" (Roces & Grace, 1985, p. 35). But this trait turns out to be variable in its effects, depending on the circumstances and contingent on other factors. So the argument that such a trait constitutes an essential attribute of Filipino physiognomy is untenable.

Demystifying Commodified Knowledge

Tourist guidebooks abound in Orientalizing indigenous reflexes (see Peplow, 1991, p. 50; Harper & Fullerton, 1993, pp. 48–54). They contrive their picture of the "Filipino" stereotype from Stanley Karnow's history, *In Our Image*, a book that draws heavily from experts like Lynch and other American scholars. Karnow echoes the platitude about Filipino behavior with an ironic or paradoxical twist: "Personal rather than institutional relationships guide Filipinos, making them less sensitive to the rules of society than to the opinions of their real or ritual kin … Hence their obsession with *hiya*, a Tagalog term that conveys the supremely important concept of 'face'. To behave decorously toward family and friends, to display respect for an elder, kindness toward an underling, deference toward a superior—all show exemplary *hiya* … Equally vital is *utang na loob*, the debt of gratitude," which, if unpaid, makes the negligent "guilty of *walang hiya*" (1989, p. 20).

Karnow's generalization postulates a Filipino transcendental essence that benefits corporate profit-making. Enriquez has already pointed out the external–internal aspect of *hiya* (shame) and its manifold nuances (1992, pp. 65–68). In reality, these patterns of negotiating transactions distinguish archaic communities in which conflicts were modulated by "indirect methods of communication" (such as *pakiramdaman)* for the sake of unity and harmony (Veneracion, 1987, p. 210; for pre-colonial customs, see Scott, 1982, pp. 96–147).

We should not ignore the framework of socioeconomic determinants of communal practices. This applies to *utang-na-loob*, that enigmatic and mystified "debt of the inner self." Usually translated as "debt of gratitude," which wrongly interprets "loob/inside) as "gratitude," "loob" is endowed with an ethical connotation. This misconstrual begets the notion that, because of the goodwill of others, returning the favor is required when the need arises, reciprocating what is given. But if there is no return in kind or token, *hiya* (translated as shame or "loss of face") follows. Such a transgression of an official code of conduct obviously functions as a regulator of interpersonal relations, but this reading again depends "on the relative status of the actors involved, or on the type of message being conveyed" (Kintanar, 1996, pp. 649, 671).

Western knowledge production thus distorts local hermeneutic endeavors in this fashion. The banking analogy imposes a contractualist background different from that which prevails in the neocolony. "*Utang*" is really not a debt in the usual commercial sense of debt–credit accounting, but a status indicator for a sense of liability or obligation. Enriquez has shown that *utang na loob* cannot be fully understood without the situational map of its usage, the lived experience of the protagonists. Thus, beyond its utilitarian/mercantile calculus, *utang na loob* manifests "a commitment to human solidarity…a value which moves to recognize, respect, promote, and at times defend the basic dignity of each person" (1992, pp. 67–68; for elaboration, see Maggay, 2002, pp. 94–95).

What has been ignored so far in the discussion of *utang na loob* is the conceptual metaphor of *loob* with its network of spatial inferences. *Loob* as inside entails *labas* as outside in a mapping operation. Given the predominantly rural/feudal milieu, the village or *barangay* defines strangers as outsiders, *taga-labas*, in contrast to those inside, *taga-looban*. The container metaphor may suggest that *utang na loob* implies a belief in obeying the norms of our common habitat. It entails affirming the trustworthiness of those inside the community. *Loob*, translated as interior, not exposed or displayed. It also signifies virtue (*giting*). In addition, the reliable *UP Diksyunaryo* (published by the State University of the Philippines) offers this signification: "*kalagayan ng pag-iisip, kapasiyahan, dalisay at taal na diwa ng pagkatao*" (Almario, 2001, p. 519), literally, the condition of the mind (thought), decisiveness, and pure and authentic spirit of personhood.

We can conclude that the notion of *utang na loob* condenses multiple strata of inferred sensorimotor entailments. Of fundamental importance is the kinesthetic image scheme of back-and-forth physical motion: *loob/labas*, inside/outside. This container schema and its metaphorical projection structure the conceptualization of "the visual field (things go in and out of sight), personal relationships (one gets in and out of a relationship), the logic of sets (sets contain their members)" (Varela et al., 2016, p. 177). Certain actions are entailed by the image schema; in other words, cognition with its epistemic infrastructure entails sensorimotor consequences. Further, spatial orientation is subsumed within the larger ontological framework of "*kapwa*," the foundational ground of SP (more on this later).

In this context, it is useful to remind ourselves that Enriquez postulates the force of the "shared inner self," the partnership of I and you; this linkage or mutuality is equivalent to his central theme of "*kapwa*," literally both/fellow being (Enriquez, 1992, pp. 43–45). From this perspective, we can judge that *utang na loob* signifies an ethos of recognizing others as integral to the acknowledgment of one's worth. Viewed dialectically, the Other serves as the necessary complement or fulfillment of one's identity. SP thus rejects the atomistic ego or monadic self of Cartesian dualism, the metaphysics of utilitarian ethics, and liberal rational-choice theory (for a critique of the latter, see Lakoff & Johnson, 1999, pp. 513–38).

Problematizing Translation

Citing another case of misrecognition might be instructive. A culturally grounded analysis of the expression "*bahala na*," often taken to be a fatalistic attitude, demonstrates the need to take account of pragmatics and lived experience. Usage supersedes abstract semantics and constrains arbitrary glosses. For the circle of competent interlocutors, "*bahala*" as a noun means: "1. Responsibility; 2. Person responsible; person in charge; 3. Management" (Panganiban, 1972, p. 98). Contrary to wild speculations, the term does not invoke a god or deity called "bathala."

To illustrate further the necessary criterion of usage, consider these multiple inflections of the phrase "*bahala na*," which excludes any hint of fatalism, as delineated by the linguist Dr. Jose Villa Panganiban:

—*Bahala ka na*. You look out and be responsible when the time comes.
—*Bahala na*. We'll consider what to do when the time comes.
—*Kabahala*. Fellow trustee.
—*Ikabahala*. To be the reason for one's feeling of concern about something.
—*Ipabahala*. To consign (x) to the responsibility of someone.
—*Mabahala*. To feel concerned or worried about something.
—*Mamahala*. To manage something.
—*Pabahala*. Something given in trust.

—*Pagkababahala*. Fact or manner of being concerned or worried about something.

—*Pamahalaan*. Government. (Panganiban, 1972, p. 98)

The tabulation above is a sample of how the term "*bahala*" acquires diverse senses, depending on the pragmatic context and conversational implicatures. This demonstrates how isolated terms designating communicative transactions cannot be understood without the appropriate socio-historical context of their usage. We contend that failure to understand Tagalog discourse (syntax, grammar, semantics), utilizing only abstract logic, leads to misleading misconstruals. This is evident with regard to such putative values/norms affiliated with such notions as *hiya* and *bahala na*, among others.

The sociologist Mary Hollnsteiner, a disciple of Lynch, observes the phenomenon *utang-na-loob* as the Filipino awareness of an "obligation to those from whom he receives favors and should repay them in an acceptable manner. Since utang-na-loob invariably stems from a service rendered, even though a material gift may be involved, quantification is impossible" (1963, p. 37). The last phrase reveals the nature of the debt as metaphoric, a matter of gain or loss, connected with the status of the landlord or peasant, worker or entrepreneur. In effect, this inner-self debt builds on a moral accounting calculus pivoting around the central role of the family and the embodied experience of organic well-being among protagonists and participants (Lakoff & Johnson, 1999, pp. 292–334).

As noted earlier, Enriquez cogently demonstrated the limits of formalist social science imported from the West. Not only were these scholars ignorant of Tagalog grammar and the semantic variations of *loob* in actual usage, but they also assumed its similarity with the contractual norms of an industrial society. They posited a disembodied mind bereft of apprehending concrete location and its sensorimotor entailments. Enriquez added that "the English-interpretations of *utang-na*-loob as reciprocity happens to be useful in promoting the image of the colonizer as benefactor" (1992, p. 67). Another inquiry has pursued the route of evaluating the term as a conceptual metaphor. It showed that the pragmatic import of *utang-na-loob* is the opposite of the Americanized gloss. The Filipino inquirer concluded that it "is therefore a value which moves to recognize, respect, promote, and at times defend the basic dignity of each person" (Enriquez, 1992, pp. 67–68). So much for the unashamed prejudice of American experts on Filipino identity and its sociocultural background.

Unfolding the Determinations

It seems superfluous to remind ourselves that life is not determined by consciousness, but consciousness is determined by life. Our brains and bodies change with social development, in particular with industry-linked technological changes that manifest "man's essential powers, the perceptibly existing human psychology" to quote Marx (1964, p. 142; Billig, 1983, p. 402). Thoughts, feelings, impulses, volitions, dreams, etc., reflect changes in the external world. And these reflections are elaborated and refined by complex mediations that crystallize in what cognitive science today calls "the embodied mind."

We can escape the trap of introspective psychologism by rejecting the premises of a priori Western philosophy. Instead, we can base our inquiries on the principle that "our conceptual system, our modes of inferring and reasoning, are anchored and crucially shaped by our perceptual and motor systems," both situated in history, in living organisms, and in the evolving environment (Lakoff & Johnson, 1999, p. 555). Perhaps SP, with its inaugural hypotheses and experimental procedures, has already anticipated the experientialist approach of cognitive science.

Enriquez's theorizing of the Filipino personality centered on "*kapwa*" as partnership-collaboration encapsulates the motivating spirit of the "embodied mind." Here are the central themes of the experientialist perspective on human thinking/action, as enunciated by George Lakoff and Mark Johnson: "Meaningful conceptual structures arise from two sources: (1) from the structured nature of bodily and social experience, and (2) from our innate capacity to imaginatively project from certain well-structured aspects of bodily and interactional experience to abstract conceptual structures. Rational thought is the application of very general cognitive processes—focusing, scanning, superimposition, figure-ground reversal, etc. to such structures" (Varela et al., 2016, p. 178). These can serve as feasible points of departure for future SP practitioners striving to sharpen SP's conceptual analytic and enlarge its range.

Subverting the Center–Periphery Binary

We agree with Enriquez and his followers that SP has a liberatory program rooted in its historical situatedness and empirical grounding. Its imperative task centers on the radical decolonization of a neocolonial polity, while recovering and affirming the validity of popular-democratic enactments. SP strives to construct a Filipino identity and national consciousness against oppressive neocolonial governance and its biopolitical apparatuses. It attempts to utilize its antecedent mentalities and practices while cultivating an open-ended methodology with local application, as attested to in current livelihood psychology, folk techniques of healing, and so on (Pe-pua & Protacio-Marcelino, 2000, p. 53).

As a historic footnote, we can comment on the early usage of the term "Filipinization." "Filipinization" acquired historic notoriety when the Washington-appointed administrator of the colony, William Cameron Forbes, halted "Filipinization' of the civil service during his term (Kramer, 2006, p. 313). According to Kramer, "Rizal was not yet a Filipino in 1889; by 1946, [Filipino] has emerged as the term for the Philippine-born population and for its national identity, molded by colonial institutions" (2006, p. 434). Colleagues are flummoxed by this wild assertion proclaimed by sophisticated American scholarship in the epoch of the empire's global war on terror. This is one more proof that SP is laboring under hegemonic surveillance camouflaged by the ironic alibis of American tutors. SP is now rendered suspect for cohabiting with indigenizing Others (some in Europe and others in Asia and non-Western regions). One can surmise that this ongoing indigenization process may now play the role of a revitalized *agent provocateur* for a more radical decolonizing drive in this new epoch inaugurated by the war in Ukraine and Gaza.

In retrospect, as many have observed, language—the imposition of the colonizer's English—was the most powerful means of producing a subservient Filipino subject (Constantino, 1975, pp. 310–312; Giddens, 1979, pp. 30–38). One way of decolonizing is by using Filipino but not refusing English as the temporary language of business and government. The vernacular is a symbol of affirming the primacy of self-determination. This mode of Filipinization, however, does not endorse world-outlook relativism—the Sapir–Whorf thesis that language mirrors the incommensurable cultural world of ethnic groups (Whorf, 1956; criticized by Schaff, 1973). To be sure, SP resorts to translation to resolve any semantic problem of differences, even though one can observe tendencies to vindicate the singularity of such SP research practices as *pagtatanung-tanong, panunuluyan, pakapakapa, pakikipagkuwentuhan, and pagdalaw-dalaw,* all underwritten by *pakiramdam* (intuitive apprehension of feelings, thoughts, etc.). These methods are all motivated by the desire to overcome the emic-etic dichotomy in anthropology (Torres, 1982; Santiago,

1982). Enriquez endorses his teacher Alfredo Lagmay's total approach: "while the method is objective and the bias scientific, the approach undeniably involves the total human being, including human judgment and human values" (1992, p. 92). "Total approach" here resembles the already mentioned cognitive science's theorizing of "the embodied mind."

Arguably, the original intent suffers from a cosmopolitan hubris. Universalization of a cultural trait begins with an empirical-oriented hypothesis and trial synthesis, not summary deduction. In his desire to be all-inclusive, Enriquez tends to be naively eclectic at the expense of the discoveries of cognitive science concerning the specificity of lived experience. He also courts the danger of forfeiting the virtues of a popular democratic counterhegemonic agenda in the midst of resurgent nationalist fervor. Nonetheless, we are assured by his partisans that "On the mentalism-behaviorism issue, SP admits both but with lesser emphasis on individual experience and with greater emphasis on the collective experience of a people with a common bond of history" (Pe-Pua & Protacio-Marcelino, 2000, p. 54). Hence, the emphasis is on ***kamalayan***, which conflates ***kaalaman, kabatiran*** (knowledge), and ***damdam*** (feeling). In this connection, the term *diwa* is considered a synonym of kamalayan, but it also denotes commonsense, gist, main idea, soul, and spirit (Vicassan, 2006, pp. 127, 307). To enrich the lexicon, I submit that *diwa* approximates the concept of "the embodied mind," the notion of the psyche, including sensorimotor capacities, moral imagination, empathy, and possibilities nesting in its as yet uncharted zones.

We have construed SP (in Enriquez's original proposition) as emancipatory in that it repudiates neocolonial hegemony and its individualizing-reifying implications. Ultimately, SP is a form of ideology critique, valorizing subversive articulations from below while locating vertical and horizontal socializations going on (Rehmann, 2014, pp. 248–249). Nevertheless, its progressive orientation and objectives are not in doubt. We sympathize with its commitment to the needs of the oppressed—the immiserated victims of imperialism that Enrique Dussell foregrounds as the organic protagonist of his *Ethics of Liberation* (2013) and of Fanon's "wretched of the earth" (Brown, 1974, pp. 96–100). At this point, we would like to recapitulate our earlier caveats: how are these subjects represented in SP without historical specification? Lacking time–space determinants, how is the *problematique* of their prefigured liberation framed?

Extrapolating Intentionality

In actuality, SP, as envisioned by Enriquez and elaborated by succeeding scholars, is not wholly a branch of an indigenizing trend. First of all, Filipinos (as they have evolved from the founding of the First Philippine Republic in 1998 to the present neocolonial conjuncture) are not the indigenes confronted by the Spanish conquistadors. Those segregated, racialized groups defined by U.S. colonizers were the non-Christian mountain tribes—the Igorots, Aetas, etc.—the lowland Manobos, and other tribal groups (now called Lumads) living side by side with the more populous Moros (Filipino Muslims) in the southern Philippines. It cannot be overemphasized that the Philippines stands out from all Asian (and "third world") countries in having undergone Spanish colonization for over three hundred years, and American domination for over a century (San Juan, 2007; Sison, 2016).

Filipinos today are neocolonized subjects, not postcolonial subalterns, struggling to free themselves from centuries of enslavement and subjugation. SP is thus a national liberation process/project coinciding with the anti-imperialist mobilization of organized workers, peasants, women, ethnic communities, youth, etc. It was inaugurated by the 1896 revolution against Spain and invigorated by the Filipino resistance against U.S. domination from 1899 to the present, more intense and flexible today when U.S. military bases have expanded within the Philippine military establishment in order to encircle a perceived enemy, China maneuvering to grab Taiwan (San Juan, 2021).

As a revolutionary movement spearheaded by intellectuals and activists, SP attempts to develop a singular project of psychology appropriate to the needs of the national-democratic mass movement in the Philippines. It is both local and global in origin and impact. As Enriquez and others have described its complex genealogy, it does not claim to invent a new tradition, a Malayan *Weltanschauung* (Paredes-Canilao & Babaran-Diaz, 2013; Yacat, 2013). Rather, it seeks to discover, appraise, and develop native cultural habits (actualized beliefs), practices, and knowledges either suppressed or marginalized by Western authorities. It also borrows from Western and Asian resources, adapting them for local purposes and survival needs.

This phenomenon can be grasped more precisely by the idea of articulation politics extrapolated from Gramsci and applied by Stuart Hall and other New Left inventors of cultural studies in the 1980s and 1990s. The anthropologist James Clifford endorses this articulation politics implemented by Native Pacific peoples struggling for "breathing space, for relational sovereignty...They are about finding ways to exist in a multiplex modernity, but with a difference, a difference derived from cultural tradition...from ongoing histories of displacement, travel and circulation" (2006, p. 183). For their part, Filipinos, as a nation-in-formation, are still in quest of sovereignty and self-determination, struggling to acquire a self-managing *habitus* and a historicizing sensibility.

Genealogy of Both/Others

Within this new paradigm, SP finds itself articulated with popular, national-democratic praxis with its own track-record of creativity and open-mindedness. It uses the residual, dominant and emergent trends of contemporary life in its counterhegemonic activities. SP's projects will be built on the foundation of the ethos and convergent experiences of Filipinos from all sectors, including the newly demarcated, multitudinous diaspora of Filipinos working abroad (labeled OFWs, Overseas Filipino Workers (San Juan, 2001, 2021, pp. 21–36), which started in the 1970s.

With a dynamic naturalist viewpoint, SP attempts to establish a framework for articulating old and new elements, not to forge a postmodern pastiche or a syncretic, hybrid artifact favored by postcolonialists. On the contrary, it endeavors to shape an integrated agency to intervene in mass political mobilization. It strives to build a research program conceptualized around the goal of forging a new subject, a new conscientious moral agency, hoping to realize what Charles Sanders Peirce calls "concrete reasonableness" (1998, p. 68; Misak, 2004, p. 170; San Juan, 2022, p. 90). This subject's horizon of engaging in transformative action, together with others, is already implicit in diverse acts of deliberative inquiry, problem-solving, and discovery of new communal values that will replace the world-outlook of the old, moribund, iniquitous feudal-comprador order—the neocolonial mode of production and reproduction of social relations (Johnson, 2014, pp. 214–217).

Further reflection will show that this new subject constructed by SP is, by necessity, a discursive, self-critical protagonist. By definition, *kapwa* cannot be a monadic, competitive entrepreneur treating everyone as antagonists. As Emile Benveniste explicated, the pronouns "I" and "you" as social positions can only signify in concrete discursive situations, given the fact that meaning is brought about by the reality of discourse inscribed in a particular symbolic order in specific time-space coordinates (Silverman, 1983, pp. 45–47). This comprehensive stance precludes such static binarism of "pantayong pananaw" versus the outsider or foreign optic. "Pantayong pananaw" proves to be an idealist fantasy or fetish because "tayo" bears no meaning without its interlocutor, its partner "*sila*" (they), or the others outside the container/locus of discourse (on "We" and "they," see Porshnev, 1970, pp. 65–108; regarding an offshoot of SP, SLK or *Sikolohiyang Panlipunan-at-Kalinangan*/Social and Cultural Psychology, see Salazar, 2004).

We can now approach the core idea of Enriquez's version of SP's articulation politics that pivots around a few key concepts. It begins with the postulation of *kapwa*, a term literally referring to "both of us," "us together." The term in use also denotes *kapareho, kauri*, literally, similarity or belonging to the same class. Immediately, we are situated in a communicative field of engagement that grounds Enriquez's task of Filipinizing personality theory. He argues that "human interaction is a highly valued aspect of life in the Philippines. For this reason, social interaction is a meaningful focus of investigation in the process of identifying and analyzing basic concepts of Filipino personality, social psychology, world view and social philosophy" (1992, p. 39).

SP's approach implies that social life is recursive, and agents self-monitor and are capable of learning from mistakes. It may be characterized as dramatistic, pragmatic, and dialectical in linking agents, discourse, feelings, perceptions, and motivations for action. We quote neuroscientist Antonio Damasio's insight in stressing the imperative of self-preservation underlying social regularities: "Social conventions and ethical rules may be seen in part as extensions of the basic homeostatic arrangements at the level of society and culture" (2003, p. 168). But simple valorization of mutuality or cooperation is somewhat redundant or tautologous, assuming that such interactions generally follow habits and end successfully. This assumption may be utopian, if not idealizing. At this juncture, let us inspect Enriquez's schema of values and associated behavior, a synthesis of shared inner perception, emotions, unconscious impulses, and its entailments in action (see Table V, Figs. 7.1 and 7.2, in Enriquez, 1992, p. 75).

It is worth recapitulating here SP's key thematizations. Salient in this foundational schema is *kapwa* (one and another; both), a shared identity, partnership, or communicative ensemble. The implied metaphor is ambivalent, susceptible to positive and negative inferences. Without further explanation, Enriquez conflates the ensemble with *pagkatao*, the public

TABLE V

Behavior Patterns and Value Structure: Surface, Core and Societal

Colonial/ Accommodative Surface Value	***hiya*** (propriety/ dignity)	***utang na loob*** (gratitude/ solidarity)	***pakikisama*** (companionship/ esteem)
Associated Behavior Pattern	***biro*** (joke)	***lambing*** (sweetness)	***tampo*** (affective disappointment)
Confrontative Surface Value	***bahala na*** (determination)	***sama/lakas ng loob*** (resentment/guts)	***pakikibaka*** (resistance)
Pivotal Inter-personal Value	***Pakiramdam*** {*Pakikipagkapwa-tao*} (shared inner perception)		
CORE VALUE	***KAPWA*** (shared identity)		{*Pagkatao*}
Linking Socio-personal Value	***Kagandahang-loob*** {*Pagkamakatao*} (shared humanity)		
Associated Societal Values	***karangalan*** (dignity)	***katarungan*** (justice)	***kalayaan*** (freedom)
Reductionist/ Functional Interpretation	"social acceptance"	"social equity"	"social mobility"

Fig. 7.1 Table reproduced from Enriquez's 1992 book, Page 75]

TABLE V

Behavior Patterns and Value Structure: Surface, Core and Societal

Colonial/ Accommodative Surface Value	***hiya*** (propriety/ dignity)	***utang na loob*** (gratitude/ solidarity)	***pakikisama*** (companionship/ esteem)
Associated Behavior Pattern	***biro*** (joke)	***lambing*** (sweetness)	***tampo*** (affective disappointment)
Confrontative Surface Value	***bahala na*** (determination)	***sama/lakas ng loob*** (resentment/guts)	***pakikibaka*** (resistance)
Pivotal Inter-personal Value	***Pakiramdam*** {*Pakikipagkapwa-tao*} (shared inner perception)		
CORE VALUE	***KAPWA*** (shared identity)		{*Pagkatao*}
Linking Socio-personal Value	***Kagandahang-loob*** {*Pagkamakatao*} (shared humanity)		
Associated Societal Values	***karangalan*** (dignity)	***katarungan*** (justice)	***kalayaan*** (freedom)
Reductionist/ Functional Interpretation	"social acceptance"	"social equity"	"social mobility"

Fig. 7.2 Behavior patterns and value structure: Surface, core and societal

manifestation of conduct and all properties (physical, mental, emotional) that comprise a unique character type. Following the *UP Diksyunaryo* definition, *pagkatao* ostensively designates the organized schema of the habitual actions of a subject-actor: "organisadong padron ng mga ugali ng isang indibidwal" (Almario, 2001, p. 629). *Pagkatao*, in its various usages, denotes the enactive person in metabolic exchange with its social and natural environment.

Eventually, this core value of *kapwa* = *pagkatao* will be subsumed in the principle of shared humanity, particularized here as *kagandahang-loob* (literally, kindness or amiability) and *pagkamakatao*. The societal virtues connected with it are the following: dignity (*karangalan*), *katarungan* (justice), and *kalayaan* (freedom). While dignity may be a quality attributed to honorable and honest conduct, it is difficult to link partnership or togetherness with much more complex categories such as justice and freedom without spelling out concretely the necessary mediations. Evidently, by fiat, Enriquez has connected *kapwa* with the idea of a social formation governed by justice, equality, and dignity—a construal of partnership or mutuality by abduction (to use C.S. Peirce's term [1998, pp. 226–241]), a method of assaying the validity of a hypothesis by finding out its conceivable practical effects. It is a visionary ideal, arguably a working hypothesis for articulating ends, purposes, and goals. To combine idea and concrete circumstance, however, we need the description of a mediatory process that will integrate enactments, feelings, and other metaphors of imaginative rationality and their practical entailments.

Passages of Recognition

What remains to be explored further is the inadequacies of SP. The unexplained exfoliation of values from the core element of "kapwa" is due to its lack of specific sociohistorical contextualization. It seems that the conceptual metaphor enabling this categorization of patterns of action inheres in the tacit assumption that "Our partnership means sharing." If not fulfilled, incompatible responses are evoked, such as *biro* (joke), *lambing* (sweetness), *tampo* (affective disappointment), and other errant syndromes (Enriquez, 1992, pp. 74–77). We encounter offshoots of colonial, accommodative surface values as *hiya* (propriety, dignity), *utang na loob* (gratitude, solidarity), and *pakikisama* (companionship, esteem), etc. They are then contrasted with confrontative surface values: *bahala* (determination), *sama/lakas ng loob* (resentment, guts), and *pakikibaka* (resistance). The latter intimates collective struggle or opposition, while the rest are personal attitudes or reactions. All these purported equivalences are imaginatively conjectured as emerging from *kapwa*, a shared identity, enabled by *pakiramdam* (the process of empathy or sharing of emotions).

Two points need clarification. Enriquez's imagined communities all cohere because *pakiramdam* is the matrix of shared humanity. It has affinities with Hegel's notion of ethical life, *Sittlichkeit* (Inwood, 1992, p. 91). It denotes empathy, an intuitive apprehension and understanding of what others are feeling and thinking. It can also be construed as a reasonable guess or felt calculation of what other sensibilities are experiencing. What Enriquez fails to underscore is the implicit marker, "*paki*," which is a prefix signaling a request to do something or for something to be done. It is a marker of enactment invested with respect or courtesy for your neighbors/compatriots to do something, as in *pakikisama, pakikibaka*, etc. It accords with the symbolic resonance of *kapwa,* the recognition of being together with someone of equal status or stature. I would like to underscore the significance of this specific prefix: the use of "paki" makes a whole world of difference in social exchange and communication in the public sphere.

Enriquez's inventory of hypothesized generative values in the prefigured Filipino personality conforms to his decisive revalidation of what is deemed "indigenous" to the natives before the Spanish and American conquests. The paramount position of *kapwa* and its entailments in SP has already been indicated before: it performs the function of synthesizing the archaic habits, folkways, beliefs, and practices of the rural inhabitants of pre-colonial Philippines. They are conceptually structured by a communal ethos of participation in collective labor and enjoyment, with its underlying feudal or pre-capitalist mode of production that Enriquez assumes as already implied in his discourse. Because this framework of historical layering is never clearly spelled out, the posited virtues of free, just, and equal sharing of work and its fruits are taken for granted. And with that being the case, this recuperated Filipino personality—combative, knowledgeable, versatile, resourceful—is then offered as the new agency for the ongoing national-democratic, popular mobilization in the Philippines today.

What is seriously lacking in Enriquez's theorizing of SP as an emancipatory project has already been indicated earlier. Enriquez has not provided a substantive analysis of colonizing ideological mechanisms in their various modalities. Glaringly absent too is any in-depth treatment of sexuality, gender, marital relations, etc., in the indigenizing agenda. Enriquez and others have, of course, already criticized Establishment theories and approaches to these aspects of social life. But the full accounting of historical socio-economic determinants is still missing. This absence of a historicizing analysis of concrete conditions delimiting the project of recovering usable folkways and habits of affective coordination vitiates the recovery program, such institutions as hospitals, prisons, public schools, media, and sports, together with surveillance agencies, as ideological apparatuses for forming acquiescent subjects, need more thorough critical scrutiny. Of course, religion and the patriarchal family remain crucial in subject formation (for the theory of subject as product of ideological processes, see Giddens, 1979, pp. 9–48, 165–197). To be sure, Enriquez has provided us with the most sensible research orientation for undertaking further inquiries into the problems discussed here.

Re-Discovering the Indigene's Psyche

After Enriquez's death, a call for renovation of SP has been made by friendly critics, colleagues, and partisans (Gastardo-Conaco, 2005; Paredes-Canilao & Babaran-Diaz, 2013; Pe-Pua, 2020; San Juan, 2007, pp. 216–248; see my previous inquiries in San Juan, 2022). One pedagogical project may be suggested here. To demonstrate its continuing relevance, SP practitioners, for instance, can engage in a rigorous analysis of the circumstances around the "1986 People Power Revolt." They can try to describe how neocolonial beliefs/attitudes were generated and reproduced, thus neutralizing any radical impulse that would have foiled the return of the oligarchy under Corazon Aquino's patronage. Such disruptions of quotidian routine, within the scope of the phenomenology of everyday life, would be one item on the agenda of future SP inquirers. Without exposing the insidious operations of these hegemonic mechanisms, the reification of work relations and the alienation saturating the whole milieu remains mystified in the formation of personality and its lived experience in everyday routine (see Ollman, 1971, pp. 131–226).

Neoliberal globalization, in this new millennium, has not only disastrously wrecked the economy of peripheral societies everywhere. It has also extensively altered traditional forms of life (Stiglitz, 2002; Yates, 2003). New powerful modes of persuasion have now submerged the ethos of *kapwa*, a fact starkly indexed by the powerful influence of electronic media and the unrelenting Americanization of Filipino dispositions and mentality. The threat of surveillance and mind control by AI and other technological innovations looms on the horizon. Unless these are criticized as ideological weapons of neocolonialism, SP and its laudable emancipatory ideals and principles will remain a utopian exercise. Notwithstanding these caveats, I believe this is not the occasion to do a thorough cognitive mapping of the terrain of the current social formation (under the bloody Duterte and now Marcos Jr. regimes) from SP's optic. But it remains a desideratum for the proponents of indigenization as a collective process of redeeming suppressed or sequestered human potential. In sum, before or coeval with any revalidation of radically liberatory, not to say redemptive, Filipino values and potential enactments, we need a wide-ranging critique of the biopower machinery in control, including its theory and practices of subjugation and domination for profit accumulation. We need to question the legitimacy of this imperial authority that continues to wreak havoc and misery on everyone who, while laboring in agonizing circumstances, can benefit from the indigenization of disciplines. We are still in search of the prophesized "Filipino" subject-on-trial, a subject in the process of rebirth and transformation.

References

Abaya, H. (1984). *The making of a subversive.* New Day Press.

Agoncillo, T., & Guerrero, M. (1970). *History of the Filipino people.* R.P. Garcia Publishing Co.

Almario, V. (Ed.). (2001). *U.P. Diksyunaryong Filipino.* University of the Philippines Press.

Billig, M. (1983). Psychology. In T. Bottomore (Ed.), *A dictionary of Marxist thought.* Harvard University Press.

Bonner, R. (1987). *Waltzing with a dictator.* Ken Incorporated.

Bourdieu, P. (1977). *Outline of a theory of practice.* Cambridge University Press.

Brown, P. (1974). *Toward a Marxist psychology.* Harper and Row.

Clifford, J. (2006). Indigenous articulations. In B. Ashcroft et al. (Eds.), *The post-colonial studies reader.* Routledge.

Constantino, R. (1975). *The Philippines: A past revisited.* Tala Publishing Services.

Constantino, R. (1978). *Neocolonial identity and counter-consciousness.* M.E. Sharpe, Inc.

Damasio, A. (2003). *Looking for Spinoza.* Harcourt.

Dussel, E. (2013). *Ethics of liberation.* Duke University Press.

Enriquez, V. G. (1992). *From colonial to liberation psychology.* University of the Philippines.

Fast, J. (1973). Imperialism and bourgeois dictatorship in the Philippines. *New Left Review, 288*(March–April), 69–96.

Gastardo-Conaco, M. C. (2005). The development of a Filipino indigenous psychology. *Philippine Journal of Psychology, 38*(2), 1–17.
Gerth, H., & Wright Mills, C. (1953). *Character and social structure.* Harvourt Brace and World.
Giddens, A. (1979). *Central problems in social theory.* University of California Press.
Grossholtz, J. (1964). *The Philippines.* Little Brown & Co.
Gurvitch, G. (1971). *The social frameworks of knowledge.* Harper Torchbooks.
Harper, P., & Fullerton, L. (1993). *Philippines handbook.* Moon Publications.
Hollnsteiner, M. (1963). Social Control and Filipino Personality. *Philippine Sociological Review, 11*(3–4), 184–188.
Inwood, M. (1992). *A Hegel dictionary.* Blackwell.
Johnson, M. (2014). *Morality for humans.* University of Chicago Press.
Johnson, M. (2018). *The aesthetics of meaning and thought.* University of Chicago Press.
Jose, V. (1984). *Mortgaging the future: The World Bank and the IMF in the Philippines.* Foundation for Nationalist Studies.
Karnow, S. (1989). *In our image: America's Empire in the Philippines.* Random House.
Kintanar, T. (1996). *Cultural dictionary for Filipinos.* University of the Philippines Press.
Kramer, P. (2006). *The blood of government.* The University of North Carolina Press.
Lakoff, G., & Johnson, M. (1980). *Metaphors we live by.* University of Chicago Press.
Lakoff, G., & Johnson, M. (1999). *Philosophy in the flesh.* Basic Books.
Lynch, F. (1973). Social acceptance reconsidered. In *Four readings on Philippine values.* Institute of Philippine Culture.
Mabini, A. (1969). *The Philippine revolution* (Leon Ma. Guerrero, Trans.). National Historical Commission.
Maggay, M. (2002). *Pahiwatig.* Ateneo University Press.
Marx, K. (1964). *The economic and philosophic manuscripts of 1844* (D. J. Struik, Ed.). International Publishers.
Misak, C. (2004). C.S. Peirce on vital matters. In C. Misak (Ed.), *The Cambridge companion to Peirce.* Cambridge University Press.
Ollman, B. (1971). *Alienation: Marx's conception of man in capitalist society.* Cambridge University Press.
Ossowska, M. (1970). *Social determinants of moral ideas.* University of Pennsylvania Press.
Panganiban, J. V. (1972). *Diksyunaryo-Tesauro. Pilipino-Ingles.* Manlapaz Publishing.
Paredes-Canilao, N. & Babaran-Diaz, M. A. (2013). Sikolohiyang Pilipino: 50 years of critical-emancipatory social science in the Philippines https://thediscussantfiles.wordpress.com/2016/05/philippines%2D%2D765783.pdf./

Peirce, C. S. (1998). *The essential Peirce* (Peirce Edition Project ed.). Indiana University Press.
Peplow, E. (1991). *The Philippines: Tropical paradise*. Passport Books.
Pe-Pua, R. (2020). From indigenous psychologies to cross-indigenous psychology—Prospects for a genuine, global human psychology. In L. Sundarajan et al. (Eds.), *Global psychology from indigenous perspectives*. Palgrave Macmillan.
Pe-Pua, R., & Protacio-Marcelino, E. (2000). Sikolohiyang Pilipino (Filipino psychology): A legacy of Virgilio Enriquez. *Asian Journal of Social Psychology, 3*, 49–71.
Pforr, C. (2013). *Coca-Cola, Krags, and Uncle Sam*. Ken Incorporated.
Pomeroy, W. (1970). *American Neocolonialism*. International Publishers.
Porshnev, B. (1970). *Social psychology and history*. Progress Publishers.
Rehmann, J. (2014). *Theories of Ideology*. Haymarket Books.
Reich, W. (1972). In L. Baxandall (Ed.), *Sex-pol: Essays 1929–1934*. Vintage Books.
Roces, A., & Grace, R. (1985). *Culture shock! Philippines*. Times Books International.
Salazar, Z. (Ed.). (2004). *Sikolohiyang Panlipunan-at-Kalinangan*. Palimbagan ng Lahi.
San Juan, E. (2001). The Filipino diaspora. *Philippine Studies, 49*(2), 255–264.
San Juan, E. (2007). *U.S. imperialism and revolution in the Philippines*. Palgrave.
San Juan, E. (2021). *Maelstrom over the killing fields*. Pantax Press.
San Juan, E. (2022). Inter/cross-cultural dialogues and postcolonial indigenization in late modernity: Introducing Filipino psychology. *ResearchGate*. www.researchgate.net/publication/366918843_InterCross-cultural_Dialogues_and_Postcolonial_Indigenization_in_late-Modernity/
Santiago, C. F. (1982). Pakapa-kapa: Paglilinaw ng Isang Konsepto sa Nayon. In R. Pe-Pua (Ed.), *Sikolohiyang Pilipino*. University of the Philippines Press.
Schaff, A. (1973). *Language and Cognition*. Mcgraw-Hill.
Schiller, N. G. (1997). Cultural politics and the politics of culture. *Identities: Global Studies in Culture and Power, 4*(1), 1–7.
Schirmer, D. B. (1987). The conception and gestation of a NeoColony. In D. B. Schirmer & S. Shalom (Eds.), *The Philippines reader*. South End Press.
Scott, W. H. (1982). *Cracks in the parchment*. New Day Publishers.
Seve, L. (1978). *Man in Marxist theory and the psychology of personality*. The Harvester Press.
Shalom, S. (1987). Counter-insurgency in the Philippines. In *The Philippines reader*. South End Press.
Silverman, K. (1983). *The subject of semiotics*. Oxford University Press.
Sison, J. M. (2016). *Continuing the struggle for national and social liberation*. International Network for Philippine Studies.
Stiglitz, J. (2002). *Globalization and its discontents*. W.W. Norton.
Torres, A. T. (1982). Pakapa-kapa as an approach in Philippine psychology. In R. Pe-Pua (Ed.), *Sikolohiyang Pilipino*. University of the Philippines Press.

Varela, F., Thompson, E., & Rosch, E. (2016). *The embodied mind*. MIT Press.
Veneracion, J. (1987). *Agos ng Dugong Kayumanggi*. Education Forum.
Vicassan. (2006). Vicassan's Pilipino-English dictionary (Abridged Edition). Manila: Anvil.
Voloshinov, V. N. (1976). *Freudianism: A Marxist critique*. Academic Press.
Vygotsky, L. (1962). *Thought and language*. MIT Press.
Wallerstein, I. (1974). *The modern world system*. Academic Press.
Whorf, B. L. (1956). *Language, thought and reality*. MIT Press.
Yacat, J. (2013). Filipino psychology. In K. Keith (Ed.), *The encyclopedia of cross-cultural psychology*. John Wiley and Sons Inc.
Yates, M. D. (2003). *Naming the system*. Monthly Review Press.

PART III

Indigenous Identities and Social Positions

CHAPTER 8

Cultural Politics, Authenticity, and (Strategic) Essentialism: Exploring How Urban Māori Youth Navigate Māori Identity

Logan Hamley

Introduction

This chapter is adapted from my PhD thesis (Hamley, 2023b), a qualitative study that was developed to explore, among other things, how young Māori construct a sense of identity as Māori in urban contexts today. It examines some ideas expressed by a group of Māori youth living in Auckland, the largest city in Aotearoa, New Zealand (henceforth, Aotearoa). Indigenous peoples who grow up in urban contexts are often positioned as less 'authentically' Indigenous because of the associations of urban spaces with Westernization and globalization (Marek, 2020; Nejad et al., 2019). I was interested in how Māori youth differently embraced or resisted such discourses of authenticity to craft their own sense of identity as Māori.

L. Hamley (✉)
Whakauae Researcher Services, Whanganui, New Zealand
e-mail: logan@whakauae.co.nz

Z. Z. Gao, M. I. Medved (eds.), *Global Perspectives on Cultural Politics in Indigenous Psychology*, Palgrave Studies in Indigenous Psychology, https://doi.org/10.1007/978-3-031-96813-6_8

Such a question has a layer of irony in it since prior to the arrival of Europeans in the late eighteenth and early nineteenth centuries, the notion of a collective Māori identity hardly existed (Ballara, 1998). Instead, there existed (and continues to exist) an array of iwi (tribe, extended kinship group), hapū (subtribe, kinship group), and whānau (extended family) groupings through which people construct(ed) their identity. These different collectives form part of whakapapa, the genealogical layers that represent the social reality that Māori move through. Whakapapa relationships also extend beyond humans, connecting to landscapes and waterscapes that nurture and support communities, as well as the wider spiritual realm (Durie, 1995; Greaves et al., 2023; Walker, 1990). However, with the arrival of Europeans (now commonly referred to as Pākehā) and the colonization of Aotearoa in the nineteenth century, Māori have experienced an array of attempts to disrupt Māori identity formation, including urbanization, assimilation, and state interventions on collective identities (Kukutai, 2004; Maddison, 2013).

However, Māori, like other Indigenous communities, have consistently resisted the impacts of colonization and imagined alternative ways of being in the world. Much of this work has been mobilized around identity, particularly the strengthening of collective identities (REF). The United Nations Declaration on the Rights of Indigenous Peoples recognizes the right of Indigenous peoples to their (UN General Assembly, 2006). Articles 11 through 16, in particular, outline the right of Indigenous peoples to their cultural practices and their revitalization. While there is a clear impetus from the United Nations, Indigenous literature has also highlighted the holistic well-being benefits of a strong cultural identity (Bourke et al., 2018). Cultural identity, for example, is seen as a protective factor against structural oppressions like racism and colonization, which negatively impact Māori well-being and more individual factors like suicidal ideation and depressive symptoms (Fox et al., 2018; Muriwai et al., 2015; Williams et al., 2018). As such, Māori scholarly work has often advocated for the strengthening of cultural identity as a formative part of both decolonizing within communities, but also as part of healing the historical trauma experienced by Māori communities.

Tensions in Strengthening Cultural Identity

While there is clear value in strengthening cultural identity, a key question emerges from it: *what* does a strong cultural identity look like for Māori? Within the literature on Māori identity, there have been various efforts to delineate what a strong cultural identity looks like, often determined by particular identity markers. These markers commonly include knowledge or fluency in te reo Māori (the Māori language), engagement with marae (an ancestral complex most commonly connected to specific iwi and hapū), and belonging to and knowledge of one's iwi, hapū, and whānau, as what constitute a strong Māori identity (Borell, 2005; Durie, 1995; Moeke-Pickering, 1996; Rata, 2015). While these markers are undoubtedly important for many Māori, their everyday experiences of these markers vary widely across Māori communities.

For example, only around one in five Māori today speak te reo Māori (the Māori language) at least fairly well (Statistics New Zealand, 2020). Similarly, 17% of Māori report not knowing their iwi, and slightly over 30% of Māori report not knowing their marae (Kukutai & Rārērē, 2015). These data are rarely reflections of individual desire to forgo cultural engagement, but more often reflections of the processes of settler colonialism and neoliberalism that have constrained the capacity for some Māori to practice culture in the ways that we did previously (Kukutai & Webber, 2011; Maddison, 2013). However, as noted by Ahuriri-Driscoll and Blake (2024), some Māori are still positioned as more or less 'authentic, ' as shaped by their upbringing or ways of enculturation to being Māori. While their research focuses on Māori adoptees (particularly those raised by non-Māori in closed adoption contexts), urban Māori and Māori youth are also often similarly positioned as holding less authentic identities as Māori (Kukutai & Webber, 2017; Meredith, 2000).

This chapter then explores some of the complexities and contradictions Māori youth encounter while constructing their own Māori culture and identity among the wider discourses of authenticity. In particular, I am interested in exploring what occurs when Māori youth are positioned as 'less' Māori, how they understand this experience, and often how they reject this positioning in favor of other approaches to describing their identity.

Method

To explore these complexities, I draw on poetic inquiry informed by semi-structured interviews with 22 young Māori men about their experiences of identity and coming to know themselves as Māori. Ethics approval was granted by the University of Auckland in July 2019, with the research being conducted between 2019 and 2022. As an Indigenous bricoleur (Hamley et al., 2021), I wove Kaupapa Māori (Pihama et al., 2015) and Indigenous story work (Archibald, 2008) with poetic inquiry to craft a broader narrative about Māori identity and culture. My approach to poetic inquiry takes the form of data poetry, where I have formed the poem from interview transcripts, focusing on surprise and intrigue as guides for dynamic poetry (Brinkmann, 2014; Prendergast, 2015). The poem, as it is composed of direct quotes from young Māori men, represents their perspectives to some degree. However, I have selected specific narratives and (re)presented their words in relation to one another. As such, the poem (*The box*) is more a mosaic that I have crafted than the unmediated voice of Māori men.

In *the box* and subsequent analysis, I seek to describe the ways that a categorical approach to identity impacts Māori youth, especially those who 'fail' to meet the criteria of 'the box.' I then explore alternative relational ways of theorizing identity that both reflect the underpinning philosophy of whakapapa and can more accurately reflect the diverse ways of being that Māori express today. Occasionally, I will expand on sections of the poem through placing them within a wider quote. In these situations, I provided the quoted Māori youth with a pseudonym.

The Box
I guess there's a box sort of thing
If you don't fit this criteria or know this about the Māori culture
I've had people be like,
How are you Māori?
You're white, you can't be Māori

If you couldn't speak the language,
If you were too light-skinned,
If you didn't fit the description of what Pākehā would say,
Then you're a
Plastic Māori

Yeah I've been called plastic
By other Māori
It's embarrassing
But on the other hand
I'm like
Can you speak it?
You can't judge me

It just kind of puts you
Into an upper class and lower class
Of your ethnicity
I doubt it's a good thing.
Only a good thing for the people on the top
Just like any other class.

Plastic is like a put down I guess
Saying that you're Māori
But
You're not quite enough to be **just** Māori

Back in year 10
I was playing cricket and was in Māori class
We had to do kapa haka
And those two clashed
Kapa haka training was on Saturdays but then I also had cricket
I had to choose

I ended up choosing cricket
I was already behind in all the words and moves for kapa haka
I just went towards cricket
I can't describe it

This year I felt like I needed to *redeem* myself
Everyone calls me a plastic Māori
Tried to prove them wrong by doing kapa haka this year
I hope that changes peoples' views

In terms of being Māori
There were a lot of things that were imparted on me
That I wasn't aware of
Language, tikanga, whakapapa
But at home it still didn't feel very Māori
Now there's a sense of what I did learn and what I did know
Were the deeper ways of being Māori

How you conduct yourself
Your character
How you relate to other people
Break the ice
Aroha, whakawhanaungatanga, manaakitanga
Brown values

At the end of the day I'm Māori
I'm Māori not necessarily because of the color of my skin
But how I choose to live my life
I represent my culture with pride
If they can't see that
It's not my problem

I think being Māori is just knowledge of your whakapapa
Of your family
Knowledge of the Māori culture
We come in all shapes and sizes
There is so much beauty in our culture
That's what I think being Māori is

Analysis

The categorization of Māori identity continues today and was a prominent feature of how Māori youth discussed Māori culture and their identities. In particular, Māori youth described a set of fixed and deterministic traits that cohered to be(come) an authentic Māori culture and identity.

If you couldn't speak the language,
If you were too light-skinned
If you didn't fit the description of what Pākehā would say,
Then you're were a
Plastic Māori

Based on the dominant representations of Māori culture, we might imagine a "*box*" based on specific "*criteria*" that determines who is Māori and who is not. Particular cultural norms within this box hold constitutive power as the dominant representation of Māori identity (Borell, 2005). Māori youth who are unable to demonstrate these criteria can have their identity contested, whether by Māori or non-Māori (cf. Kukutai & Webber, 2017). This section then focuses on the 'box' of Māori culture and identity, considering how a categorical description of Māori culture and identity, when embedded in broader colonial power relations, leaves some Māori youth in compromised identity spaces. This argument centers on how repressive authenticities, lateral violence, and the drive for (re) connection can shape ambivalent identity experiences because of the larger systems of oppression that shape Māori identity possibilities.

Authenticity, Power, and Plasticity

Māori youth were highly attuned to dominant discourses of Māori identity and the various criteria that can restrict them from holding an 'authentic' Māori identity. In Māori youth contexts, this authenticity was often described by who/what was and was not 'plastic'; Māori who did not fit into the criteria of the box were seen as plastic. The criteria of the box included physical characteristics, te reo Māori, and knowledge of traditions in determining who could be classified as authentically Māori. Plastic then serves to label someone who is perceived as inauthentic and not a 'real' Māori. Performing culture 'correctly' then be(comes) a crucial requirement for Māori youth who want to avoid a subordinate plastic identity.

Maddison (2013) highlights how a fixed idea of Indigeneity constructs a hierarchy of authenticity among Indigenous peoples. In this way, plasticity is invariably tied to wider power relations, linked to claims-making about who is a 'real' Māori and who is not. Māori youth describe how the idea of plastic Māori constructs a hierarchy of "*upper class and lower class*" Māori. Using plastic as an insult then can create a power imbalance, where the utterer is positioned as authentically Māori "*upper class*" and therefore higher in the hierarchy than the person who is "plastic" (and thus inauthentically Māori and "*lower class*"). Theoretically, then, "*upper class*" Māori could be able to deploy the term 'plastic' as a way of reinforcing their power of making claims over other Māori.

In this way, tradition as authentic Māori identity could be(come) a strategy that empowers particular claims/people (Hokowhitu, 2013). Kukutai and Webber (2011) highlight that in contexts where cultural credentials are esteemed, those who hold those credentials can enact a particular kind of (valorized) Māori identity. Māori who do not necessarily look, speak, or live 'traditionally' can then be readily dismissed as not Māori enough in spaces where authenticity is required to hold power. If "*you're not quite enough to be just Māori*," you risk being marginalized in spaces where there are implicit or explicit expectations to perform a particular Māori identity.

Plastic Identity and Lateral Violence

For Māori youth, the impacts of authenticity and culture were higher during discussions where their own identity had been questioned by other Māori, most often other Māori youth. Matiu described how plastic, as a term, was a common form of lateral violence within Māori youth contexts to describe Māori youth who did not fit within the 'box':

Matiu *The things that I use to differentiate plastic and not plastic is usually just if they can speak [te reo Māori], how knowledgeable they are I guess, how aware of the culture's customs, and then probably personality a little bit, maybe, maybe not.*
Logan *Have you ever been called plastic or anything like that by someone?*
Matiu *Yeah, only by other Māori.*
Logan *What is it like when someone calls you plastic?*
Matiu *One side of the hand that's embarrassing but then on the other side, who are you to say that? Like can you speak it, like, you can't judge me, what are you? That's the way I see, I haven't really had someone who was a hearty Māori say that to me. It's just been the boys at school who are just as plastic or maybe just a little bit less so I kind of just disregard it but at the same point I do feel embarrassed.*

In this account, Matiu highlights how Māori youth can shore up their identity by marginalizing other Māori youth who are not able to 'hold' the valorized identity of Māori. Within a colonial context where Māori youth may themselves be positioned as marginal, one way of asserting their identity may be to marginalize others. As such, plastic can be used not only by those who are "*upper class*" Māori, but also those who are, in this analogy, "*lower class*" too.

Māori youth then might use this 'tool' even when they had their own experiences of being called plastic and the intimate knowledge of how it had made them feel lesser compared to someone else. In this sense, derogating others for being 'plastic' could be effective for them (in that it achieves its intended outcome of bolstering one's identity), but it could also quickly become undermined by others who use it against them. This back-and-forth was associated with a sense of embarrassment, shame, pain, and anger. "*[Y]ou*" (who called me plastic) have no right to "*judge me.*' You are as precarious in this hierarchy as I am (you cannot speak te reo Māori and therefore should not be able to position yourself at a higher level). However, this awareness of pain did not stop some Māori youth from continuing to use it as a way of (re)accruing cultural capital and affirming their (Māori) identity over others.

Māori youth could also resist the claim of being plastic in other ways. Taika described his approach this way:

> *oh yeah I've had people be like, 'how are you Māori? You're white and you can't be Māori. You're plastic'. I hear that like heaps of times but I don't really pay attention to that because it's negative energy. It's just not something that I want to take on… over the years, after you hear it, you sort of realize, that's not what I think, I think I'm this and I'm going to represent my culture with pride and I don't care what you say. You know, at the end of the day I'm Māori and I represent my culture with pride and if they can't see that then not my problem.*

Taika in this excerpt, highlights that he could be positioned as 'plastic' by others. However, he was able to construct an alternative narrative of Māori identity and culture that was centered around whakapapa and pride as the core tenets of 'being' Māori. This formulation of Māori identity is harder to derogate since it is connected to genealogy. If you have Māori whakapapa, you belong and are therefore Māori (Burgess & Painting, 2020).

Plastic, a term that circulates around Māori youth spaces, highlights the ways in which cultural identity continues to be contested. Māori identity, particularly in school contexts, became a performance that could be validated or, more often, invalidated by others. An identity paradox can then occur within school contexts, where being diminished as 'less Māori' than others becomes a common identity experience for Māori youth. Plastic, as a challenge to identity, is another form of lateral violence that is enacted against Māori youth (Berryman & Eley, 2019; Whyman et al., 2021).

How plastic identity is taken up could also have broader impacts than just individualized pain for Māori youth. Wolfe (1994) draws on the concepts of repressive authenticity to highlight how Indigenous peoples must perform a 'precolonial' Indigeneity to be considered legitimate. Settler societies require Indigenous peoples to 'perform' a particular expression of culture to receive symbolic and material recognition from the state. Indigenous peoples who are unable to perform these limiting representations of Indigenous cultures are often in a precarious space of being 'eliminated', having their Indigeneity not recognized by the State (cf. Wolfe, 2006).

Within the context of Aotearoa, 'plastic' can serve as a settler-colonial tool that can 'eliminate' Māori. Deploying 'plastic Māori' can be a way of diminishing someone's authority to speak as Māori (their perspective is plastic; it is not a real or authentic Māori perspective). 'Plastic' Māori thus require no special (cultural) considerations or resourcing (cf. Maddison, 2013). Plasticity becomes a term for a form of cultural disconnection that equates to being Pākehā. That is to say, if someone is 'plastic', they 'act' or 'are' Pākehā. A binary is constructed where those who do not fit within a Māori 'box' are then forced into a Pākehā 'box'. Ultimately, this practice of assessing 'authenticity' can reduce the number of Māori who can make legitimate claims about Māori culture or even require/receive specific support and resourcing 'as Māori.' By shaping who can claim a legitimized Indigenous identity, the settler state can restrict the number of Indigenous people it must engage with (Wolfe, 2006). This elimination is the ultimate goal of the settler colonial nation, ensuring 'successful' replacement of the Indigenous nation(s) by the colonial one (Wolfe, 1994).

Maddison (2013) argues that the definition of Indigenous identities has been one of the most powerful technologies of settler colonialism. Hierarchies of authenticity, as rooted in the notion of a fixed (colonial) Māori identity, can enable large-scale disenfranchisement of Māori, not only of their whakapapa but also of their ability to mobilize around a Māori identity. These contestations regarding 'authentic' Māori identity are thus rooted in the colonial and structural violence that seeks to regulate, control, and eliminate Indigenous identity. Plastic identity, in marginalizing Māori from an affirming Māori identity, can then represent one form of assimilation-as-elimination that further ensnares Māori in colonial imaginings of Indigeneity as historic and outmoded.

It is for these reasons I am ultimately wary of how Māori take up and (re)produce 'plastic' (or any marginalizing phrase) as an insult because it can quickly be(come) aligned with the colonial strategy of elimination. My wariness is not the same as stating that Māori cannot hold one another accountable if we reproduce coloniality. I agree with Watego (2021), who states that we must be able to recognize that Indigeneity is relational, embodied, and reflexive, and thus open to dialogue and challenge. However, as Watego (2021) urges, we must be sovereign over our stories and selves in ways that do not further enmesh us within colonial narratives of Māori identity. This requires Māori to reflect on whether concepts like plastic can garner the futures and change we want to see. Ultimately, I argue that terms like plastic are too rooted in settler coloniality representations of authenticity to be able to liberate Māori from coloniality.

Reconnection: An Easy Answer?

Often related to plastic identity is the language of (re)connection. Plastic Māori who wish to reject this label are often encouraged to undergo a process of (re)connection, which is considered to transform them into an authentic Māori (cf. Maddison, 2013). Connected then to a discourse of authenticity is also the idea of connection to culture (and identity). To have a strong and positive identity as a Māori is to be connected to the dominant markers of Māori culture. This idea of cultural connection has been described in various ways: cultural efficacy (Greaves, 2017), engagement (Durie, 2001), or embeddedness (Fox et al., 2018). Māori who are versed in these markers then provide them to Māori who are 'disconnected', providing them with an 'authentic' Māori identity to improve their well-being and sense of self.

In this way, a dominant description of identity reconnection often assumes a common form. Reconnection becomes a neat, linear, unidirectional journey of culture reclamation: a person becomes 'reconnected' with their Māori identity and builds a positive sense of self, which then enables them to flourish. While reconnection to Māori culture can be a positive experience, the over-representation of this narrative at the expense of different possibilities I argue can be unhelpful. In particular, a simplistic and linear journey from being disconnected to (re)connected ignores the many ways in which this process of cultural engagement can be complex, nonlinear, and deeply ambivalent for Māori youth (or any Māori).

Atama described how his engagement with kapa haka (Māori performing arts) was a response to being challenged about being 'plastic':

> *I was in Māori class and we had to do kapa haka. And, I remember those two being a clash because kapa haka training was on Saturdays but then I also had cricket and I had to choose and I ended up choosing cricket probably because I was already behind in all the words and moves for kapa. I can't describe it but I just went towards cricket. Then this year I felt like I needed to redeem myself cause everyone calls me silver tongue or just like a plastic Māori, and so I tried proving them wrong by doing kapa haka this year and yeah. I hope that changes views.*

Rather than being a way of engaging with Māori ways of being and knowing or even finding a community at school where being Māori is nurtured, for Atama, performing kapa haka is a way of proving people "*wrong*" about his status as "*plastic.*" Cricket was not 'Māori' and so Atama choosing to do cricket over kapa haka meant he was 'inauthentically' Māori at school. To resist this claim, Atama required redemption through 'reconnecting' with an authentic Māori identity using kapa haka. This act, he hoped, would shift the perception of other Māori students and render him 'authentic'.

Other Māori youth similarly described how learning te reo Māori could enable them to challenge the idea that they were 'less' Māori than others. Engagement with Māori culture can be(come) what Māori youth feel they *have* to perform to prove something about themselves to others (they were a 'real' Māori). Engaging in what could be joyful, exciting, and affirming cultural practices like kapa haka then take on more ambivalent affect positions. Practices that are part of the 'box' of Māori identity can be(come) coercive through how other Māori may discipline you for not performing culture (correctly).

These processes highlight the complexities of creating meaningful connections to different elements of Māori culture when the Māori identity is readily contested. Tensions (or coercion) can 'push' Māori youth to engage in 'Māori' things, but perhaps in ways which may lead to them resenting this process:

> *I went to*
> *one of them you know fully immersive primary schools*
> *threw me off learning the language*
> *I didn't like my time there*
> *I didn't fit in there*
> *Didn't speak*
> *It made me distance myself from aspects of*
> *being Māori*
> *lots of Māori can't speak it*
> *so it's not like I'm the odd one out*

When the box plays out in the lives of Māori youth who have had limited access to these markers of culture, it can create an array of different possibilities for them. Rather than kura kaupapa Māori (Māori-immersion primary school) presenting as an opportunity for joyous (re)connection, some youth felt excluded because of their limited knowledge of te reo Māori. Because the language often features heavily within the dominant representations of Māori identity, this led some youth to also forgo engaging with other expressions of Māori culture.

Interestingly, some youth could construct an alternative affirming Māori identity through asserting the number of Māori who do not speak te reo. Both positions (real Māori speak te reo Māori or lots of Māori do not speak te reo Māori so it does not matter if I do not) represent different ends of the disappointing spectrum of coloniality. I argue both positions can reproduce settler coloniality; the first eliminates the majority of Māori from valorized identities (creating 'upper class' and 'lower class' Māori), while the second reproduces the colonial marginalization of te reo Māori (and dominance of English). This binary reveals the broader challenges where Māori identity is variously undermined and shaped by the politics of settler colonialism (Hamley, 2023a).

Equally, customary practices and spaces outside of the school context could also create complex identity journeys for Māori youth. Ihaka spoke about the complexities of a whānau tangihanga (funeral). Commonly, tangihanga are opportunities for whānau and community to come together to both collectively grieve and celebrate the life of a loved one who has passed on (Nikora et al., 2012; Nikora & Te Awekotuku, 2016). As such, the cultural practices at a tangihanga provide opportunities for Māori to come together as Māori and perform social practices that are otherwise widely absent from urban life. However, this process can be complicated for Māori youth, who may be constrained in their ability to perform different roles on the marae due to the impacts of colonialism and urbanization on their whānau.

These opportunities for (re)connection with whānau and a certain kind of Māori culture may not seem as meaningful when they have not been present in the life of Māori youth outside of tangihanga:

Ihaka	*I went to my other great uncle's funeral. A couple months back…I mean, a whole lot of people, a whole lot of great-aunts and uncles that I never even knew I had.*
Logan	*And what was that like?*
Ihaka	*That was pretty. It was like, it wasn't overwhelming. But it was just like, wow, there's a lot of family here that knows me. But I don't know them. And they're like, I saw you when you're this height. And I'm like, I don't know you. Yeah."*

Ihaka described the asymmetry that can occur in these relational spaces, where his whānau had known him when he was "*this*" height (suggesting when he was very young) but that he did not "*know*" them. The implication behind these phrases hints at the ways in which whānau may once have been involved in this young person's life but had not been there for a long time. While his whānau had fond memories of him, he did not recognize any of them and therefore could not reciprocate their excitement. Going to the tangihanga was not "*overwhelming*" (in that it was a negative experience which discouraged him from engaging in Māori culture), nor was it a formative moment which encouraged him to explore his identity and whānau background more. It simply was *an* experience of identity he recounted that others assumed *should* be impactful. However, for him, it was not (at least at the time he described it to me). Although tangihanga are positioned as a formative process for reforging bonds within whānau, this may not necessarily be the case. Reconnection as a process is more than simply bringing Māori youth into Māori contexts; there is deeper work required.

Problematizing Reconnection in Colonial Contexts

In exploring narratives of Māori youth, I argue that we need a new language for describing our collective aspirations for Māori. Most Māori desire a future in which Māori youth can speak te reo Māori, practice Māori culture, and collectively flourish. I, too, dream of this for my nephews and for all others who come after me. But I think our language, centered on connection (whether dis- or re-connection), is poorly equipped to achieve that future. When Māori are pathologized or pitied as plastic/disconnected, and (re)connection to culture is positioned as *the* answer to resolving the issues they face, we create an array of cultural tensions.

A static, precolonial culture once again becomes reified as central to an 'ideal' Māori identity, one that risks reinforcing a colonial context that further disenfranchises Māori (youth). Within this colonizing context, connection can set up an implicit deficit framing of Māori who are (imagined as) 'disconnected'. Māori become defined by what they lack ('connection') as opposed to what they create in response to the (presumed) lack of 'connection' to Māori culture. This lack of culture becomes the focus of conversation. 'Disconnected' Māori cannot be viewed as vibrant and self-determining people making decisions based on their contexts and aspirations (Borell et al., 2020). How Māori youth (and other Māori) continue to embody Māori practices and repurpose them in their everyday lives is foregone.

Further, considering the discourses of neoliberal personal responsibility that pervade society, 'disconnected' Māori are now increasingly impelled to engage in the process of constructing a particular kind of Māori identity, despite the many barriers to doing so within (urban) contemporary spaces (Borell et al., 2020). Those who are unable to 'reconnect' are considered at fault for being unable to do so or are positioned as passive victims of colonization. A narrative of disconnection then draws us into gazing at (disconnected) people, enabling the colonial conditions and systems that constrain Māori from becoming 'connected' to remain unquestioned. The colonial systems that reproduce Māori inequities continue to be(come) the natural and normal conditions that we must (re)build connections within.

It is impossible for Māori to be disconnected from our whakapapa; we are always part of a broader set of relationships, whether we are (fully) aware of these relationships or not (Burgess & Painting, 2020). However, the nuances of whakapapa can often be marginalized within the context of colonization and discourses of authenticity and plasticity that circulate in our social milieu. The challenges lie not in simply rejecting people's experiences of disconnection (in that they may *feel* disconnected) but in locating that within a colonial legacy. There are many intersecting complexities for those growing up feeling 'disconnected'; a term like disconnection erases these nuances. When trying to revitalize, regenerate, or (re)create Māori customs, I argue that we must also resist individualizing the harms of colonization and expecting individuals to undo intergenerational trauma. This requires us to move beyond the individual 'disconnected' Māori to thinking about strategies of dismantling coloniality.

Beyond the Box?

The previous sections highlighted how the dominant cultural 'box' positions Māori in fixed categories (McIntosh, 2005; Rata, 2015). These identity positions have differential power possibilities, where plastic/disconnected identities are often derogated. This derogation can be uncomfortably linked to repressive authenticity that enables the assimilation of marginalized Indigenous peoples. This process of elimination also creates spaces where lateral violence among Māori youth generates harm and pain, complicating the ability for Māori youth to nurture affirming identities as Māori. Even idealized notions of (re)connection as resistance can be(come) complicated in a sociocultural context where Māori youth are *expected* to perform a particular expression of Māori culture to have a valorized identity. While there are many ways in which Māori youth would like support to (re)connect to Māori culture, a focus on filling the 'gaps' left by colonization also marginalizes the many ways in which Māori youth continue to express Māori identities in (k)new ways.

Of course, this process needs to acknowledge the reclamation of Māori identity and culture which has occurred over the past 50 years. Part of this reclamation has involved the strategic essentialism (Spivak, 2006) of Māori being essentially different than Pākehā. When a group has been economically, socially, and politically marginalized by colonization, drawing on strategic essentialism can be a pragmatic decision. Essentialism has been a resource Māori have drawn on to gain (material) resources from the state (or state agencies). It is difficult to say if legislative change, funding schemes, kaupapa Māori organizations, or the myriad of other political actions Māori have taken could have been successful without some sort of fixed view of culture.

However, I am critical of whether strategic essentialism can enable the re-configuration of power relations needed for self-determination and Māori emancipation. A discourse of authenticity can slide all too easily into colonial binaries that fix us as historic and colonial partners (cf. Ahuriri-Driscoll & Blake, 2024). If researchers, practitioners, or whānau perceive Māori youth as solely plastic or disconnected it marginalizes the many ways in which Māori youth are fostering a positive sense of Māori culture on their own terms. The final section of this chapter directs our attention towards this task.

Plasticity and New Directions for Māori Youth Identity

Dudgeon (2016) emphasizes the need for Aboriginal peoples in Australia to critically reflect on what their cultures mean to them, how that culture is expressed, and who can determine what culture is for their nation(s). To me, she is speaking about looking at the nexus of tradition, colonization, strategic essentialism, and history, and then thinking about what can or should be brought into the future. This is crucial and ongoing work as part of a broader reclamation and journey of Indigenous pride and futurism, something which the colonial project worldwide has sought to eliminate in Indigenous peoples.

When looking at this spiraling nexus in Aotearoa, I see much hope. "*Deeper ways of being Māori*" were commonly discussed as important to Māori youth. This could be a conscious engagement with the culture (speaking te reo Māori, doing kapa haka) or an embodied and spiritual engagement with the culture (performing roles and values like "*break the ice*" or "*brown values*"). This potentiality can be nurtured within the everyday whānau contexts in both urban and rural spaces that are constantly reshaped and reformed to meet their needs and aspirations. Often these values and expressions were considered the foundational values and practices of the culture, suggesting that these are still relevant to young people today (King et al., 2018; Le Grice et al., 2017).

Equally, Māori youth bring with them new ways of being Māori. They do not simply accept inequity or marginalization; they actively resist and challenge ideas of being "plastic." I want to appropriate the language of plastic to highlight Māori youth *plasticity*, their ability to bend and shape, as a skill and talent that should be recognized and celebrated. Māori youth plasticity does not spring from a space of deficit or disconnection but rather from a space of potential. Māori youth plasticity asserts that Māori youth have a key role in the process of culture making and the ability to be agentic in asserting diverse expressions of Māori culture as part of their identity development. Māori youth can stretch and bend, snapping 'back' to customary practices or extending to reach new horizons of possibilities for Māori. Whether in the arts, sports, technology, or the many various passions of Māori youth, they unfurl new possibilities for future generations through their plasticity. This plasticity resonates with the term routed hybridity discussed by Gonzalez (2010). In her research with members of Ngāti Kahungunu (an iwi of the East Coast of the North Island of New Zealand), Gonzalez highlights how Ngāti Kahungunu identity persists in urban contexts but is transformed through engagements with urban contexts.

I want to close with a recognition of the relationality of Māori culture to help foster a broader space for imagining Māori identity and culture. The foundations of whakapapa emphasize that we connect to one another and that whakapapa guides our relationships with the world around us. Similarly, we need to center our recognition of Māori identity on this relationality. Māori are not and have never been a homogenous group. Our connections to one another may be partial (whether coming from different iwi, hapū, and whānau, speaking or not speaking te reo Māori); however, this partiality is not an invalidation of Māori identity as a collective one. We do not have to be 'the same' in order to qualify as having a meaningful and rich social identity. Indeed, as Māori, our diversity is too rich to conform to an essentialized identity. Our culture has always been fluid. It has moved and shifted as our ancestors moved across the Pacific, encountering new contexts which have shaped their practices. We are entitled to the same potential today.

Conflicts of Interest The author declares no conflicts of interest.

References

Ahuriri-Driscoll, A., & Blake, D. (2024). Contesting the margins of coloniality: Māori adoptee identities in the context of Māori identity scholarship. *Identities*, 1–20. https://doi.org/10.1080/1070289X.2024.2309823

Archibald, J. A. (2008). *Indigenous storywork: Educating the heart, mind, body, and spirit*. UBC press.

Ballara, A. (1998). *Iwi: The dynamics of Māori tribal organisation from c.1769 to c.1945*. Victoria University Press.

Berryman, M., & Eley, E. (2019). Student belonging: Critical relationships and responsibilities. *International Journal of Inclusive Education, 23*(9), 985–1001. https://doi.org/10.1080/13603116.2019.1602365

Borell, B. (2005). *Living in the city ain't so bad: Cultural diversity of South Auckland rangatahi: A thesis submitted in partial fulfilment of a Masters of Philosophy in Psychology* [Masters]. Massey University.

Borell, B., Waru Rewiri, K. T., Barnes, H. M., & McCreanor, T. (2020). Beyond the veil: Kaupapa Māori gaze on the non-Māori subject. *Journal of Sociology, 56*(2), 197–212. https://doi.org/10.1177/1440783319893503

Bourke, S., Wright, A., Guthrie, J., Russell, L., Dunbar, T., & Lovett, R. (2018). Evidence review of indigenous culture for health and wellbeing. *The International Journal of Health, Wellness, and Society, 8*(4), 11–27. https://doi.org/10.18848/2156-8960/CGP/v08i04/11-27

Brinkmann, S. (2014). Doing without data. *Qualitative Inquiry, 20*(6), 720–725. https://doi.org/10.1177/1077800414530254

Burgess, H., & Painting, T. K. (2020). Onamata, anamata: A whakapapa perspective of Māori futurisms. In A.-M. Murtola & S. Walsh (Eds.), *Whose futures?* (pp. 207–233). Economic and Social Research Aotearoa.

Dudgeon, P. (2016). Decolonising identities: Aboriginal Asian identity. *The Journal of Critical Psychology, Counselling and Psychotherapy, 223*, 223–232.

Durie, M. (2001). *Mauri Ora: The dynamics of Maori health*. Oxford University Press.

Durie, M. H. (1995). Te Hoe Nuku Roa framework: A Maori identity measure. *The Journal of the Polynesian Society, 104*(4), 461–470.

Fox, R., Neha, T., & Jose, P. E. (2018). Tū Māori Mai: Māori Cultural Embeddeness Improves Adaptive Coping and Wellbeing for Māori Adolescents. *New Zealand Journal of Psychology, 47*(2), 14–24.

Gonzalez, C. M. (2010). *Be(com)ing Ngāti Kahungunu in the Diaspora: Iwi Identity and Social Organisation in Wellington* [Master's thesis, Victoria University of Wellington]. https://openaccess.wgtn.ac.nz/articles/thesis/_Be_com_ing_Ngati_Kahungunu_in_the_Diaspora_Iwi_Identity_and_Social_Organisation_in_Wellington/16973926?file=31398202

Greaves, L. (2017). *He Pōkēkē Uenuku I Tū Ai: A quantitative exploration of Māori identity, political attitudes, and behaviour* [Doctor of Philosophy, University of Auckland]. http://hdl.handle.net/2292/37064

Greaves, L. M., Lindsay Latimer, C., Li, E., & Hamley, L. (2023). Well-being and cultural identity for Māori: Knowledge of iwi (tribal) affiliations does not strongly relate to health and social service outcomes. *Social Science & Medicine, 329*, 116028. https://doi.org/10.1016/j.socscimed.2023.116028

Hamley, L. (2023a). Intergenerational affect, language trauma, and pride: Young Māori men's emotional experiences of Te Reo Māori. *Journal of Language, Identity & Education, 1–14.* https://doi.org/10.1080/15348458.2023.2281955

Hamley, L. (2023b). *Whakapapa, "the box", and beyond: Poems, (re)presentations and the potentiality of rangatahi tāne identities in Auckland* [PhD]. University of Auckland.

Hamley, L., Groot, S., Le Grice, J., Gillon, A., Greaves, L., Manchi, M., & Clark, T. (2021). "You're the One That Was on Uncle's Wall!": Identity, Whanaungatanga and Connection for Takatāpui (LGBTQ+ Māori). *Genealogy, 5*(2), 54. https://doi.org/10.3390/genealogy5020054

Hokowhitu, B. (2013). Producing indigeneity. In C. Andersen & E. J. Peters (Eds.), *Indigenous in the City: Contemporary identities and cultural innovation* (pp. 354–376). UBC Press.

King, P., Hodgetts, D., Rua, M., & Morgan, M. (2018). When the Marae Moves into the city: Being Māori in urban Palmerston North. *City & Community, 17*(4), 1189–1208. https://doi.org/10.1111/cico.12355

Kukutai, T. (2004). The problem of defining an ethnic group for public policy: Who is Māori and why does it matter? *Social Policy Journal of New Zealand, 23*, 86–108.

Kukutai, T., & Rārērē, M. (2015). *Te ao hurihuri: Iwi identification in the census (NIDEA Brief)* (pp. 1–4). National Institute of Demographic and Economic Analysis (NIDEA). https://hdl.handle.net/10289/9764

Kukutai, T., & Webber, M. (2011). Navigating the "space between": Authenticity and identity in "Maori" Social Science. *New Zealand Sociology, 26*, 4–20.

Kukutai, T., & Webber, M. (2017). Ka Pū Te Ruha, Ka Hao Te Rangatahi: Maori identities in the twenty-first century. In A. Bell, T. Elizabeth, T. McIntosh, & M. Wynyard (Eds.), *A Land of Milk and Honey? Making Sense of Aotearoa New Zealand* (pp. 71–82). Auckland University Press.

Le Grice, J., Braun, V., & Wetherell, M. (2017). "What I reckon is, is that like the love you give to your kids they'll give to someone else and so on and so on": Whanaungatanga and matauranga Maori in practice. *New Zealand Journal of Psychology, 46*(3), 88–97.

Maddison, S. (2013). Indigenous identity, 'authenticity' and the structural violence of settler colonialism. *Identities, 20*(3), 288–303. https://doi.org/10.1080/1070289X.2013.806267

Marek, S. A. (2020). Indigenous urban geographies of empowerment: Māori Urban Geographies of Whakamanatanga. *Espace Populations Sociétés, 2020/1*–2020/2. https://doi.org/10.4000/eps.10001

McIntosh, T. (2005). Maori identities: Fixed, fluid, forces. In J. H. Liu, T. McCreanor, T. McIntosh, & T. Teaiwa (Eds.), *New Zealand identities: Departures and destinations* (pp. 38–51). Victoria University Press.

Meredith, P. (2000, February 22). *Urban Maori as 'New Citizens': The Quest for Recognition and Resources* [Paper]. Revisioning Citizenship in New Zealand Conference, University of Waikato. http://lianz.waikato.ac.nz/PAPERS/paul/URBAN%20MAORI.pdf

Moeke-Pickering, T. (1996). *Maori identity within whanau: A review of literature.* University of Waikato. https://hdl.handle.net/10289/464

Muriwai, E., Houkamau, C. A., & Sibley, C. G. (2015). Culture as cure? The protective function of Māori cultural efficacy on psychological distress. *New Zealand Journal of Psychology, 44*(2), 13.

Nejad, S., Walker, R., Macdougall, B., Belanger, Y., & Newhouse, D. (2019). "This is an Indigenous city; why don't we see it?" Indigenous urbanism and spatial production in Winnipeg. *The Canadian Geographer / Le Géographe Canadien, 63*(3), 413–424. https://doi.org/10.1111/cag.12520

Nikora, L. W., Masters-Awatere, B., & Awekotuku, N. T. (2012). Final arrangements following death: Maori indigenous decision making and Tangi: Maori indigenous decision making and Tangi. *Journal of Community & Applied Social Psychology, 22*(5), 400–413. https://doi.org/10.1002/casp.2112

Nikora, L. W., & Te Awekotuku, N. (2016). Moehewa: Death, lifestyle & sexuality in the Māori world. *Journal of Indigenous Wellbeing Te Mauri - Pimatisiwin, 1*(2), 2–8.

Pihama, L., Southey, K., Tiakiwai, S., Te Kotahi Research Institute, Waikato-Tainui College for Research and Development, & Ngā Pae o te Māramatanga (Organization). (2015). *Kaupapa rangahau: A reader: A collection of readings from the Kaupapa Māori Research workshop series led by Associate Professor Leonie Pihama and Dr Sarah-Jane Tiakiwai.*

Prendergast, M. (2015). Poetic Inquiry, 2007–2012: A Surrender and Catch Found Poem. *Qualitative Inquiry, 21*(8), 678–685. https://doi.org/10.1177/1077800414563806

Rata, A. (2015). The Māori identity migration model. *MAI Review, 4*(1), 3–14.

Spivak, G. C. (2006). Subaltern studies. Deconstructing historiography. In *In other worlds: Essays in cultural politics.* Routledge, Taylor & Francis Group.

Statistics New Zealand. (2020). *More than 1 in 6 Māori people speak Te reo Māori.* https://www.stats.govt.nz/news/more-than-1-in-6-maoripeople-speak-te-reo-maori/

UN General Assembly. (2006). *United Nations Declaration on the Rights of Indigenous Peoples.* United Nations. https://social.desa.un.org/sites/default/files/migrated/19/2018/11/UNDRIP_E_web.pdf

Walker, R. (1990). *Ka whawhai tonu matou =: Struggle without end.* Penguin Books.

Watego, C. (2021). *Another day in the colony.* University of Queensland Press. https://go.openathens.net/redirector/umoncton.ca?url=https%3A%2F%2Febookcentral.proquest.com%2Flib%2Fumoncton-ebooks%2Fdetail.action%3FdocID%3D6786847

Whyman, T., Adams, K., Carter, A., & Jobson, L. (2021). Lateral violence in Indigenous peoples. *Australian Psychologist, 56*(1), 1–14. https://doi.org/10.1080/00050067.2021.1893595

Williams, A. D., Clark, T. C., & Lewycka, S. (2018). The associations between cultural identity and mental health outcomes for indigenous Māori youth in New Zealand. *Frontiers in Public Health, 6*, 1–9. https://doi.org/10.3389/fpubh.2018.00319

Wolfe, P. (1994). Nation and miscegenation: Discursive continuity in the Post-Mabo era. *Social Analysis: The International Journal of Social and Cultural Practice, 36*, 93–152. JSTOR.

Wolfe, P. (2006). Settler colonialism and the elimination of the native. *Journal of Genocide Research, 8*(4), 387–409. https://doi.org/10.1080/14623520601056240

CHAPTER 9

What Is Black Indigenous Diasporic Psychology?

Rashelle Litchmore and Cheryl Cadogan-McClean

Introduction

What is Black diasporic indigenous psychology? We set out to answer this question due to what we have identified as limited psychological research on Black populations outside of the United States. We chose to focus our examination on Black, English-speaking populations in the Caribbean, and on Black people of Caribbean ancestry in Canada, given their immediate interconnections—Black Caribbean Canadians are members of the Caribbean diaspora, and after the United States, Canada is the top migration destination for Caribbean migrants (Lorenzi & Batalova, 2022). We also chose to focus on Canada and the Caribbean, given the geographical, political, and cultural proximity of these two regions to the United States. Through globalization processes, the United States, both through

R. Litchmore (✉)
Department of Human Development, Connecticut College,
New London, CT, USA
e-mail: rlitchmor@conncoll.edu

C. Cadogan-McClean
The University of the West Indies, Cave Hill Campus, Bridgetown, Barbados

Z. Z. Gao, M. I. Medved (eds.), *Global Perspectives on Cultural Politics in Indigenous Psychology*, Palgrave Studies in Indigenous Psychology, https://doi.org/10.1007/978-3-031-96813-6_9

cultural production and through the proliferation of psychological theories and methods, has had significant reach across the world. We argue that these influences are particularly significant for the regions of the Caribbean and Canada.

For populations categorized as “Black” in these regions, there are compounded implications. The identity of “Black” is often interpreted to mean “African American” in popular discourse (Adams, 2020), resulting in a conflation of the experiences of African Americans with those who may also be identified as “Black” around the world. This is particularly significant for Black-Caribbean and Black-Caribbean-Canadian populations due to the shared histories of the transatlantic slave trade and colonization with each other and with the United States. Additionally, the field of Black Psychology was initiated in the United States, with a stated intention of being applicable to, and accounting for the experiences of peoples of African descent around the world (Grills et al., 2018). We are therefore interested in expanding psychological research in these regions by using indigenized theories and methodologies that account for both shared histories, as emphasized through Black Psychology, as well as through attention to these regions’ unique sociocultural contexts.

Our own identities and experiences also inform our writing on this topic. Both authors were born in the Caribbean. The first author emigrated from Jamaica to Canada as an adolescent where she received all of her post-secondary education, and now resides in the United States. The second author has lived most of her life in Barbados and received her post-secondary education in Trinidad and the United States. Consequently, we sought to imagine what indigenous psycholog(ies) for Black diasporic populations might look like, while accounting for, or attempting to at the very least, the complex histories of colonization and neocolonialism, transatlantic slavery, immigration, and cultural evolution and fusion that shape, inform, and are constitutive of the psychological experiences of these populations.

Terminology

Before beginning our discussion, we would like to first benchmark for our readers what we mean when we use the terms “Black,” “diaspora,” “culture,” as well as our conceptualization of indigenous psychology, with specific attention to the field of Black Psychology.

"Black"

In this chapter, we treat the label and category of "Black" as a complex signifier, with sociohistorical, phenotypic, and power implications. Philogene (1994) notes that in the US context, the label of "Black" coexisted with other labels, "African," "Negro," "Coloured" during the period of slavery, and had broadly negative connotations. The Black Power movement of the 1960s brought about deliberate efforts to shift this label away from these negative connotations and to make it a political signifier of racial pride.

Caribbean historian Walter Rodney also points to the Black Power movement in the Caribbean, in contextualizing his use of the term. Rodney argues that "the white world defines who is Black" (Rodney, 2019, Chap. 2). Using this context of colonization and racialization in the Caribbean, Rodney (2019) uses the term Black to signify people of all ethno-racial backgrounds who were not defined by European colonial powers as "white" (Rodney, 2019). However, Rodney also left room for the label to signify people of African descent in particular, and their unique histories and circumstances in the Caribbean.

The vast diversity of Black Canadian communities has informed historical disagreement among scholars regarding the use of the term "Black" in Canada. Some scholars (e.g., Anderson, 1993) have argued that it risks homogenizing a highly diverse group of people. Others have used it to signify the processes of racialization that these diverse communities experience, which lead to common experiences associated with race (Mensah, 2010). Canadian scholar Rinaldo Walcott (2018) therefore argues for flexibility in the use of the term "Black-Canadian", the meaning of which is never fully settled, while simultaneously imbued with particular histories of power and power relations.

Taking this overall context together, we follow Walcott's lead in treating the meaning of "Black" as never fully settled, as primarily referential to people of African ancestry, but contextually flexible in relation to the shared experiences of colonization and racial subjugation of both Black and Brown people. While originally applied as a derogatory label by enslavers and European colonialists, this label has been deliberately reclaimed through the Black Power movements in the 1960s as one of empowerment. We therefore also treat the term as a signifier of historical racialized power relations. Perhaps most importantly, in the discipline of psychology and research contexts, we prioritize individual self-identification with the term.

Diaspora

Gilroy (1994) discusses diaspora as "a relational network, characteristically produced by forced dispersal and reluctant scattering" (p. 207). In defining diaspora as such, Gilroy points to both the forced displacement of people from the African continent around the world through the transatlantic slave trade, as well as the continued sociopolitical and economic factors that underlie purportedly voluntary migration in the present day. Gilroy cautions against any fixed notions of "source" and "destination" countries or nation-states. Consequently, neither countries of origin nor diasporic contexts can be assumed to be historically or presently culturally uniform and consistent. Gilroy instead emphasizes communication networks—networks that are becoming increasingly accessible and efficient in the present day (e.g. social media)—that enable "dispersed populations to converse, interact, and even synchronize elements of their social and cultural lives" (p. 211). With increasing access to affordable travel, physical movement between the "source", "destination," and other countries on an ongoing basis also becomes more seamless, and further reinforces ongoing cultural connections and transformation.

Similarly, Bhatia (2007) describes diaspora as a condition, rather than as a descriptor, as "produced through and embedded in particular historical, sociocultural, economic and political experiences of movement, dislocation and displacement" (p. 307). These conceptualizations orient us to the multiplicity of diaspora for people of African descent around the world. Indeed, people of African descent in the Caribbean are considered to be a part of the African diaspora, and people of Caribbean descent in Canada are also considered to be members of the Caribbean diaspora. If these individuals identify as being of African descent, they are also considered to be members of the African diaspora. Definitions are therefore relative and context-dependent, requiring attention to processes and the meanings associated with them, as opposed to locations and identifications that may be treated as concrete, objective, and finalized.

Culture

Cultural psychologists treat culture not as an independent variable but as an interpretive concept (Bhatia, 2007). Hammack (2011) further argues that culture "is not something we *have*; it is something we *do*. And it is something we *talk about* doing—both to ourselves and to others—thereby reproducing the material and dis-cursive conditions of a society" (emphasis in original, Hammack, 2011, p. 22). In treating culture and mind as "mutually constitutive," we no longer focus solely on how an external variable of culture may "impact" our choices; for example, a Caribbean migrant's practice of eating only Caribbean foods in Canada due to their cultural heritage. Instead, we attend to the processes at play that shape, for example, access to "cultural" foods (e.g., political, economic, and social factors that impact the importation of Caribbean products to Canada) and socialized preferences (e.g., experiences pre-immigration that may have shaped the meanings associated with these foods). These determinations position culture as far more historically, politically, and socially situated than it has been traditionally treated and also highlight the various intersections of culture and mind that would be difficult to separate on a moment-by-moment basis.

Indigenous Psychology

Our understanding of the label "Black" and the concepts of culture and diaspora consequently guide the paradigm of indigenous psychology, which we seek to use in this work. Prior conceptualizations of indigenous psychology include approaches which seek to understand people in their cultural context in order to develop psychological knowledge that is specific to individual cultures, which may then be combined into a universal psychology (Yang, 2000). In these approaches, culture is defined as a set of shared meanings and beliefs fixed to specific geographical regions. In contrast, Bhatia and Priya (2019) argue for a critical indigenous psychology, one that treats culture as socially constructed and shaped within sociohistorical and political contexts. They emphasize epistemological and methodological approaches that prioritize an empathetic researcher–participant relationship, where the participant's voice is foregrounded, and where the presentation of research findings is geared toward participant empowerment, as opposed to outlining cultural generalizations.

Notably, Indigenous psychologies are typically contrasted with Western/Euro-American/mainstream psychology. The goal of this contrast is to highlight the marginalizing impacts of Western psychology in attempting to establish universal theories and methodologies that do not account for local contexts (Ciofalo, 2019). Implicit in this contrast is the dichotomization of Western and non-Western/indigenous. However, as Bhatia and Priya (2019) argue, such dichotomization does not adequately account for transnational movement and global media access, which make distinguishing between local and global contexts difficult at best. The implications of transnationalism and globalization are especially applicable to our populations of interest. Black Caribbean people and Black Caribbean Canadians have been historically displaced from their "indigenous" context, the continent of Africa, and currently live within muti-ethnic, multi-language, and multicultural settings that include, and are in many ways dominated by, Westernized ways of being. In this chapter, we intend to account for the multiplicity of these contexts in our conceptualization of indigenous psychologies for these populations.

Black Psycholog(ies)

Although developed in the United States, the broad subfield of Black Psychology is an indigenous psychology intended to be applicable to, and has been applied to Black diasporic populations around the world, as well as in the continent of Africa (Grills et al., 2018). Originating in the early twentieth century, the field has grown over the past several decades and has reoriented research with people of African descent toward challenging traditional Eurocentric psychological frameworks, as well as deficit conceptualizations of Blackness that were customary in the discipline prior to Black Psychology's inception (Stevens, 2015).

Grills et al. (2018) outline what can be treated as three strands of Black Psychology: (1) Black Psychology, (2) Africa-centered psychology, and (3) African Psychology, although the discipline does not consistently make these distinctions. Black Psychology initially utilized mainstream Western frameworks to challenge racist framings of African American psychological and social issues within the discipline (Stevens, 2015). This included, for example, the famous Clark doll experiments, which influenced the *Brown v Board of Education* decision (Stevens, 2015). Models of racial identity development, such as the Cross Nigrescence theory (Cross, 1978), which relied, in part, on mainstream Euro-American identity development and measurement frameworks, were also developed through Black Psychology. Africa-centered psychology, by contrast, emphasizes an African worldview, "drawing on African philosophy, African traditional religion, African traditional medicine, and African epistemological methods that value self-knowledge and intuition in addition to the observable" (Grills et al., 2018, p. 799). Finally, African Psychology can be seen as a combination of Black Psychology and Africa-centered psychology. It centers on Indigenous African knowledge systems while also recognizing the value of Western psychological models in studying specific questions within specific contexts (Grills et al., 2018).

A central tenet of Black/African/Africa-centered psychology is challenging Eurocentric psychological models that have historically worked to reinforce racist understandings of peoples of African descent, and in turn, elevating an Afrocentric worldview and African epistemology (Nobles, 2013). Carroll (2018) argues that an Afrikan worldview involves "common interpretive processes" (p. 4) that people of African descent draw on in understanding their experiences and reality more broadly. This worldview is based on "Being, Felt-time, Communalism, and Harmony-with-Nature" (Carroll, 2018, p. 7). This is contrasted with the Euro-American worldview, which emphasizes "Doing, Future-time, Individualism, and Mastery-over-nature" (p. 7). Africa-centered psychologists have therefore engaged in theory development through examination of precolonial, colonial, and post-colonial African histories (Ebede-Ndi, 2016; Grills et al., 2018), as well as through tracing the histories of Euro-American psychological sciences in order to establish this contrast.

However, the concept of common interpretive processes, or common African Identity among peoples of the African diaspora has come under scrutiny. Zeleza (2006) argues that "[t]he idea of "Africa" is a complex one with multiple genealogies and meanings, so that extrapolations of 'African' culture, identity or nationality, in the singular or plural, any explorations of what makes 'Africa' 'African,' are often quite slippery as these notions tend to swing unsteadily between the poles of essentialism and contingency" (p. 14). The sociohistorical, political, and discursive processes that have constructed "Africa" as a place, and as an idea over the centuries, must therefore be attended to in any discussion associated with framing a pan-African or diasporic Black identity.

Pan-African scholars in Black/African/Africa-centered psychology note the impacts of the transatlantic slave trade and colonialism on the psychological trajectories of people of African descent (Nobles, 2013), as well as, they would argue, the shared cultural characteristics of African descendent peoples. However, transnational Black psychologists have also contended with what it means to identify as "Black," as well as how the concept of Blackness has been approached in psychology (Stevens et al., 2017). These scholars advocate, as we do in this chapter, for non-essentialist understandings of Blackness. Following this, Dei (2000) argues that "[i]ndigenous knowledges do not 'sit in pristine fashion' outside of the effects of other knowledges" (p. 5). In turning to indigenous African knowledges to inform how we understand the experiences of people of African descent around the world, we must also foreground "local, specific and historically informed analyses grounded in spatial and cultural contexts" (Dei, 2000, p. 6). Indigenous psychologies for African descendent people in the Caribbean, as well as the Black Caribbean diaspora in Canada, must account for the diversity of cultural, political, economic, and historical influences that inform the experiences of these populations today. We emphasize indigenous *psychologies*, plural, as we do not seek to advocate for a singular approach to studying these two populations, which are in and of themselves diverse. Instead, we seek to bring attention to two geographical regions within the African diaspora that have received less attention in the psychological literature, and to use them as exemplars for how research pertaining to any population categorized as, or within which individuals who self-identify as "Black" may be approached.

To that end, the remainder of this paper will attend to the unique contexts of these regions and consider how indigenous psychologies may continue to be developed to account for these contexts. We propose five guideposts for developing indigenous psychologies focused primarily on people of African descent—or people who self-identify as "Black" in these regions:

1. Recognition and incorporation of the socio-politico-historical contexts that are consistently working to shape and impact the shared meanings and beliefs of the populations of interest. This includes acknowledgment of the cultural diversity between, and within these populations, while also attending to cultural fluidity, hybridization, and dispersal among them. For both populations, this includes recognition that these "groups" do not, and have never, existed in isolation from other populations in their regions. For the Canadian population, this also includes the explicit consideration of generation status.

2. Explicit consideration of epistemology and ontology in framing and carrying out research, including the co-construction of meaning between the researcher and the researched by prioritizing participant voices. If more positivist approaches are used, explicit framing of the benefits and limitations of these approaches in supporting social justice outcomes for populations of interest.
3. Incorporation of decolonial and intersectional approaches. This includes the explicit consideration of processes of racialization and those associated with social class, gender, etc., versus relying on taken-for-granted racial categories and other axes of power.
4. Attempts to address social justice and social problems for the populations under study include examinations of community strengths and everyday life, and explicit efforts to interrupt discourses of deficit. This includes acknowledgment of the role of community in addressing mental health issues.
5. Incorporation of the insights and successes from other psychologists using indigenous approaches with other groups outside of the Afro-Caribbean and Black-Canadian communities.

Recognition and Incorporation of Socio-Politico-Historical Contexts: Blackness in the Caribbean and Canada

The Caribbean

The Caribbean region is inclusive of islands with shores bound by the Caribbean Sea and the continental countries of Belize on the coast of Central America and Guyana, French Guiana, and Suriname on the coast of South America. It includes overseas territories, independent states, and the republics. It is a linguistically diverse region with diverse ethnic groups speaking several languages (including Arabic, English, Dutch, Hindi, French, Kreyol, Spanish, and different patois), and having had ancestral ties to Africa, Asia, Europe, and the Middle East, as well as those who are indigenous to the region, including Amerindians, Garifuna, and Kalinago. The cultural potpourri that ensues is, in part, due to racial mixing. The cultural and ethno-racial diversity gives the Caribbean its unique nature, and yet adds to the complexity of defining the region as one body and deciphering the psycholog(ies) of its peoples.

Caribbean countries have a shared history of thriving Indigenous populations prior to European colonization, which started with the arrival of Christopher Columbus in 1492. Colonialization peaked with the slaughter of large numbers of Amerindians. This was accompanied by the transportation of enslaved Africans to the Caribbean to service plantation labor for the cash crops of sugar, tobacco, and others, and the later addition of indentured laborers from Europe and Asia to supplement slave labor (Wilson et al., 2018). Resultantly, the demographic composition of most English-speaking and French-speaking countries is majority peoples of African descent, while Spanish-speaking and Dutch-speaking countries have larger portions of other ethno-racial groups.

The psychological profiles of Afro-Caribbean people are regarded as being directly impacted by enslavement, colonialization, and the resultant social and economic issues in the region (Hickling, 2020). European conquest resulted in a disconnect from people's original cultural contexts through forced removal and migration, as well as voluntary migration to the region. The ongoing effects of colonization have implications for social and psychological outcomes, including changes in family structure and economic dependence, as well as impacts on individual identity formation (Nicolas & Wheatley, 2013). Colonial relationships persist, with some countries having remained territories of their colonizing European nations. In post-colonial societies, the oppressor–oppressed relationship continues with class struggles between the wealthy and the poor within each nation.

The Black Power movement in the Caribbean, although originating in North America, provided an opportunity for Caribbean citizens to openly explore their African ancestry and to seek political and economic freedoms from the existing post-colonial oppressive systems of governing (Lux, 1972). Blackness has both physical and cultural connotations in Caribbean society. Individuals who identify as Black are mainly those who are able to trace their ancestry back to the continent of Africa (Sutherland, 2011). However, people of Indian and Chinese heritage in the Caribbean may also identify with the struggle of Afro-Caribbeans due to their own engagement in the Black Power movement in the 1970s.

All Caribbean countries are made vulnerable by natural disasters, as they are situated in a geographic area prone to hurricanes, volcanic activity, and earthquakes. Experiences with natural disasters have had an impact on the economic, social, and psychological states of Caribbean people. The experience of devastating earthquakes in Haiti, hurricanes, and recent volcanic eruptions in St. Vincent and Montserrat, and changes in weather due to climate change, have resulted in stress, anxiety, depression, and post-traumatic stress disorder (Devirios et al., 2018; Cloos et al., 2023). Economically, the need to divert funds to address natural disasters takes funds away from capacity building in areas like mental health. However, the recognition of the effect of natural disasters on Haiti has led to the development of more educational programs in psychology in Haiti, funded by external aid organizations (Rich & Jean-Charles, 2022).

Geopolitically, Caribbean countries are small island developing states in the Global South. Post-colonial economic dependence on developed countries has made the financial impacts of natural disasters and pandemics like COVID-19 hard to manage without receiving aid from more developed countries and their funding agencies, e.g. the European Union, the Inter-American Development Bank, and the International Monetary Fund. In addition, reliance on vulnerable industries like tourism and agriculture has limited countries' ability to generate income and allocate funds to mental health service provision.

The Canadian Context

Blackness in Canada. In order to understand the present-day socio-political-cultural-economic contexts of Black Caribbean Canadians, we must first comprehend the histories and discourses related to Blackness in Canada overall. The Black experience in Canada is typically contrasted with that in the United States. Canada is often cited as a destination on the Underground Railroad for enslaved African Americans in pursuit of freedom (Maynard, 2017). However, far less attention is typically given to the over 200 years of slavery that existed in regions of the country from the late 1600s to its abolition in the mid-1800s (Maynard, 2017). Slavery existed on a smaller scale than in the United States and was not plantation-based, but as Maynard argues, it was no less brutal or inhumane and worked to establish Black populations as inherently inferior. Early established Black populations in Canada also included Black loyalists and refugees from the American Revolutionary War, continuous waves of free African Americans, as well as those who escaped bondage in the US, and Maroons from Jamaica, many of whom subsequently departed for Sierra Leonne (Winks, 1997). These populations were met with mixed reception in Canada, some welcomed on the grounds of their ability to contribute to building the country. However, given the already established racial hierarchy in the country, as the number of Black arrivals increased, prejudice across the country also rose (Winks, 1997).

Several scholars have documented the material and discursive consequences of this historical context for people of African descent in Canada. The dehumanization of Blackness over the centuries resulted in, for example, the establishment of segregated schooling in the 1800s and the early 1900s (Chan, 2007), restrictive immigration policies for Black populations from the Caribbean (Satzewich, 1989), and the continent of Africa (Tetty & Puplampu, 2005). In the present day, there is documented overpolicing and state violence against Black Canadians (Maynard, 2017; Tator & Henry, 2007), disproportionate placement in child welfare services (James et al., 2010), as well as disproportionate experiences of academic exclusion (James & Turner, 2017). Consequently, despite official Canadian multiculturalism policies, and the widespread perception of Canada as a kinder, gentler nation in comparison to the United States, much of the existing research literature pertaining to Black-Canadian experiences is, in fact, slanted toward Black disenfranchisement. Nonetheless, Black communities have claimed space in the Canadian mosaic. Black Canadian civil rights activist Viola Desmond was placed on the Canadian $10 bill in 2020. Foods and products from the Caribbean and Africa are relatively easily accessible in Canadian metropolitan centers. Celebrations such as Afrofest and the Toronto Caribbean Carnival in Toronto, Carifiesta in Montreal, and others signify the cultural space that these communities hold all over the country. Political representatives at the federal, provincial, and municipal levels also include several individuals from long-standing and more recently established Black communities in Canada.

Today, Black Canadians comprise 4.3% of Canada's population (Statistics Canada, 2023). The majority (40%) of people who identify as "Black" in the Canadian census were born in Canada, and 21% were born in the Caribbean (Statistics Canada, 2022). Additionally, approximately 25% of Black Canadians reported being of more than one ethnic origin (Statistics Canada, 2022). This indicates vast diversity within this population and a continuous process of cultural fusion, fissure, and evolution over the centuries that is uniquely Canadian. Consequently, any attempted study of Black Caribbean Canadians in particular can never be separated from the overall context that has brought this multiethnic, multigenerational group of people together to be categorized as "Black" in Canada.

Black Caribbean Presence in Canada

Canadian immigration policy of the late 1800s invited new immigrants to contribute to Canadian nation-building. However, the prevalence of scientific racism and "racial naturalism" at the time swiftly shifted immigration policies to restricting arrivals from non-Western European countries (Walker, 2012). Black immigrants were therefore deemed to be "mentally, morally, physically and socially inferior" (Calliste, 1993, p. 133), and it was believed that they would have difficulties adapting to the Canadian climate, leading to an inability to contribute their labor to the Canadian economy (Satzewich, 1989). Black Caribbean women, in particular, were regarded as moral liabilities, likely to become single parents, and dependent on social welfare (Calliste, 1993). There were also fears that they would induce "race relations" problems in the country in a manner similar to issues occurring in the United States and Britain, which would also be harmful to the Canadian economy (Satzewich, 1989).

Consequently, immigration from the Caribbean was vastly restricted until the 1950s, when slight improvements came with a revamped Caribbean Domestic Scheme (Darden, 2006) that allowed increased numbers of female migrants from the Caribbean to be admitted as domestic workers after 1955 (Anderson, 1993). In the 1960s, explicit racial discrimination in immigration policy was officially removed, and the "points system"—where immigrants are accepted based on their potential contribution to the Canadian economy—was implemented (Anderson, 1993). Despite these official changes in immigration policy, the Department of Citizenship and Immigration still employed practices that sought to restrict Black Caribbean migration, including the delayed establishment of immigration offices in the Caribbean and racist descriptions of applicants (Satzewich, 1989). Darden (2006) argues that these historical immigration restrictions have had longstanding consequences for the composition of Black Caribbean families and, ultimately, for the social and economic outcomes. This includes a disproportionate number of sole-parent, female-led households for people of Caribbean ancestry in Canada, which, in turn, contributes to higher rates of poverty and consequent intergenerational impacts.

Psychological Implications of Socio-Politico-Historical Contexts

The socio-politico-historical contexts previously described shape and inform the psychological functioning of Afro-Caribbean and Afro-Caribbean Canadian peoples. In relation to Caribbean populations, scholars have argued that efforts to fight for freedom and develop societies coming out of a colonial past have had a psychological impact on these peoples. These histories have impacted individual and collective psychological well-being, including the development of internalized oppression and colonial mentality, as well as intergenerational trauma with mental health outcomes that can lead to depression, anxiety, aggression, and other psychosocial outcomes (Nicolas & Wheatley, 2013).

Caribbean psychologists and those in the diaspora have made efforts to use an indigenous approach to create theories and models that explain the behavior of Caribbean peoples and the application of these models to treatment. Some researchers include Gopaul-McNicol (1993) and Hickling (2020), who developed theories to explain the Caribbean psyche through their work with Caribbean immigrants in North America and Britain and nationals living in the English-speaking Caribbean. Applying theory to clinical practice with individuals and families in the Caribbean and the diaspora, Gopaul-McNicol developed a multicultural/multimodal/multisystem approach to treatment. Hickling (2020) developed psycho-historiographic cultural therapy and Dream-A-World Therapy. Dudley-Grant (2016), in the US Virgin Islands, developed Family Therapy Under the Tamarind Tree and Family Dinners.

In reviewing the relevant Canadian psychological literature, we found very little research that focused explicitly on Black Caribbean-Canadian populations (e.g., Goddard-Durant et al., 2022, 2023; Jackson & Naidoo, 2012; Litchmore et al., 2016; Schreiber et al., 2000). Instead, the vast majority of articles on the topic of Black Canadian psychological experiences[1] focused on a broader category of "Black." We believe that this broader focus is likely a reflection of researchers' emphasis on the previously discussed context of racialization in Canada, where focus is given to

[1] Search terms used in Psych Info and Google Scholar were "Black Canadian," "Caribbean," "West Indies," "psychology," "identity," "culture." Additional targeted searches were conducted for papers by scholars who research Black-Canadian experiences in the fields of psychology, psychiatry, and public health. This included scholars in the newly established Black Psychology section of the Canadian Psychological Association (CPA, 2022).

the comparative histories of enslavement in Canada and the United States (e.g., Cénat et al., 2024; Smith & Lalonde, 2003) as well as experiences of discrimination, and disparities associated with being racialized as Black in majority white countries (e.g., Cénat et al., 2021; Joseph & Kuo, 2009; Lalonde et al., 2008).

The specific context of racialization in Canada is highly relevant to the psychological experiences of Afro-Caribbean Canadians and should continue to be studied; however, this also needs to be coupled with a deeper examination of immigrant and multigenerational cultural expression and experiences. For example, in their study of Black Caribbean Canadian women's experiences with depression, Jackson and Naidoo (2012) categorized first- and second-generation Indo-Caribbean and Afro-Caribbean women as "Black," which they describe as a political rather than a racial category, pointing to shared histories of slavery and indentureship and resistance to colonial rule in the Caribbean, which act as both "unifying and divisive" (p. 226) for these communities. They describe these women's self and social positionings as "strong" and as developed through processes of immigration and racialization, which have led to a lack of reliable and ongoing social support.

Examination of immediate social contexts within Canada must also be considered. As previously discussed, the Black Canadian population is highly diverse. Examination of psychological experiences within this context of vast ethnic and cultural diversity would be beneficial for apprehending the uniqueness of Black Canadian and Afro-Caribbean Canadian identities. Litchmore et al. (2016), for example, examined how adolescents of Caribbean and African heritage negotiated racial and ethnic labels, and the meanings that young people associated with these labels. In this study, the label of "Black" was not taken for granted, but was examined as something that young people of various ethnic backgrounds who may be racialized as Black may or may not opt into.

Our review of these broader contexts, while brief and inevitably incomplete, is uniquely Caribbean and Canadian. We therefore contend that any psychological research related to people of African descent in these regions must account for these complexities.

Considerations of Epistemology and Ontology, Including co-Construction of Meaning between Researcher and Researched

As previously outlined, Black psychologists have introduced Black/African/Africa-centered psychology as an alternative epistemological framework to examine the experiences of people of African descent around the world. Black psychologists have argued that Western Euro-American models of psychology have had the effect of centering deficits in the psychological functioning of people of African descent (Stevens, 2015). However, researchers also note that Western Euro-American models do not need to be rejected outright, as they have proven to be useful entry points for anti-racist advocacy in mainstream spaces, for example, research on stereotype threat (Belgrave & Allison, 2018). We therefore do not argue for a single approach to understanding the experiences of our populations of interest. Rather, we argue that researchers must explicitly name and justify their epistemological choices in their work.

The use of Euro-American theories and models to inform psychological research and practice in the Caribbean is thus widespread. Efforts have also been made to develop psychometric tools that are culturally specific to Black Caribbean people, for example, the Caribbean Symptom Checklist (CSC) and Behavioural and Emotional Assessment for Children of Caribbean Heritage (BEACCH; Lambert et al., 2016). However, researchers have also expanded their epistemological orientations by turning to everyday relational practices in Caribbean communities such as "liming" and "ole talk," as strategies for capturing day-to-day experiences in culturally relevant ways (Wilson et al., 2018). Researchers enter these informal meeting spaces to gather information on relevant research topics, centering participant voice in the framing and shaping of how research is done, and enabling the co-construction of meaning between the researcher and the researched. Notably, quantitative and qualitative research methods are both valuable for informing policies and policymakers' decisions on mental health.

Communalism is viewed as one very relevant Africanism of importance to how Caribbean people of African descent navigate life and manage adversity (Sutherland, 2011). Indigenous approaches to theorizing the resilience of the peoples in the region have taken into account how community ties, such as supportive parents, teachers, and other mentors, influence individuals' ability to overcome adversity (Robertson-Hickling,

2008; Goddard-Durant, 2019). Through the oral approach of capturing the life stories of Caribbean people, a conceptual framework for studies on idioms of resilience has also been undertaken (Andreassen et al., 2023). Caribbean psychologists are therefore being encouraged to develop a more African-centered approach to psychology in the region, acknowledging the relevance of Africanism to Caribbean peoples' social identity and its relevance to their mental health (Sutherland, 2011).

Canadian psychological research has seen very little integration of African-centered epistemologies. At least one study has attempted to assess African-centered worldviews of participants using Euro-American frameworks. Joseph and Kuo (2009) used experimental methods to assess whether, and under what conditions Black Canadians employed Africultural coping strategies in response to life stressors. These researchers adopted their Africultural coping strategies measure from their work with African Americans, which assessed coping strategies through qualitative focus group research (Utsey et al., 2000). However, Joseph and Kuo did not themselves examine the cultural backgrounds of their Black Canadian participants or whether specific culturally based practices or traditions might inform their coping strategies. This study was therefore valuable in introducing Africultural worldviews to the discussion of Black-Canadian psychological well-being, but stopped short of a comprehensive examination of whether and how such worldviews may manifest in the ethnically diverse population of Black Canadians, including Afro-Caribbean participants.

Fante-Coleman et al. (2023) used Community-Based Participatory research (CBPR) to examine how Black Canadians manage mental health in relation to religious practices. CBPR, while challenging to implement, represents a shift away from the power dynamics typically imposed through traditional Eurocentric research models by seeking collaboration between researchers and participants (Stanton, 2014). Using CBPR allowed the researchers to understand that that religion, which included Christianity, Islam, and Agnosticism, could have both stigmatizing and beneficial roles in Black Canadian young people's mental health. The community-based, participatory epistemological orientation of this research allowed for an understanding of the dynamic role of religion, rather than starting with a premise of significance and attempting to measure the degree of this significance. These researchers also did not report the specific cultural backgrounds and generation status of their participants, and it is unclear whether this diversity would have played a role in their findings. However, the majority of their participants self-identified as "Black," perhaps indicating that this was the identity that was most salient for participants.

Incorporation of Decolonial and Intersectional Approaches

Decolonial and intersectional approaches are specific examples of alternative epistemological orientations that explicitly account for the histories and current life circumstances of Afro-Caribbean people living in the Caribbean and Canada. Decolonial psychologists bring attention to the history of psychological sciences as representing "the other," that is, non-Western and indigenous populations as inferior and deviant, and the legacy of such representations today (Bhatia, 2018). The concept of "coloniality" emphasizes not simply the colonial relationship between Europe and the territories it claimed but the resultant knowledge systems and relationships embedded in unequal power relations, which are maintained through present-day popular and academic culture, including psychological constructions of subjectivity (Bhatia, 2018). Decolonial scholarship is therefore an ongoing enterprise, seeking to understand and eventually deconstruct these knowledge systems and power relationships.

Caribbean scholars have started to make deliberate attempts to address how the impact of the colonial past on mental health could be addressed through decolonizing efforts in research and practice (Hickling, 2020). One effort toward a decolonizing approach is the work of community psychologists in the Spanish-speaking Caribbean. This work enables clients to use self-determination and autonomous organizing to address how communities respond to and rebuild after natural disasters and includes the clients' viewpoint in proposed solutions. In this way, client voices are central (Ortiz-Torres, 2020).

Goddard-Durant et al. (2022) propose a decolonizing, intersectional, Black feminist approach to studying Black Caribbean Canadian mothers' resilience. Goddard-Durant et al. question mainstream "euro-Western" approaches to understanding human development and the concept of resilience, which do not account for how racialized and gendered experiences may shape the outcomes of Black women. They turn to US Black feminist epistemologies (Hill Collins, 2009) to provide an alternative framework for understanding Black Caribbean Canadian women's experiences. These researchers also rely on a decolonized version of Constructivist

Grounded Theory (Charmaz, 2014) to examine how participants' experiences, as well as the research process itself, may be shaped by colonial, neocolonial, and neoliberal ideologies.

These studies represent thoughtful approaches to studying our populations of interest that explicitly account for the ongoing impacts of colonization rather than treating it as an event to be left in the distant past. Future research must continue to examine these contexts when working with these populations.

Attempts to Address Social Justice and Social Problems

Caribbean social problems include chronic non-communicable diseases, crime and violence, work and environmental attitudes, poverty, families, gender discrimination, disease stigmatization, concerns related to educational performance, and mental health and wellness. Remote acculturation is also one area of concern which stems from the close social, monetary, and practical connections with family and friends who migrated. Caribbean people, especially the youth, develop a type of transnational or cosmopolitan identity (Ferguson, 2016). Remote acculturation in this context produces Caribbean youth who integrate an Americanized culture with their lived experiences on the islands. This hybridized culture adds a new dimension to identity and identity issues that can impact mental health.

There have been isolated attempts to address these issues, but there has been no systematic attempt to develop a framework to address Caribbean social problems through a comprehensive psychological research lens (Thompson, 2016). An approach that is needed. Some examples of the researchers and a snapshot of their work include Chadee et al. (2020) exploration of crime and perceptions of crime, Devonish (2018) examining work attitudes and performance, Maynard (2018) reviewing educational psychology research in the English-speaking Caribbean, and Roopnarine et al. (2023) addressing intimate partner violence. There is a need to move away from a piecemeal approach to researching Caribbean social problems and develop frameworks and processes that can be used to enable research to inform social policies and practices.

Similarly, as previously mentioned, research on Black Caribbean Canadian communities has been largely subsumed under the umbrella of the Black Canadian population writ large. Therefore, less attention has been given to how the migratory and transnational contexts of Black Canadians of Caribbean heritage may uniquely impact and inform and potentially alleviate disparate experiences in Canada. Disparities in educational achievement, mental health, child welfare, and state violence have all been documented across various fields. Focused psychological research conducted through the epistemological framings previously discussed, would go a long way in proposing both individually focused, and systemic interventions to support long-term psychological well-being of Black Caribbean Canadians.

Incorporation of Insights from Other Indigenous Psychologies: The Way Forward

Black Caribbean and Black Caribbean Canadian researchers can embrace Indigenous psychology as a vibrant discipline that represents a vast range of peoples who have survived the experience of colonization (Waitoki et al., 2018). However, due to their diasporic social, cultural, and geographical positioning, these populations do not come by indigeneity in a manner similar to indigenous peoples in the Americas, Australia, Asia, or Africa, who still live in their places of origin. Migration features prominently in the lives of the two groups we study, that is, forced migration through slavery from Africa, resulting in adopted homelands, as well as through post-colonial migration to Canada in search of better opportunities.

Turning to examples of how indigenous psychologies have been developed for other populations may therefore be challenging due to these differences. However, the main aim of indigenous psychology is to bring to the fore ways of being, and epistemologies, that are informed by local contexts and are outside of dominant Euro-Western practices and knowledge systems. We have argued in this chapter that making a clear distinction between "western" and "non-western" culture, particularly for our populations of interest, can be a difficult endeavor. However, as we have seen from other indigenous psychologies, including African/Black Psychology, developing an understanding of alternative ways of being, even within colonial contexts and histories, is a highly necessary endeavor to counteract the harms imposed by these histories. Similar to work with Native Hawaiians (McCubbin & Marsella, 2009), explorations of traditional conceptualizations of the self, the roles of nature, spirituality, and family in the psychology of these peoples, and how it has been shaped by their collective socio-historical political past, is a strong starting point.

Conclusions

The development of indigenous psychologies for Black Caribbean and Black Caribbean Canadian peoples will require the collaborative efforts of psychologists from both regions. The regional conferences of psychology organized by the Caribbean Alliance of National Psychological Associations (CANPA, 2023) have been an avenue for sharing research, discourse, and strategizing on the development of Caribbean psychology. The more recently established Black Psychology section of the Canadian Psychological Association (CPA, 2022) can also be a space that leads to the development of collaborative projects aimed at informing teaching, research, and practice in both regions. We believe that the guideposts that were elaborated through our discussion can be integral to the development of indigenous psychologies for these regions and populations. Our emphasis on critical attention to historical and present-day contexts, prioritization of collaborative research approaches, and orientation toward indigenous or traditional ways of being for peoples of African descent can support further development of novel research approaches while addressing the diverse psychological needs of these populations.

Conflict of Interest The authors declare that there is no conflict of interest.

References

Adams, C. (2020). Not all Black people are African American. Here's the difference. *CBS News*. https://www.cbsnews.com/news/not-all-black-people-are-african-american-what-is-the-difference/

Anderson, W. W. (1993). *Caribbean immigrants: A socio-demographic profile*. Canadian Scholars' Press Inc.

Andreassen, K. E., Kirkengen, A. L., & Johansen, M. (2023). "I base my life on sadness": Apparently paradoxical sources of resilience among young Haitians. *Transcultural Psychiatry, 60*(6), 985–996. https://doi.org/10.1177/13634615231202094

Belgrave, F. Z., & Allison, K. W. (2018). *African American psychology* (4th ed.). SAGE Publications. https://bookshelf.vitalsource.com/books/9781506333410

Bhatia, S. (2007). Rethinking culture and identity in psychology: Towards a transnational cultural psychology. *Journal of Theoretical and Philosophical Psychology, 27–28*(2–1), 301–321. https://doi.org/10.1037/h0091298

Bhatia, S. (2018). *Decolonizing psychology: Globalization, social justice, and Indian youth identities.* Oxford University Press.

Bhatia, S., & Priya, K. R. (2019). From representing culture to fostering 'voice': Towards a critical indigenous psychology. In K. H. Yeh (Ed.), *Asian indigenous psychologies in the global context* (pp. 19–46). Palgrave Macmillan. https://doi.org/10.1007/978-3-319-96232-0_2

Calliste, A. (1993). Race, gender and Canadian immigration policy: Blacks from the Caribbean 1900–1932. *Journal of Canadian Studies, 28*(4), 131–148. https://doi.org/10.3138/jcs.28.4.131

CANPA. (2023). Empowering Caribbean Psychologists. https://www.wearecanpa.com

Carroll, K. K. (2018). Africana studies and research methodology revisiting the centrality of the Afrikan worldview. In I. M. Flannery (Ed.), *An introduction to Black psychology* (pp. 2–23). Cognella, Inc. https://bookshelf.vitalsource.com/books/82508-1B

Cénat, J. M., Darius, W. P., Dalexis, R. D., Kogan, C. S., Guerrier, M., & Ndengeyingoma, A. (2024). Perceived racial discrimination, internalized racism, social support, and self-esteem among Black individuals in Canada: A moderated mediation model. *Cultural Diversity & Ethnic Minority Psychology, 30*(1), 118–129. https://doi.org/10.1037/cdp0000542

Cénat, J. M., Kogan, C., Noorishad, P. G., Hajizadeh, S., Dalexis, R. D., Ndengeyingoma, A., & Guerrier, M. (2021). Prevalence and correlates of depression among Black individuals in Canada: The major role of everyday racial discrimination. *Depression and Anxiety, 38*(9), 886–895. https://doi.org/10.1002/da.23158

Chadee, D., Williams, D., & Bachew, R. (2020). Victims' emotional distress and preventive measures usage: Influence of crime severity, risk perception, and fear. *Journal of Community Applied Social Psychology, 30*, 14–30. https://doi.org/10.1002/casp.2418

Chan, A. S. (2007). Race-based policies in Canada: Education and social context. In L. Johnson & R. Joshee (Eds.), *Multicultural education policies in Canada and the United States* (pp. 131–143). UBC Press.

Charmaz, K. (2014). *Constructing grounded theory: A practical guide through qualitative analysis.* Sage.

Ciofalo, N. (2019). Indigenous psychologies: A contestation for epistemic justice. In N. Ciofalo (Ed.), *Indigenous psychologies in an era of decolonization* (pp. 1–38). Springer Nature Switzerland AG. https://doi.org/10.1007/978-3-030-04822-8_1

Cloos, P., Belloiseau, M., McPherson, N., Harris-Glenville, F., Joseph, D. D., & Zinszer, K. (2023). Discussing linkages between climate change, human mobility and health in the Caribbean: The case of Dominica. A qualitative study. *The Journal of Climate Change and Health, 11*. https://doi.org/10.1016/j.joclim.2023.100237

CPA. (2022). *Psychology month Profile: Dr. Jude Mary Cénat, Dr. Helen Ofosu, Anita Shaw, Kafui Sawyer, Dr. Erin Beettam, and Dr. Monnica Williams, Black Psychology Section*. https://cpa.ca/psychology-month-profile-dr-jude-mary-cenat-dr-helen-ofosu-anita-shaw-kafui-sawyer-dr-erin-beettam-and-dr-monnica-williams-black-psychology-section/

Cross, W. E., Jr. (1978). The Thomas and Cross models of psychological Nigrescence: A review. *Journal of Black Psychology, 5*, 13–31. https://doi.org/10.1177/009579847800-500102

Darden, J. T. (2006). The impact of Canadian immigration policy on the structure of the Black Caribbean family in Toronto. In E. Fong (Ed.), *Inside the mosaic* (pp. 146–168). University of Toronto Press. https://doi.org/10.3138/9781442676176-008

Dei, G. J. S. (2000). Rethinking the role of indigenous knowledges in the academy. *International Journal of Inclusive Education, 4*(2), 111–132. https://doi.org/10.1080/136031100284849

Devirios, D., Cénat , J. M., Karray, A., Guiller-Pasut, N., Cadiction, J. M., Baptiste, L., Joseph, N. E., Brolles, L., & Mouchenik, Y. (2018). Resilience in Haiti: Is it culturally pathological? *The British Journal of Psychiatry, 15*(4), 79–80. https://doi.org/10.1192/bji.2017.25

Devonish, D. (2018). Effort-reward imbalance at work: The role of job satisfaction. *Personnel Review, 47*(2), 319–333. https://doi.org/10.1108/pr-08-2016-0218

Dudley-Grant, R. (2016). Innovations in clinical psychology with Caribbean peoples. In J. L. Roopnarine & D. Chadee (Eds.), *Caribbean psychology: Contributions to a global discipline*. American Psychological Association.

Ebede-Ndi, A. (2016). A critical analysis of African-centered psychology: From ism to praxis. *International Journal of Transpersonal Studies, 35*(1), 9. https://doi.org/10.24972/ijts.2016.35.1.65

Fante-Coleman, T., Allen, K., Booker, M., Craigg, A., & Jackson-Best, F. (2023). "If you prayed more, you would feel better": The dual nature of religion and spirituality on Black youths' mental health and access to care in Canada. *Child and Adolescent Social Work Journal*, 1–18. https://doi.org/10.1007/s10560-023-00932-1

Ferguson, G. M. (2016). Remote acculturation and the birth of an Americanized Caribbean youth identity on the islands. In J. L. Roopnarine & D. Chadee (Eds.), *Caribbean psychology: Indigenous contributions to a global discipline* (pp. 97–117). American Psychological Association. https://doi.org/10.1037/14753-005

Gilroy, P. (1994). Diaspora. *Paragraph, 17*(3), 207–212. http://www.jstor.org/stable/43263438

Goddard-Durant, S. (2019). "Resilience" in Barbados: Bein' uh work in progress. Dissertation. Guelph University.

Goddard-Durant, S. K., Doucet, A., Tizaa, H., & Sieunarine, J. A. (2022). A decolonizing, intersectional, Black feminist approach to young Black Caribbean-Canadian mothers' resilience. *Journal of Family Studies, 29*(4), 1946–1966. https://doi.org/10.1080/13229400.2022.2105737

Goddard-Durant, S. K., Doucet, A., Tizaa, H., & Sieunarine, J. A. (2023). "I don't have the energy": Racial stress, young Black mother hood and Canadian social policies. *Canadian Review of Sociology, 60*(4), 542–566. https://doi.org/10.1111/cars.12457

Gopaul-McNicol, S. (1993). *Working with West Indian families.* The Guildford Press.

Grills, C., Nobles, W. W., & Hill, C. (2018). African, Black, neither or both? Models and strategies developed and implemented by the association of Black psychologists. *Journal of Black Psychology, 44*(8), 791–826. https://doi.org/10.1177/0095798418813660

Hammack, P. L. (2011). *Narrative and the politics of identity: The cultural psychology of Israeli and Palestinian youth.* Oxford University Press.

Hickling, F. W. (2020). Owing our madness: Contributions of Jamaican psychiatry to decolonizing global mental health. *Transcultural Psychiatry, 57*(1), 19–31. https://doi.org/10.1177/1363461519893142

Hill Collins, P. (2009). *Black feminist thought: Knowledge, consciousness, and the politics of empowerment* (2nd ed.). Routledge.

Jackson, F. Z., & Naidoo, K. (2012). "Lemeh check see if meh mask on straight": Examining how Black women of Caribbean descent in Canada manage depression and construct womanhood through being strong. *Southern Journal of Canadian Studies, 5*(1–2), 223–240. https://doi.org/10.22215/sjcs.v5i1.296

James, C., Este, D., Thomas Bernard, W., Benjamin, A., Lloyd, B., & Turner, T. (2010). *Race and well-being: The lives, hopes and activism of African Canadians.* Fernwood Publishing.

James, C. E., & Turner, T. (2017). *Towards race equity in education: The schooling of Black students in the greater Toronto area.* York University. https://youthrex.com/report/towards-race-equity-in-education-the-schooling-of-black-students-in-the-greater-toronto-area/

Joseph, J. C., & Kuo, B. C. H. (2009). Black Canadians' coping responses to racial dis-crimination. *Journal of Black Psychology, 35*, 78–101. https://doi.org/10.1177/009579840-8323384

Lalonde, R. N., Jones, J. M., & Stroink, M. L. (2008). Racial identity, racial attitudes and race socialization among Black Canadian parents. *Canadian Journal of Behavioural Science, 40*, 129–139. https://doi.org/10.1037/0008-400X.40.3.129

Lambert, M. C., Sewell, W. C., & Levitch, A. H. (2016). Metamorphosing euro American psychological assessment instruments to measures developed by and for English-speaking Caribbean people. In J. L. Roopnarine & D. Chadee (Eds.), *Caribbean psychology: Contributions to a global discipline* (pp. 327–355). American Psychological Association. https://doi.org/10.1037/14753-014

Litchmore, R. V. H., Safdar, S., & O'Doherty, K. (2016). Ethnic and racial self-identifications of second-generation Canadians of African and Caribbean heritage: An analysis of discourse. *Journal of Black Psychology, 42*(3), 259–242. https://doi.org/10.1177/0095798414568454

Lorenzi, J., & Batalova, J. (2022). *Caribbean immigrants in the United States.* Migration Policy Institute. https://www.migrationpolicy.org/

Lux, W. R. (1972). Black power in the Caribbean. *Journal of Black Studies, 3*(2), 207–225.

Maynard, D. (2018). Research in educational psychology in the English-speaking Caribbean: A systematic literature review. *Caribbean Journal of Psychology, 10*(1), 18–53.

Maynard, R. (2017). *Policing Black lives: State violence in Canada from slavery to the present.* Fernwood Publishing.

McCubbin, L. D., & Marsella, A. (2009). Native Hawaiians and psychology: The cultural and historical context of indigenous ways of knowing. *Cultural Diversity and Ethnic Minority Psychology, 15*(4), 374–387. https://doi.org/10.1037/a0016774

Mensah, J. (2010). *Black Canadians* (2nd ed.). Fernwood Publishing.

Nicolas, G., & Wheatley, A. (2013). Historical and socio-political perspectives on mental health in the Caribbean region. *Interamerican Journal of Psychology, 47*(2), 167–176.

Nobles, W. W. (2013). Shattered consciousness, fractured identity: Black psychology and the restoration of the African psyche. *Journal of Black Psychology, 39*(3), 232–242. https://doi.org/10.1177/0095798413478075

Ortiz Torres, B. (2020). Decoloniality and community-psychology practice in Puerto Rico: Autonomous organising (autogestion) and self-determination. *International Review of Psychiatry, 32*(4), 359–364. https://doi.org/10.1080/09540261.2020.1761776

Philogene, G. (1994). "African American" as a new social representation. *Journal for the Theory of Social Behaviour, 24*, 89–109. https://doi.org/10.1111/j.1468-5914.1994.tb00248.x

Rich, G. J., & Jean-Charles, W. (2022). Psychology in Haiti. In G. J. Rich & N. A. Ramkumar (Eds.), *Psychology in Oceania and the Caribbean. International and cultural psychology*. Springer. https://doi.org/10.1007/978-3-030-87763-7_15

Robertson-Hickling, H. (2008). Resilience: Secrets of success in African-Caribbean people. In F. W. Hickling, B. K. Matthies, K. Morgan, & R. C. Gibson (Eds.), *Perspectives in Caribbean psychology* (pp. 70–92). CARIMENSA.

Rodney, W. (2019). *The groundings with my brothers*. Random House Publishing Services. https://bookshelf.vitalsource.com/books/9781788731171

Roopnarine, J. L., Ong'ayi, D. M. M., Krishnakumar, A., Ali, A., & Primus, M. A. (2023). Maternal depressive symptoms and physical intimate partner violence and children's internalizing and externalizing behaviors in Guyanese families: Mediating role of constructive conflict behavior. *American Journal of Orthopsychiatry, 93*(3), 236–244. https://doi.org/10.1037/ort0000671

Satzewich, V. (1989). Racism and Canadian immigration policy: The government's view of Caribbean migration, 1962–1969. *Canadian Ethnic Studies, 21*(1), 77–97. https://www.proquest.com/scholarly-journals/racism-canadian-immigration-policy-governments/docview/1293245023/se-2

Schreiber, R., Noerager Stern, P., & Wilson, C. (2000). Being strong: How Black West-Indian Canadian women manage depression and stigma. *Journal of Nursing Scholarship, 32*(1), 39–45. https://doi.org/10.1111/j.1547-5069.2000.00039.x

Smith, A., & Lalonde, R. N. (2003). "Racelessness" in a Canadian context? Exploring the link between Black students' identity, achievement, and mental health. *Journal of Black Psychology, 29*(2), 142–164. https://doi.org/10.1177/0095798403029002002

Stanton, C. R. (2014). Crossing methodological borders: Decolonizing community-based participatory research. *Qualitative Inquiry, 20*(5), 573–583. https://doi.org/10.1177/1077800413505541

Statistics Canada. (2022). The Canadian census: A rich portrait of the country's religious and ethnocultural diversity. https://www150.statcan.gc.ca/n1/daily-quotidien/221026/dq221026b-eng.htm

Statistics Canada. (2023). Black history month 2023…by the numbers. https://www.statcan.gc.ca/en/dai/smr08/2023/smr08_270

Stevens, G. (2015). Black psychology: Resistance, reclamation and redefinition. In I. Parker (Ed.), *Handbook of critical psychology* (pp. 181–189). Taylor & Francis. https://bookshelf.vitalsource.com/books/9781317537175

Stevens, G., Bell, D., Sonn, C., Canham, H., & Clennon, O. (2017). Transnational perspectives on black subjectivity. *South African Journal of Psychology, 47*(4):459–469. https://doi.org/10.1177/0081246317737929

Sutherland, M. E. (2011). Toward a Caribbean psychology: An African-centered approach. *Journal of Black Studies, 42*(8), 1175–1194. https://doi.org/10.1177/0021934711410547

Tator, C., & Henry, F. (2007). *Racial profiling in Canada: Challenging the myth of 'a few bad apples'*. University of Toronto Press.

Tetty, W. J., & Puplampu, K. P. (2005). *The African diaspora in Canada: Negotiating identity and belonging*. University of Calgary Press. https://press.ucalgary.ca/books/9781552381755/

Thompson, A. D. (2016). Toward a Caribbean psychology: Context, imperatives, and future directions. In J. L. Roopnarine & D. Chadee (Eds.), *Caribbean psychology: Contributions to a global discipline* (pp. 15–44). American Psychological Association. https://doi.org/10.1037/14753-002

Utsey, S. O., Adams, E. P., & Bolden, M. (2000). Development and initial validation of the Africultural coping systems inventory. *Journal of Black Psychology, 26*(2), 194–215. https://doi.org/10.1177/0095798400026002005

Waitoki, W., Dudgeon, P., Nikora, L.W. (2018). Indigenous Psychology in Aotearoa/New Zealand and Australia. In: Fernando, S., Moodley, R. (Eds.), *Global Psychologies*. Palgrave Macmillan, London. https://doi.org/10.1057/978-1-349-95816-0_10

Walcott, R. (2018) *Black like who? Writing Black Canada*. 20th anniversary edition. Insomniac Press.

Walker, B. (2012). Introduction: From a property right to citizenship rights—The African Canadian legal odyssey. In B. Walker (Ed.), *The African Canadian legal odyssey: Historical essays* (pp. 3–46). University of Toronto Press. http://www.jstor.org/stable/10.3138/j.ctt2tv2wh.5

Wilson, S., Nakhid, C., Fernandez-Santana, A., & Nakhid-Chatoor, M. (2018). An interrogation of research on Caribbean social issues: Establishing the need for an indigenous Caribbean research approach. *AlterNative, 15*(1), 3–12. https://doi.org/10.1177/1177180118803692

Winks, R. W. (1997). *Blacks in Canada: A history*. McGill-Queen's University Press. https://www.jstor.org/stable/j.ctt7zq6b

Yang, K.-S. (2000). Monocultural and cross-cultural indigenous approaches: The royal road to the development of a balanced global psychology. *Asian Journal of Social Psychology, 3*(3), 241–263. https://doi.org/10.1111/1467-839X.00067

Zeleza, P. T. (2006). The inventions of African identities and languages: The discursive and developmental implications. In O. F. Arasanyin & M. A. Pemberton (Eds.), *Selected proceedings of the 36th annual conference on African linguistics* (pp. 14–26). Cascadilla Proceedings Project.

CHAPTER 10

Using Indigenous Cultural Resources to Negotiate Diasporic Belonging: A Case Study of Chinese Roots-Related Metaphors

Katherine Bischoping, Zed Zhipeng Gao, and Edmund Siu

Introduction

People say *luoyeguigen* (fallen leaves return to the roots), but I won't.
—Research respondent Lindsay

Members of ethnic minority groups often experience a transnational life in a dynamic space between their home country and the host country. This

K. Bischoping (✉)
Department of Sociology, York University, Toronto, ON, Canada
e-mail: kbischop@yorku.ca

Z. Z. Gao
Department of Psychology, Health and Gender, The American University of Paris, Paris, France
e-mail: zgao@aup.edu

E. Siu
Independent Scholar, Toronto, ON, Canada

Z. Z. Gao, M. I. Medved (eds.), *Global Perspectives on Cultural Politics in Indigenous Psychology*, Palgrave Studies in Indigenous Psychology, https://doi.org/10.1007/978-3-031-96813-6_10

liminal status contributed to the development of two scholarly areas—acculturation research and diaspora studies—that can be distinguished in terms "forward looking" and "backward looking" perspectives. The scholarship of acculturation, as implied by the concept, originated from a concern with how immigrants acclimate to their host society (Sam, 2006). Even though later versions of acculturation theory displayed greater openness to immigrants' desire to preserve their heritage culture, acculturation scholars tend to reflect a "forward looking" mindset by emphasizing the link between immigrants and the host society. The populations of interest to acculturation researchers and diaspora scholars may well overlap, yet diaspora studies takes a "backward looking" perspective, in that it is more interested in how immigrants address their ties to their regions of origin, from which they have been dispersed (Brubaker, 2005).This is where we position our research: we are interested in how members of a diaspora address the indigenous culture they carry—or refuse to carry—in the journey away from their homeland. Indigenous culture, we suggest, plays a key role in how diaspora communities navigate their transnational trajectory, as it informs who they are as well as where they feel to belong.

We choose to focus on members of the Chinese diaspora's use of indigenous cultural resources to address their relations with the homeland partly in light of the latest fragmentation of global Chinese diasporic communities. At a time of heightened international geopolitics surrounding China, overseas Chinese—whether naturalized citizens of the West, international students, or visitors—have become severely divided in their attitudes toward the Chinese state. Reports of jingoistic overseas Chinese glorifying their home country exist alongside public events of political dissent such as those of artist Ai Weiwei. Such a contentious relation between the diaspora and its home state forms the backdrop of our analysis.

Regardless of their different relations to the home state, members of Chinese diasporic communities share many time-honored, distinct indigenous cultural traditions. If, as popularly assumed, culture serves as a basis for the formation of a common ethnic identity, how do Chinese immigrants articulate their political differences while speaking from a shared cultural framework? We address this question of cultural politics by examining how Chinese immigrants use the indigenous resource of roots-related metaphors to speak of belonging. Of course, many cultures use such metaphors: one may "put down roots" in a host country or long to "return to one's roots" in one's homeland; one's roots may be considered constructed or essential, located in one's relationships or in a culture, ethnicity, place, or state. This chapter will first trace the genealogy of a more distinctively Chinese idiom, *luoyeguigen* — "fallen leaves return to the roots," to highlight how a roots metaphor, as an indigenous cultural resource, can become politicized. This is consequential, for metaphors are no mere discursive bit players but rather are rhetorical devices that powerfully influence beliefs and values (Lakoff & Johnson, 1980; Musolff, 2016; Tay, 2014).

It should be noted that in this approach, we meld two definitions of the concept of culture. One, which uses what Baldwin et al. (2006) call an "intergroup perspective" (p. 17), is concerned with how groups are constructed through processes of identifying with, distinguishing among, and comparing groups. Such processes predominate in how our research participants speak of belonging and exclusion in China and Canada. In so doing, they draw on linguistic resources that may be culturally distinctive and, indeed, it could be said that our attention to distinctive metaphors itself acts to constitute people into cultural groups. That said, we view culture to be neither static nor neutral. As Yuval-Davis (2006) theorizes, the large collectives in which we may experience belonging or exclusion are ongoingly constructed through "active and situated imagination" (p. 204) and through a "dirty business of boundary maintenance" (p. 204) that inherently involves both hegemonic forces and those contesting them. Thus, our analysis will combine the intergroup perspective on culture with what Baldwin et al. (2006) term a "culture as power" (p. 18) perspective. We seek to understand how the linguistic resources of roots-related metaphors enter into struggles between hegemonic and counter-hegemonic forces.

Having presented the genealogy of *luoyeguigen*, we next turn to a specific recent juncture—2019, in Toronto, Canada—and a sample of immigrants from the People's Republic in China. We examine how they tapped into an extended family of roots-and-leaves metaphors involving soil, branches, seeds, and the like to express the complex nature of their belonging, or rather, for some, the nature of what Gao (2023) theorizes as their unbelonging. Influenced by cultural theorist Stuart Hall (1999), we explore how these participants navigated between using such metaphors for agentic self-expression and using them in ways that instantiated or contested the kind of hegemonic discourse about roots and belonging that is championed by the Chinese state.

Methods and Data

The first genealogical component of the analysis uses a sample drawn from our wide search for sources in which the *luoyeguigen* idiom appears in the simplified Chinese characters in use in the People's Republic of China and occasionally in English translation. Among these sources were news reports, a Buddhist text, poetry, a film, social media posts, songs, and academic studies, dating from the Ming Dynasty to the 2020s. In analyzing these literary and discursive instantiations of *luoyeguigen*, we draw inspiration from Raymond Williams' (1976) study, *Keywords*, albeit focusing on a key idiom. That the factual content of idioms is slight makes them potentially applicable to numerous contexts, where they can richly convey affects and attitudes (Sidtis & Sidtis, 2018). Through repeated use, idioms gain in familiarity for listeners and gain in rhetorical might: they come to appeal to what they implicitly represent to be widely held truths (Drew & Holt, 1988). In the Chinese language, four-character idioms such as *luoyeguigen*, which may originate in peasant colloquialisms, literary works, political slogans, and more, play a far more vibrant and central role in communication than the recurring idioms used in English (Rohsenow, 2001). This is in part because their populist appeal and the value of creating a common political language had been championed by Mao Zedong, himself a deft coiner of idioms (Rohsenow, 2001; Jiang & González, 2021).

On the one hand, Williams (1976) views keywords as instantiating the discourses available in a particular time, place, and configuration of social forces, but on the other hand, he points out that "some important social and historical processes occur *within* language" (1976, p. 22). That is, the contestations over a keyword's meaning can themselves bring about social and historical change. Our analysis seeks to identify how changing national and transnational events, relations, and power struggles are connected to the changing meanings and messages associated with *luoyeguigen*. The idiom can thus be used to do—and to resist—different kinds of ideological work in various national circumstances and transnational configurations.

Next, our interview-based analysis draws on semi-structured qualitative interviews coauthor Gao conducted in mid-2019 with 39 first-generation immigrants from mainland China who were living in the Greater Toronto Area in Canada. Participants gave informed consent and the project received approval from the Research Ethics Office of York University. Participants had varied citizenship statuses (including Canadian citizens, permanent residents, international students, short-term visitors, and undocumented status), and all self-identified as being ethnically Chinese. The interviews, conducted in Mandarin, addressed their decisions to come to Canada, relations with locals in Canada, relations with family and friends in China, experiences with Chinese social media, and views of Canadian-Chinese international relations. Central to the last of these topics was the ongoing controversy about Huawei executive Meng Wangzhou, who had been arrested in Canada in 2018 and who, at the time of the interviews, was still awaiting a court decision about whether Canada should extradite her to the USA to face charges there. In the meantime, the Chinese government performed a few seemingly retaliatory actions, including trade sanctions and the detention of two Canadian citizens.

A theme running through the interviews was the participants' sense of belonging, whether in China, Canada, or neither (Gao, 2023). Through a close reading of the transcripts, we identified 11 participants who made reference to roots and related metaphors of branches and stems, soil, leaves, and seeds. As "roots" was not purposefully included among the interview questions, when it arose, it was nearly always at the participants' initiative. It is these transcripts, from participants ranging in age from 23 to 55 years, who had been living in Canada for 1 to 19 years, that we analyze. All names used in this chapter are pseudonyms.

Research Findings Part I: A Transnational Genealogy

A Naturalistic Roots-and-Leaves Metaphor

In tracing the meanings of the cultural resource of the *luoyeguigen* idiom, we recognize that this idiom, due to its metaphoric flexibility, can symbolize a diversity of phenomena. For example, one might ask: Who or what is the leaf, how does it fall, what are the roots, how does the leaf return to the roots, and is this return inevitable? One of the earliest and most influential answers comes from China, where the idiom appears in a Ming Dynasty (1368–1644 AD) text named *Diamond Sutra and the Sutra of Hui-Neng*, purporting to collect the teachings of the Buddhist master Hui-Neng (638–713 AD). In the scene that is key for our purposes, Hui-Neng is anticipating his death and calls for a boat to take him back to his hometown. When his disciples plead with him to remain with them, Hui-Neng replies that his physical body will inevitably die before he enters nirvana. The disciples then beseech him to return after his hometown visit, but Hui-Neng decisively closes that discussion with "*luoyeguigen*" (Price & Wong, 1990, pp. 148–149). In this exchange, Hui-Neng's hometown is characterized in an essentialist way as the root to which he, a leaf that will fall through his body's death, ought to be returned, a conclusion with the inevitability of a natural phenomenon. Over centuries, ideas related to *luoyeguigen* gained traction in Chinese culture, animating individuals' nostalgic attachment to their hometowns.

Leaves Across the Pacific Ocean

We fast forward to the mid-nineteenth century, when the *luoyeguigen* idiom crossed the Pacific as Chinese immigrants arrived in North America to work in the burgeoning rail and mining industries, only to be met with opposition from white workers who came to regard them as competitors (Almaguer, 1994; Lee, 2002). These immigrants were perniciously racialized and their access to mobility and citizenship limited, whether through the "head tax" imposed in Canada (1885–1923) or the Exclusion Acts in place in Canada (1923–1947) and the USA (1882–1943) (Chan, 2020). Particularly germane for our investigation of the *luoyeguigen* idiom is that Chinese could be excluded from mainstream cemeteries and relegated to less dignified burial grounds (Hom, 2002; Maxwell, 2007). In response, mutual assistance groups in Chinese immigrant communities emphasized returning their ill and aging members to China to pass away in their home communities, or repatriating deceased members' remains (Hom, 2002; Yip, 2018). Either was considered in keeping with *luoyeguigen*. In this transnational instantiation of the idiom, the leaves became members of a group of immigrants spurned and embattled in North America. While for Hui-Neng, the Buddhist master of our earlier example, return to the root was positioned as simply natural, for these immigrants to fail to return to the gravesites of one's patrilineal ancestors would mean becoming a lonely spirit adrift in a foreign land (Yip, 2018).

Yet the *luoyeguigen* idiom may not always have spoken to the beliefs and experiences of Chinese in North America during this era. Chen (2000) argues that despite their experiences of discrimination, they nonetheless established connections and community within Chinatowns and through strong transnational ties: not all were sojourners longing to return to their country of origin. Wang (2005) proposes that following the USA Exclusion Act's repeal, a competing idiom *luodishenggen* (p. 782), meaning "[leaves/seeds] fall to/land on the ground and take root," better represented this experience of forming connections that fostered local belonging. In conveying a notion of roots as emergent and constructed within the new social context in which a person can land, rather than as fixed, essential, and related to the cessation of life, *luodishenggen* profoundly differs from *luoyeguigen*.

The Politicization of Roots-Related Metaphors in China

In the meantime, back in China, roots-related metaphors were about to undergo a different transformation. With the 1949 founding of the People's Republic of China, the term "roots" was turned to a sharply new politicized meaning, grounded initially in revolution, class struggle, and loyalty to the Party. A vivid illustration is a 1963 song celebrating communist hero Lei Feng, who had been orphaned in childhood owing to landlord oppression of his impoverished proletarian parents. Succored by the Party, he went on earn Mao Zedong's acclaim for daily performing good deeds in a collectivist spirit. The song begins,

> Study Lei Feng, a good role model
> Loyal to the revolution, loyal to the Party
> Clearly distinguish what to love from what to hate, don't forget [your] *ben*
> (CCTV, 2017, 0:02 translation ours)

As *ben* means both "roots" and "origin," the third line of the song is understood to be praising Lei Feng for his lucid understanding of class struggle and for conducting himself in ways inspired by his class background and by the Party, the origin of his communist subjectivity. Since the post-communist China began to open to the outside world in the late 1970s, the hegemonic discourse's emphasis on revolution and class struggle has diminished, but it incorporated new notions of loyalty. This new hegemonic rendering of the *luoyeguigen* discourse has come to hold that all people of Chinese descent naturally belong to China, whether in an ancestral, cultural, national, or geographic sense. In this way, the cultural resource of roots-related ideas came to be mobilized to bolster Chinese nationalism among both those living in China (as "leaves") and those overseas (as "fallen leaves").

A Global United Front?

Concerning overseas Chinese, the Chinese government, especially the Overseas Chinese Affairs Office, has been promoting multiple outreach activities (To, 2014). Since the 1980s, China sponsored *xungen* (root-seeking) camps, where overseas Chinese explored their culture and ancestral ties (To, 2014). Among the highlights of *xungen* tourism is a colossal and ancient pagoda tree popularly believed to be the site from which, in 1370–1417, most of the Chinese population was forcibly dispersed from Shanxi Province to the rest of China (iMedia, 2024). The story of the pagoda tree visualizes the roots-related metaphors, fleshes them out with historical details, and nominates a physical site for tourist exploration. Later, the outreach activities expanded to the TV screen. The year 2012 saw the launch of a televised reality singing competition named *The Voice of China*, which has actively recruited not only Chinese citizens but also non-citizens of Chinese descent. In interviews and in lyrics, its overseas participants express a longing to return to their Chinese roots (Jiang & González, 2021). Activities such as these aimed to forge a united front coalescing around a global Chinese identity.

The Chinese government sometimes avails itself of roots-related discourses in addressing international relations. For example, when reporters asked Deng Xiaoping about the agreement he had signed with the UK to transfer sovereignty of Hong Kong to China, he replied, "*luoyeguigen*" (as cited in Mah, 2012, p.3), invoking a quasi-natural law to assert China's sovereignty over Hong Kong. Further, this reply strikes a chord to Chinese ears, portraying a nostalgic longing for reunification. However, as mentioned earlier, given the multiplicity of roots-related expressions, there are counter-discourses such as *luodishenggen* available. Take, for example, Singapore, a small island country that makes up for its lack of natural resources with highly successful international trade, involving not only neighboring Asian countries but also the West. With a majority of its population comprised of Chinese descendants, Singapore has the thorny task of addressing the role of Chinese identity in its nationhood. As Ng (2021) discusses, the Singaporean government tends to emphasize that Singaporean Chinese culture is distinct from that of China. For instance, on Singapore's National Day in 2022, Prime Minister Lee Hsien Loong (2022) gave a speech in which he entreated his country's Chinese community to *luodishenggen* (land on the ground and take root) and identify with Singaporean priorities rather than considering themselves *luoyeguigen* who should align with China. In so doing, Loong took advantage of a Chinese cultural resource to turn the tables on China.

Recent Developments

The status of Chinese emigration has shifted in recent decades, sometimes valorized by the Chinese state as well as the emigrants themselves, and other times a matter of tension. When China joined the World Trade Organization around the turn of the twentieth-first century, the Chinese government hailed its expatriates as patriots for expanding China's international business opportunities (Nyíri, 2001). Two decades later, China entered a new phase of geopolitical tension which coincided with its Covid-19 lockdowns. As a result, Chinese official discourse about overseas Chinese shifted from the previous focus on business exchanges to a globally based ethnonationalism. In May 2020, the overseas edition of *People's Daily* published an article entitled "*Shu gao qianzhang gen zai Zhongguo*" [A tree ten thousand feet tall has its roots in China], praising its audience for donating in aid of China's Covid-19 response despite their not living in China (Yan, 2020, p.1). This depiction might have held true in the early stage of the pandemic. Yet, soon many overseas Chinese found themselves unable to return to China due to its stringent border lockdowns, leading to difficulties with their visa status, finances, and healthcare (Gao, 2023). Stranded overseas Chinese sometimes resorted to the roots-and-leaves discourse to enhance their cases. For example, in 2020, a Chinese vlogger in Argentina related the story of a son pleading on behalf of his father who, while suffering liver cancer, would not have been allowed to enter China (Yun zai Agenting, 2020). The video employed the *luoyeguigen* idiom to contend that the father had a right to return. The story gains rhetorical force by synthesizing the early sense of the idiom, in which the ill and aging naturally return to their roots, and the hegemonic sense, in which the state has actively encouraged the far-flung "fallen leaves" to picture themselves being welcomed "home" in China.

Research Findings Part II: Roots-Related Metaphors Used by Chinese Immigrants

Hegemonic and Counter Discourses

In the above, we have sketched a genealogy of roots-related metaphors, with particular attention to how these metaphors became politicized. While the germinal story of Hui-Neng likened burial ceremony to the imagery of leaves returning to the roots in a naturalistic fashion, later, the roots metaphors became frequently used to make assertions about whether one is entitled and obliged to belong in a territorial, cultural, and national sense. Consistent with the notion of cultural politics, we observe the competition between *luoyeguigen, a* hegemonic discourse often sponsored by the nation state, and *luodishenggen* as an alternative idiom used to contend for non-essentialized identities. In the following, we flesh out the dynamic between the hegemonic discourse and the counter discourse by looking at how our Toronto interview respondents talk about their sense of belonging.

Flexible Use of the Roots Metaphors

We begin with Yang, a professor employed in a Chinese university and Party member, who in the following passage seemed to express a staunchly essentialist position:

> Chinese immigrants who oppose Huawei, what are they thinking? I feel when some people are going about things, they should never be forgetting [their] roots. Where's [their] origin? Whatever your country is, you're someone who came from there: this is the root. No matter what your country does that's not good for you, you came from there. If that country isn't good to you, and you oppose today's government, then on the surface you're opposing the government and in actuality, you're opposing the people. If this government has benefited the people, let the people develop and live and work in peace. If back then [the government] wasn't good to you, and now you're still holding grudges in [your] heart, still looking for trouble, that means we aren't looking at things from a development perspective.

Of interest here is that Yang characterizes Chinese immigrants in Canada as having roots in China—rather than simply in their family or hometown. To Yang, one's roots command loyalty of a specifically political kind. In his interpretation, opposition to Huawei and indeed any opposition to the Chinese government is tantamount to opposition to this root. In keeping with the hegemonic Party argument, Yang maintains that because the government has provided the people of China with economic development and peace, to criticize it is indicative of both flawed reasoning ("What are they thinking?") and the flawed morality of a self-centered trouble-seeking grudge-bearer. A further moral freighting is achieved in the final sentence of this passage by Yang's transition from the imagined "you" who is a grudge-bearer, to a paternalistic "we" who can sensibly arrive at a development perspective. This use of "we" is a common rhetorical device in Chinese political speeches (Liu, 2022).

Later in the interview, however, Yang took a turn toward a constructivist notion of roots.

> People undergo change as their experiences change. *Interviewer: Are you worried about your children coming here and forgetting their roots?* I think that we adults have a certain root, and whatever roots a child may have, I respect him. This is his freedom. He's of the next generation.

Here, he invokes the social constructivist notion that experience alters people, and then explains that although he considers the roots of adult Chinese immigrants to be immutable, children who come to Canada should be at liberty to conceive of their roots as they will. As Yang continues, he would expound on the idea that a child migrating from China would be ineligible to criticize China, unless China harmed him in some way:

> If after he [a child] comes here, life is good, the two countries' relationship is good, certainly it'd be fortunate. But no matter what happens, if China hasn't done anything bad to him, at the least he can't take a stance against China; if he has this notion, until China did something bad to him, he can't behave like this.

In these quotations, it has become evident that the through-line in the views Yang has expressed is neither essentialism nor constructivism. Rather, he appears to be using essentialism and constructivism flexibly to the rhetorical effect of staunchly defending China against criticism in the public sphere, whether by an adult immigrant with essentially Chinese roots or by a child immigrant lacking bad experience in China and constructing his own roots.

The Choice of Silence

While Yang spoke in depth on the connection of "roots" to the subordination of individuals to the Chinese state, some other respondents alluded to roots when explaining problems in communication within the Chinese communities. Among them, Charlotte, who had been living in Canada for 11 years, mentioned an instance when another Chinese person living in Canada had given a vague reply when a media interviewer asked whether the USA was untrustworthy. Charlotte surmised that the interviewee had been concerned that a concrete answer might lead to the allegation that he or she was a "*wangben de damaozi*," a "root-forgetting big hat." By using the expression "big hat," which refers to an unjustifiably applied and hyperbolically negative political label, Charlotte signals that the interviewee probably did not feel safe to express an honest opinion, and that this lack of freedom of speech is problematic. Another problem pointed out by Charlotte is disinformation, such as the online theory that an American plot to kill Chinese technicians had been at the heart of the disappearance of Malaysian Airlines Flight 370. According to Charlotte, while naive individuals fall for such clearly unsubstantiated conspiracy theories, those with good judgment would choose to stay silent about them. The choice of silence, however, is not one easily made. In her own case, Charlotte went through many bitter debates with friends in the Chinese communities, before making a vow that she would never speak about these contentious topics again.

Another respondent, Louise, who had lived in Canada for 16 years, similarly expressed an acute lack of social belonging exacerbated by the choice of silence. This came to light when she was asked what she thought of the balance between communicating with Chinese using social media and visiting China once a year, which was typical among those in the sample with Canadian citizenship. Initially, she said that being in Canada as a single person, her home "has no roots." Thus, "Every year I go back to China and feel my home is there. Here [in Canada] there's little emotional support. With people there [in China] communication is better." Note that she utilizes a sense of roots as being ongoingly *socially* constructed via the shared intimacy of a family environment—a sense sharply contrasting with Yang's *political* one. However, Louise continued despondently, "In this environment (China), you still face problems, never can talk with family, they don't understand. They don't understand at all." In consequence, Louise silenced herself when political and cultural differences she experienced between the countries came to mind. This left her conversing only about topics she called "very superficial," which could be interpreted to be damaging her subjective sense of familial roots, intimacy, and belonging. She concluded these reflections:

> To be honest, I don't know what choice I will make [about where to live] when I retire. Emotionally, I don't know where my home is either. On the other hand, my situation is special. It would be different if I had a family here.

Countering Hegemonic Discourse

We turn next to two participants who use roots metaphors in voicing their resistance to the hegemonic discourse. The first of these is Cynthia, a small business owner and lapsed Party member. She dates her decision to emigrate from China to the moment when the Chinese government crushed the democratic movement of 1989. While Cynthia does not feel she belongs politically in China, she has a strong sense of cultural belonging and takes time to maintain her familiarity with traditional Chinese arts and literature. The divide she feels between these two senses of belonging is epitomized by how she explained her political decision to leave by drawing on her cultural repertoire, reciting lines from an elegant pre-Qin Dynasty (221–206 BC) poem in which a girl decides to depart for a paradise-like land after suffering the exploitations of a rat, a creature popularly understood to symbolize a corrupt and greedy governor (Balcom, 2001).

Rather than bluntly arguing against the hegemonic roots metaphor, Cynthia expresses herself through the alternative roots metaphor *luodishenggen*, discussed earlier, in which to migrate is to generate roots. For instance, when asked about her experience as a Chinese person who had thus far been living in Canada for one year, she replied:

> We came of our own volition, because of what we wanted to participate in, and we knew what that was before we came. The process [we] experienced is mainly to complete the construction of a local social network and establish a regular source of income. It's a process of transplantation, of finding good soil. For seeds to fall [instead] on stone—that would be too stupid for me to do. [It's a matter of] strengthening your root system.

This quotation is thoroughly constructivist. In her extended use of the roots metaphor, Cynthia positions herself as a seed, her migration as transplantation, and Canada as potentially good soil in which to develop roots. To Cynthia, roots are not an essential characteristic that one automatically possesses so much as they result from a process of constructing them via an intelligent systematic approach to social and economic integration. In all, Cynthia uses this sense of roots in positioning herself as an effective, agentic author of her social and economic belonging in Canada, and thus sidesteps the hegemonic discourse in which her roots would be essentially Chinese.

We turn last to Lindsay, the respondent who had set us on this chapter's analytic path through her statement "People say fallen leaves return to the roots, but I won't," and thereby expressing her opposition to the Communist Party of China. She says:

> Given China is the way it is, if my father [who lives in China] passes away, I might never go back. The reason is this country makes me feel it has lost its basic morality. If I went back, I'd feel unsafe. When I travel to Japan, I just carry [gestures as if to a backpack] on my shoulders. Would you dare to in China? Children are kidnapped, snatched away. Crossing the road, no one gives way [to pedestrians]. It's not safe. […] There's nothing people won't stoop to.

This quote stands out for how Lindsay positions Japan, a country often reviled in China for its conduct in the Sino-Japanese War, as a foil to China. Japan, she says, is safe, while China has become fundamentally unsafe. Japan-China comparisons are often a theme in Lindsay's interview, for instance, elsewhere she speaks of traveling in Japan and seeing "genuine" and "peaceful" smiles between people, rather than smiles given for economic motivation. Substantial passages of Lindsay's interview are concerned with how, in her view, people living in China have become beset by greed through undemocratic politics and Party policies that leave the poor to struggle while rewarding the corruption of the wealthy. To Lindsay, political and economic unbelonging have driven social and even moral unbelonging.

Yet, when asked whether she desired to return to China, Lindsay replied, "Yes," and then "If China had no money [i.e., were incorruptible], in that case, I still would, because it is the soil where I grew up." Whereas Cynthia had implicitly refuted the hegemonic essentialist use of roots by offering an alternative constructivist root metaphor, here we see Lindsay embrace the *luoyeguigen* idiom's essentialist notion of roots, and turn it against the hegemony of the Communist Party. "To put it simply," she concludes, "the country that the Communist Party of China is in is not my country. There is no reason to go back."

Conclusion

In this chapter, we have analyzed the cultural politics of roots-related metaphors. We show that although overseas Chinese of the nineteenth century had used this idiom to refer to a longing to be buried in their hometowns, the idiom has since been politically assimilated by the Chinese Party-state, which has used it to promote an ethno-nationalist belonging both domestically and overseas. In other words, we established how roots-and-leaves metaphors, as a Chinese cultural resource, have become imbued with politics. Second, we turned to Chinese living in Canada to examine how they use roots-and-leaves metaphors to construct and negotiate their sense of belonging in relation to China. While immigrants have long been known to have an unsettled or contested sense of belonging, contemporary overseas Chinese arguably experienced this in the extreme given the geopolitical tensions surrounding China. We demonstrate that our research participants used diverse roots-and-leaves metaphors that permitted them to agentically express their fraught sense of belonging and signal their political alignments.

We chose to focus on roots-related metaphors as an exemplary case of cultural politics. Among Chinese communities, the roots-related metaphors are commonly known as affectively potent articulations of individuals' relation with China. We view these metaphors to be cultural resources in the sense that they are curated products in a repertoire of meanings available for individuals who are part of the culture. Yet, these metaphors do not exist in an insulated cultural sphere. As we have shown, the historical evolution as well as the contemporary usages of the roots-related metaphors are saturated with political significance.

The next question is: how does culture enable politics? We suggest that, sometimes, the roots-related metaphors offer certain pre-structured definitions about one's entitlement and obligation with regard to one's country of origin. The notion of *luoyeguigen*, for example, makes one such hegemonic, essentializing definition readily available to Chinese immigrants. However, we hasten to add that, far from determining Chinese immigrants' sense of belonging, the roots-related metaphors allow diverse interpretations that accommodate the complex nature of belonging and, indeed, unbelonging. The elements of root and soil, for example, could symbolize the nation-state, one's hometown, social network, or cultural heritage. This permits Chinese immigrants to choose among multiple types of belonging: ethno-national belonging, cultural belonging, social belonging, etc. Further, the relations among various elements of the tree system—including soil, roots, branches and leaves—are open to interpretation. As salient as the hegemonic discourse is about the leaves' obligation to the roots that had nourished them, it is possible for Chinese immigrants to subvert this narrative with an alternative assertion that fallen leaves should grow new roots wherever they may land. If there is one thing that makes roots-related metaphors interesting, it is the organic nature of the tree system. Trees keep evolving, not without structural constraints but always containing possibilities of change. In a metaphoric spirit, we suggest that this also characterizes the evolution of Chinese diasporic belonging mediated by cultural heritage.

References

Almaguer, T. (1994). *Racial fault lines: The historical origins of white supremacy in California*. University of California Press.

Balcom, J. (2001). Big Rat, Big Rat: Multiple translations of a Chinese poem. *Translation Review, 62*(1), 35–41. https://doi.org/10.1080/07374836.2001.10523798

Baldwin, J. R., Faulkner, S. L., & Hecht, M. L. (2006). A moving target: The illusive definition of culture. In J. R. Baldwin, S. L. Faulkner, M. L. Hecht, & S. L. Lindsley (Eds.), *Redefining culture: Perspectives across the disciplines* (1st ed., pp. 3–26). Taylor and Francis. https://doi.org/10.4324/9781410617002

Brubaker, R. (2005). The 'diaspora' diaspora. *Ethnic and Racial Studies, 28*(1), 1–19. https://doi.org/10.1080/0141987042000289997

CCTV Zhongguo Zhongyang Dianshitai [CCTV China Central Television]. (2017, August 1). *Celebrating the 90th anniversary of Chinese People's Liberation Army | CCTV* [Video]. YouTube. https://www.youtube.com/watch?v=h6eTaW1wzYs

Chan, A. (2020, June 3). Chinese head tax in Canada. *The Canadian Encyclopedia*. https://www.thecanadianencyclopedia.ca/en/article/chinese-head-tax-in-canada

Chen, Y. (2000). *Chinese San Francisco, 1850–1943: A trans-Pacific community*. Stanford University Press.

Drew, P., & Holt, E. (1988). Complainable matters: The use of idiomatic expressions in making complaints. *Social Problems, 35*(4), 398–417. https://doi.org/10.2307/800594

Gao, Z. (2023). The politics of Chinese immigrants' double unbelonging and deglobalization. *Theory & Psychology, 33*(2), 266–283. https://doi.org/10.1177/09593543221130728

Hall, S. (1999). Encoding, decoding. In S. During (Ed.), *The cultural studies reader* (2nd ed., pp. 507–517). Routledge.

Hom, M. K. (2002). Fallen leaves' homecoming: Notes on the 1893 Gold Mountain Charity Cemetery in Xinhui. *Chinese America: History and Perspectives*, 36–52. https://link.gale.com/apps/doc/A105160298/AONE?u=anon~695d177e&sid=googleScholar&xid=3660abac

iMedia. (2024, January 6). The truth about the big locust tree in Hongdong, Shanxi. https://min.news/en/culture/8d09646274f5e456ad6cccaea2490cec.html

Jiang, X., & González, A. (2021). <China Dream> and <root-seeking>: The rhetoric of nationalism in *The Voice of China. Journal of Contemporary China, 30*(132), 1014–1026. https://doi.org/10.1080/10670564.2021.1893553

Lakoff, G., & Johnson, M. (1980). *Metaphors we live by.* University of Chicago Press.

Lee, E. (2002). The Chinese Exclusion example: Race, immigration, and American gatekeeping, 1882–1924. *Journal of American Ethnic History, 21*(3), 36–62. https://doi.org/10.2307/27502847

Lee, H. (2022, August 21). National Day Rally 2022. [Video]. https://www.youtube.com/watch?v=KlFA5qxz4iA

Liu, A. H. (2022). Pronoun usage as a measure of power personalization: A general theory with evidence from the Chinese-speaking world. *British Journal of Political Science, 52*(3), 1258–1275.

Mah, A. Y. (2012). *A thousand pieces of gold: A memoir of China's past through its proverbs.* HarperCollins Publishers.

Maxwell, J. (2007). Chinese cemeteries and grave markers in B.C.: A research guide. *British Columbia History, 40*(4), 13–17.

Musolff, A. (2016). Metaphor and persuasion in politics. In E. Semino & S. Demjén (Eds.), *The Routledge handbook of metaphor and language* (pp. 309–322). Routledge.

Ng, A. (2021). The divisiveness of Chinese identities in Singapore. *International Communication of Chinese Culture, 8*(4), 465–481. https://doi.org/10.1007/s40636-021-00235-z

Nyíri, P. (2001). Expatriating is patriotic? The discourse on "new migrants" in the People's Republic of China and identity construction among recent migrants from the PRC. *Journal of Ethnic and Migration Studies, 27*(4), 635–653. https://doi.org/10.1080/13691830120090421

Price, A. F., & Wong, M. (Trans.). (1990). *The Diamond Sutra and the Sutra of Hui-Neng*. Shambhala.

Rohsenow, J. (2001). *ABC dictionary of Chinese proverbs*. University of Hawaii Press.

Sam, D. L. (2006). Acculturation: Conceptual background and core components. In D. L. Sam & J. W. Berry (Eds.), *The Cambridge handbook of acculturation psychology* (pp. 11–26). Cambridge University Press. https://doi.org/10.1017/CBO9780511489891.005

Sidtis, D. V. L., & Sidtis, J. J. (2018). The affective nature of formulaic language: A right-hemisphere subcortical process. *Frontiers in Neurology, 9*, 573. https://doi.org/10.3389/fneur.2018.00573

Tay, D. (2014). Lakoff and the theory of conceptual metaphor. In J. Littlemore & J. R. Taylor (Eds.), *The Bloomsbury companion to cognitive linguistics* (pp. 49–59). Bloomsbury Academic.

To, J. J. H. (2014). *Qiaowu: Extra-territorial policies for the overseas Chinese*. Brill.

Wang, L. C. (2005). Chinese in the United States. In M. Ember, C. R. Ember, & I. Skoggard (Eds.), *Encyclopedia of diasporas: Immigrant and refugee cultures around the world* (pp. 769–785). Springer.

Williams, R. (1976). *Keywords: A vocabulary of culture and society*. Oxford University Press.

Yan, Y. (2020, May 18). A tree ten thousand feet tall has its roots in China, *People's Daily* (Overseas edition). http://paper.people.com.cn/rmrbhwb/html/2020-05/18/content_1987506.htm

Yip, H. (2018). Institutionalizing charity: Hong Kong and the homebound burial of Chinese Americans, 1900–1949. *Chinese America, History and Perspectives*, 1–11. https://link.gale.com/apps/doc/A581024570/AONE?u=anon~7e8169bb&sid=googleScholar&xid=b0bff010

Yun zai Agenting (Director). (2020, June 26). *Sick Chinese compatriot wishes to receive treatment in China, fallen leaves return to the roots, but when will flights resume?* https://www.ixigua.com/6842489295433892367?logTag=a41b98d90e17682d2a8a

Yuval-Davis, N. (2006). Belonging and the politics of belonging. *Patterns of Prejudice, 40*(3), 197–214. https://doi.org/10.1080/00313220600769331

PART IV

Indigenous Resistance

CHAPTER 11

Indigenous Resurgence as Radical Healing Among Native Hawaiians

Laurie D. McCubbin, Christine Park, and Fei Bi Chan

Indigenous Resurgence as Radical Healing Among Native Hawaiians

The dispossession and disconnection from ancestral homelands are one of the main forms of colonial violence impacting Indigenous peoples today. As original stewards of the land, connection to ʻāina (land) is essential for

Please note all authors contributed equally to this manuscript.

L. D. McCubbin (✉)
Educational, School, and Counseling Psychology, University of Kentucky, Lexington, KY, USA
e-mail: laurie.mccubbin@uky.edu

C. Park
Adler Graduate School, Minnetonka, MN, USA

F. B. Chan
University of Louisville, Louisville, KY, USA

Z. Z. Gao, M. I. Medved (eds.), *Global Perspectives on Cultural Politics in Indigenous Psychology*, Palgrave Studies in Indigenous Psychology, https://doi.org/10.1007/978-3-031-96813-6_11

the wellness (mental, physical, and spiritual health) of the Kānaka ʻŌiwi (Native Hawaiians; Casken, 2001; Keli'iholokai et al., 2020; McCubbin & Marsella, 2009). Since the overthrow of the Hawaiian kingdom through today, Kānaka have not stopped fighting for Native Hawaiian rights, including land and water preservation and sovereignty (McCubbin & Marsella, 2009). Expanding on Bhatia's (2019) vision of justice in Indigenous Psychology (IP), this chapter advocates for the inclusion of Indigenous resistance and resurgence in the discussion of global IP; being Indigenous in a globalized world is resistance. Indigenous resistance, including activism, refers to individual- and collective-based cognitions and behaviors that sustain Indigenous peoples' capacity to protect, restore, and celebrate Indigenous knowledge, values, and ancestral connections (French et al., 2020; Goodyear-Kaʻōpua, 2017). This chapter provides an overview of recent land rights activism among Kānaka, such as the Mauna Kea protest the Thirty Meter Telescope (TMT) and the Red Hill water crisis. These land rights activism events illustrate Native Hawaiian resistance, refusal of settlers' gifts, and resurgence of Indigenous ways of being, serving as pathways inclusive of radical healing and social justice.

Overview of IP

IP has evolved over time and has recently garnered attention in modes of scholarship in the Western, Educated, Industrialized, Rich, and Democratic framework (WEIRD; Henrich, et al., 2010). The WEIRD framework equates WEIRD empirical methodologies as universal despite the majority of research emerging from the United States (USA). The WEIRD acronym allows us to acknowledge the western cultural encapsulation, particularly within the field of psychology, and redefine other ways of knowing in Indigenous cultures and respective alternative frameworks. Indigenous epistemologies have existed since time immemorial, and these epistemologies and their respective methodologies remain today passed down from generation to generation through cultural language, stories, rituals/ceremonies, and practices. The traditions, values, frameworks, and healing practices are essential when discussing Indigenous Psychology including among Kānaka ʻŌiwi.

In the 1970s, Global South[1] scholars pioneered IP as a response to the supremacy of mainstream psychology (see Allwood & Berry, 2006 for perspectives on the origins of IP). IP seeks to disrupt and decenter Euro-American perspectives in psychology and, with it, dismantle ethnocentrically based representation of communities and cultures of the Global South (Bhatia, 2019). To do so, IP deliberately approaches the study of human behavior from the lens of localization and specificity; understanding people within their local, social, political, historical, and cultural contexts (Kim et al., 2006). Since its conception, the conceptualization of IP has expanded in its dimensionality as a result of international scholarly contributions from Africa (e.g., Oppong, 2022); Māori (e.g., Groot et al., 2018); Filipino (e.g., Gastardo-Conaco, 2005); India (e.g., Sinha, 1998); Indonesia (e.g., Muluk et al., 2018); Latin America (e.g., Pavón-Cuéllar, 2022); South Africa (e.g., Matoane, 2012); and Taiwan/China (e.g., Hwang, 2005), to name a few.

While some scholars view the lack of uniformity of IP, its definition, function, and application, as an inherent weakness (e.g., Jahoda, 2016), others have embraced the coexistence of and exchanges between heterogenous, diverse epistemologies and methodologies within IP as a function of multiplicities and complexities of indigeneity (Bhatia, 2019; Shams, 2002; Sundararajan, 2019). Additionally, scholars in IP have highlighted the need to consider the ways in which Indigenous peoples make meaning of their identities and cultures within the present-day globalized, post/neo/settler-colonial world (Bhatia, 2019; Kirschner, 2019; Shams, 2002; Sundararajan, 2019). Indigenous peoples and their cultures do not exist in a vacuum. Rather, they are disproportionately impacted by colonial politics, policies, and practices that seek to eliminate their persons and/or ways of being (Alfred & Corntassel, 2005; Kashyap, 2019; Wolfe, 2006). Bhatia (2019) posits the need to include politics within the cultural discourse of IP; he envisions IP as a justice-oriented platform that problematizes structures and social conditions that oppress Indigenous communities.

[1] Regions within Latin America, Asia, Africa, and Oceania.

Indigenous Peoples and Politics within IP: Liberation

Indigenous Psychology can be understood alongside different frameworks and schools of thought, for example, liberation psychology and cross-cultural psychology. In examining these fields from a broad lens, each emphasizes the importance of social justice, challenging oppression, and understanding cultural context. IP weaves social justice, decolonization, and empowerment through the validation of Indigenous ways of knowing and self-determination (Groot et al., 2018). With resources and access to movement, culture can manifest in more authentic ways. Liu et al. (2014) state that Indigenous populations that have been able to organize and mobilize against injustice to transform power structures have aligned IP with mainstream cross-cultural psychology, emphasizing the critical role of cultural context. However, for Indigenous populations that remain under colonized conditions and have limited resources or ability to impact power and political structures, IP holds stronger emphasis on liberation (Liu et al., 2014). Thus, aligning more closely with liberation psychology and centering around recognizing and disrupting oppressive systems and contexts.

From a systems perspective, the devastating impacts of colonization are evident, ranging from the loss of language and culture to the loss of life, violence, and genocide. These impacts result in downstream effects such as health disparities, poverty, substance abuse, incarceration rates, and other disproportionate outcomes. From a trauma-lens, historical trauma recognizes the impact of intergenerational trauma and destructive historical events, offering a collective understanding of trauma rather than focusing solely on individuals and broken systems (Liu et al., 2014). The socio-political landscape is also a factor to consider. Liu et al. (2014) identified that some Indigenous groups who have lived and continue to live under greater colonized conditions have greater responsibility in educating non-Indigenous folx. In this context, revitalizing, maintaining, and strengthening Indigenous identity and integrity among social, political, and environmental landscapes are essential to cultural liberation and determinism. Resistance and resurgence efforts are complex, and by weaving cross-cultural, liberation, and global perspectives, we can better recognize and honor the resistance and resurgence of Indigenous peoples.

The political nature of IP reveals the many complex layers and dimensions of the impacts of colonization, cultural genocide, and social injustice, as well as the resistance and resurgence efforts of Indigenous people.

To understand politics from the perspective of IP, we explore the creative, strategic, and empowering efforts of Kānaka ʻŌiwi and the ways in which culture can heal. The emphasis of these efforts is from *within*, rather than as a separate construct from *without*. It is centered on beliefs, practices, and existence that is in alignment with Indigenous ways of knowing and being (Groot et al., 2018). Through culture and efforts of resistance, protection, and resurgence, Indigenous communities endure settler colonial violence, capitalism, and the commodification of Indigenous culture. Culture from within is core to the efforts of resistance, protection, and resurgence, and Indigenous knowledge, values, and practices are needed in response to the structural colonial oppression and for healing across generations. This begins with understanding cultural origins and the collective understanding and strength that transcends time.

Defining Indigenous Resistance Among Hawaiians: Protectors and Resurgence

The Kumulipo is the Hawaiian creation chant and origin story, which connects Kānaka ʻŌiwi, to the kalo (taro) plant, who is seen as the elder sibling of all people. In the origin story, people are called to care for the ʻāina and all natural resources. ʻĀina is more than a geographic place. In examining the root of the word, "ai" is to eat, and represents the relationship Kānaka ʻŌiwi have with the land, which is that of reciprocity. The land feeds and in return, Kānaka care for the land. The relationship with the ʻāina is a familial one. The ʻāina is an extension of family and the physical manifestation of gods and ancestors (Sproat & Palau-McDonald, 2022). Centered around the connection to ʻāina and the natural world, Indigenous resistance among Kānaka ʻŌiwi has grown in momentum since the Hawaiian cultural renaissance of the 1960s and 1970s. However, resistance movements among Kānaka ʻŌiwi go back almost a hundred years prior, to the Bayonet Constitution which resulted in diminished power of the Hawaiian monarchy, removal of Native Hawaiian land rights, and voting rights given to foreign landowners. During this period, Kānaka ʻŌiwi and supporters of King Kālakaua formed *hui* (organizations), which held protests to return power and rights to the Hawaiian people. After the overthrow of Queen Liʻliuokalani, the Kūʻe petitions, which collected tens of thousands of signatures, were taken to Washington in support of the Queen and in protest of the annexation of the Kingdom of Hawai'i.

Since the annexation and statehood, resistance efforts have continued and are evident today as seen through the protests for Kahoʻolawe, Mauna Kea, and Red Hill. Discussed in more detail later in this chapter, all these movements demonstrate resistance against the loss of land, culture, and the embodiment of values and the protection of the Kānaka ʻŌiwi Indigenous ways of being. These movements and efforts demonstrate radical healing among Kānaka ʻŌiwi. The land and water protectors are at an apex between interlocking systems of oppression including the stealing and desecration of the ʻāina and the systematic genocide and erasure of Indigenous peoples and protecting the ʻāina for Indigenous peoples and maintaining Indigenous ways of knowing through liberation and social justice. Protecting the ʻāina is a holistic endeavor for radical healing (e.g., see French et al., 2020). Before we can talk about the process of radical healing, we need to be clear about what Kānaka ʻŌiwi face under colonial systems and structures of oppression.

Settler Colonial Violence in Hawaiʻi

Settler colonialism refers to efforts (social and political) and actions to eliminate, remove, and/or replace people (Native and Indigenous) from their homelands and ways of being to secure or control land and territory for foreign (non-Native) benefit, and at the expense of Indigenous societies (Darrah-Okike, 2020; Whyte, 2018). Settlers destroy Indigenous homelands to create new settler homesteads and, in the process, create a narrative that deems settler actions as moralized and necessary while covering up violent, immoral, and unethical actions (Whyte, 2018). Often under a narrative of the "doctrine of discovery," settler colonialism states are built on the stolen and occupied lands of Indigenous people (Darrah-Okike, 2020).

An example of settler colonialism and settler colonial violence is seen in the illegal overthrow of the Hawaiian Kingdom. Once a thriving nation, the Independent Kingdom of Hawaiʻi was annexed in 1893. White American businessmen organized a coup d'etat with the backing of the US military and overthrew the Queen to control the Hawaiian Islands (Arvin, 2019; Darrah-Okike, 2020). In 1898, Hawaiʻi became a territory of the USA without the vote of Native Hawaiians (McCubbin et al., 2023).

Prior to the illegal overthrow and occupation, British and American businessmen owned and developed plantations to grow crops, mainly sugar, which was a driving force for colonialism in the tropical regions

(Arvin, 2019; Kessler, 2014). After annexation and through reciprocity treaties in the 1870s, plantation owners gained duty-free access to US markets and Hawai'i became a major exporter of sugar and later pineapple (Kessler, 2014; Mak, 2015). Laborers from China, Japan, Korea, Portugal, the Philippines, and Puerto Rico, among others, were brought to Hawai'i to work on the plantations (Darrah-Okike, 2020). During the plantation period, there were many oppositional views on sugarcane harvesting and land use. Missionaries claimed that Kānaka 'Ōiwi farming practices were inferior and that Kānaka 'Ōiwi were ineffective planters and farmers (Kessler, 2014). This is because Kānaka 'Ōiwi farming practices were rooted in conservation and kuleana (responsibility) to 'āina and future generations, directly opposing the colonial objectives of exerting control over profits, land, and land use for immediate resource and economic gains. For example, clearcutting, a high yield harvesting method commonly employed by foreign (non-Native) planters and farmers, made the 'āina more susceptible to foreign and invasive species as well as other destructive environmental impacts (Kessler, 2014). Foreign planters, farmers, and business owners considered their methods superior because of their high yield and profit outcomes, using these beliefs to justify extending their influence and exerting force. As plantation profits became unstable, these businessmen turned to tourism as a new avenue to expand their wealth, power, and influence, disregarding the ecological health of the land they exploited.

In 1902, a three-person committee organized by the Merchants' Association of Honolulu reported that it was necessary to promote the permanent immigration of whites[2] who they felt were of more desirable character above Kānaka 'Ōiwi and other migrant plantation workers (Mak, 2015). The strategy was to promote white tourism in order to recruit permanent white residents. In 1903, the Hawaii Promotion Committee (HPC), later becoming the Hawaii Tourism Bureau (HTB) and most recently the Hawaii Visitors and Convention Bureau, was developed as a private organization, but funded through the Territorial Government, to promote tourism and farming to mainland farmers to persuade more to immigrate to Hawaii (Mak, 2015). Marketing shifted from farming to tourist destinations. Efforts to market the islands as an exotic paradise were seen through promotions in the 1940s for hula shows that targeted military and tourist audiences (Kaeppler, 2002). The version of the hula

[2] The word "white" is intentionally in lower-case to decenter whiteness.

on display was an appropriated, westernized, and romanticized version of hula. Traditional ways of being, including hula and the Hawaiian language had been banned post-overthrow. Film depictions of Hawai'i and residents from the 1900s to the 1940s displayed Hawai'i and the way of life as part of the past and the Hawaiian people as being primitive, while western American views and ways of life were superior and the ways for the future (Miyose & Morel, 2019). Women were sexualized and presented as objects that were willing and eager to provide favors to white male visitors among exotic landscapes (Miyose & Morel, 2019). The Aloha Spirit, a cultural value that is rooted in community as a sense of respect and responsibility, was also commodified and capitalized on, marketed, and sold to consumers as a guarantee that they would be welcomed and served (Arvin, 2019; Miyose & Morel, 2019). The marketing of tourism paid off as it is one of the top three leading economic forces alongside construction and the military (State of Hawaii, 2025).

The multi-ethnic diversity in Hawai'i, partially born out of the need for immigrant plantation workers, has resulted in a conglomerate of cultural pluralism. Narratives have also sold Hawai'i as a cultural paradise that is free of racism and a place where a true "melting pot" exists of a plethora of cultures (Arvin, 2019; Darrah-Okike, 2020; Fojas et al., 2018). However, this narrative is problematic, and scholars have pushed back against this narrative (Arvin, 2019). How could Hawai'i be free of racism when political and social structures rooted in racist settler colonialism structures continue to exist? The narrative that Hawai'i is a cultural paradise distorts and promotes an appropriated version of the "Aloha Spirit," which is touted to advance a tourist paradise agenda that overshadows the dispossession of and loss experienced by Kānaka 'Ōiwi (Arvin, 2019; Darrah-Okike, 2020; Fojas et al., 2018).

After decades of whitewashing, promotion of a cultural paradise, and marketing appealing to a "more desired population," cultural resurgent efforts surfaced through the Hawaiian Renaissance and continue into contemporary times. Efforts to protect the environment, language, culture, and traditions continue today and are evidence that settler colonialism continues to oppress Indigenous people in current times. The exploited narrative of the Aloha Spirit and dependence on tourism, construction, and the military promotes oppressive institutional policies and perspectives that perpetuate settler-colonial injustices and provides continued evidence of the impact of settler colonialism and settler-colonial violence. This evidence is also present in a closer examination of capitalism and the commodification of Hawai'i. Examples are continually demonstrated through capitalism and the commodification of values and ways of being. For example, the trademarking of Aloha Spirit and Aloha. In recent years, American businesses have been met with protest and frustration for trademarking aspects of Hawaiian Culture that is understood by Kānaka 'Ōiwi, and others that respect and support Hawaiian culture, as something that cannot and should not be owned.

Capitalism and the Commodification of Hawai'i

In their analysis of the dynamic entanglements between settler colonialism and capitalism, Ramones and Merry (2021) concluded that capitalism created the conditions that enabled the creation of settler colonies in Hawai'i and the subsequent loss of Hawaiian autonomy. Capitalism is an economic and socio-political system based on exploitative wage-labor relations and commodity production in service of capital accumulation (Marx, 1867). The emergence of global capitalism shifted the purpose of producing goods from subsistence, trade, and/or tribute to the pursuit of wages (workers) and profits (capitalists) (Marx, 1867). Within a capitalist system, individuals become private actors who engage in the free market as propertyless workers and/or property-owning capitalists with the core goal of securing capital and attaining consumption privileges. Whereas capitalists own the means of production (e.g., resources, tools, knowledge), workers whose labor is central to the production process are forced to sell their labor to capitalists for wages and in turn rely on capitalists for the supply of life-sustaining goods (e.g., shelter, food, clothing) due to the lack of capital and means to produce goods for their own survival (Fulcher, 2015). Under this configuration of inequitable labor-wage relations, not only does the product of labor become a commodity, but the workers, their milieu, and their labor are also systematically privatized and reduced into inanimate objects that can be exchanged for capital and controlled by capitalists to structure social life (Marx, 1932). Simply, people who work for wages no longer possess inherent worth and their labor is no longer their own. The privatization of labor also makes it so that the act of labor is concealed, and workers are confined to and defined by the production process, thus alienating workers from their humanity, self-determination, and relationality (Marx, 1932). The shift of labor-capital relations through the adoption of capitalism facilitated and fueled the subordination of

Indigenous communities globally (Wolf, 1982), as in the case of Kānaka ʻŌiwi.

In the 1800s, threats to Hawaiian sovereignty were rampant. To secure the right to govern their lands and people, aliʻi (chiefs) and kamaʻāina (people of the land or commoners) undertook the process of adopting capitalist agriculture (e.g., sugar plantation, sandalwood trade) as a strategy to gain recognition from imperialist powers at the time (Ramones & Merry, 2021). Sensing the economic potential of the agricultural endeavors, settlers, missionaries, and foreign elites seized the opportunity to establish their presence on the islands (formation of settler communities) and infuse themselves into social/cultural, political, and economic spheres in Hawaiʻi (Ramones & Merry, 2021). Responding to the daily exchanges between Kānaka ʻŌiwi and foreign settlers as well as the overwhelming presence and influence of settler communities, capitalism and related Euro-American ideologies, knowledge, and values gradually spread beyond the agricultural sector into other systems of governance (e.g., land tenure, taxation, and marriage), fundamentally shifting the systems of law, governance, and social structure in Hawaiʻi (Ramones & Merry, 2021).

Prior to western contact, reciprocity and redistribution served as the foundation in which the relationships between labor, people, and ʻāina and the means of production are sustained (Osorio, 2002, 2021). In addition to labor privatization, the institutionalization of capitalism in Hawaiʻi in the nineteenth century engendered the privatization of land that dismantled the communal- and land-based system and facilitated the mass dispossession of Kānaka ʻŌiwi from their homelands. Expanding on Marx's (1932) notion of alienation, as experienced by the worker, Osorio (2002) examined the ways loss, appropriation, and privatization of the land have alienated Kānaka ʻŌiwi from the land. Coupled with the illegal overthrow of the Hawaiian kingdom, land alienation has led to the "dismemberment" of the lāhui (nation, people) and its ontological bases (Osorio, 2002). The severing of human-ʻāina interconnectedness made it so that lands were not primarily recognized as relatives or ancestors nor used for subsistence. Rather, land is treated as a commodity that can be packaged, sold, owned, and ceaselessly extracted of its' resources in service of capital accumulation (Haunani-Kay, 2000; Ryoo & McLaren, 2010). In response to the ongoing oppression of the Kānaka ʻŌiwi, Indigenous resurgence emerged as a transformative movement whereby Kanaka ʻŌiwi find individual and collective ways to refuse settler colonial violence and restore all their relations including the ʻāina.

Indigenous Resurgence: Activism as Healing

Indigenous resurgence is the revitalization of Indigenous culture, language, and traditions, serving as evidence that oppression and suppression rooted in colonialism continue to exist. Through cultural revitalization efforts, land and environmental stewardship, protection and conservation acts, political and legal activism, and community engagement, empowerment, and education, Indigenous culture is revitalized and perpetuated. The Hawaiian Renaissance is an example of resurgent efforts that moved forward the Hawaiian culture through language, education, art (including song and dance), environmental stewardship, and political activism. Culture is healing, and protecting the Indigenous way of life is a means to help future generations survive and thrive. Central to Indigenous resistance is the environmental movement, which emphasizes the importance of connection to the natural environment and the importance of conservation in ensuring the survivance of Indigenous peoples and their culture.

Land and Water Protectors

The embodiment of Indigenous resistance and resurgence embedded in activism and liberation can be seen among Kānaka ʻŌiwi land and water protectors. These protectors have demonstrated the creation of radical healing at Kaho'olawe, Mauna Kea, and Red Hill. Radical healing involves being in the dialectics—the simultaneous processes of resisting systems (institutional, interpersonal, and internalized) of oppression while envisioning realities where justice and psychopolitical freedom reside (French et al., 2020). The mechanism of healing is grounded in critical consciousness, cultural authenticity and self-knowledge, radical hope, and envisioning possibilities, collectivism, and strength and resistance (French et al., 2020). In these spaces, Kānaka ʻŌiwi, with Indigenous epistemology and lahui, come together to preserve the land and water for generations to come, and to stop settler colonial violence against the land, water, and Indigenous people.

Kaho'olawe

The island of Kaho'olawe and the protests and political action toward protecting this land were considered a watershed moment for the Hawaiian Renaissance and its people. The ʻāina has consistently been the center of

Indigenous sovereignty and has multiple spiritual and cultural meanings for Kānaka ʻŌiwi. The preservation of land and water and the determination for Indigenous peoples to be in connection with this land is part of Kānaka epistemology, gods, and way of life. A key value is aloha ʻāina, the love for the land and the responsibility to mālama (protect) the ʻāina. In the 1970s, Kaho'olawe was at the center of a political movement, protecting this island and challenging the US military's control of Hawaiian lands (McGregor, 2002). Kaho'olawe is the smallest of the Hawaiian Islands and was taken over by the US Navy for live fire exercises and combat training in preparation for World War II. In 1976, Kaho'olawe became a center point for Hawaiian resistance when a group of Kānaka ʻŌiwi took occupation of the island. Gathering knowledge from Kūpuna (elders), the sacredness of this island began to emerge with the island being a physical manifestation of the Hawaiian god of the ocean, Kanaloa (McGregor, 2002). This rediscovery of Kaho'olawe as a sacred island led to the revival of the traditional Hawaiian value of aloha ʻāina. Acknowledgment of the ancestry of this land is an essential part of bearing responsibility to protect the land and its resources (McGregor, 2002). This process and political fighting continued into the 1990s resulting in the island being officially returned to the State of Hawai'i. This renaissance movement encompassed multiple acts including establishing Hawaiian language immersion schools, re-diverting water back from plantations for Native stream ecosystems, and the emergence of hula halaus (e.g., schools dedicated to teaching the traditional Hawaiian dance and chants; McGregor, 2002). Kaho'olawe represents the reclamation of Indigenous lands, the rematriation of this sacred space, and the need for Indigenous people to have the land back under Indigenous care for future generations. The land and water protectors are guided by Kānaka ʻŌiwi epistemology, customs, and values, and create radical healing by reconnecting the Kānaka ʻOiwi spiritually and culturally to the land.

Mauna Kea

At the time this chapter was written, the issues with the Thirty Meter Telescope on Mauna Kea continued to persist and have not been resolved. The sacredness and cultural significance of Mauna Kea compounded with the repetitive misuse and the loss of Native Hawaiian land, illustrates a perpetual loss for the Kānaka ʻŌiwi. Mauna Kea is a dormant volcano and one of the tallest mountains in the world. It is the highest point in Hawaiʻi and has tremendous cultural significance to Kānaka ʻŌiwi. Mauna Kea is the home of *Wākea* (sky god) and is the *piko* (summit) where the heavens and earth meet. In the historic district of Mauna Kea, there are ancient shrines and other properties that are sacred (Hoʻomanawanui et al., 2019). From the perspective of the scientific world, Mauna Kea also holds significance. With its unique position in the Pacific, its tall reach into the atmosphere, and low light emissions from the surrounding area, Mauna Kea is in prime position to view into space. Beginning in the 1960s, Mauna Kea garnered attention from astronomers and the scientific world, and many astronomical breakthroughs came from observatories positioned on or near the summit of Mauna Kea. In 1968, the Hawaiʻi State Land Board issued the first lease to construct the first telescope on Mauna Kea (Hoʻomanawanui et al., 2019). The University of Hawaii Institute for Astronomy has maintained the lease on the land at approximately 3700 meters elevation and above (Hoʻomanawanui et al., 2019; Osorio, 2021). However, advocates maintain the existence of long-standing misuse and abuse of the land on Mauna Kea. In 2011, the TMT was approved for construction. However, the construction of the telescope was much contested. Native Hawaiian and environmental groups maintained that the construction of the telescope would be culturally, historically, and environmentally devastating. To add to the argument was the question of who and what entity should be the rightful steward of the land. In 2015, attempts were made to build the TMT; however, these efforts were met with protests and a back-and-forth in the courts. Protests to protect the *Mauna* reached their peak around 2019 when the courts approved construction to resume. Under the central principle of *kapu aloha* (nonviolent action, the highest standard rooted in dignity and keeping aloha sacred), a *puʻuhonua* (place of refuge) was created at the base of the mountain and *Kiaʻi* (protectors) formed in droves to protect the *Mauna* (Manuel-Sagon, 2020; Osorio, 2021). Cultural classes were held on the *Mauna* to educate others about the importance and significance of Mauna Kea and teach and model traditional practices such as traditional protocol, pule (prayer), *oli* (chant), *hula* (dance), *mele* (song), and other practices (Johnson, 2020; Osorio, 2021). The *Kiaʻi* recognized that this movement was more than an opportunity to stop the construction of the TMT. It was also an opportunity to educate and further advance the Hawaiian culture and sovereignty movement by investing in the protection of the ʻāina and each other (Osorio, 2021).

Red Hill

The Red Hill Facility is made up of pipelines and massive fuel tanks that can hold in excess of 250 million gallons of fuel, all of which were built in the World War II era. In 1978, Hawai'i Senator Dan Inouye called attention to the need for renovations to the tanks (Jedra, 2022). In 2014, approximately 27,000 gallons of fuel leaked into the water supply for the local community. In November of 2021, complaints about water quality began to roll in. The Hawai'i Department of Health began to receive reports about residents falling ill and the water having an oily film and a fuel-like smell (Hofschneider, 2023; Jedra, 2022). Families and residents in the area were advised to avoid drinking and using the water, however, the military denied any problems. Water testing conducted by the Department of Health retrieved samples from the Red Hill area including the Joint Base Pearl Harbor-Hickam. Samples indicated the presence of petroleum hydrocarbons in the water at greater than 350 times the action level and more than double the action level for drinking water in the Aiea Halawa shaft area (Miko et al., 2023). The Navy test sample reports, however, indicated levels that were below the level of action and that there was no crisis (Hofschneider, 2023; Miko et al., 2023). Almost a month after the initial reports were received by the Department of Health, the Navy issued a letter confirming a jet propellant leak just one hundred feet above an aquifer that serves as a primary source of water for the island of O'ahu (Jedra, 2022; Miko et al., 2023). Over 70 organizations rallied and advocated for environmental protection. The O'ahu Water Protectors, a grassroots organization, among others, such as the Sierra Club called for the shutdown of Red Hill. In October of 2023, the military began draining the fuel from Red Hill. The efforts of the Water Protectors alongside other advocacy groups yielded progress in protecting sacred natural resources. The issues of Red Hill are still ongoing.

Indigenous Resistance

As seen through the kia'i movement of Mauna Kea and Red Hill, and the embodied principles of Aloha 'Āina and Kapu Aloha, engaging in cultural activism is healing, and Indigenous resistance can move healing and culture forward. Kanahele (2005, p. 23) writes "I am the land, and the land is me." The connection to 'āina in the Aloha 'Āina movement is more than environmental activism. Aloha 'Āina is a political movement and a cultural value turned legal requirement. Sproat and Palau-McDonald (2022) cite *Ching v. Case* in which two Native Hawaiian cultural practitioners sued the Hawai'i Board of Land and Natural Resources (BLNR) and Department of Land and National Resources (DLNR) for failing to adequately care for and manage the land and resources that were leased to the military. Attorneys for the plaintiffs argued that the Hawai'i Constitution holds that BLNR and DLNR are required to protect trust lands, some of which were leased to the military for the Pōhakuloa training facility. Similar to leased lands on Mauna Kea, in 1964 the BLNR leased 23,000 acres to the military for just one US dollar a year (Sproat & Palau-McDonald, 2022). Several parcels of ceded land were in the lease. Ceded lands or public trust lands were the property of the sovereign monarchs and government of the Hawaiian Kingdom (Sproat & Palau-McDonald, 2022). In 1959, the USA transferred these lands to the State of Hawai'i, and as a result, under the management of the Board of Natural Resources and DLNR. The lawsuit highlights the kuleana (responsibility) we have toward environmental stewardship and is a legal recognition of the importance of caring for the 'āina, representing the efforts of Indigenous resistance and resurgence. The duty to malama 'āīna, care for the land, and aloha 'āina, is rooted in the Native Hawaiian tradition and value of caring for and respecting natural resources (Sproat & Palau-McDonald, 2022), and is evidenced throughout the cases presented in this chapter.

Refusal of Settler-Colonial Gifts

In the case examples of Kaho'olawe, Mauna Kea, and Red Hill, Kānaka 'Oiwi demonstrate a refusal of settler-colonial *gifts*, such as the Thirty Meter Telescope and military occupation. Nguyen (2012) examined the concept of a "gift" and challenged the notion of gifts, framing it through larger implications of power and oppression. While the reference Nguyen made was regarding *gifts of freedom* among Vietnamese refugees in the USA, the concept of injustice and marginalization is mirrored in the context of *settler-colonial gifts* described in this chapter. *Gifts* are part of a larger narrative that perpetuates colonial control. *Gifts* are framed by the giver as a benefit to the receiver. The *gifts* perpetuate a colonial power-over entitlement that reinforces and justifies colonization while masking ongoing injustices and rationalizing colonization as benevolent. Simpson (2014) describes refusal as a movement juxtaposed with the policies and practices of cultural recognition. Rather than purely advocating for cultural recognition, Indigenous movements have emphasized resurgence and refusal in which Indigenous peoples refuse to accept settler-colonial conditions. As such, contemporary political conceptualization examines *resurgent refusal* (Maile, 2019, p.64). Resurgent refusal, resistance, and resurgence movements emphasize protection over protesting, and *protectors* have stood to protect their connection to culture, ancestors, and ways of knowing (Goodyear-Ka'ōpua, 2017). At the core of this connection is the 'āina. Critical Indigenous Pedagogy of Place emphasizes the connection to place and provides a "culture- and place-specific" framework (Trinidad, 2011). The 'āina is integral to the health and well-being of Kānaka 'Ōiwi. Colonial Euro-American policy was strategic in stripping Kānaka of land rights and connection to land. Centuries later, these policies continue to impact the health and well-being of Kānaka. Thus, contemporary movements to protect the 'āina are more than just land protests. In fighting for the 'āina, protectors are also fighting to maintain and perpetuate a connection to ancestors, culture, language, and ways of being, all of which intersect with the overall health and well-being of Kānaka 'Ōiwi, current and future generations to come.

Conclusion

The movements and activism of the land and water protectors in these places demonstrate the healing that occurs through Indigenous Psychology. As stated earlier, IP considers Indigenous peoples in their local, social, political, historical, and cultural contexts (Kim et al., 2006). At the heart of IP is the study of peoples through a localized and specified lens taking ecological layers into consideration. The radical healing framework (French et al., 2020) for Indigenous people centers the land and the importance of place and knowing one's familial ties to that place. These places represent the intersection of both the interlocking systems of oppression through military, capitalism, and settler colonial violence and the spaces for liberation and justice through mālama 'āina (protecting the land). According to Indigenous scholars, healing occurs when one fits "within the overall cosmology" (Duran et al., 2008). It is through the preservation of these sacred places that one can connect with the cosmology and spirituality of the Kānaka 'Ōiwi. In these sacred places, Kānaka 'Ōiwi can return to their Indigenous ways of knowing through mele, hula, oli, and 'olelo (language). The healing of the 'āina is the healing of the lāhui and its people. Radical hope and healing exist in these sacred spaces through acts of becoming water and land protectors, refusing of settler gifts, and the resurgence of Hawaiian sovereignty. The first author was taught as a young Hawaiian girl by her Kūpuna, "As a Hawaiian you need to know your place. You need to know your mountain, your valley, and your ocean." These words are a reminder as an Indigenous person to be centered; to heal, one needs to go back to the land.

References

Alfred, T., & Corntassel, J. (2005). Being Indigenous: Resurgences against contemporary colonialism. *Government and Opposition, 40*(4), 597–614. https://doi.org/10.1111/j.1477-7053.2005.00166.x

Allwood, C. M., & Berry, J. (2006). Origins and development of Indigenous psychologies: An international analysis. *International Journal of Psychology, 41*(4), 243–268. https://doi.org/10.1080/00207590544000013

Arvin, M. (2019). *Possessing Polynesians: The science of settler colonial whiteness in Hawai'i and Oceania*. Duke University Press.

Bhatia, S. (2019). Searching for justice in an unequal world: Reframing Indigenous psychology as a cultural and political project. *Journal of Theoretical and Philosophical Psychology, 39*(2), 107–114. https://doi.org/10.1037/teo0000109

Casken, J. (2001). Improved health status for Native Hawaiians: Not just what the doctor ordered. *Wicazo Sa Review, 16*(1), 75–89.

Darrah-Okike, J. (2020). Theorizing race in Hawai'i: Centering place, indigeneity, and settler colonialism. *Sociology Compass, 14*(7), 1–18. https://doi.org/10.1111/soc4.12791

Duran, E., Firehammer, J., & Gonzalez, J. (2008). Liberation psychology as the path toward healing cultural soul wounds. *Journal of Counseling and Development, 86*(3), 288–295. https://doi.org/10.1002/j.1556-6678.2008.tb00511.x

Fojas, C., Guevarra, R. P., & Sharma, N. T. (Eds.). (2018). *Beyond ethnicity: New politics of race in Hawai'i*. University of Hawai'i Press.

French, B. H., Lewis, J. A., Mosley, D. V., Adames, H. Y., Chavez-Dueñas Nayeli, Y., Chen, G. A., & Neville, H. A. (2020). Toward a psychological framework of radical healing in communities of color. *The Counseling Psychologist, 48*(1), 14–46. https://doi.org/10.1177/0011000019843506

Fulcher, J. (2015). *Capitalism: A very short introduction* (2nd ed.). Oxford University Press.

Gastardo-Conaco, M. C. (2005). The development of a Filipino Indigenous psychology. *Philippine Journal of Psychology, 38*(2), 1–17.

Goodyear-Ka'ōpua, N. (2017). Protectors of the future, not protestors of the past: Indigenous Pacific activism and Mauna a Wākea. *South Atlantic Quarterly, 116*(1), 184–194. https://doi.org/10.1215/00382876-3749603

Groot, S., Le Grice, J., & Nikora, L. W. (2018). Indigenous psychology in New Zealand. In *Asia-Pacific perspectives on intercultural psychology* (pp. 198–217). Routledge.

Haunani-Kay, T. (2000). Tourism and the prostitution of Hawaiian culture. *Cultural Survival Quarterly, 24*(1), 21–22. https://www.culturalsurvival.org/publications/cultural-survival-quarterly/tourism-and-prostitution-hawaiian-culture

Henrich, J., Heine, S. J., & Norenzayan, A. (2010). Most people are not WEIRD. *Nature (London), 466*(7302), 29–29. https://doi.org/10.1038/466029a

Hofschneider, A. (2023, October 19). Water Protectors in Hawai'i Took on the U.S. Military and won. *Grist*. https://grist.org/global-indigenous-affairs-desk/water-protectors-in-hawai%CA%BBi-took-on-the-u-s-military-and-won/

Ho'omanawanui, K., Fujikane, C., Kagawa-Viviani, A., Long, K. K., & Perry, K. (2019). Teaching for Maunakea: Kia'i perspectives. *Amerasia Journal, 45*(2), 271–276. https://doi.org/10.1080/00447471.2019.1686318

Hwang, K.-K. (2005). From anticolonialism to postcolonialism: The emergence of Chinese Indigenous psychology in Taiwan. *International Journal of Psychology, 40*(4), 228–238. https://doi.org/10.1080/00207590444000177

Jahoda, G. (2016). On the rise and decline of 'Indigenous psychology'. *Culture & Psychology, 22*(2), 169–181. https://doi.org/10.1177/1354067X16634052

Jedra, C. (2022, March 14). How Hawaii activists helped force the military's hand on Red Hill. *Honolulu Civil Beat*. https://www.civilbeat.org/2022/03/how-hawaii-activists-helped-force-the-militarys-hand-on-red-hill/

Johnson, G. (2020). Engaged Indigeneity: Articulating, anticipating, and enacting tradition on Mauna Kea. In S. E. Kraft, B. O. Tafjord, A. Longkumer, G. D. Alles, & G. Johnson (Eds.), *Indigenous Religion(s): Local Grounds, Global Networks* (pp. 154–181). Routledge. https://doi.org/10.4324/9781003021513

Kaeppler, A. L. (2002). Music and dance as export and import: A case study of Japan in Europe and Hawai'i in Japan. *Journal for the Anthropological Study of Human Movement, 12*(1), 22–40.

Kanahele, P. (2005). I am this land, and this land is me. *Hūlili: Multidisciplinary Research on Hawaiian Well Being, 2*(1), 21–30.

Kashyap, M. B. (2019). Unsettling immigration laws: Settler colonialism and the U.S. immigration legal system. *Fordham Urban Law Journal, 46*(3), 548–579.

Keli'iholokai, L., Keaulana, S., Antonio, M. C. K., Rogerson, I., Deitschman, K., Kamai, J. A., Albinio, L., Wilson, K., Kepa, D., Makua, K. L., Vegas, J. K., Chung-Do, J. J., Ho, K., Jr., & Ho-Lastimosa, H. I. (2020). Reclaiming "Āina

Health in Waimānalo. *International Journal of Environmental Research and Public Health, 17*(14), 5066. https://doi.org/10.3390/ijerph17145066

Kessler, L. H. (2014). A Plantation upon a Hill; Or Sugar without Rum: Hawai'i's Missionaries and the Founding of the Sugarcane Plantation System. *Pacific Historical Review, 84*(2), 129–162.

Kim, U., Yang, K.-S., & Hwang, K.-K. (2006). Contributions to Indigenous and Cultural Psychology: Understanding People in Context. In U. Kim, K.-S. Yang, & K.-K. Hwang (Eds.), *Indigenous and cultural psychology: Understanding people in context* (pp. 3–25). Springer Science + Business Media. https://doi.org/10.1007/0-387-28662-4_1

Kirschner, S. R. (2019). Indigenous psychology compared to what? Some complexities of culture, language, and social life. *Journal of Theoretical and Philosophical Psychology, 39*(2), 98–106. https://doi.org/10.1037/teo0000110

Liu, J. H., Aho, K. L. T., & Rata, A. (2014). Constructing identity spaces for First Nations people: Towards an Indigenous psychology of self-determination and cultural healing. *Psychology and Developing Societies, 26*(2), 143–153.

Maile, D. M. (2019). Resurgent refusals: Protecting Mauna a Wākea and Kanaka Maoli decolonization. *Hūlili: Multidisciplinary Research on Hawaiian Well-Being, 11*(1), 57–69.

Mak, J. (2015). *Creating "Paradise of the Pacific": How Tourism Began in Hawaii.* College of Social Sciences, Department of Economics.

Manuel-Sagon, K. (2020). An awakening of the Hawaiian way of life: Framing Kapu Aloha and the Mauna Kea controversy. *PURE Insights, 9*(1), 5.

Marx, K. (1867). *Capital: A critique of political economy* (Vol. 1). Retrieved January 30, 2024, from https://www.marxists.org/archive/marx/works/1867-c1/index.htm

Marx, K. (1932). *Economic and philosophic manuscripts of 1844* (M. Milligan, Trans.). Retrieved January 30, 2024, from https://www.marxists.org/archive/marx/works/1844/manuscripts/preface.htm

Matoane, M. (2012). Locating context in counselling: The development of Indigenous psychology in South Africa. *Psychotherapy and Politics International, 10*(2), 105–115. https://doi.org/10.1002/ppi.1263

McCubbin, L. D., & Marsella, A. (2009). Native Hawaiians and Psychology: The cultural, and historical context of indigenous ways of knowing. *Cultural Diversity and Ethnic Minority Psychology, 15*(4), 374–387.

McCubbin, L. D., Alex, R. M., Bergkamp, J., Malone, C. M., Wang, C. D., & Reynolds, A. L. (2023). Returning the colonizers gaze: Critiquing Whiteness in our training programs. *Training and Education in Professional Psychology, 17*(1), 14–21. https://doi.org/10.1037/tep0000436

McGregor, D. P. (2002). Kaho'olawe: Rebirth of the sacred. *Amerasia Journal, 28*(3), 69–83. https://doi.org/10.17953/amer.28.3.8x71282m37025w8v

Miko, S., Poniatowski, A. R., Troeschel, A. N., Felton, D. J., Banerji, S., Bolduc, M. L., et al. (2023). Community health impacts after a jet fuel leak contaminated a drinking water system: Oahu, Hawaii, November 2021. *Journal of Water and Health, 21*(7), 956–971.

Miyose, C. Y., & Morel, R. (2019). Eh… You Hawaiian? Examining Hawaii Five-0's "Hawaiian". *Prism, 15*(1), 66–80.

Muluk, H., Hudiyana, J., & Shadiqi, M. A. (2018). The development of psychology of culture in Indonesia. In *Asia-Pacific perspectives on intercultural psychology* (pp. 140–156). Routledge.

Nguyen, M. T. (2012). *The gift of freedom: War, debt, and other refugee passages.* Duke University Press.

Oppong, S. (2022). Indigenous psychology in Africa: Centrality of culture, misunderstandings, and global positioning. *Theory & Psychology, (20220622).* https://doi.org/10.1177/09593543221097334

Osorio, E. K. (2021). Struggle for Hawaiian cultural survival. *Ballard Brief, 2021*(1), 2. Retrieved January 25, 2024, from https://scholarsarchive.byu.edu/cgi/viewcontent.cgi?article=1017&context=ballardbrief

Osorio, J. K. K. (2002). *Dismembering Lāhui: A history of the Hawaiian nation to 1887.* University of Hawai'i Press.

Pavón-Cuéllar, D. (2022). Colonialism, subjectivity, and psychology in Latin America. *Journal of Theoretical and Philosophical Psychology.* https://doi.org/10.1037/teo0000217

Ramones, I., & Merry, S. E. (2021). Capitalist transformation and settler colonialism: Theorizing the interface. *American Anthropologist, 123*(4), 741–752. https://doi.org/10.1111/aman.13655

Ryoo, J. J., & McLaren, P. (2010). Chapter 1: Aloha for Sale: A Class Analysis of Hawai'i. *Counterpoints, 355*, 3–17. http://www.jstor.org/stable/42980563

Shams, M. (2002). Issues in the study of Indigenous psychologies: Historical perspectives, cultural interdependence, and institutional regulations. *Asian Journal of Social Psychology, 5*(2), 79–91. https://doi.org/10.1111/1467-839X.00096

Simpson, A. (2014). *Mohawk interruptus: Political life across the borders of settler states.* Duke University Press.

Sinha, D. (1998). Changing perspectives in social psychology in India: A journey towards indigenization. *Asian Journal of Social Psychology, 1*(1), 17–31. https://doi.org/10.1111/1467-839X.00003

Sproat, D. K., & Palau-McDonald, M. J. (2022). The duty to aloha 'āina: Indigenous values as a legal foundation for Hawai'i's public trust. *Harvard Civil Rights-Civil Liberties Law Review, 57*(2), 525–576.

State of Hawaii, Department of Business, Economic Development & Tourism. (2025). Quarterly Statistical & Economic Report. dbedt.hawaii.gov/economic/qser

Sundararajan, L. (2019). Whither Indigenous psychology? *Journal of Theoretical and Philosophical Psychology, 39*(2), 81–89. https://doi.org/10.1037/teo0000115

Trinidad, A. M. O. (2011). Sociopolitical development through critical indigenous pedagogy of place: Preparing Native Hawaiian young adults to become change agents. *Hūlili: Multidisciplinary Research on Hawaiian Well-Being, 7*(1), 185–214.

Whyte, K. P. (2018). A brief introduction to Indigenous environmental studies. *Dædalus, 147*(2), 136–147. https://doi.org/10.1162/DAED_a_00497

Wolf, E. (1982). *Europe and the People without History*. University of California Press.

Wolfe, P. (2006). Settler colonialism and the elimination of the native. *Journal of Genocide Research, 8*(4), 387–409. https://doi.org/10.1080/14623520601056240

CHAPTER 12

Popular Power and Contra-Power within Mexican Indigenous Psychologies

Nuria Ciofalo

Popular Power and Contra-Power within Mexican Indigenous Psychologies

Indigenous cultures have their distinctive cosmovisions, epistemologies, axiologies, and praxes. Western social science developed under Western paradigms that expanded as ideological regimes to colonize other world-views and epistemologies (Almeida & Sánchez Díaz de Rivera, 2014; Grosfoguel, 2008; Maldonado-Torres, 2007; Mignolo, 2009; Rivera Cusicanqui, 2012; Santos, 2018; Smith, 2012). Decolonizing knowledge implies inclusivity of other ways of knowing that promotes epistemic equity. We must ask, what does cultural power mean under Indigenous epistemologies? What are the specific contextual and external structures that facilitate or inhibit expressions of Indigenous autonomy and self-determination? What are the impacts of governmental policies on

N. Ciofalo (✉)
M.A/Ph.D Depth Psychology Program, Pacifica Graduate Institute, Carpinteria, CA, USA
e-mail: Nciofalo@pacifica.edu

Z. Z. Gao, M. I. Medved (eds.), *Global Perspectives on Cultural Politics in Indigenous Psychology*, Palgrave Studies in Indigenous Psychology, https://doi.org/10.1007/978-3-031-96813-6_12

Indigenous forms of community power? What kind of cultural politics promotes decoloniality and self-determination? These questions were addressed through a review of Indigenous literature authored by the Zapatista movement, scholarship from the Global South, and reflections on my collaboration with Indigenous communities in northern, central, and southern Mexico for several decades. To dismantle colonial regimes of knowledge and promote epistemic equity and ecological wellbeing, we need to learn from Indigenous cosmovisions, epistemologies, axiologies, and praxes.

This chapter revisits the Zapatista movement in Mexico, also known as Zapatismo, and its impacts worldwide as a cultural-political philosophy and pedagogy of *Lekil Kuxlejal*, in Maya Tseltal (good living) that embraces a deep spiritual connection with all living beings, including animals, humans, ancestors, and nature within accountability to the individual self as inseparable from community, promoting holistic and cosmic wellbeing (López Intzin, n.d.). It centers the inclusion of Indigenous epistemologies in understanding the relationship between culture and politics. The first sections address the review of the concepts of culture, power, and politics in Latin America under the critical analysis of the impacts of colonization and ongoing coloniality. The following section focuses on different forms of coloniality of power on knowledge, nature, culture, and gender. I review the resistance, refusals, and contestations of these various forms of power by the Indigenous struggles for autonomy and self-determination and the political, cultural, and pedagogical impacts of Zapatismo. The analysis of power follows, understood as autonomous community empowerment composed of popular power that strengthens community cohesion and solidarity, and contra-power directed against the structural violence of capitalism and neoliberalism. This analysis is applied to the main lessons learned from Zapatismo. The conclusions refer to the role played by the Zapatista autonomous community organizations and the Indigenous forms of cultural-political power in contributing to ecological sustainability.

The Coloniality of Power

Annibal Quijano (2000) addressed the inquiry about power as the main manifestation of the dominance of the European hegemonic culture constituted during colonization and that evolved as ongoing coloniality using global power. The main axis of coloniality is the classification of the world population under the social construct of race following the Euro-centric rationality imposed everywhere, independent of cultural context. The race construct divides the world population into those declared superior from the conquerors' bloodlines and all others from other races who need to be conquered for progress and civilization, which is the rational myth of empire. The other axis of power is the control of labor by integrating all historically previous forms of domination, such as slavery and serfdom, through the regulations of world capital.

The colonization of the Americas became the project of modernity imposed worldwide. Race became power to dominate and subjugate based on the phenotypical differences and justified as biological determinants of hierarchy. The Europeans, who at first were the Spaniards, the Portuguese, and the British, became the hegemonic ideology that tamed beliefs and spiritual traditions, knowledge systems, and human and natural habitats according to their ideology of capital accumulation, control, and exploitation of people and nature. According to Quijano's analysis of the constitution of this global power, race became the most important categorical differentiation brought about by the modern world order. In one part of the American continent, where the Spaniards and Portuguese established their racial supremacy, the Indians were categorized as inferior and later as Mestizos and Afro-descendent populations. In Anglo-America conquered by the British, the Africans were displaced and enslaved, experiencing the most violent form of domination and exploitation. The Indians were attacked violently as well, and genocide occurred when the British occupied their lands under the myth of *terra nullius* (empty land) and manifest destiny (the right to seize it for profit and imperial expansion as private property to maximize personal and national gain). Quijano (2000) added, "As time went by the colonizers codified the phenotypic trade of the colonized as color, and they assumed it as the emblematic characteristic of racial category" (p. 533). Race became the most powerful ideological category of modernity to support the domination of labor for the capitalist world order.

The global control of labor under racial categories has capital production as its main goal. Resources have been distributed unequally according to racially determined geo-political regions that separated the colonies from Europe as the central node of power. The national struggles for independence accomplished only the location of power in the colonies' elites who descended from the colonizers and have been governing the so-called ex-colonized world, struggling for autonomy. Racial classifications assisted the Europeans in determining the right to wage labor owned only by the superior white race. The Indians were allowed to become serfs, and the Africans were completely deprived of any right to paid or compensated labor, using slavery. Quijano (2000) asserted,

> The historical process is, however, very different. To start with, in the moment that the Iberians conquered, named, and colonized America (whose northern region, North America, would be colonized by the British a century later), they found a great number of different peoples, each with its own history, language, discoveries and cultural products, memory and identity. The most developed and sophisticated of them were the Aztecs, Mayas, Chimus, Aymaras, Incas, Chibchas, and so on. Three hundred years later, all of them had become merged into a single identity: Indians. This new identity was racial, colonial, and negative. The same happened with the peoples forcefully brought from Africa as slaves: Ashantis, Yorubas, Zulus, Congos, Bacongos, and others. In the span of three hundred years, all of them were Negroes or blacks. (pp. 551–552)

In the same way, knowledge became a product of this coloniality of power used to dominate the inferior races and their geopolitical regions. This is a specific, hegemonic type of knowledge that is Eurocentric, capitalist, and modernist. It is based on evolutionary conceptions of historical linear change, attributing the move from nature-based to civilized societies built according to the European way of life. Non-European races were placed in a historical past and thus uncivilized and primitive, following a linear universality that made white supremacy analogous with civilization and legitimized knowledge production, commodified as science and technology. The cultural production of the inferior races needed to be erased, extinguished, and replaced with the Euro-centric, supremacist culture that supported an only-one-world mentality. As Arturo Escobar asserted (2022), "One-World World (a world made of a single globalized world) vision of reality has increasingly occupied other visions, disabling their world-making practices and potential to a significant degree" (cited in Escobar et al., 2022, p. 105).

The European worldview appropriated modernity and rationality as its exclusive cognitive components and codified cultural and intersubjective relations with the rest of the world under the "new categories: East-West, primitive-civilized, magic/mythic-scientific, irrational-rational, traditional-modern—Europe and not Europe" (Quijano, 2000, p. 542). In this way, the European hegemony dominated and appropriated the colonized culture, politics, and knowledge for the benefit of their capitalistic accumulation. The imposition of Judo-Christian religiosity also contributed to the control of the colonized spirituality, intending to erase their cosmovisions. This Euro-centric imposition glorifies its antiquity based on Greco-Roman legacies, devaluing the legacies of other non-European cultures such as the Mayans and the Aztecs—among others, who developed scientific systems informed by mathematics, astronomy, medicine, and practiced secular and religious beliefs that could be considered equivalent to a different kind of rational modernity. Dussel (1995) called it "transmodernity" to differentiate it from the hegemonic European model.

Another important consequence of the coloniality of power is the separation of body, spirit, human, and nature. These separations were promoted by the Christian worldview that considered the body an object and the soul detached from the material world, possessing the capacity to exist eternally. Reason exists in the soul and the body is close to nature. For this reason, the non-Europeans were considered irrational and objectified bodies and were classified under racial categories to be exploited and disposed of. According to Quijano (2000), the configuration of imperial power was created in the United States after the Independence by becoming a powerful nation-state. The Black population was dominated violently under slavery to produce its might and abundant goods, and the Indians were targeted for extermination to possess their lands. The southern regions also had their independence struggles, but "Mexico (1910) and Bolivia (since 1952) came along the road of social decolonization through a revolutionary process, during which the decolonization of power was able to gain substantial ground before being contained and defeated" (p. 564).

Decolonization did not occur, given the hegemonic white minorities continued to depend on the powerful European elites who possessed the means of production. The southern regions in the American continent, called Latin America, did not have the political capacity and the power to become independent nation-states. A re-articulation of the coloniality of power over new institutional structures controlled by global capital occurred.

The Coloniality of Nature, Culture, and Gender

Another axis of the coloniality of power has been the separation of nature and culture. It has justified the project of progress and civilization carried on by colonization to invade peoples and territories. A characteristic of the patriarchal civilized white human has been their capacity to control nature and extract its resources for their privilege and benefit. Asher (2017) alerted us that among the strongest social movements of our contemporary times are the struggles for territoriality of Indigenous and Afro-descendant populations that have not separated nature from culture and embedded the latter within the former. This struggle for cultural and political power to defend the wellbeing of the Earth has become one of the focus of ecofeminists, such as Gayatri Spivak in India and Silvia Rivera-Cusicanqui in Bolivia. Spivak (1988) reminded us of the impossibilities and inevitability of representing the colonized, which she defined as "the subaltern," without incurring the possibility of replicating the colonial domination of their subjectivities and identities. This critique is based on Spivak's delinking from positivism and essentialism and constant questioning of the effects of colonization on the marginalized and racialized subaltern. For Spivak (1999), postcolonial rationality misrepresented the non-European populations as an idealized Third World that could become an agent of political change, unaltered by the impacts of Eurocentric cultural imperialism. Spivak invited us to learn from "the ecological philosophers of the world" and be critical of romanticizing and essentializing the non-Western relation to nature (cited in Asher, 2017, pp. 518–519).

In Bolivia, Aymara Indigenous scholar-activist Silvia Rivera Cusicanqui (2012) took a different angle to the critique of representing colonized populations, ending in essentialists discussions of multiculturalism or hybridity. Such discourses tend to deprive the Indigenous actors of access to political and cultural power that have generated national changes. Rivera Cusicanqui (2012) critiqued the work of scholars who have engaged in the modernity/coloniality/decoloniality discourse, appropriating the contributions of Indigenous scholars who remain in the trenches of localized social struggle instead of only acting from the vantage point of the academic ivory towers of the Global North. In contrast to this critique, Rivera Cusicanqui emphasized the significant contributions of Indigenous women, who have been engaged in labor and territorial struggles and impacting national policies, causing the election of the first Indigenous president in Bolivia, Evo Morales, and the 2009 constitutions that granted

Indigenous rights as well as, for the first time in world history, the rights to the Earth.

Regarding this denunciation of invisibility of the Indigenous and Afro-descendant women's contributions to access cultural and political power, Asher (2017) added,

> Indigenous women too often fall through the cracks of the shifting terrains of class, ethnic, and cultural politics. For example, women migrants doing domestic work in urban areas are treated as "Indigenous" and earn less than the normal minimal wage. However, they are designated as mestizos and thus denied access to Indigenous rights. By highlighting the contradictions and dilemmas of Indigenous women's identity and work, Rivera Cusicanqui's writing helps complicate discussions about how Indigenous women contribute to decolonial futures. (p. 522)

Feminist decolonial and postcolonial scholars can significantly contribute to understanding how Indigenous struggles are intersectional and multifaceted and not simply relations of nature and culture, but embedded in an interplay of political economy, neoliberal policies, and cultural politics (Asher, 2017).

The Argentinian, feminist Maria Lugones (2008) revised Anibal Quijano's analysis of the coloniality of power under the Eurocentric patriarchal capitalist and modernist system by understanding how domination, exploitation, and the consequent generation of conflict impacted gender. Quijano's analysis of the competition around "sexual access, its resources, and products" and who has access can be understood as a gender system under the coloniality/modernity matrix that is patriarchal, heterosexual, and oppressive, determining a hegemonic and violent modernity/colonial/gender system (p. 6). Lugones dismantled the allegiance to this gender system of domination at the intersection of race and the heterosexual binary of men/women, making visible the violence incurred to women of color, particularly Black and Indigenous women. The Eurocentric one-world worldview introduced gender binaries where there were none, such as in African and many Native American cultures throughout the American continent. Lugones (2008) asserted that Paula Gunn Allen referred to "gynecratic egalitarianism" in communities where the sacred Woman is at the center, and everything needs her blessing (p. 9). Lugones invited us,

> ...to begin a conversation and a project of collaborative, participatory, research and popular education to begin to see in its details the long sense of the processes of the colonial/gender system enmeshed in the coloniality of power into the present, to uncover collaboration, and to call each other to reject it in its various guises as we recommit to communal integrity in a liberatory direction. (p. 16)

Confronting our complicity in this violent system can contribute to communal transformation. In this same venue, Albán and Rosero (2016) analyzed how nature became colonized to support the Eurocentric myth of development and civilization. The authors asserted that nature was conceived under the project of modernity/coloniality that made it a natural resource to be exploited and extracted indefinitely for the benefit of capital. It superimposed an anthropomorphic superiority to the human being that generated the nature/culture dichotomy tailored to satisfy the greedy needs of the capitalist enterprise.

The violent relationship between nature and the Anthropos, who impose "culture" on a wild nature to domesticate it and extract its resources, promoted environmental devastation and ecocide, and its consequent climate change conceived as an imperative crisis of civilization. The authors stated,

> The commercialization of nature and its consequent colonization is measured by the production of knowledge that within industrial spaces and in many cases, academic cases, is being made of it, leaving outside ways of proceeding, acting, living, and being in communities that have constructed different forms than the western and Eurocentric rationality. The coloniality of nature, maybe beyond its colonization, must be understood as a form of construction of hegemonic discourses that exclude in regard to those who have a right to know, exploit, protect, and preserve it. (p. 30)

Those who adjudicate themselves the latter right are the capitalist, extractivist, and neoliberal corporations and the Western environmentalists. Their organizations and governments impose rules and regulations on the most biodiverse areas in the world, where their Indigenous guardians, who have maintained its wellbeing for generations, are prohibited from accessing nature, not even to continue tending it for wholistic survival (Albán & Rosero, 2016; Ciofalo, 2019, 2022). As Dussel (2010) stated, the irrationality of Western rationality erased the presence of Indigenous peoples who refuse to relate to technological developments that have desecrated nature by commodifying it without remorse and ethical accountability. Dussel (2019) elaborated a liberation pedagogy that emerges from below, from the community, and is anti-bureaucratic, dismantling the oppressive structures of society and creating a new revolutionary culture that erupts "... as new aesthetic" (p. 186).

Indigenous communities of Bolivia and Ecuador have proclaimed the need to incorporate the rights of the Earth as *sumac kawsay* or buen vivir in Quechua and Spanish (well-being) (Gudynas, 2014; Escobar et al., 2022), *lekil kuxlejal* in Tseltal (López Intzin, n.d.) as the testimony of this new aesthetic. This became a movement first embraced by the South American Indigenous Women Movement for Buen Vivir (SAIWM), who are Mapuche from Patagonia and have formed a collective to protect the Earth from "*terricide*," the violence committed against the life of the planet, killing physical and living ecosystems as well as their knowledge systems and spiritual relations with nature (Escobar et al., 2022, p. 107). In countercurrent to terricide, this devastation and crisis of civilization and Western rationality, we must learn to *senti-pensar* (feeling thinking) with the Earth (Escobar, 2016; Fals-Borda, 1984) and from Indigenous movements that have enacted a social and poHlitical struggle against the coloniality of power, nature, culture, and gender.

The Zapatista Movement: A Hopeful Cultural Politics, Decolonial Philosophy, and Pedagogy

On January 1, 1994, powerfully organized Maya Indigenous peoples from the state of Chiapas marched silently to loudly oppose the political war strategies of the Mexican state against their territories, cultures, and lives. Their struggle for autonomy offers pathways toward a decolonial cultural politics that, as Callahan (2005) asserted, has become a growing Zapatismo beyond the Lacandon Rainforest of Chiapas, where it is anchored using its key flourishing elements: (1) a politics of refusal, (2) dignity and hope, (3) to lead by following, (4) never again a world without us, (5) everything for everyone and nothing for ourselves, and, lastly, (6), the most demanding element of refusal, enough is enough, "*Ya Basta,*" co-constructing an alternative world in which many worlds are possible.

The Zapatista autonomy and new form of democratic communalism are guided by seven principles: (1) *Obedecer y no mandar—mandar obedeciendo* (to obey and not to rule—rule by obeying); (2) *representar y no suplantar* (to represent and not to replace); (3) *bajar y no subir* (down and not up); (4) *servir y no servirse* (to serve and not self-serve); (5) *convencer y no vencer* (to persuade and not conquer); (6) *construir y no destruir* (to construct and not destroy); (7) *proponer y no imponer* (to propose and not impose) (Enlace Zapatista, 2022—my translation).

The movement demands the end of the neoliberal monster with many heads, the capitalist hydra, and the government's war against life, "*la tormenta* (the storm)," by voicing the *Ya Basta* (enough is enough) epistemology and praxeology. Other deeply inspiring statements are "*caminamos preguntando* (we walk asking); *nunca jamás un mundo sin nosotros* (never again a world without us)," and "*un mundo donde quepan muchos mundos* (a world where many worlds fit)," based on their key organizational principle, "*mandar* obedeciendo" (pp. 10–11). Elements, principles, and statements constitute the main structures of the Zapatista philosophy and pedagogy. Yet, the Zapatistas do not define Zapatismo as a philosophy or political ideology but as a bridge to co-construct another world.

The Zapatismo is a cultural politics that has mobilized collectivities and individuals who incorporate their identity as theirs to guide the collective struggle against the capitalist hydra, the monster with many heads (EZLN, 2015). Callahan (2005) proposed that the "Zapatismo is a political and cultural practice… [an] ethical, creative and disciplined …inspiration" that has reached both local and global impacts using its capacity to convene people from diverse backgrounds and regions in numerous "*encuentros*" (pp. 7–8). This author asserted that during "the March for Indigenous Dignity in 2001, it was not unusual to hear: 'We are all Indigenous!' 'We are all Zapatistas!' 'We are all Marcos!' Not surprisingly, supporters claiming the Zapatista rebel identity have been generously embraced by the Zapatistas" (p. 9). According to Esteva (1999), the Zapatismo is a paradox and a movement that did not intend to seize power yet has gained significant popular power with an army that claims to be both non-violent and peaceful, singular and typical, radical and traditional. Most importantly, the Zapatistas are exposing the truth that no one dared to voice and the deep disappointment with the myth of democracy carried on by hegemonic minorities in search of their interests. Esteva asserted this is "a struggle that does not aim to conquer 'democratic power' but to widen, strengthen and deepen the space where people can exert their own power" (p. 154).

The Zapatistas centered the topic of autonomy for Indigenous communities in their political discourse of recognition, respect, and dignity as they exercise sovereignty, regulating their communities and territories under their terms practiced for generations, also known as *usos y costumbres* (practices and customs). Esteva added,

> Marcos Sandoval, a young Triqui leader, says: "Westerners represent justice as a blind-folded woman; we want her with eyes wide open, for her to notice what is happening." Jurisdiction does not imply a sphere of application of the law or a section of the centralized government, but an autonomous space which limits state and economic power in applying flexible principles for thought and behavior, giving historical continuity to tradition without freezing it. (p. 163)

The contributions of the social movements led by Zapatista women were brought to the center by the Mexican feminist scholar-activist, Sylvia Marcos (2022) as they reclaim their autonomy and women's rights based on their own *saberes ancestrales* (ancestral knowledges) to confront the coloniality of gender and nature because both are deeply imbricated. This position is in countercurrent to the hegemonic arrogance of the imposed superiority of "some knowledge forms over others" that do not assume "just one race over another, prevailing since the conquest and colonization of Mexico" and that are implicit in "the epistemic subjugation of local forms of comprehending the world that prevail in the Indigenous cosmovisions" (p. 397—my translation).

In an "Intergalactic Encounter," as the Zapatista women called it, one representative, "la mayor Ana María," declared the powerful epistemic paradox: "*somos iguales porque somos diferentes* (we are equals because we are different)" based on the profound Maya cosmovisions of equal and different elements that are complementary to conform with harmony (p. 398). Marcos (2022) embraced this profound statement as epistemic pluriversality that allows one to cross the abyssal line clearly sketched by Santos (2009), rendering some forms of knowledge valuable and others primitive or bare superstition because these are incommensurable by the standards of Western rationality. Bastida (2019) asserted that the Zapatismo's most important characteristic is that it started as a local movement and became global in its influence in Mexico, Latin America, and elsewhere. It is a discursive rather than an armed movement performed in many artistic, cultural, and political forms and stages in the streets, social media networks, and other spaces.

The Zapatismo disseminates its teachings in articles published in various popular social media networks, academic books, journals, stories, and tales by Subcomandante Marcos in different languages. These stories, besides being entertaining are provocatively educational, reaching diverse populations from the Indigenous activists to the intellectuals, youths, and children in privileged households. The *Declaraciones de la Comandancia Clandestina Revolucionaria Indígena* and the abundant documentary videos, music, and theater performances carried on in vivo in various localities of the Lacandon Rainforest and the Highlands of Chiapas are transmitted online, reaching global audiences and promoting enthusiastic support and solidarity. Bastida (2019) added,

> These examples of advertising enterprises, totally foreign to the Zapatismo, demonstrate that the 2001 March of the Color of the Earth to Mexico City was an algid moment of their resonances, a truly communicative explosion with a proliferation of musical concerts, Indigenous ceremonies, pictorial and theatrical expressions, debate forums, creation of free media, video editing and or novellas dedicated to the mobilization. There were tens of informative products about one of the most important mobilizations in Mexican history. (10—my translation)

Between 2002 and 2012, the Zapatistas created autonomous communication means such as *Radio Insurgente* and *Enlace Zapatista* webpages. In 2006, they launched *La Sexta Declaración de la Selva Lacandona*, where they declared their anti-capitalist autonomy and refusal of the electoral process. They also expanded their informational outreach with the goal, as Marcos assured, "…to make the word grow from below and to construct the collective ear for that. But technology and science to network with the most distant comrades are still missing (*hacer crecer la palabra de abajo y construir el oído colectivo para ella. Pero faltan todavía la ciencia y la técnica para enlazar a l@s compas más lejanos*)" (Subcomandante Marcos (2006), cited in Bastida, 2019, p. 12—my translation).

In December 2006 and January 2007, the Zapatistas made a large encounter with the world, and prestigious national and international intellectuals and leaders participated as part of the *Escuelita* (The Little School) Zapatista in Oventik. This encounter continued in July 2007 in autonomous communities called *Caracoles* (Snails) ruled by their *Juntas del Buen Gobierno* (Assemblies of Good Government). In December, known international scholar activists met with the Zapatistas, such as "Immanuel

Wallerstein, John Berger, Francois Houtart, Peter Rosset, Jean Robert, Naomi Klein; Mexicans such as Carlos Antonio Aguirre Rojas, Silvia Marcos, Pablo González Casanova, Gustavo Esteva, Enrique Dussel," and representatives of international and national social movements, culminating with the Encounter of the Women of the World, where *Comandanta* Ramona and other Zapatista women met with "2000 women from 30 countries" (p. 13 my translation).

From 2008 to 2009, the *Festival de la Digna Rabia* (The Festival of the Dignified Rage) took place, in Zapatista words: "*mostrar su lucha y su coraje...la dignidad y la rabia se harán arte y cultura, música y canto, porque la rebeldía también se baila. Y con palabras el dolor se hará esperanza* (to show its struggle and anger...the dignity and rage will become culture, music, and song because the rebellion is also danced. And with words of pain, hope will be made)" (cited in Bastida, 2019, p. 13—my translation). It followed a period of silence not without international impacts of the Zapatista struggle or other struggles such as the Arab Spring, Occupy, the Spanish *Indignados*, and others inspired by the Zapatistas' anti-capitalist philosophy of *lekil kuxlejal, buen vivir.* Bastida (2019) called the third phase: "the Indigenization of the artistic and communication politics of Zapatismo," which began with the biggest silent march in its history, "la *Marcha de Silencio,*[...] on the Maya cycle of the 13 *baktun,*" on December 21, 2012, in San Cristóbal de las Casas, Chiapas (p. 23 my translation). After the impactful march, it was announced loudly: "*A quien corresponda. ≃Escucharon? Es el sonido de su mundo derrumbándose. Es el del nuestro resurgiendo. El día que fue el día, era noche. Y noche será el día que será el día* (To whom it may concern. Did you listen? It is the sound of a rumbling world. It is ours resurging. The day that was day was night. And the night will be the day that will be the day)" (EZLN, 2012, cited in Bastida, 2019, p. 24—my translation).

In 2018, the first Indigenous Zapatista woman, Marichuy, appeared as a presidential candidate. Unfortunately, the impositions of the Mexican political oligarchy shifted votes in favor of Manuel Lopez Obrador, who had belonged to the powerful Institutional Revolutionary Party (PRI) and constituted a new party called *Movimiento de Regeneración Nacional* (Morena) (National Regeneration Movement) attracting the hope of disillusioned Mexicans who were looking for a promising change. The Zapatistas are strengthening their Buen Gobierno delinking from the Mexican government, yet their struggle against its constant violent interventions continues to date. In 2022, the Zapatista organized a journey to the insurrection of Europe, sailing the Atlantic Ocean as a metaphor of "counter-colonization" to meet with solidary communities in different localities, share their struggle, teachings, and inspirations for the co-construction of a better world.

Currently, the Zapatismo focuses on the maintenance and nourishment of their Indigenous cultures, languages, and territories, and the demands to preserve their ecological resources, such as waters and lands that are considered sacred, in their refusal and resistance against the capitalist hydra, and exercising their political self-determination and sovereignty.

Understanding Power, Culture, and Politics in Latin America: Popular Power and Contra-Power

The Colombian sociologist Orlando Fals-Borda (1986) defined power in two components: popular power and contra-power in his book *Conocimiento y Poder Popular* (*Knowledge and Popular Power*). He conceived of popular power as a force, a strength, or an endogenous social energy that belongs to autonomous groups through processes of collective organization to defend their territories, culture, needs, dreams, and desires. Contra-power resists external agents such as state institutions and corporate capital through community mobilization, protest, and concerted action. It can be retrieved, stored, and used at other times when the environment is appropriate, like a feedback system (Hirschman, 1984). Contra-power is also exercised to promote political alliances with other organizations or groups (Ciofalo, 2014).

Popular power is formed through the processes of collective organization to defend the peoples' legitimate interests, fostering shared goals for social change and political participation. Fals-Borda (1986) stated that popular power is a process that simultaneously includes adult education, collaborative research, and political action. Everyday experience, as a source/cause of popular power, produces knowledge to generate popular power for social action, transforming from process to outcome of autonomous community empowerment. Community members become organic intellectuals who apply their endogenous knowledge for holistic community wellbeing (Ciofalo, 2014).

Contra-power manifests through internal and external processes facilitated by the Indigenous organizations that resist external agents such as state institutions and corporate capital through empowerment outcomes such as community mobilization, protest, and concerted action. Contra-power is analogous to the concept of counterhegemonic globalization proposed by Santos (2009), which base communities mobilize through international solidarity with professionals, activists, worker unions, and student organizations, conforming to "trans-border activism" (p. 231). Transformative and equitable class, ethnic, and racial alliances promote the formation of cohesive and cooperative communities or organizations to develop "...diverse institutional forms and conceptions to the project of socialization of power according to their diverse, multiple epistemologies" (Grosfoguel, 2008, p. 20).

The Zapatista movement evidences the application of these power dynamics. Popular power is evidenced in their sophisticated forms of community organization to promote wellbeing, reinforce their cultural ways of knowing within individual, family, and community life generation and regeneration, and to strengthen their culture. The movement applies contra-power to resist the neoliberal threats against their lives, "*las tormentas* (the storms)," the enactment and performance of cultural celebrations to strengthen their internal and external solidarity among themselves and with national and international organizations to resist the capitalist hydra, and the constitution of their own Buen Gobierno, independent of the Mexican state.

Participatory Action Research (PAR) is a methodology of empowerment (popular power and contra-power) based on the knowledge of the base communities (Fals-Borda, 1984, 1986). Community members become co-researchers as organic intellectuals, who design, implement, and evaluate the research process and outcome. Their involvement in knowledge generation for social change strengthens community organizations such as health and educational committees, community cooperatives, and the like, which constitute outcomes of empowerment that may generate community autonomy and wellbeing. PAR researchers represent the community interests and may become empowering leaders and change agents who maintain horizontal relationships and plan from below (Ciofalo, 2014).

PAR has been shaping its presence in the scientific and political context in Asia, Africa, Latin America, and some regions in Europe, the United States, and Canada. PAR has become a process of knowledge generation by scholars, practitioners, and activists of colonized countries who struggle for liberation (Ciofalo, 2014). Fals-Borda (1986) added that its formative conceptual ingredients emerged in the 1960s from dependency theory

(Cardoso, Furtado), theories of exploitation (Gonzalez Casanova), contra-theory of subversion (Camilo Torres), liberation theology (Freire, Gutierrez, Martin-Baró), the theory and praxis of dialogue (Freire), and interpretations of theories proposed by Marx and Gramsci. PAR researchers resist subordinate relations and co-construct knowledge with the community, cultivating dignified and reciprocal relationships. They respect the community's traditional culture and learn from its history and epistemologies. PAR researchers are critically self-reflexive of their privilege, positionality, and attachment to academic knowledge based on Western scientific paradigms to avoid the reproduction of coloniality. The engaged community confronts and refuses feelings of inferiority and submission, valuing their traditional knowledge and culture in understanding social transformation (Freire, 1972; Martin-Baró, 1986; Ciofalo, 2014, 2019). PAR counters the monopoly of knowledge generation (Fals-Borda, 1986). It facilitates community participation in research as an emancipatory, empowering process that Freire (1972) called "consciousness raising" (Ciofalo, 2014).

The Zapatismo applies this PAR methodology to gain collaborative knowledge from the base communities "*desde abajo y a la izquierda* (from below and to the left)" as the Zapatista would say, and to engender organizing structures that address health, education, sustainable agricultural production, and ways of resistance against the bad government. The Zapatista communities came together to learn about neoliberalism and how it has impacted their individual, family, and community lives in the various national and international encounters. They reflected on how they could organize to confront these impacts within their local communities and with national and international scholar-activists and organizations. The Zapatistas apply these enriched local knowledge systems to co-construct their own Buen Gobierno based on self-determination and sovereignty and for *lekil kuxlejal* based on deep spiritual respect to all living beings and accountability to the self-embedded in the community (López Intzin, n.d.).

The social community psychologist from Venezuela, Maritza Montero (2003), defined community power as "*fortalecimiento comunitario*," demonstrating alignment between some Western definitions of this construct and Latin American definitions (pp. 63–65). Three main objectives to facilitate the emergence of sources/causes, processes, and outcomes of empowerment as defined in Latin America are: (1) to raise critical awareness (conscientization) that stimulates liberation from exploitation (Freire, 1972; Martin-Baró, 1986; Montero, 2003), (2) to build consensus, collaboration, and horizontal relationships of mutual recognition, and (3) sharing power with the community and organic intellectuals for transformative action applying contra-power against internal or external threats (Almeida & Sánchez Díaz de Rivera, 2001, 2005, 2014; Fals-Borda, 1986; Montero, 2013). The Zapatista movement evidences the performance and enactment of these three dynamics of community empowerment. Critical awareness of the war against life carried on by the Mexican government is applied as everyday collaborative praxis based on horizontal relationships that recognize the community members' contributions. Furthermore, the movement built consensus within class, ethnic, and racial alliances (i.e., base community and professionals) as demonstrated in the national and international encounters with prestigious scholar-activists who facilitated trust and concerted action for social, cultural, epistemic, linguistic, spiritual, and ecological justice.

Power as Empowerment, Autonomy, and Self-Determination

Autonomy conceived as Indigenous sovereignty and self-determination is a necessary social, economic, cultural, and political process in countries that have been colonized and continue to be threatened by neo-colonization perpetuating inequitable distribution of resources and opportunities, exploitation, cultural genocide, and environmental destruction (ecocide). Leff (1995) defined this kind of community autonomy as,

> ...[the] ongoing social struggles for the appropriation of production conditions by indigenous peoples and peasant communities and for building a ... new society ...in a preserved environment [rather than in] sterile deserts—cemeteries of resources—the probably legacy of capitalism without development. (p.129)

Empowerment manifests in diverse forms: (1) as a process of autonomy and self-determination (popular power); (2) as a process stimulated by external agents such as enabling, non-governmental organizations, or (3) as a synergistic process formed by the collaborative efforts of community members and critical change agents who promote its emergence (Ciofalo, 2014).

In Mexico, there has been a history of peasant and Indigenous movements to address the unequal provision of services, allocation of production credits, and their cultural and land rights. At the end of the nineteenth century, several court determinations took place to return the land to the Indigenous *campesinos* (peasants), and regional confrontations against the state and the agricultural bourgeoisie occurred during the 1960s and 1970s. Indigenous communities organized to resist the violence of the Mexican government against their uprising and protests (Ciofalo, 2014).

Besides the Zapatismo, another example of an impressive outcome of this organized resistance in the Northern Highlands of the State of Puebla is the regional cooperative, the *Tosepan Titataniskej*, formed in a Nahuat community represented by 800 members representing 60 communities, including 200 indigenous women (Sánchez Díaz de Rivera & Almeida, 2005). An important struggle of this regional cooperative was the search for cultural and political power. One of its members became municipal president from 1986 to 1989 following their *usos y costumbres*, uses and customs, and traditional judiciary systems such as popular assemblies that occurred regularly, including other communities in the region.

Almeida (1988) asserted that assemblies are participatory schools where decisions are made collectively. The numerous peasant and Indigenous movements searched for autonomy and popular power nourished by their spirituality and culture. These movements used popular power, enacting rituals, ceremonies, annual celebrations, and contra-power against the government to demand their land, cultural, spiritual, and political rights (Ciofalo, 2014, 2019). In the same venue, the Zapatismo has been promoting cultural, spiritual, and political power to enact community empowerment that enabled self-determination using an autonomous Buen Gobierno and defense for their sacred sites and resources. Their popular power occurs as everyday resistance in various educational, health, agricultural activities, and community organizations. Contra-power is practiced by dancing, singing, and protesting in public performances to disseminate their teachings, principles, and statements to end the war against life for a better world in which many worlds are possible.

Conclusions: The Cultural Politics of Popular Power and Contra-Power

The Zapatista movement manifests popular power in the form of cultural-political-organizational-educational-and spiritual empowerment. It is a valuable example of decolonizing pedagogy and community praxis. This movement proved that commitment and perseverance in forming transformative relations of solidary conviviality promote the "transmodern decolonial socialization of power" (Grosfoguel, 2008, pp. 20–21). Under Indigenous epistemologies, this kind of socialization of power is analogous to cultural-spiritual-community empowerment (Ciofalo, 2014, 2019, 2022). It is a demand for Indigenous rights for social, political, economic, cultural, ecological, and epistemic equity. Granda Henao (2022) asserted that the Zapatista autonomy merged and grew from the communitarian position the Zapatista communities maintain, co-constructing "a longer framework of struggles for land and territory, political and religious militancy, collective works and everyday political practices of resistance and conviviality" (p. 173). Arturo Escobar et al., (2022) added,

> Autonomy is sometimes thought of as the radicalization of direct democracy and a new manner of conceiving and enacting politics. It involves reimagining politics as the inescapable process that emerges from the entanglement of humans among themselves and with the Earth but is oriented to reconfiguring power in less hierarchical ways based on principles such as sufficiency, mutual aid, and the self-determination of the norms of living. (cited in Escobar et al., 2022, p. 114)

The Zapatistas created their own government, *El Buen Gobierno*, which rules by obeying the peoples' will and its autonomous judiciary system based on Indigenous *usos y costumbres.* In this way, they are doing politics in their own way. Valentina, a Zapatista woman and leader from the *Caracol* Roberto Barrios stated,

> The politics that our peoples and their autonomous governments focus on is the construction of autonomy, then our own thought and plan is to change the situation that our peoples suffer because of the bad government of the rich people, such as poverty, inequality, exploitation, injustice. We fight for having a life with dignity for all the children, young people, men,

> women and elders and that we all have the same opportunities and place, without any exclusion. (EZLN, 2013, 72; cited in Granda Henao, 2022, p. 12)

As Xochitl Leyva (2018) asserted, the Zapatista pedagogy has taught us to practice "*La Otra Política y la Otra Teoría*" (p. 199) that were co-constructed in educational and cultural settings such as workshops, festivities, celebrations, everyday activities, and encounters through its resistant and rebellious "*Ya Basta* epistemic," informed by their ancestral cosmovisions, their communitarian relationality with human, animals, plants, ancestors, and the Earth (p. 205). This is a holistic and powerful cultural politics against the capitalist hydra to return to a dignified life on our planet, where after the end of the Anthropocene and Capitalocene, the death of the capitalist hydra, the Ecocene can exist and thrive.

Conflict of Interest Statement: There is no conflict of interest to be disclosed related to this article.

References

Albán, A., & Rosero, J.R. (2016). La colonialidad de la naturaleza: imposición tecnológica e imposición epistémica? Intercururalidad, desarrolo, y re-existencia. *Nómadas, 45,* 27–41. Universidad Central de Colombia.

Almeida, E. (1988, October, 26). *La capacitación en el proyecto de transformación social en una comunidad Nahuat: Quinto ciclo de conferencias sobre la teoría y la práctica de la educación de adultos y su relación con el mundo de trabajo.* Universidad Autónoma de Mexico, Mexico City.

Almeida, E., & Sánchez Díaz de Rivera, M. E. (Coords.) (2001). *Conocimiento y acción en Tzinacapan: Autobiografías razonadas.* Universidad Iberoamericana del Golfo Centro, Universidad Veracruzana, and Universidad Autónoma del Estado de Mexico.

Almeida, E., & Sánchez Díaz de Rivera, M. E. (2005). *Las veredas de la incertidumbre: Relaciones interculturales y supervivencia digna.* Universidad Iberoamericana de Puebla, Universidad Autónoma de San Luis Potosí, Universidad Juárez de Tabasco, Universidad Veracruzana, Universidad Autónoma de Sinaloa, El Colegio de Puebla, Escuela Libre de Psicología de Chihuahua, and Consejo Nacional de Enseñanza e Investigación en Psicología.

Almeida, E., & Sánchez Díaz de Rivera, M.E. (2014). *Comunidad: Interacción, conflicto y utopía. La construcción del tejido social.* Universidad Iberoamericana.

Asher, K. (2017). Spivak and Rivera Cusicanqui on the dilemmas of representation in postcolonial and decolonial feminism. *Feminist Studies, 43*(3), 512–524.

Bastida, M. L. (2019). Anotaciones sobre un cuarto de siglo decultura u comunicación crítica Zapatista. *Grupo Estudios Críticos de Comunicación, ECCO. Universidad de Almería.*
Callahan, M. (2005). Why not share a dream? Zapatismo as political and cultural practice. Special issue. *Humboldt Journal of Social Relations, 29*, 5–37.
Ciofalo, N. (2014). Cultural-religious empowerment, popular power, and contra-power: A demand for indigenous rights. *Psicología Social Comunitaria. Segunda Época, 3*, 452–481.
Ciofalo, N. (Ed.). (2019). *Indigenous psychologies in an era of decolonization.* Springer Nature.
Ciofalo, N. (2022). Making the road *caminando de otra manera*: Co-constructing decolonial community psychologies from the global south. *American Journal of Community Psychology, 69*(3–4), 426–435. https://onlinelibrary-wiley-com.pgi.idm.oclc.org/doi/full/10.1002/ajcp.12562
Dussel, E. (1995). *The invention of the Americas: Eclipse of the other and the myth of modernity.* Continuum.
Dussel, E. (2010). *El giro descolonizador dsde el pueblo y hacia la segunda descolonización.* Universidad Autonóma de México, Departamento de Filosofía.
Dussel, E. (2019). *Pedagogics of liberation: A Latin American philosophy of education.* Punctum Books, Earth, Mikyway.
Enlace Zapatista. (2022, May 20). La Red Grietas, presenta el primer número de la publicación Grietas: Una revista de pensamiento y horizontes Zapatistas. https://enlacezapatista.ezln.org.mx/2022/05/20/la-red-sexta-grietas-del-norte-presenta-el-primer-numero-de-publicacion-grietas-una-revista-de-pensamiento-y-horizontes-zapatistas/
Escobar, A. (2016). Thinking-feeling with the earth: Territorial struggles and the ontological dimensions of the south. *Revista de Antropología Iberoamericana en Red, 11*(1), 12–33.
Escobar, A., Tornel, C., & Lunden, A. (2022). On design, development and the axes of the pluriversal politics. *Nordia Geographical Publications, 51*(2), 103–122.
Esteva, G. (1999, Summer). The Zapatismo and peoples' power. *Capital & Class, 22*(68), 153–182.
EZLN (Ejército Zapatista de Liberación Nacional) Sixth Commission. (2015). *Critical thought in the face of the capitalist hydra.* AK Press.
Fals-Borda, O. (1984). Participatory action research development. *Seeds for Change, 2*, 18–20.
Fals-Borda, O. (1986). *Conocimiento y poder popular: Lecciones con campesinos de Nicaragua, Mexico y Colombia.* Punta de Lanza, Siglo Veintiuno.
Freire, P. (1972). *Pedagogía de la emancipación.* Editorial Siglo Veintiuno.
Granda Henao, S. (2022). El pueblo manda y el gobierno obedece: Decolonizing politics and constructing worlds in the everyday through Zapatista autonomy. In F. D. Márquez Duarte & V. E. Espinoza Valle (Eds.), *Decolonizing politics and theories from Abya Yala.* E-International Relations. https://www.e-ir.info/

Grosfoguel, R. (2008, July). *Transmodernity, border thinking, and global coloniality* (pp. 1–23). Eurozine.
Gudynas, E. (2014). Derechos de la naturaleza: Ética biocéntrica y políticas ambientales. Programa Democracia y Transformación Global (PDTG), Red Peruana por una Globalización con Equidad (redGE), CooperAcción, and Centro Latino Americano de Ecologia Social (CLAES).
Hirschman, A. (1984). *Getting ahead collectively: Grassroots experiences in Latin America*. Pergamon Press.
Leff, E. (1995). *Green production: Toward an environmental rationality*. The Guilford Press.
Leyva, X. J., Alonso, R. A., Hernández, A., Escobar, A. K., et al. (2018). *Prácticas otras de conocimiento(s): Entre crisis, entre guerras*. Cooperativa Editorial Retos.
López Intzin, J. L. (n.d.). *Ich'el ta muk': Insights from the construction of Lekil Kuxlejal. Towards a visibilization of "other" knowledges from the matrix of the Tseltal feel-thinking and feel-knowing*. Hemi Press. https://resistantstrategies.hemi.press/ichel-ta-muk-insights-from-the-construction-of-lekil-kuxlejal-towards-a-visibilization-of-other-knowledges-from-the-matrix-of-the-tseltal-feel-thinking-and-feel-k/.
Lugones, M. (2008, Spring). The coloniality of gender. In *Worlds and Knowledges Otherwise* (Vol. 2, pp. 1–12). Duke University Press.
Maldonado-Torres, N. (2007, March). On the coloniality of being: Contributions to the development of a concept. *Cultural Studies, 21*(2–3), 240–270.
Marcos, S. (2022). Indigenous spirituality and the decolonization of religious beliefs. In W.S. Goldstein, & J.P. Reed. (Eds.), *Religion in rebellions, revolutions, and social movements* (231–245). Rutgers.
Martin-Baró, I. (1986). Hacia una Psicología de la Liberación. *Boletín de Psicología, No., 22*, 219–231.
Mignolo, W. D. (2009). *Local histories/global design: Coloniality, subaltern knowledge, and border thinking*. Princeton University Press.
Montero, M. (2003). *La Psicología Comunitaria: La tensión entre comunidad y sociedad*. Paidos.
Montero, M. (2013). Social consortium: A partnership of community agents. *Global Journal of Community Psychology Practice, 4* (2), 2–4. Retrieved August 8, 2013, from http://www.gjcpp.org.
Quijano, A. (2000). Coloniality of power, eurocentrism and Latin America. In A. Quijano & M. Ennis (Eds.), *Nepantla: Views from the south 1.3* (pp. 533–580). Duke University Press.
Rivera Cusicanqui, S. (2012). Ch'ixinakax utxiwa: A reflection on the practices and discourses of decolonization. *The South American Quarterly, 11*(1), 95–109.
Santos de Souza, B. (2009). *Una epistemología del sur*. Siglo Veintiuno Editores.

Santos de Souza, B. (2018). *The end of the cognitive empire*. Duke University Press.
Smith, L. T. (2012). *Decolonizing methodologies: Research and indigenous peoples*. Zed Books Ltd.
Spivak, G. (1988). Can the subaltern speak? In C. Nelson & L. Grossberg (Eds.), *Marxism and the interpretation of culture*. University of Illinois Press.
Spivak, G. (1999). *A critique of postcolonial reason: Toward a history of the vanishing present*. Harvard University Press.

CHAPTER 13

Unpacking Cultural Politics in Indigenous Psychology: Sweetgrass Method to Mental Health Services Among American Indian/Alaska Natives

Mark Standing Eagle Baez and C. Allison Baez

For years, substance use has plagued many American Indian and Alaska Native (AI/AN) communities. Research indicates that significantly more American Indians and Alaska Natives needed treatment for alcohol or illicit drug use in the prior year than people from other ethnic groups, according to Kwon et al. (2024). Substance use disorders have been seen as a more dominant mental health issue among AI/ANs compared to the general population in the United States. AI/AN, descendants of the indigenous people, are a diverse population group growing yearly. According to Arias et al. (2014), studies suggest that AI/ANs have a lower life expectancy, mortality rate, and quality of life than the general US

M. S. E. Baez (✉)
Bemidji State University, Bemidji, MN, USA
e-mail: mark.baez@bemidjistate.edu

C. A. Baez
Independent Scholar, Bemidji, MN, USA

Z. Z. Gao, M. I. Medved (eds.), *Global Perspectives on Cultural Politics in Indigenous Psychology*, Palgrave Studies in Indigenous Psychology, https://doi.org/10.1007/978-3-031-96813-6_13

population. In the past, many psychologists attempted to tackle these problems by introducing Western evidence-based strategies that failed to recognize indigenous values such as spirituality, the wisdom of elders, and family relationships.

Moreover, indigenous people were rarely invited to participate in designing solutions. Over time, it became clear that these Western practices did not work (Brockie et al., 2022). Many Indigenous communities are concerned with the seriousness of substance abuse problems and mental health effects and are eager to advance effective solutions for their people's health and welfare. However, these communities are also concerned about the perpetuation of colonizing, stigmatizing approaches to mental health, and social narratives about mental health practitioners who apply techniques that look at the three braiding strands: introspective (self-reflection/self-care), communication (with clients/other professionals), and continuity (continued culturally responsive support services) as a means of developing healthy and successful outcomes for the client. The SGM is a community-based participatory practice approach incorporating practice-based evidence (PBE), which looks at what works for this community setting. The SGM can be used to understand the cultural differences in how patients view illness and healthcare by engaging family and tribal community members in addiction treatment. The SGM is a self-motivated process that prevention/intervention practitioners can use to begin a healthy dialogue with AI/AN clients by incorporating self-reflection, communication, and the continuation of tailored services. The SGM is taking the strengths of our indigenous ways of knowing and evidence-based practices and weaving them together to provide practice-based evidence tailored for AI/AN people.

Introduction

Statement of the Problem: Risk Factors for AIAN Youth

Too often, children face adversity in life because of their history, culture, and identity. AI/AN children have a higher predisposition for Adverse Childhood Experiences (ACEs), which directly impact their thoughts, behaviors, health and wellness, self-esteem, choices in life, and emotions. According to Caetano et al., 2013, the National Violent Death Reporting System of AI/AN suicide tested for alcohol showed 36% were officially inebriated at the time of death. There were proportionally more positive test results for alcohol among AI/AN deceased than for any other racial or ethnic group (Caetano et al., 2013). In 2011, AI/AN people had the highest proportion of current prohibited drug use (13.4%) among those ages 12 or older contrasted to any other racial/ethnic group, and illicit drug use is a risk factor for suicide. The overall rate for all racial/ethnic groups was 8.7% (SAMHSA, 2012). Substance use and behavioral health conditions among AI/AN populations are higher, almost across the board, than those in other demographics, and obstacles to treatment (such as ineffective access and stigma) are more evident. Substance Abuse and Mental Health Services Administration (SAMHSA, 2012) suggests that 13% of Native Americans need substance use treatment, but only 3.5% receive any. SAMHSA data found a lack of cultural understanding and culturally sensitive programs as reasons for the underutilization of therapy and low retention rates among AI/AN clients. Generational trauma among AI/AN populations has produced a gap of trust between people in need in those communities and programs that have been almost entirely constructed by—and *for*—white people. Stigma, mistrust, not knowing who they are, and fear of being judged are barriers. Not understanding who they are—the therapists and counselors they work with may think we are all alike as indigenous people. The reaction among AI/AN clients is natural. Attempts to eliminate AI/AN culture—such as forced relocation, removal of children to boarding schools, prohibition of the practice of native language and cultural traditions, and outlawing of traditional religious practices—have affected multiple generations of AI/AN people and contribute to high rates of suicide among them (Brave Heart & DeBruyn, 1998; HHS, 2010).

Understanding disparities among Indigenous people would be an essential step toward health equity. Providing a recipe for success will be challenging if we know their story. Listening patiently and participating in cultural traditions is just as important as the content of those stories is the act itself. Sometimes, even sharing one's own stories as a practitioner may lend to building trust with the client. Telling stories is culturally appropriate and builds a better understanding and healthy relationship. Building relationships by asking them what tribe they are from and also sharing traditions is how we start our conversations. There should be an effort to improve AI/AN mental health care disparities through culturally competent clinical interventions. In working toward this goal, it is essential to identify the existing inequalities in mental health care delivery and outcomes among AI/ANs. This will help guide the steps necessary for improved outcomes and reduced health disparities. Alaska Native tribal members with more excellent adaptation to the mainstream culture reported increased psychosocial stress, less happiness, and greater use of drugs or alcohol to cope with the stress of navigating cultural differences (Wolsko et al., 2016). In some American Indian tribes, there is more pressure to acculturate, significant conflict regarding traditional cultural practices, and a high suicide rate among adolescents and young adults (Olson & Wahab, 2006). Also, studies of American Indian youth found that discrimination was as important a predictor of suicidal ideation as poor self-esteem and depression (Walls et al., 2007; Yoder et al., 2006).

Methods and Approaches (Western, Limited AIAN Literature)

AI/ANs face some of the highest tasks to the Mental Health and well-being of any racial or racial group in the United States. Mental health-related mortality is a priority. A recent study (Shiels et al., 2017) of death certificate data from the US National Center for Health Statistics showed that premature deaths among AI/ANs were highest and increased each year from 1999 to 2014, primarily due to magnitudes of mental health and substance use conditions such as liver disease and cirrhosis, suicide, and injuries. An estimated 6600 excess premature deaths occurred in AI/ANs ages 25–49 during this time frame. The intergenerational burden of mental health and substance use disorders was also apparent in high prevalence rates of one-lifetime mental health or substance use disorder (43%) or two or more lifetime disorders (31.6%) among these youth's caregivers (Whitbeck et al., 2004). Another study by Brave Heart and colleagues (Brave Heart et al., 2016) suggests that urban AI/ANs demonstrated that approximately 70% and 63% of AI/AN men and women, respectively, contrasted to 62% and 53% of non-Hispanic White women and men, met the criteria for a lifetime psychiatric disorder. Despite disparities, there is significant heterogeneity in mental health and substance use disorders by age, region, gender, and tribal context. There is also a great need to understand the historical and current stressors that serve as root causes impacting mental health and well-being, as well as the unique role that strengths play in overcoming these inequities within AI/AN communities.

Cultural Protective Factors (Storytelling?)

Cultural protective factors that address resiliency include spirituality, family, respect for elders, ceremonial rituals, oral traditions, tribal identity, and traditional healing practices, many of which are rooted in positivity. Our Native stories have always been woven into our daily lives to create our resiliency and lead us to be culture rich in history and tradition for hundreds of years. The passing down of our stories through our cultural lens benefits our community, especially our children. Culture is noted to impact resilience, individually and as a community. Research by Brockmeier and Carbaugh with AI/ANs reveals that protective factors for positive outcomes include culture, family, and community. Commitment to tribal cultural spirituality (spirituality deriving from traditions predating European contact) is significantly associated with reducing suicide attempts. Garroutte et al. (2003) suggest that people with a high level of cultural and spiritual orientation have a reduced frequency of suicide compared with those with low levels of cultural and spiritual positioning. Family connectedness: Connectedness to family and discussing problems with family and friends are protective against suicide attempts among AI/AN youth (Garroutte et al., 2003). Storytelling and story circles honor traditional wisdom but allow participants to speak their truth, honor their identity, and learn values and skills contributing to self-efficacy. It is the transmission of these values that lays the foundation for resilience. According to Hodge et al. (2022), storytelling offers an opportunity to continue traditions by passing down stories orally and in writing. Storytelling benefits future families because they can continue how they were once used and use stories to learn traditional lifestyles and practices. Storytelling is an attempt to reinforce values and beliefs and allows future generations to connect to their ancestral roots through stories. Due to colonialism, it is hard to keep traditions, so they could only be taught through stories. Stories provide a means by which Indigenous people can identify and reconnect with ancient tribal traditions. Traditional Native stories have been handed down within a tribe for centuries and often have extremely ancient origins. These stories may reflect social and physical environments in preservation eras and long before, thus giving present-day listeners insight into past realities (Hodge et al., 2022) (Fig. 13.1).

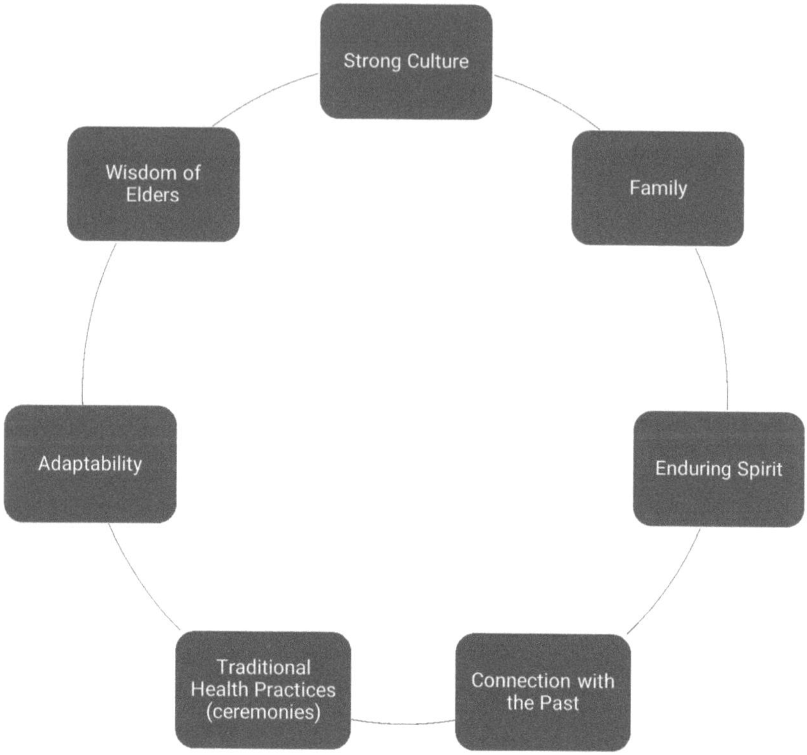

Fig 13.1 Present-day listeners insight into past realities (Hodge et al., 2022)

Counter-Cultural Considerations/Implications (Cultural Politics)

Mental health and substance use as priority areas in Native communities have prompted increased literature on treatment. Theoretical and empirical articles have attempted to understand treatment utilization, barriers to seeking mental health care, and treatment preferences. Stigma has appeared as one of the most constant obstacles to care across several studies for Native communities. AI/ANs have described stigma about obtaining services associated with concerns about being inadequate and how others will see them (Duran et al., 2005; Freitas-Murrell & Swift, 2015; Venner et al., 2012). Other barriers include maintaining privacy about their presenting psychiatric complaint, trusting providers, and absence of transportation, time, economic income, and social support (Duran et al., 2005; Venner et al., 2012). AI/AN ethnic identification may also have implications for engaging in mental health treatment. In a study of AN college students, those with higher levels of Caucasian identity demonstrated positive attitudes (i.e., openness in therapy, willingness to seek help, and stigma) about seeking mental health therapy (Freitas-Murrell & Swift, 2015). In contrast, in a separate study of AI college students, those with strong tribal identification reported negative attitudes (i.e., self-reported need for therapy, stigma, openness in therapy, and confidence in service providers; McNeill, 1992).

Numerous authors have identified colonialism (i.e., European contact, land theft, genocidal acts, forced assimilation), its lasting effects (e.g., historical trauma or historical loss; Brave Heart & DeBruyn, 1998; Whitbeck et al., 2004) and continuing oppression (e.g., discrimination) as root causes of Indigenous mental health inequities (Brave Heart, 2003; Duran & Duran, 1995; Goodkind et al., 2015; Gone & Trimble, 2012; Smith, 1999). Colonialism and continued discrimination impact specific tribes differently (e.g., historical events and the current context of racism). There is also a general sense of shared suffering (Heart et al., 2011) that may be reflected in the population-level mental health disparities. Research has shown a direct link between historical trauma (also called historical loss) and depression, anxiety, substance abuse, and indirectly to suicide ideation (e.g., Armenta et al., 2016; Grayshield et al., 2015; Whitbeck et al., 2004, 2009; Wiechelt et al., 2012). Burgeoning viewpoints assert that if colonialism and intergenerational historical loss are recognized as the identified problem, it follows that interventions with AI/ANs should be focused on cultural reassertion and revitalization at the individual and community level (Heart et al., 2011; Gone & Trimble, 2012; Goodkind et al., 2015). In a qualitative study, AI elders discussed that healing from intergenerational historical trauma involves tribal cultural reclamation, including speaking one's native language and spirituality (Grayshield et al., 2015).

Cultural resilience can be defined as the ability of a cultural community to face adversity and change while continuing to progress. For AI/ANs, it is helpful to find inner strength rooted in cultural grounding and a belief system. Sharing and teaching about resilience with our youth is significant for their health and well-being as well as the sustainability of our culture. For Native American communities to continue to be resilient and heal, the connection to culture is paramount. Alaska Native tribal members following a more traditional way of life reported greater happiness, more recurrent use of religion and spirituality to manage stress, and less repeated use of drugs and alcohol to manage stress. Alaska Native tribal members often adhere to more traditional cultural practices. Studies of Native American youth in the Midwest indicate that a strong ethnic and cultural identity is associated with greater resilience to acculturative stress and a reduced risk of suicidal ideation.

VULNERABLE

- Historically, AI/ AN populations have been vulnerable in both physical and mental health.
- Historically, AI/AN communities have been disproportionately represented in education, foster care, juvenile crimes, poverty, and more.

RESILIENT

- AI/ANs draw strength from traditional ways of living, places, relationships, and collective successes. Their resilience is built through culture, spirituality, shared values, and a strong sense of identity, accountability, and responsibility.

The Sweetgrass Method

American Indians/First Nations people have held sweetgrass (Óhonte Wenserákon) sacred for a long time. Sweetgrass is used to purify oneself—mentally, emotionally, physically, and spiritually—in hopes of grounding the person in healing. The SGM is a culturally responsive framework designed to enhance services for AI/AN people (Baez, 2011, 2023; Baez & Isaac, 2013; Baez et al., 2016, 2022). This framework strongly emphasizes community, fostering a deep connection to the natural world, respect for elders and traditions, and a holistic perspective on health and well-being. The SGM weaves the best of evidence-based practices with the very best of Indigenous practice-based evidence to serve the population or individuals best. The SGM (Fig. 13.2) divides sweetgrass into three sections, each representing a central strand: Introspection, Communication, and Continuation. These three central strands encompass numerous sub-strands within their core areas (i.e., the Introspection strand includes self-reflection, cultural humility, and the application of the best aspects of Western and Indigenous methodologies, along with Communication and

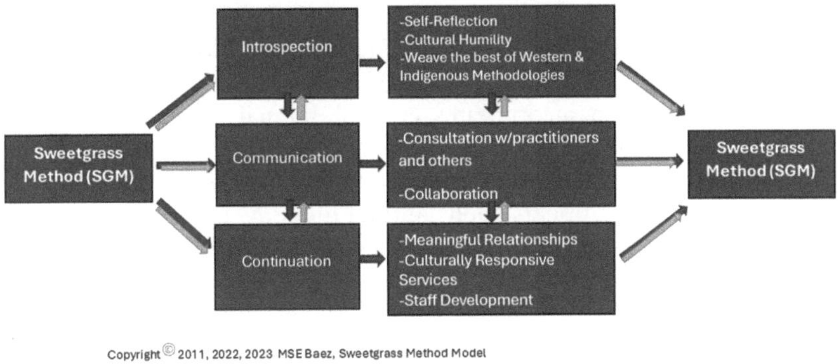

Fig. 13.2 (SMG) Model (Copyright © Baez, 2011, 2013, 2022, 2023)

Continuation, among others). We weave this braid tightly together to symbolize the strength of the intentions set forth—Introspection, Communication, and Continuation—enabling practitioners and educators to address social barriers that lead to disparities in student success. Providing a safe place of H.O.P.E. or honoring our people's experiences without judgment (Baez et al., 2016) is essential when developing services for Indigenous families. Non-AI/AN providers can communicate respect for their AI/AN clients' stories, feelings, and understanding of what they are experiencing through H.O.P.E.

First Strand: Introspection

A commitment to self-reflection, life-long practice, weaving in the best Western evidence-based practices and the best Indigenous practice-based evidence for the individuals serviced. Also, recognizing one's culture and how it influences behavior is necessary but insufficient for working effectively in a multicultural society (Baez et al., 2022). Such awareness is particularly critical for professionals providing services to Indigenous populations, as they must be respectful and non-judgmental and avoid assumptions and expectations to serve their clients best (Baez, 2011, 2023; Baez & Isaac, 2013; Baez et al., 2022). This cannot happen if we are not grounded introspectively. Introspection includes reflecting on professional competencies and practicing self-care to promote spiritual, emotional, physical, and mental wellness to bring understanding, clarity, and preparedness to prevention strategies and support. The Introspection strand of the SGM braid also allows educators to be examples of healthy leaders for the AI/AN and Indigenous individuals to whom they provide services.

Introspection also incorporates cultural humility. Cultural humility starts with a commitment to exploring one's cultural beliefs and values because responding effectively to others is hard without understanding yourself. When practitioners apply cultural humility, they ask sincere and curious questions about, for example, the client's ethnicity, gender, sexual identity, sexual orientation, social needs, and language. Practitioners knowledgeable of AI/AN perspectives of mental health also understand that the primary goal of psychological helping to address special education needs is to explore issues related to a client's reason to act out and help them find healing (Baez et al., 2022; Baez & Baez, 2023). Through introspection, we have the opportunity to assist our clients in finding healing and provide support for their academic and social-emotional growth.

Second Strand: Communication

The second strand of the braid, Communication, refers to how the work becomes action with others. Partnerships with families and communities are critical when supporting AI/AN clients. In particular, the community is essential to supporting the growth and success of individuals dealing with substance use disorder issues. This second strand in the SGM braid is an evolving process that calls for active participation from contributing professionals, families, community, and clients, all of whom engage in shared problem-solving and decision-making to achieve a common goal (Baez, 2011, 2023; Baez & Isaac, 2013; Baez et al., 2022). All these different groups must communicate well to work together effectively. However, this can be challenging when the partnerships include AI/AN and non-AI/AN members.

Non-AI/AN providers can communicate respect for their Indigenous clients' stories, feelings, and understanding of what they are experiencing through H.O.P.E. For example, most AI/AN people understand the use of sweetgrass, which is used to cleanse the mind, spirit, and body. According to C.A. Baez, "the culturally responsive technique of the SGM discusses how professional clinicians would approach with openness to honoring our people's experiences" (personal communication; April 2015). This means embracing the experiences that AI/AN clients may factor into choices.

It is essential to communicate the possible support strategies available to family members in a culturally responsive and appropriate manner, mainly when working with the family of a client dealing with substance use. For AI/AN clients and extended family members, trust is essential in any conversation, mainly when working with non-AI/AN providers. Based on historical trauma, AI/AN caregivers have many reasons not to trust clinical personnel. Family members may not feel comfortable or be receptive to discussions about their family member's drug use when they do not know, let alone trust, the person sharing such information.

Third Strand: Continuity

The third strand in the SGM braid involves maintaining a continuum of action-oriented cultural Intentionality practices, fostering cultural understanding, improving student well-being, and providing enhanced academic engagement. This includes support for the client and their extended support, community, and staff development. Providing ongoing culturally responsive approaches is vital to improving social-emotional and academic outcomes for AI/AN and Indigenous youth (Baez et al., 2022; Baez, 2023). This strand also focuses on continued research on new prevention strategies and ongoing social support services that weave together Western approaches and AI/AN traditional methodologies for clients with disabilities.

Although consistently continuing services may sound intuitive as best practice, it *only sometimes happens.* Moreover, when systems break down, Indigenous families may feel abandoned by providers who fail to continue to "show up" for them. Practitioners reach out to a family and should be honest and transparent about their current state in the services that must be provided. Communicating with clients about what is happening is essential and helpful for the client's progress and success. Even asking families for their suggestions and support is very useful. Maintaining continuity can be challenging, especially in areas experiencing shortages of

Native educational providers. There may be situations where a provider needs help to follow through, even though they are committed and want to because they have too large a caseload or too many mandated evaluations to complete.

As a braid, the strands of SGM are interwoven and overlap. Thus, communication and continuity are often closely connected. For example, as practitioners, educators, and administrators, there is a need for continuity of communication with families and the community. Providers can achieve this by communicating when there is a concern with services not being provided for the client or some support for the person identified with mental health issues (Baez et al., 2022; Baez, 2023). A phone call or note home to share a success—large or small—can go a long way toward continuing to build trust and maintain relationships. Generally speaking, continuity of support services requires continuing a healthy dialogue to preserve relationships with AI/AN clients.

In addition, there is a need for continuity of support services in and outside of school for special education services. Ongoing collaborative care improves outcomes, particularly for people with complex needs (Henderson et al., 2019). This often requires partnerships with other professionals and community resources, particularly those familiar with local knowledge and traditions. Practitioners, other professionals, and community partners must be flexible in deciding the appropriate and relevant methods for their particular tribe or community.

Three-Step Process to the Sweetgrass Method for Clients with SUD

The first step in the SGM process is the *initial consultation and needs identification.*

When practitioners work with clients with mental health issues, beginning with a communication process that builds relationships and promotes information sharing is essential. Practitioners begin this initial consultation with cultural humility. This is essential when working with Indigenous clients because it is grounded in embedding traditional cultural methods and authentic content into practitioners' approaches (Baez et al., 2022; Baez & Baez, 2023). Next, the practitioner identifies and prioritizes the client's needs, asking for examples of substance use disorder needs and focusing on specific target areas. Practitioners set goals and develop strategies for the classroom and home. Identifying the needs during the initial assessment helps practitioners determine what must be accomplished to reach expected treatment goals. This needs identification to inform an overall plan and approaches. For example, the initial consultation and needs identification regarding substance use may determine the forms of the particular substance use disorder, if the behavior warrants intervention, and how often the client's needs continue after repeated practitioner intervention (Baez et al., 2022; Baez & Baez, 2023).

The second step is a *needs analysis* to identify the reasons for the problem and how to overcome the gap between what is and should be. As practitioners, we are trained in this area to conduct a behavioral assessment, but the question is, how should one administer a behavioral assessment to AI/AN clients? In facilitating this assessment among AI/AN clients, the practitioner should have an approach incorporating cultural relevancy and cultural sustainability. The initial cultural dialog with the client is essential in developing cultural understandings and knowledge when identifying behavioral, healthy social, and emotional needs. The SGM intentionally has the practitioner focus on cultural humility as a strand for developing successful approaches.

The last step is the *needs evaluation*. This step involves collaborators reviewing the data collected by the team of professionals. This data gathering allows the practitioner to determine the child's progress regarding the intervention and the services' overall success. The practitioner and consultees share feedback throughout the consultation to enable immediate modifications to the treatment plan when needed. The data from a needs assessment assists practitioners in determining why clients are not succeeding, some of the barriers they face, and their strengths. This last step can assist practitioners in identifying client needs, informing behavioral strategies to address those needs, and pinpointing the high-need areas for small groups. A suggested meeting or consultation time with the clients/clients is up to three or four meetings that would need to occur for support and direction for the client/client. A suggested time would be 45–60 minutes per meeting. These steps will weave in the SGM to incorporate a culturally responsive approach to service delivery for the Indigenous clients that are being serviced.

Case Example: An SGM Approach to SUD

Johnny White Horse is an AI/AN sent to meet with mental health therapist Jeff, having been court-ordered to attend Substance abuse classes. Applying the SGM (see Fig. 13.2), Jeff would begin with introspection. This would include thinking through what he knows and does not know about Johnny's culture and reflecting on where there may be similarities and differences between Johnny's traditions and his own. It would also mean assessing self-care and how calm and equipped he felt to handle Johnny's case.

Communication with Johnny would begin from a place of cultural humility and curiosity to build trust. Jeff might thank Johnny for coming to the meeting and explaining that he cares about him and where he comes from, so they must discuss what happened. Gazing around the room without staring directly at Johnny, Jeff could start by sincerely wanting to learn about Johnny and asking him about preferred terms or his Tribal name. Like most discussions with clients about complex issues, the conversation would likely carefully and patiently explore Jeff's perspective about the difficulties with Johnny's academics or social-emotional needs, with Jeff checking for understanding.

It would be necessary for a practitioner applying SGM to communicate to Johnny that addressing academic deficiencies requires ongoing collaboration with his caregivers. Thus, Jeff would want to be clear with Johnny about all plans to speak with his parent(s) or guardian(s) before connecting with his family. Applying the fundamentals of the SGM Communication braid, Jeff would invite Johnny's caregiver(s) for a meeting to discuss the special education issue and ensure they know they have a voice and a valued perspective. Jeff would aim to establish an equal partnership with Johnny's family and avoid any implication that, as a school staff member, he was more of an expert or held more power than the caregivers. Instead, Johnny's family members are the experts on Johnny, and by hearing their stories and honoring their experiences, Jeff will be better equipped to support him.

Addressing Johnny's special education needs would be ongoing and collaborative. Jeff would need to "show up" consistently and work patiently to establish and maintain the trust needed to work with Johnny to change his behavior. Consistent communication with Johnny's family would also be essential. For example, Jeff might call home periodically to check in for updates or to share successes when Johnny has made progress toward his behavioral goals. The three strands of the SGM braid would remain woven throughout the process, and through reflection, Jeff would continue to learn and strengthen his skills for working with AI/AN communities.

The Unique Needs and Context of SUD Among AI/AN

Individuals who experience trauma or are incarcerated or homeless are more likely to need mental health care and addiction treatment. Indigenous peoples are disproportionately overrepresented in these vulnerable populations. AI/ANs are also at greater risk for mental health problems, suicide, drug and alcohol abuse, and involvement in the juvenile justice system (Singh et al., 2024). These outcomes are attributed to a variety of causes, such as lack of support from parents and family members, poor academic skills, poor client–teacher relationships, lack of a sense of belonging in schools, linguistic and cultural barriers, low expectations, and client transfer and mobility (Reyhner & Singh, 2010; Sarche & Spicer, 2008). To effectively address this range of critical needs, we must provide services that reflect best practices grounded in cultural awareness. Although there is literature on the effectiveness of substance abuse programs, little research is available to inform our understanding of substance abuse disorder and suicidality within the AI/AN context, its consequences among AI/AN clients, and what prevention approaches are culturally aligned for AI/AN people. However, for professionals working with AI/AN clients, any framework to prevent and address substance use disorders and suicidality must consider cultural context as a critical component of addressing specific issues. Although substance abuse disorders can compound existing vulnerabilities for people from marginalized populations, research on culturally responsive prevention programs is limited, particularly for American Indian/Alaska Native (AI/AN) communities. This chapter will explain how a culturally responsive approach to mental and behavioral health, the Sweetgrass Method (SGM; Baez, 2011; Baez et al., 2022), can address substance use disorders.

Suggestions for a Positive Path

When mental health services focus on mind, body, and spirit, there is a connection to cultural and traditional teachings. These connections are considered cultural protective factors: concepts that are key to the "cultural context, identity, adaptability, and perseverance" of AI/ANs. Cultural protective factors include holistic healing methods and the promotion of well-being for one's community. Culture is a strength and primary protective factor within AI/AN communities and in our youth's identity. Our history, stories, and traditions have carried Native families in times of adversity and celebration going back seven generations and will keep us moving forward for seven generations.

Conclusions

Developing culturally responsive clinical skills is critical to improving behavioral health services among Indigenous clients. Although mental health facilities are ever more diverse, many new practitioners have few opportunities to develop multicultural competency before on-the-job experiences. Unfortunately, it is clients of color who are disproportionately affected. Decolonizing mental health and therapy is a process that challenges the legacy of colonialism, imperialism, and systemic oppression in mental health and healing. Recognizing the impact of colonization and decolonizing mental health involves acknowledging how Western psychiatric knowledge has marginalized non-Western models of knowledge and healing (Baez, 2025). What is most disturbing is that these circumstances are not new for minority clients, and efforts to change the adverse outcomes have been largely unsuccessful. Gomes (2018) states that much of federal policy, statute, and case law (especially Federal Indian Law and past and present policies) affect the health of Indigenous Nations, Peoples, and communities in the United States and US territories. Colonization, which is ongoing and pervasive in federal policy, continues to affect the health of Indigenous Peoples and communities negatively. By incorporating cultural methods into the initial supports/strategies for the client, we are more likely to see better outcomes. Practitioners can continually improve their culturally responsive practices by practicing Introspection, Communication, and Continuity, building trusting relationships with AI/AN clients, and providing reliable community support as a resource. As practitioners, we can make healthy changes by building relationships with our clients and partnerships with our AI/AN communities. Understanding AI/AN clients is essential for beginning a healthy dialogue between the client and the practitioner. This also allows the practitioners to develop healthy, meaningful approaches to mental health that are culturally responsive for AI/AN clients. As practitioners and counselors, we must determine ways to involve teaching and learning development within a cultural framework. With an understanding of the SGM represented through the description above, the practitioner is given an approach to search the fundamentals of cross-cultural connections formed in a mutual relationship with the client's family and community as the SGM applies community-based participatory practices in a partnership approach that involves Indigenous community members, Indigenous and other organizational representatives, and academic professionals in all aspects of the process. As we have argued, now is the time for dialogue between Indigenous and non-indigenous peoples about their understanding of culturally responsive methodologies and ways to disseminate these services among non-indigenous practitioners working with Indigenous clients. The emerging literature reveals that mental health scholars from the global north and south need to reflect further on the language and views concerning culturally responsive methodologies for Indigenous clients. Such reflections must address how colonialism and the resulting social disadvantages have led to dislocation, the loss of land rights, and disruption to traditional livelihoods, resulting in violence, substance abuse, and mental health issues. These factors are recognized as correlated to high impairment rates, and meaningful dialogue about the experiences of impairment and mental health amongst indigenous peoples cannot occur in a historical vacuum.

Conflict of Interest The authors declare that there is no conflict of interest.

References

Arias, E., Xu, J., & Jim, M. A. (2014). Period life tables for the non-Hispanic American Indian and Alaska Native population, 2007–2009. *American Journal of Public Health, 104*(Suppl 3), S312–S319. https://doi.org/10.2105/AJPH.2013.301635

Armenta, B. E., Whitbeck, L. B., & Habecker, P. N. (2016). The Historical Loss Scale: Longitudinal measurement equivalence and prospective links to anxiety among North American indigenous adolescents. *Cultural Diversity & Ethnic Minority Psychology, 22*(1), 1–10. https://doi.org/10.1037/cdp0000049

Baez, M. (2025, March 4). *Indigenous spirituality: Resilience in decolonizing mental health.* Crushing Colonialism. https://crushingcolonialism.org/indigenous-spirituality-resilience-in-decolonizing-mental-health/

Baez, M. S. E., (2011, March/April). Significant partnerships with native American Students, parents, and schools: A Sweetgrass method. *National Association of School Psychologists (NASP) communiqué.* http://www.nasponline.org/publications/cq/39/6/Student-Connections.aspx

Baez, M. S. E. (2023, November). Applying the Sweetgrass Method to address bullying for indigenous. *National Association of School Psychologists (NASP) communiqué.* https://www.nasponline.org/resources-and-publications/periodicals/communiqu%C3%A9-volume-52-number-3-(november-2023)/applying-the-sweetgrass-method-to-address-bullying-for-indigenous-youth

Baez, M. S. E., & Baez, C. A. (2023). Cultural-emotional learning among American Indian/Alaska native students. *Journal of Indigenous Research.* https://digitalcommons.usu.edu/kicjir/vol11/iss1/1/

Baez, M. S. E., Baez, C. A., Lavallie, B., & Spears, W. (2022). Sweetgrass Method: A culturally responsive approach to mental health. *Journal of Indigenous Research*. https://digitalcommons.usu.edu/cgi/viewcontent.cgi?article=1174&context=kicjir

Baez, M. S. E., & Isaac, P., (2013). Sweetgrass method to bullying prevention for native American Youth. *Journal of Indigenous Research*. https://digitalcommons.usu.edu/kicjir/vol3/iss1/1/

Baez, M. S. E., Isaac, P., & Baez, C. A., (2016). H.O.P.E. for indigenous people battling intergenerational trauma: The Sweetgrass method. *Journal of Indigenous Research*. https://digitalcommons.usu.edu/kicjir/vol5/iss2/2/

Brave Heart M. Y. (2003). The historical trauma response among natives and its relationship with substance abuse: A Lakota illustration. *Journal of psychoactive drugs, 35*(1), 7–13. https://doi.org/10.1080/02791072.2003.10399988

Brave Heart, M. Y., & DeBruyn, L. M. (1998). The American Indian holocaust: Healing historical unresolved grief. *American Indian and Alaska Native Mental Health Research: journal of the National Center, 8*(2), 56–78.

Brave Heart, M. Y., Lewis-Fernández, R., Beals, J., Hasin, D. S., Sugaya, L., Wang, S., & Blanco, C. (2016). Psychiatric disorders and mental health treatment in American Indians and Alaska Natives: Results of the National epidemiologic survey on alcohol and related conditions. *Social Psychiatry and Psychiatric Epidemiology, 51*, 1033–1046. https://doi.org/10.1007/s00127-016-1225-4

Brockie, T. N., Hill, K., Davidson, P. M., Decker, E., Krienke, L. K., Nelson, K. E., Nicholson, N., Werk, A. M., Wilson, D., & Around Him, D. (2022). Strategies for culturally safe research with Native American communities: an integrative review. *Contemporary nurse, 58*(1), 8–32. https://doi.org/10.1080/10376178.2021.2015414

Caetano, R., Kaplan, M. S., Huguet, N., McFarland, B. H., Conner, K., Giesbrecht, N., & Nolte, K. B. (2013). Acute alcohol intoxication and suicide among United States ethnic/racial groups: Findings from the National Violent Death Reporting System. *Alcoholism: Clinical and Experimental Research, 37*(5), 839–846. https://doi.org/10.1111/acer.12038

Duran, E., & Duran, B. (1995). *Native American postcolonial psychology*. State University of New York Press.

Duran, B., Oetzel, J., Lucero, J., Jiang, Y., Novins, D. K., Manson, S., Beals, J., & American Indian Service Utilization and Psychiatric Epidemiology Risk and Protective Factors Project Team, University of Colorado Health Sciences Center. (2005). Obstacles for rural American Indians seeking alcohol, drug, or mental health treatment. *Journal of Consulting and Clinical Psychology, 73*(5), 819–829. https://doi.org/10.1037/0022-006X.73.5.819

Freitas-Murrell, B., & Swift, J. K. (2015). Predicting attitudes toward seeking professional psychological help among Alaska Natives. *American Indian and Alaska Native Mental Health Research, 22*(3), 21–35.

Garroutte, E. M., Goldberg, J., Beals, J., Herrell, R., Manson, S. M., & the AI–SUPERPFP Team. (2003). Spirituality and attempted suicide among American Indians. *Social Science & Medicine, 56*(7), 1571–1579.

Gomes, A. (2018). Indigenous peoples and colonialism: Global perspectives, by Colin Samson and Carlos Gigoux. *Anthropological Forum, 28*(3), 301–302. https://doi.org/10.1080/00664677.2018.1461589

Gone, J. P., & Trimble, J. E. (2012). American Indian and Alaska Native mental health: diverse perspectives on enduring disparities. *Annual review of clinical psychology, 8*, 131–160. https://doi.org/10.1146/annurev-clinpsy-032511-143127

Goodkind, M., Eickhoff, S. B., Oathes, D. J., Jiang, Y., Chang, A., Jones-Hagata, L. B., Ortega, B. N., Zaiko, Y. V., Roach, E. L., Korgaonkar, M. S., Grieve, S. M., Galatzer-Levy, I., Fox, P. T., & Etkin, A. (2015). Identification of a common neurobiological substrate for mental illness. *JAMA psychiatry, 72*(4), 305–315. https://doi.org/10.1001/jamapsychiatry.2014.2206

Grayshield, L., Rutherford, J. J., Salazar, S. B., Mihecoby, A. L., & Luna, L. L. (2015). Understanding and healing historical trauma: The perspectives of Native American elders. *Journal of Mental Health Counseling, 37*(4), 295–307. https://doi.org/10.17744/mehc.37.4.02

Heart, M. Y., Chase, J., Elkins, J., & Altschul, D. B. (2011). Historical trauma among Indigenous Peoples of the Americas: concepts, research, and clinical considerations. *Journal of psychoactive drugs, 43*(4), 282–290. https://doi.org/10.1080/02791072.2011.628913

Henderson, D. X., Walker, L., Barnes, R. R., Lunsford, A., Edwards, C., & Clark, C. (2019). A Framework for Race-Related Trauma in the Public Education System and Implications on Health for Black Youth. *The Journal of school health, 89*(11), 926–933. https://doi.org/10.1111/josh.12832

Hodge, F. S., Pasqua, A., Marquez, C. A., & Geishirt-Cantrell, B. (2022, January). Utilizing traditional storytelling to promote wellness in American Indian communities. *Journal of Transcultural Nursing, 13*(1), 6–11. https://doi.org/10.1177/104365960201300102

Kwon, S. C., Kabir, R., Saadabadi, A. Mental Health Challenges in Caring for American Indians and Alaska Natives. [Updated 2024 Feb 12]. In: StatPearls [Internet]. Treasure Island (FL): StatPearls Publishing; 2025 Jan-. Available from: https://www.ncbi.nlm.nih.gov/books/NBK570587/

McNeill, D. (1992). *Hand, and Mind: What Gestures Reveal about Thought*. The University of Chicago Press.

Olson, L. M., & Wahab, S. (2006). American Indians and suicide: a neglected area of research. *Trauma, violence & abuse, 7*(1), 19–33. https://doi.org/10.1177/1524838005283005

Reyhner, J., & Singh, N.K. (2010). Cultural Genocide in Australia, Canada, New Zealand, and the United States: The Destruction and Transformation of Indigenous Cultures. *Indigenous Policy Journal, 21*(4), 1–26.

Sarche, M., & Spicer, P. (2008). Poverty and health disparities for American Indian and Alaska Native children: current knowledge and future prospects. *Annals of the New York Academy of Sciences, 1136*, 126–136. https://doi.org/10.1196/annals.1425.017

Shiels, M. S., Chernyavskiy, P., Anderson, W. F., Best, A. F., Haozous, E. A., Hartge, P., Rosenberg, P. S., Thomas, D., Freedman, N. D., & Berrington de Gonzalez, A. (2017). Trends in premature mortality in the USA by sex, race, and ethnicity from 1999 to 2014: an analysis of death certificate data. *Lancet (London, England), 389*(10073), 1043–1054. https://doi.org/10.1016/S0140-6736(17)30187-3

Singh, G. K., Lee, H., Kim, L. H., & Williams, S. D. (2024). Social Determinants of Health Among American Indians and Alaska Natives and Tribal Communities: Comparison with Other Major Racial and Ethnic Groups in the United States, 1990-2022. *International journal of MCH and AIDS, 13*, e010. https://doi.org/10.25259/IJMA_10_2024

Smith, J. A. (1999). Identity development during the transition to motherhood: An interpretive phenomenological analysis. *Journal of Reproductive and Infant Psychology, 17*(3), 281–299. https://doi.org/10.1080/02646839908404595

Substance Abuse and Mental Health Services Administration (SAMHSA). (2012). Results from the 2011 national survey on drug use and health: Volume I. Summary of national findings. Rockville, MD: Author. http://www.samhsa.gov/data/NSDUH/2k11Results/NSDUHresults2011.htm#2.1

U.S. Department of Health and Human Services. (2010). *To live to see the great day that dawns: Preventing suicide by American Indian and Alaska Native youth and young adults.* Rockville, MD: Substance Abuse and Mental Health Services Administration. https://store.samhsa.gov/product/To-Live-To-See-the-Great-Day-That-Dawns-Preventing-Suicide-byAmerican-Indian-and-Alaska-Native-Youth-and-Young-Adults/SMA10-4480

Venner, K. L, Greenfield, B. L, Vicuña, B, Muñoz, R, Bhatt, S, & O'Keefe, V (2012). "I'm not one of them": Barriers to help-seeking among American Indians with alcohol dependence. *Cultural Diversity & Ethnic Minority Psychology, 18*, 352–362. https://doi.org/10.1037/a0029757

Walls, M. L., Chapple, C. L., & Johnson, K. D. (2007). Strain, emotion, and suicide among American Indian youth. *Deviant Behavior, 28*(3), 219–246.

Whitbeck, L. B., Adams, G. W., Hoyt, D. R., & Chen, X. (2004). Conceptualizing and measuring historical trauma among American Indian people. *American journal of community psychology, 33*(3–4), 119–130. https://doi.org/10.1023/b:ajcp.0000027000.77357.31

Whitbeck, L. B., Walls, M. L., Johnson, K. D., Morrisseau, A. D., & McDougall, C. M. (2009). Depressed affect and historical loss among North American Indigenous adolescents. *American Indian and Alaska native mental health research (Online), 16*(3), 16–41. https://doi.org/10.5820/aian.1603.2009.16

Wiechelt, S., Gryczynski, J., Johnson, J., & Caldwell, D. (2012). Historical trauma among urban American Indians: Impact on substance abuse and family cohesion. *Journal of Loss and Trauma, 17*(4), 319–336. https://doi.org/10.1080/15325024.2011.616837

Wolsko, C., Ariceaga, H., & Seiden, J. (2016). Red, white, and blue enough to be green: Effects of moral framing on climate change attitudes and conservation behaviors. *Journal of Experimental Social Psychology, 65*, 7–19. https://doi.org/10.1016/j.jesp.2016.02.005

Yoder, K., Whitbeck, L. B., Hoyt, D. R., & LaFromboise, T. D. (2006). Suicidal ideation among American Indian youth. *Archives of Suicide Research, 10*, 177–190. https://doi.org/10.1080/13811110600558240

Index[1]

[1] Note: Page numbers followed by 'n' refer to notes.

Z. Z. Gao, M. I. Medved (eds.), *Global Perspectives on Cultural Politics in Indigenous Psychology*, Palgrave Studies in Indigenous Psychology, https://doi.org/10.1007/978-3-031-96813-6

Kolibri 360 GmbH
Ferdinand-Jühlke-Straße 7
99095 Erfurt, Deutschland
produktsicherheit@kolibri360.de